Explorations in
Reading and Writing

Explorations in Reading and Writing

Tom Zaniello
Northern Kentucky University

Random House New York

For my parents, Anthony and Augusta
(Tony and Gussie)

First Edition
987654321
Copyright © 1987 by Random House, Inc.

Library of Congress Cataloging-in-Publication Data

Explorations in reading and writing.

Includes index.
1. College readers. 2. English language—
Rhetoric. 3. Interdisciplinary approach in education.
I. Zaniello, Tom, 1943–
PE1417.E955   1986   808'.0427   86-20440
ISBN 0-394-34292-5

Cover Illustration: Kurt Schwitters, *Cherry Picture.* 1921. Collage of colored papers, fabrics, printed labels and pictures, pieces of wood, etc., and gouache on cardboard background.

Collection, The Museum of Modern Art, New York. Mr. and Mrs. A. Atwater Kent, Jr., Fund.

Photograph © 1987 The Museum of Modern Art, New York.

Cover Design: Lorraine Hohman

Manufactured in the United States of America

Permissions

Preface: To the Instructor

Explorations in Reading and Writing may be used in writing courses in three distinct ways:

(1) It may be used as a *reader,* as it offers numerous essays which may be assigned on either a topical or a rhetorical basis.

(2) It may be used as a *controlled research text,* since it offers a variety of self-contained readings on each topic.

(3) It may be used as a *cross-disciplinary text,* in that it provides readings from different disciplines on each topic.

The text offers students the opportunity to read and write about six important topics from different perspectives. I designed the collection for use in both first- and second-semester composition courses but, because of its flexibility, it can also be used in advanced composition and honors courses. The flexibility in the use of the text is for you to experiment with, but I had in mind at least three ways in which the materials could be used:

(1) An essay in the text may serve as a starting-point or as a model for a student's essay.

(2) A group of essays from different disciplines may provide the student with different viewpoints with which to interpret a given topic.

(3) Using an essay or group of essays as a base, the student may follow suggestions from the "Assignments," "Explorations," or

"Sources," and do research outside the classroom and, in many instances, outside the library as well.

The flexibility of the text is also built in to the chapters themselves. Each chapter is divided into four sections, representing a full range of informational, polemical, and expressive writing as well as models of professional and student writing:

(1) *Discursive essays and fictions:* the traditionally more "literary" materials give a general view of the topic. Although a number of classic writers have been included in this section, the emphasis throughout the text is on some fine contemporary writers who are typically underrepresented in textbooks.

(2) *Essays from the disciplines:* academic or formal essays that are written from the perspective of a single discipline or, in some cases, with a cross-disciplinary emphasis, including an appropriate methodology and reference style.

(3) *Documentary materials:* journalistic and archival pieces which offer some of the "raw" stuff of a research project. In some instances, these have been seen in print only rarely.

(4) *Student essays:* actually written for one of the "Assignments," these pieces close each of the chapters. The sample pieces may be expository essays based on the materials of a single chapter, research papers involving library or other kinds of research, or essays which have resulted from a "creative writing," or more open-ended, assignment.

Each selection is complete as originally published, unless noted otherwise. Since I have attempted to reproduce the text as it originally appeared in every instance, one will occasionally encounter the use of the masculine pronoun to denote persons of both sexes. For the few selections which have been excerpted from longer essays or from books, I have added my own title in brackets. I have also identified the primary discipline related to the selection or to the type of writing it represents.

Although certain disciplines may be expected in a given chapter, students may be encouraged to move out from the territory of a discipline familiar to them toward the consideration of the points of view of other disciplines. Thus, within Chapter 4, "Investigating Murder," students may combine both sociological and psychological ways of looking at murder. Additionally, after studying Chapter 5, "Perspectives on Salem," students may use the disciplines and methods applied to the analysis of the more social problems of Salem to confront the seemingly quite individual cases of murder presented in Chapter 4.

Accompanying every selection is an "Introduction" which places the selection in the context of its topic and explains whatever disciplinary and rhetorical features are of note. Whenever possible, the introduction also covers the kind of periodical or book in which the selection originally appeared, and its intended audience. If the selection incorporates notes or references of any kind, its specific reference style is explained briefly in the "Appendix: Reference Styles." Every chapter includes "Questions for Discussion" to bring out important issues in the chapter at hand as well as in related readings in other chapters, "Assignments" which may be completed using only this book, and others which may require additional research, "Sources," an annotated list of published materials, and "Explorations" of other open-ended ways students may follow up on the topics.

The assignments fall into two major groups: The first set can be done with only the materials *within the chapter* itself; the remaining ones reach *beyond the chapter* in various ways, either by taking the student outside the text (interviews, visiting sites, etc.) or by offering additional readings or sources to pursue. I would urge you to be selective in your choice of assignments—there are too many for a one-semester course! Do not assume that the first one necessarily provides the best way for your class to begin. I have included a fairly large number of assignments in case you wish to vary the disciplinary mix from semester to semester. The *Instructor's Manual* contains numerous suggestions geared specifically to the assignments. (You may find that, in the *Manual*, I have included a fair amount of the information which often is included in a text itself, so please consult the *Manual* often.) The "Explorations" and "Sources" also offer numerous possibilities for assignments you can construct yourself.

Because I do not believe it is possible to represent all disciplines fairly and equally in a single text, I have concentrated instead on using materials and assignments which have already proven successful in introducing the ideas and writing habits associated with a cross-disciplinary approach to composition.

I would very much like to hear how the text has worked for

you. Please write to me: c/o Literature Program, Northern Kentucky University, Highland Heights, KY 41076.

ACKNOWLEDGMENTS

For advice and support over the years, as I developed this book, my thanks go first of all to my teaching colleagues at Northern Kentucky University: Judy Bechtel, Carmine Bell, Bob Collier, Paul Ellis, Bill McKim, Bob Wallace, Ted and Mary Ann Weiss, Jeff Williams, and Fran Zaniello. For helpful administrative support over the years, I am indebted to Darryl Poole, Bill McKim, and Frank Stallings.

The students whose "sample" essays appear here are but seven of the many fine students I have taught at Northern Kentucky University. Without their cooperation, a text like this would have been impossible. I have also benefited from the suggestions made by students at the George Meany Center for Labor Studies in Silver Spring, Maryland.

The support staff at Northern Kentucky University has also been very helpful: I would like to thank Edith Armstrong and Vanessa Johnson, secretaries in the Literature Program; Mary Ellen Rutledge and Connie Mulligan, librarians; and Debbie Tucker, Mary Kelm, and Sharon Taylor, interlibrary-loan staff.

I have been inspired by the active assignments created by two teachers from other universities: W. Keith Kraus, of Shippensburg State, developed the *New York Times* "murder" assignment in Chapter 4, and Herbert F. Crovitz originated the combination of Duncker's problems with Ogden's Basic English, featured in Chapter 2.

John Hall of the University of Missouri has given me valuable suggestions for Chapter 6, specifically the Jonestown transcript, although the version printed here is my own. Bonnie Winters provided both helpful and timely typing service.

I have also learned much from two very different books. An anti-textbook, Leonard A. Greenbaum's and Rudolf B. Schmerl's *Course X,* served as a reminder of how students can often get lost in the shuffle called Freshman English. A fine little textbook by Walker Gibson, *Seeing and Writing,* demonstrated to me how well challenging readings and active writing assignments go together.

The notes provided by Dixie Goswami and Harold Douglass for their session at the 1976 Conference on College Composition and

Communication helped me to understand the importance of process in teaching writing.

I would like to thank Sylvan Barnet and X. J. Kennedy, my undergraduate English teachers at Tufts University, for demonstrating how to combine good teaching and good text-writing.

I am very grateful for the advice and help from Random House, especially from Steve Pensinger, Cynthia Ward, and Lisa Haugaard.

My children, Sarah and Benjamin, always kept me going by asking: "Are you finished with your book yet?"

TOM ZANIELLO

Preface: To the Student

Here is "A Little Fable," written by Franz Kafka:

> "Alas," said the mouse, "the whole world is growing smaller
> every day. At the beginning it was so big that I was afraid, I kept
> running and running, and I was glad when at last I saw walls far away
> to the right and left, but these long walls have narrowed so quickly
> that I am in the last chamber already, and there in the corner stands
> the trap that I must run into."
> "You only need to change your direction," said the cat, and ate
> it up.

Too often you have been in the unfortunate position of that
mouse, facing an assignment which looks like a trap, while an instructor—who bears a striking resemblance to the cat—stands by,
whispering, "Change your direction! change your direction!" Kafka
was a great writer, though a very anxious one, yet I'm sure that even
he did not have writing classes in mind when he wrote his fable. Since
this fable *does* describe many classrooms I have been in, I have tried
to design a book which will help both you and your instructor
"change directions," a book which presents writing as an active exploration and partnership, not a pursuit with baited traps.

The readings and assignments, organized by disciplines but
within a cross-disciplinary framework, will help you read, do research, discuss, and write about important and compelling problems
in human experience and thought.

The "Introductions" will explain the characteristic disciplines
and approaches to writing of the individual selections. The "Appen-

dix: Reference Styles" at the end of the text will help you through the maze of problems associated with footnoting. And finally, there are "Questions for Discussion," "Assignments," and "Explorations," all designed to help you study the materials in the text.

Your reaction to the text is important to me. Write and let me know how it has worked for you: c/o Literature Program, Northern Kentucky University, Highland Heights, KY 41076.

TOM ZANIELLO

Contents

CHAPTER 6 *Approaching Jonestown* 351

Explorations in
Reading and Writing

CHAPTER ONE

The American Scene

The novelist Henry James called his book of essays about visiting his native America after a twenty-year absence *The American Scene*. With that title and his novelist's eye for detail, he attempted to capture the people, places, and stories which typified the America of 1904–1905. His by then well-entrenched European manners were somewhat ruffled by the powerful sights which greeted him—immigrants turning New York City neighborhoods into foreign lands, the "strange and inordinate charm of the Jersey shore," and the behavior of the "new rich." Although today James might find America just as amusing and shocking, we currently tend to accept more readily the kaleidoscope which reflects, and sometimes even distorts, the American scene—its mix of distinctive characters, landscapes, strange creatures, and tales which help to define the variety and vigor of American life. It is with this mix we begin.

A sense of place dominates the selections in this chapter, many of which complement the geographer's feel for the land. Geography has always meant more than places on a map, and a skillful story or essay about the land can transform such places into territories you feel you have visited or at least should visit. While you could visit many of the places described in this chapter, the "Assignments," "Sources," and "Explorations" are meant to convince you that these places—or their equivalents—are probably, in some ways, in your own backyard. Finding them is a matter of reorienting yourself. When David Lowenthal wrote *his* essay called "The American Scene" (see "Sources"), he argued that "landscapes are formed by landscape tastes," that is, what is out there is strongly influenced by how we go about looking for it.

This chapter comes close to a "cultural geography" of selected American scenes, since the interaction of people, behavior, technology, and place mark so many of the selections. This chapter will encourage you to see the diversity of American culture because, in the words of Wilbur Zelinsky (see "Sources"), there may not be a "single physical American environment, or even a dominant one, or any sensible possibility of arriving at a meaningful *average* environment." In "mapping" some of that diversity—whether the maps are physical, psychological, or even cultural—you might begin to "read" your own landscape as if it is no longer simply (and perhaps boringly) your own backyard.

The selections in "Discursive Essays and Fictions" emphasize the identity, perhaps even the symbiosis or beneficial exchange, between a special personality and a specific place. Freeman's short story about a woman who becomes dependent upon her neighbors, and Trillin's portrait of a man and "his" city reveal the "character" of everyday life; Le Sueur's and McPhee's essays attempt broader visions by revealing both the economic and physical characteristics of an era. In "Essays from the Disciplines" Stewart offers a method for looking at our places: Through prose and photographs he uncovers the layers of human occupancy sometimes visible, sometimes hidden, on the "open road." (Compare this with Chief Seattle's speech from Chapter 3 about his landscape—western Washington State—in which both the living and the spirits of the dead are present.)

The second selection in "Essays from the Disciplines," and all those in "Documentary Materials," survey some of the most characteristic features of the American scene—monsters, both real and imaginary, as well as storytellers, real and imaginative. The American scene has been constantly enlivened by "things that go bump in the night," and some that show off during the day too. Some of the liveliest have been the hardest to see. These legendary and "fearsome creatures" make up a distinctive presence on the American scene.

In terms of the disciplines represented, this chapter is quite diverse: Geography and travel writing dominate, with fiction and folklore running a close second. In addition to offering the "objectivity" of journalism, I have added an essay in physics by a writer who doesn't trust mists over lakes as the best means to see water monsters, even if many people believe that they are native to large American lakes.

DISCURSIVE ESSAYS AND FICTIONS

SHORT STORY

MARY E. WILKINS FREEMAN

Our first short story employs dialect and a rural Massachusetts setting to present an intriguing problem about a woman's strength. Freeman published "A Church Mouse" in her first successful book of short stories, A New England Nun and Other Stories, *in 1891. In that volume, she concentrated on the women of Massachusetts rural life, creating a group of powerful and memorable fictional characters, such as Louisa Ellis of "A New England Nun," Sarah Penn of "The Revolt of 'Mother,'" and the grandmother known as "Old Woman Magoun." Hetty Fifield, "a church mouse," is such a woman as well since she speaks in a voice that is characteristic of New England folk, but one that never loses the power of her own individuality. She had, the narrator tells us, "the reputation of always taking her own way, and never heeding the voice of authority."*

In her short stories, Freeman often chose to present these women in adversity; her heroines were indigenous to the countryside in dress, speech, manners, and especially, in their problems. Hetty, poor as a "church mouse," takes up residence in the church, and the village people are, of course, shocked: "Hetty as a church sexton was directly opposed to all their ideas of church decorum and propriety in general." Her struggle to find a home and to support herself are heroic within the context of her community, the "little settlement of narrow-minded, prosperous farmers." Of course the issue of "woman's work" is at the bottom of the controversy, for Deacon Caleb Gale has trouble imagining a woman ringing the church bell or tending the fires in the wood-stoves. The plot and resolution of Hetty's problem may strike us today as very modern, for Freeman's fiction, ignored for so long, is finally coming into its own once more.

Freeman's popularity in the late nineteenth century was widespread, but in our century she tends to be regarded as only a regional, or "local color," writer, a status which erroneously implies that

*she speaks only for a limited section of the American scene. That she
employs local speech patterns is certainly part of her strength as a writer;
that she also confronts enduring human problems is part of her
universality.*

A Church Mouse

"I never heard of a woman's bein' saxton."

"I dun' know what difference that makes; I don't see why they
shouldn't have women saxtons as well as men saxtons, for my part,
nor nobody else neither. They'd keep dusted 'nough sight cleaner.
I've seen the dust layin' on my pew thick enough to write my name
in a good many times, an' ain't said nothin' about it. An' I ain't goin'
to say nothin' now again Joe Sowen, now he's dead an' gone. He did
jest as well as most men do. Men git in a good many places where
they don't belong, an' where they set as awkward as a cow on a
hen-roost, jest because they push in ahead of women. I ain't blamin'
'em; I s'pose if I could push in I should, jest the same way. But there
ain't no reason that I can see, nor nobody else neither, why a woman
shouldn't be saxton."

Hetty Fifield stood in the rowen hay-field before Caleb Gale.
He was a deacon, the chairman of the selectmen, and the rich and
influential man of the village. One looking at him would not have
guessed it. There was nothing imposing about his lumbering figure
in his calico shirt and baggy trousers. However, his large face, red and
moist with perspiration, scanned the distant horizon with a stiff and
reserved air; he did not look at Hetty.

"How'd you go to work to ring the bell?" said he. "It would
have to be tolled, too, if anybody died."

"I'd jest as lief ring that little meetin'-house bell as to stan' out
here an' jingle a cow-bell," said Hetty; "an' as for tollin', I'd jest as
soon toll the bell for Methusaleh, if he was livin' here! I'd laugh if
I ain't got strength 'nough for that."

"It takes a kind of a knack."

"If I ain't got as much knack as old Joe Sowen ever had, I'll give
up the ship."

"You couldn't tend the fires."

"Couldn't tend the fires—when I've cut an' carried in all the wood I've burned for forty year! Couldn't keep the fires a-goin' in them two little wood-stoves!"

"It's consider'ble work to sweep the meetin'-house."

"I guess I've done 'bout as much work as to sweep that little meetin'-house, I ruther guess I have."

"There's one thing you ain't thought of."

"What's that?"

"Where'd you live? All old Sowen got for bein' saxton was twenty dollar a year, an' we couldn't pay a woman so much as that. You wouldn't have enough to pay for your livin' anywheres."

"Where am I goin' to live whether I'm saxton or not?"

Caleb Gale was silent.

There was a wind blowing, the rowen hay drifted round Hetty like a brown-green sea touched with ripples of blue and gold by the asters and golden-rod. She stood in the midst of it like a May-weed that had gathered a slender toughness through the long summer; her brown cotton gown clung about her like a wilting leaf, outlining her harsh little form. She was as sallow as a squaw, and she had pretty black eyes; they were bright, although she was old. She kept them fixed upon Caleb. Suddenly she raised herself upon her toes; the wind caught her dress and made it blow out; her eyes flashed. "I'll tell you where I'm goin' to live," said she. *"I'm going' to live in the meetin'-house."*

Caleb looked at her. *"Goin' to live in the meetin'-house!"*

"Yes, I be."

"Live in the meetin'-house!"

"I'd like to know why not."

"Why—you couldn't—live in the meetin'-house. You're crazy."

Caleb flung out the rake which he was holding, and drew it in full of rowen. Hetty moved around in front of him, he raked imperturbably; she moved again right in the path of the rake, then he stopped. "There ain't no sense in such talk."

"All I want is jest the east corner of the back gall'ry, where the chimbly goes up. I'll set up my cookin'-stove there, an' my bed, an' I'll curtain it off with my sunflower quilt, to keep off the wind."

"A cookin'-stove an' a bed in the meetin'-house!"

"Mis' Grout she give me that cookin'-stove, an' that bed I've allers slept on, before she died. She give 'em to me before Mary Anne Thomas, an' I moved 'em out. They air settin' out in the yard now, an' if it rains that stove an' that bed will be spoilt. It looks some like rain now. I guess you'd better give me the meetin'-house key right off.''

"You don't think you can move that cookin'-stove an' that bed into the meetin'-house—I ain't goin' to stop to hear such talk."

"My worsted-work, all my mottoes I've done, an' my wool flowers, air out there in the yard."

Caleb raked. Hetty kept standing herself about until he was forced to stop, or gather her in with the rowen hay. He looked straight at her, and scowled; the perspiration trickled down his cheeks. "If I go up to the house can Mis' Gale git me the key to the meetin'-house?" said Hetty.

"No, she can't."

"Be you goin' up before long?"

"No, I ain't." Suddenly Caleb's voice changed: it had been full of stubborn vexation, now it was blandly argumentative. "Don't you see it ain't no use talkin' such nonsense, Hetty? You'd better go right along, an' make up your mind it ain't to be thought of."

"Where be I goin' to-night, then?"

"To-night?"

"Yes; where be I a-goin'?"

"Ain't you got any place to go to?"

"Where do you s'pose I've got any place? Them folks air movin' into Mis' Grout's house, an' they as good as told me to clear out. I ain't got no folks to take me in. I dun' know where I'm goin'; mebbe I can go to your house?"

Caleb gave a start. "We've got company to home," said he, hastily. "I'm 'fraid Mis' Gale wouldn't think it was convenient."

Hetty laughed. "Most everybody in the town has got company," said she.

Caleb dug his rake into the ground as if it were a hoe, then he leaned on it, and stared at the horizon. There was a fringe of yellow birches on the edge of the hay-field; beyond them was a low range of misty blue hills. "You ain't got no place to go to, then?"

"I dun' know of any. There ain't no poor-house here, an' I ain't got no folks."

Caleb stood like a statue. Some crows flew cawing over the field. Hetty waited. "I s'pose that key is where Mis' Gale can find it?" she said, finally.

Caleb turned and threw out his rake with a jerk. "She knows where 'tis; it's hangin' up behind the settin'-room door. I s'pose you can stay there to-night, as long as you ain't got no other place. We shall have to see what can be done."

Hetty scuttled off across the field. "You mustn't take no stove nor bed into the meetin'-house," Caleb called after her; "we can't have that, nohow."

Hetty went on as if she did not hear.

The golden-rod at the sides of the road was turning brown; the asters were in their prime, blue and white ones; here and there were rows of thistles with white tops. The dust was thick; Hetty, when she emerged from Caleb's house, trotted along in a cloud of it. She did not look to the right or left, she kept her small eager face fixed straight ahead, and moved forward like some little animal with the purpose to which it was born strong within it.

Presently she came to a large cottage-house on the right of the road; there she stopped. The front yard was full of furniture, tables and chairs standing among the dahlias and clumps of marigolds. Hetty leaned over the fence at one corner of the yard, and inspected a little knot of household goods set aside from the others. There were a small cooking-stove, a hair trunk, a yellow bedstead stacked up against the fence, and a pile of bedding. Some children in the yard stood in a group and eyed Hetty. A woman appeared in the door— she was small, there was a black smutch on her face, which was haggard with fatigue, and she scowled in the sun as she looked over at Hetty. "Well, got a place to stay in?" said she, in an unexpectedly deep voice.

"Yes, I guess so," replied Hetty.

"I dun' know how in the world I can have you. All the beds will be full—I expect his mother some to-night, an' I'm dreadful stirred up anyhow."

"Everybody's havin' company; I never see anything like it," Hetty's voice was inscrutable. The other woman looked sharply at her.

"You've got a place, ain't you?" she asked, doubtfully.

"Yes, I have."

At the left of this house, quite back from the road, was a little unpainted cottage, hardly more than a hut. There was smoke coming out of the chimney, and a tall youth lounged in the door. Hetty, with the woman and children staring after her, struck out across the field in the little footpath towards the cottage. "I wonder if she's goin' to stay there?" the woman muttered, meditating.

The youth did not see Hetty until she was quite near him, then he aroused suddenly as if from sleep, and tried to slink off around the cottage. But Hetty called after him. "Sammy," she cried, "Sammy, come back here, I want you!"

"What d'ye want?"

"Come back here!"

The youth lounged back sulkily, and a tall woman came to the door. She bent out of it anxiously to hear Hetty.

"I want you to come an' help me move my stove an' things," said Hetty.

"Where to?"

"Into the meetin'-house."

"The meetin'-house?"

"Yes, the meetin'-house."

The woman in the door had sodden hands; behind her arose the steam of a wash-tub. She and the youth stared at Hetty, but surprise was too strong an emotion for them to grasp firmly.

"I want Sammy to come right over an' help me," said Hetty.

"He ain't strong enough to move a stove," said the woman.

"Ain't strong enough!"

"He's apt to git lame."

"Most folks are. Guess I've got lame. Come right along, Sammy!"

"He ain't able to lift much."

"I s'pose he's able to be lifted, ain't he?"

"I dun' know what you mean."

"The stove don't weigh nothin'," said Hetty; "I could carry it myself if I could git hold of it. Come, Sammy."

Hetty turned down the path, and the youth moved a little way after her, as if perforce. Then he stopped, and cast an appealing glance back at his mother. Her face was distressed. "Oh, Sammy, I'm afraid you'll git sick," said she.

"No, he ain't goin' to git sick," said Hetty. "Come, Sammy." And Sammy followed her down the path.

It was four o'clock then. At dusk Hetty had her gay sunflower quilt curtaining off the chimney-corner of the church gallery; her stove and little bedstead were set up, and she had entered upon a life which endured successfully for three months. All that time a storm brewed; then it broke; but Hetty sailed in her own course for the three months.

It was on a Saturday that she took up her habitation in the meeting-house. The next morning, when the boy who had been supplying the dead sexton's place came and shook the door, Hetty was prompt on the other side. "Deacon Gale said for you to let me in so I could ring the bell," called the boy.

"Go away," responded Hetty. "I'm goin' to ring the bell; I'm saxton."

Hetty rang the bell with vigor, but she made a wild, irregular jangle at first; at the last it was better. The village people said to each other that a new hand was ringing. Only a few knew that Hetty was in the meeting-house. When the congregation had assembled, and saw that gaudy tent pitched in the house of the Lord, and the resolute little pilgrim at the door of it, there was a commotion. The farmers and their wives were stirred out of their Sabbath decorum. After the service was over, Hetty, sitting in a pew corner of the gallery, her little face dark and watchful against the flaming background of her quilt, saw the people below gathering in groups, whispering, and looking at her.

Presently the minister, Caleb Gale, and the other deacon came up the gallery stairs. Hetty sat stiffly erect. Caleb Gale went up to the sunflower quilt, slipped it aside, and looked in. He turned to Hetty with a frown. To-day his dignity was supported by important witnesses. "Did you bring that stove an' bedstead here?"

Hetty nodded.

"What made you do such a thing?"

"What was I goin' to do if I didn't? How's a woman as old as me goin' to sleep in a pew, an' go without a cup of tea?"

The men looked at each other. They withdrew to another corner of the gallery and conferred in low tones; then they went downstairs and out of the church. Hetty smiled when she heard the door shut. When one is hard pressed, one, however simple, gets wisdom as to vantage-points. Hetty comprehended hers perfectly. She was the propounder of a problem; as long as it was unguessed, she was sure of her foothold as propounder. This little village in which she had lived all her life had removed the shelter from her head; she being penniless, it was beholden to provide her another; she asked it what. When the old woman with whom she had lived died, the town promptly seized the estate for taxes—none had been paid for years. Hetty had not laid up a cent; indeed, for the most of the time she had received no wages. There had been no money in the house; all she had gotten for her labor for a sickly, impecunious old woman was a frugal board. When the old woman died, Hetty gathered in the few household articles for which she had stipulated, and made no complaint. She walked out of the house when the new tenants came in; all she asked was, "What are you going to do with me?" This little settlement of narrow-minded, prosperous farmers, however hard a task charity might be to them, could not turn an old woman out into the fields and highways to seek for food as they would a Jersey cow. They had their Puritan consciences, and her note of distress would sound louder in their ears than the Jersey's bell echoing down the valley in the stillest night. But the question as to Hetty Fifield's disposal was a hard one to answer. There was no almshouse in the village, and no private family was willing to take her in. Hetty was strong and capable; although she was old, she could well have paid for her food and shelter by her labor; but this could not secure her an entrance even among this hard-working and thrifty people, who would ordinarily grasp quickly enough at service without wage in dollars and cents. Hetty had somehow gotten for herself an unfortunate name in the village. She was held in the light of a long-thorned brier among the beanpoles, or a fierce little animal with claws and teeth bared. People were afraid to take her into their families; she had the reputation of always taking her own way, and never heeding the voice of authority. "I'd take her in an' have her give me a lift with the work," said one sickly farmer's wife; "but, near's I can find out, I couldn't never be sure that I'd get molasses in the beans, nor saleratus° in my sour-milk cakes, if she took a notion not to put it in. I don't dare to risk it."

Stories were about concerning Hetty's authority over the old woman with whom she had lived. "Old Mis' Grout never dared to say her soul was her own," people said. Then Hetty's sharp, sarcastic sayings were repeated; the justice of them made them sting. People did not want a tongue like that in their homes.

Hetty as a church sexton was directly opposed to all their ideas of church decorum and propriety in general; her pitching her tent in the Lord's house was almost sacrilege; but what could they do? Hetty jangled the Sabbath bells for the three months; once she tolled the bell for an old man, and it seemed by the sound of the bell as if his long, calm years had swung by in a weak delirium; but people bore

---

° saleratus: baking soda.

it. She swept and dusted the little meeting-house, and she garnished
the walls with her treasures of worsted-work. The neatness and the
garniture went far to quiet the dissatisfaction of the people. They had
a crude taste. Hetty's skill in fancy-work was quite celebrated. Her
wool flowers were much talked of, and young girls tried to copy
them. So these wreaths and clusters of red and blue and yellow wool
roses and lilies hung as acceptably between the meeting-house windows as pictures of saints in a cathedral.

Hetty hung a worsted motto over the pulpit; on it she set her
chiefest treasure of art, a white wax cross with an ivy vine trailing
over it, all covered with silver frost-work. Hetty always surveyed this
cross with a species of awe; she felt the irresponsibility and amaze-
ment of a genius at his own work.

When she set it on the pulpit, no queen casting her rich robes
and her jewels upon a shrine could have surpassed her in generous
enthusiasm. "I guess when they see that they won't say no more,"
she said.

But the people, although they shared Hetty's admiration for the
cross, were doubtful. They, looking at it, had a double vision of a
little wax Virgin upon an altar. They wondered if it savored of
popery.° But the cross remained, and the minister was mindful not
to jostle it in his gestures.

It was three months from the time Hetty took up her abode in
the church, and a week before Christmas, when the problem was
solved. Hetty herself precipitated the solution. She prepared a boiled
dish in the meeting-house, upon a Saturday, and the next day the
odors of turnip and cabbage were strong in the senses of the worship-
pers. They sniffed and looked at one another. This superseding the
legitimate savor of the sanctuary, the fragrance of peppermint lo-
zenges and wintergreen, the breath of Sunday clothes, by the homely
week-day odors of kitchen vegetables, was too much for the sensibilities of the people. They looked indignantly around at Hetty,
sitting before her sunflower hanging, comfortable from her good
dinner of the day before, radiant with the consciousness of a great
plateful of cold vegetables in her tent for her Sabbath dinner.

Poor Hetty had not many comfortable dinners. The selectmen
doled out a small weekly sum to her, which she took with dignity

---

° popery: of the pope; that is, Roman Catholic. Hetty's white wax cross reminds the
Protestant/Puritan congregation of Catholic ways of worship.

as being her hire; then she had a mild forage in the neighbors' cellars and kitchens, of poor apples and stale bread and pie, paying for it in teaching her art of worsted-work to the daughters. Her Saturday's dinner had been a banquet to her: she had actually bought a piece of pork to boil with the vegetables; somebody had given her a nice little cabbage and some turnips, without a thought of the limitations of her housekeeping. Hetty herself had not a thought. She made the fires as usual that Sunday morning; the meeting-house was very clean, there was not a speck of dust anywhere, the wax cross on the pulpit glistened in a sunbeam slanting through the house. Hetty, sitting in the gallery, thought innocently how nice it looked.

After the meeting, Caleb Gale approached the other deacon. "Somethin's got to be done," said he. And the other deacon nodded. He had not smelt the cabbage until his wife nudged him and mentioned it; neither had Caleb Gale.

In the afternoon of the next Thursday, Caleb and the other two selectmen waited upon Hetty in her tabernacle. They stumped up the gallery stairs, and Hetty emerged from behind the quilt and stood looking at them scared and defiant. The three men nodded stiffly; there was a pause; Caleb Gale motioned meaningly to one of the others, who shook his head; finally he himself had to speak. "I'm 'fraid you find it pretty cold here, don't you, Hetty?" said he.

"No, thank ye; it's very comfortable," replied Hetty, polite and wary.

"It ain't very convenient for you to do your cookin' here, I guess."

"It's jest as convenient as I want. I don't find no fault."

"I guess it's rayther lonesome here nights, ain't it?"

"I'd 'nough sight ruther be alone than have comp'ny, any day."

"It ain't fit for an old woman like you to be livin' alone here this way."

"Well, I dun' know of anything that's any fitter; mebbe you do."

Caleb looked appealingly at his companions; they stood stiff and irresponsive. Hetty's eyes were sharp and watchful upon them all.

"Well, Hetty," said Caleb, "we've found a nice, comfortable place for you, an' I guess you'd better pack up your things, an' I'll carry you right over there." Caleb stepped back a little closer to the other men. Hetty, small and trembling and helpless before them, looked vicious. She was like a little animal driven from its cover, for whom there is nothing left but desperate warfare and death.

"Where to?" asked Hetty. Her voice shrilled up into a squeak.

Caleb hesitated. He looked again at the other selectmen. There was a solemn, far-away expression upon their faces. "Well," said he, "Mis' Radway wants to git somebody, an'—"

"You ain't goin' to take me to that woman's!"

"You'd be real comfortable—"

"I ain't goin'."

"Now, why not, I'd like to know?"

"I don't like Susan Radway, hain't never liked her, an' I ain't goin' to live with her."

"Mis' Radway's a good Christian woman. You hadn't ought to speak that way about her."

"You know what Susan Radway is, jest as well's I do; an' everybody else does too. I ain't goin' a step, an' you might jest as well make up your mind to it."

Then Hetty seated herself in the corner of the pew nearest her tent, and folded her hands in her lap. She looked over at the pulpit as if she were listening to preaching. She panted, and her eyes glittered, but she had an immovable air.

"Now, Hetty, you've got sense enough to know you can't stay here," said Caleb. "You'd better put on your bonnet, an' come right along before dark. You'll have a nice ride."

Hetty made no response.

The three men stood looking at her. "Come, Hetty," said Caleb, feebly; and another selectman spoke. "Yes, you'd better come," he said, in a mild voice.

Hetty continued to stare at the pulpit.

The three men withdrew a little and conferred. They did not know how to act. This was a new emergency in their simple, even lives. They were not constables; these three steady, sober old men did not want to drag an old woman by main force out of the meeting-house, and thrust her into Caleb Gale's buggy as if it were a police wagon.

Finally Caleb brightened. "I'll go over an' git mother," said he. He started with a brisk air, and went down the gallery stairs; the others followed. They took up their stand in the meeting-house yard, and Caleb got into his buggy and gathered up the reins. The wind blew cold over the hill. "Hadn't you better go inside and wait out of the wind?" said Caleb.

"I guess we'll wait out here," replied one; and the other nodded.

"Well, I sha'n't be gone long," said Caleb. "Mother'll know how to manage her." He drove carefully down the hill; his buggy wings rattled in the wind. The other men pulled up their coat collars, and met the blast stubbornly.

"Pretty ticklish piece of business to tackle," said one, in a low grunt.

"That's so," assented the other. Then they were silent, and waited for Caleb. Once in a while they stamped their feet and slapped their mittened hands. They did not hear Hetty slip the bolt and turn the key of the meeting-house door, nor see her peeping at them from a gallery window.

Caleb returned in twenty minutes; he had not far to go. His wife, stout and handsome and full of vigor, sat beside him in the buggy. Her face was red with the cold wind; her thick cashmere shawl was pinned tightly over her broad bosom. "Has she come down yet?" she called out, in an imperious way.

The two selectmen shook their heads. Caleb kept the horse quiet while his wife got heavily and briskly out of the buggy. She went up the meeting-house steps, and reached out confidently to open the door. Then she drew back and looked around. "Why," said she, "the door's locked; she's locked the door. I call this pretty work!"

She turned again quite fiercely, and began beating on the door. "Hetty!" she called; "Hetty, Hetty Fifield! Let me in! What have you locked this door for?"

She stopped and turned to her husband.

"Don't you s'pose the barn key would unlock it?" she asked.

"I don't b'lieve 'twould."

"Well, you'd better go home and fetch it."

Caleb again drove down the hill, and the other men searched their pockets for keys. One had the key of his corn-house, and produced it hopefully; but it would not unlock the meeting-house door.

A crowd seldom gathered in the little village for anything short of a fire; but to-day in a short time quite a number of people stood on the meeting-house hill, and more kept coming. When Caleb Gale returned with the barn key his daughter, a tall, pretty young girl, sat beside him, her little face alert and smiling in her red hood. The other selectmen's wives toiled eagerly up the hill, with a young daughter of one of them speeding on ahead. Then the two young girls stood close to each other and watched the proceedings. Key after key was tried; men brought all the large keys they could find, running importantly up the hill, but none would unlock the meeting-house door. After Caleb had tried the last available key, stooping and screwing it anxiously, he turned around. "There ain't no use in it, any way," said he; "most likely the door's bolted."

"You don't mean there's a bolt on that door?" cried his wife.

"Yes, there is."

"Then you might jest as well have tore 'round for hen's feathers as keys. Of course she's bolted it if she's got any wit, an' I guess she's got most as much as some of you men that have been bringin' keys. Try the windows."

But the windows were fast. Hetty had made her sacred castle impregnable except to violence. Either the door would have to be forced or a window broken to gain an entrance.

The people conferred with one another. Some were for retreating, and leaving Hetty in peaceful possession until time drove her to capitulate. "She'll open it to-morrow," they said. Others were for extreme measures, and their impetuosity gave them the lead. The project of forcing the door was urged; one man started for a crow-bar.

"They are a parcel of fools to do such a thing," said Caleb Gale's wife to another woman. "Spoil that good door! They'd better leave the poor thing alone till to-morrow. I dun' know what's goin' to be done with her when they git in. I ain't goin' to have father draggin' her over to Mis' Radway's by the hair of her head."

"That's jest what I say," returned the other woman.

Mrs. Gale went up to Caleb and nudged him. "Don't you let them break that door down, father," said she.

"Well, well, we'll see," Caleb replied. He moved away a little; his wife's voice had been drowned out lately by a masculine clamor, and he took advantage of it.

All the people talked at once; the wind was keen, and all their garments fluttered; the two young girls had their arms around each other under their shawls; the man with the crow-bar came stalking up the hill.

"Don't you let them break down that door, father," said Mrs. Gale.

"Well, well," grunted Caleb.

Regardless of remonstrances, the man set the crow-bar against the door; suddenly there was a cry, "There she is!" Everybody looked up. There was Hetty looking out of a gallery window.

Everybody was still. Hetty began to speak. Her dark old face, peering out of the window, looked ghastly; the wind blew her poor gray locks over it. She extended her little wrinkled hands. "Jest let me say one word," said she; "jest one word." Her voice shook. All her coolness was gone. The magnitude of her last act of defiance had caused it to react upon herself like an overloaded gun.

"Say all you want to, Hetty, an' don't be afraid," Mrs. Gale called out.

"I jest want to say a word," repeated Hetty. "Can't I stay here, nohow? It don't seem as if I could go to Mis' Radway's. I ain't nothin' again' her. I s'pose she's a good woman, but she's used to havin' her own way, and I've been livin' all my life with them that was, an' I've had to fight to keep a footin' on the earth, an' now I'm gittin' too old for't. If I can jest stay here in the meetin'-house, I won't ask for nothin' any better. I sha'n't need much to keep me, I wa'n't never a hefty eater; an' I'll keep the meetin'-house jest as clean as I know how. An' I'll make some more of them wool flowers. I'll make a wreath to go the whole length of the gallery, if I can git wool 'nough. Won't you let me stay? I ain't complainin', but I've always had a dretful hard time; seems as if now I might take a little comfort the last of it, if I could stay here. I can't go to Mis' Radway's nohow." Hetty covered her face with her hands; her words ended in a weak wail.

Mrs. Gale's voice rang out clear and strong and irrepressible. "Of course you can stay in the meetin'-house," said she; "I should laugh if you couldn't. Don't you worry another mite about it. You sha'n't go one step to Mis' Radway's; you couldn't live a day with her. You can stay jest where you are; you've kept the meetin'-house enough sight cleaner than I've ever seen it. Don't you worry another mite, Hetty."

Mrs. Gale stood majestically, and looked defiantly around; tears were in her eyes. Another woman edged up to her. "Why couldn't she have that little room side of the pulpit, where the minister hangs his hat?" she whispered. "He could hang it somewhere else."

"Course she could," responded Mrs. Gale, with alacrity, "jest as well as not. The minister can have a hook in the entry for his hat. She can have her stove an' her bed in there, an' be jest as comfortable as can be. I should laugh if she couldn't. Don't you worry, Hetty."

The crowd gradually dispersed, sending out stragglers down the hill until it was all gone. Mrs. Gale waited until the last, sitting in the buggy in state. When her husband gathered up the reins, she called back to Hetty: "Don't you worry one mite more about it, Hetty. I'm comin' up to see you in the mornin'!"

It was almost dusk when Caleb drove down the hill; he was the last of the besiegers, and the feeble garrison was left triumphant.

The next day but one was Christmas, the next night Christmas Eve. On Christmas Eve Hetty had reached what to her was the flood-tide of peace and prosperity. Established in that small, lofty room, with her bed and her stove, with gifts of a rocking-chair and table, and a goodly store of food, with no one to molest or disturb her, she had nothing to wish for on earth. All her small desires were satisfied. No happy girl could have a merrier Christmas than this old woman with her little measure full of gifts. That Christmas Eve Hetty lay down under her sunflower quilt, and all her old hardships looked dim in the distance, like far-away hills, while her new joys came out like stars.

She was a light sleeper; the next morning she was up early. She opened the meeting-house door and stood looking out. The smoke from the village chimneys had not yet begun to rise blue and rosy in the clear frosty air. There was no snow, but over the hill there was a silver rime of frost; the bare branches of the trees glistened. Hetty stood looking. "Why, it's Christmas mornin'," she said, suddenly. Christmas had never been a gala-day to this old woman. Christmas had not been kept at all in this New England village when she was young. She was led to think of it now only in connection with the dinner Mrs. Gale had promised to bring her to-day.

Mrs. Gale had told her she should have some of her Christmas dinner, some turkey and plum-pudding. She called it to mind now with a thrill of delight. Her face grew momentarily more radiant. There was a certain beauty in it. A finer morning light than that which lit up the wintry earth seemed to shine over the furrows of her old face. "I'm goin' to have turkey an' plum-puddin' today," said she; "it's Christmas." Suddenly she started, and went into the meeting-house, straight up the gallery stairs. There in a clear space hung the bell-rope. Hetty grasped it. Never before had a Christmas bell been rung in this village; Hetty had probably never heard of Christmas bells. She was prompted by pure artless enthusiasm and grateful happiness. Her old arms pulled on the rope with a will, the bell sounded peal on peal. Down in the village, curtains rolled up, letting in the morning light, happy faces looked out of the windows. Hetty had awakened the whole village to Christmas Day.

NARRATIVE ESSAY

MERIDEL LE SUEUR

On the American frontier, stories about "displaced peoples" were usually cruelly reserved for Native Americans. (See Chief Seattle's speech in Chapter 3, for example.) But in Le Sueur's essay, the white pioneers are the ones who are in turn displaced by a more aggressive breed of nonsettler—the capitalists like "Old Andy," Andrew Carnegie. The tale is also epic in its telling of the confrontation between Eastern capitalists and lawyers opposed to the Western trailblazers and frontiersmen. The end of Le Sueur's story is also like Seattle's in its inclusion of a people displaced, the ghosts of a family (the Merritts) overlooking the Kitchi Gammi—itself an Indian name—and the rise of a new era (that of monopoly capitalism). This work is politicized folklore; what the author calls elsewhere in North Star Country *(1945), the source of this essay, "the hieroglyphics of all man's communication, both obvious and subterranean, as he struggles with growing society, changing tools, to create a place, a community, a nation."*

In form, then, Le Sueur's essay is a narrative of the American scene, but an unusual one. The actual events cover the period at the end of the nineteenth century and the beginning of the twentieth century when the great Eastern capitalists, like Carnegie, were buying up land, minerals, companies, and *individuals. Le Sueur colors her narrative with details, anecdotes, folk sayings, and other tidbits to give a sense of an oral, or "people's," history, as if it were a tale told by her as the voice of the people, "from the bottom up."*

Old Andy Comes to the North Star Country

This opulent city, cradle of enterprise from the first settler in 1856, is now a bankrupt, instead of being the seat of wealth and independence as its advantages dictate. It only serves as a monument to identify the spot where "wise" men were mistaken; where the man of industry took a recess, the speculator knocked him down and the five per cent ate him up. You didn't cultivate land, you speculated. All this arises from the impudence not the necessity of man. It is a nightmare.

I saw a beast, dreadful and terrible and strong exceedingly and it had great iron teeth. I saw him devour the healthy merchant, break to pieces the farmer, mechanic, and everything that fell between its iron teeth. At last I saw him force entry into our little home. I saw my wife weep and the children cry and we were turned into the street without covering for our backs. My tongue lost its action and I was in great distress.

All we pioneers have suffered in life are comforts compared to this vision. The bitter fruit of three and five percent mortgages. Three and five per cent is the fourth Beast seen by the prophet Daniel in his vision of the night.

—REMARKS OF J. E. MCKUSICK AT AN "OLD SETTLERS' " MEETING

It was in a hotel room in Duluth that Andy Carnegie first came to the North Star Country,° representing a faceless new kind of giant —the monopoly. It was there that the financial East met the West for a showdown. On one side of the table were the battery of lawyers —many bought up by Old Andy—a preacher, and poker-faced speculators. On the other side were the people represented by the Daniel Boones of the Northwest—the seven surveying Merritt brothers.

The sons of tiny Hepzibah Merritt didn't have the chance of a snowball in a blast furnace. They were old-fashioned Americans and they still believed that there was enough for all, and they thought the people in a country should own it and wanted the claims to the richest soft-ore basin in the world to be taken up by the common people, wanted to make Duluth the steel capital of the world and thus create wealth for everyone.

They had traveled every foot of the range, misery bands holding the packs suspended from their foreheads, struggling through with ax and compass. "I understand woodcraft better than anything

○ North Star Country: the "new" territories of the Northwest, but specifically Minnesota.

else," Leonidas the strong one said. They were tough, they had all the guts of the frontiersman, pioneer, woodsman, but they were lost from the beginning amidst the roaring sound of Eastern blast furnaces opening their maws for iron ore.

They were lost because the first year they came to the range Henry Bessemer learned how to burn iron into cheap steel and Mr. Carnegie needed cheap ore to support the vast consolidations of his monopoly—forcing the cost of steel down and down. America was bawling for steel for skyscrapers, giant bridges, railroad ties, steel plows for the growing wheat harvest. The seven brothers were lost because they believed that the rich resources of nature were for the use of the common people. Mark Hanna° shocked Leonidas by saying to him, "The common people be damned!"

And they were lost because of the kind of men they were—sitting across from the poker faces, from Mr. Frick who, as Leonidas said, "cut me off short and bulldozed me"; and because just when they could have cashed in hands down, made them a pile, retired as nabobs, they were still digging, working, turning up new claims, busy as beavers struggling through the woods with axes and compass. These were men whose every adventure and effort was a saga, part of the heroic struggle of men of all times to make new paths through the wilderness, create new tools, take the earth's wealth and put it back again.

At midnight in his office in Duluth Leonidas, the bushwacker, appealed to the citizens to save him from the eastern capital:

> *Put some cash in the Mis-sa-be,*
> *Lend a helping hand to others,*
> *Others who are working for you.*
> *Let us bind with bands of iron*
> *The Mis-sa-be to the Zenith.*

But they would not.

Carnegie was at his hunting lodge in Scotland when Oliver, the plowmaker, told Frick about cheap ore in the open pits of the Biwabik which could be loaded into cars with one scoop of the shovel. "No shaft, no air compressors, no upkeep—" Frick had been wounded two days before by an anarchist who thought it his duty

---

° Mark Hanna: merchant, politician, and senator.

to call attention to the offensive power of steel in the Monongahela. He was so excited he forgot his annoyance at the striking workmen at Homestead. He had blast furnaces and rolling mills, and he needed cheap iron ore. And he got it, beating the Homestead strikers, and skinning the Merritts.

The hotels in Duluth were full of frenzied speculators, incorporating to the tune of five million a day, secret bargaining, backstair deals, the stock watered, doubling, zooming.

At last by devious devices of chicanery the Merritts came back from New York stripped, without, as Alf put it, a "soo-markee."° Their backs to the wall, they had been forced to sell their entire consolidated stock to Mr. Rockefeller. They had barely enough left to get home and then were without streetcar fare.

Eighteen years after their discovery of iron ore—when thirty million tons had been shipped out and Charles Schwab testified that probably three hundred and thirty-three million dollars would be a fair estimate of the value of the Mesabi° property—in 1911 Leonidas sat in a long room in Washington, facing notables and authorities in a silence that was full of strange askings, defenses, challenges, accusations, and the sorrow of Leonidas, who at times could not speak. He remembers that he and his brothers found the Mesabi—he remembers the thirty years that preceded their discovery. He remembers those great days of cold and hardship and excitement and their fantastic belief that iron ore lay under the lake country and that they would find it. The touch of the Homeric storyteller is in the way he tells it; the dignity of their labor, the greatness of their faith, and the belief still that he was right in the way he wanted to develop it, so that the earth should belong to the people that he knew.

Leonidas says that he has cultivated a forgetter. He says that when he came back from the journey to New York, where he sold the consolidated stock of the entire Merritt clan to Mr. Rockefeller in 1894, he nearly lost his mind. His family didn't have streetcar fare. "I could not conceive that I could go down with millions—how in hell I could within those few months, without spending a cent above my board bill, have lost all those millions."

"I blame myself," he says.

Congressman Stanley cannot stand the beleaguering of the big

° soo-markee: slang, based on French, for a coin of practically no value.
° Mesabi: the range of hills in northeastern Minnesota, rich in iron ore.

woodsmen by the brilliant lawyers. "I went to the state of Minnesota," he says in Leonidas' defense, "I went to the city of Duluth, went to the range, went among the lumbermen with whom they, the Merrits, had explored in the snow, and found that not one man but the people of Minnesota regarded these men in a way as we regard Boone of Kentucky, and as they regard Houston in Texas, with gratitude, with reverence."

The Merritts were poor after that and they stuck together.

Their mother Hepzibah said, "Have you done anything wrong? Then the Lord will care for you."

Mr. Rockefeller said, "Probably the most generous people in the world are the very poor, who assume each other's burdens in the crisis which comes so often to the hardpressed!"

So an era ended.

In the early days, industry, mills, timber, and mines were often owned by individuals like the Merritts or George Stuntz,° but when the Rockefellers, the Fricks, the Morgans entered the North Star Country contending for the vast mineral resources, bespeaking the ore "forever," the pattern changed and produced a new alignment of forces.

So the political supremacy of agriculture was broken and a new industrial dynasty was born having its own night talk, jokes, backfence badinage, and argument high up in office buildings:

> A timber baron claimed: We took the backwoods, cleared the land in less than fifty years; our efforts transformed the wild timber lands into a modern economic state.
>
> The farmer heard about the bank crash while he was in the hay mow. He jumped five feet into the air, slid down the rick and took off across the field. By the time he got to the north forty he stopped and asked himself, Why am I runnin'? I haven't got a dime in the bank!
>
> Do you know the banker has a glass eye? Do you know how you can tell it's the right one that's glass? There's a gleam of kindness in the glass eye!
>
> I've been blackmailed and hoodooed. I cut my own hair, shave myself with an ax. I'm a blacksmith, a tinsmith and a barrel-maker. I am anything from a bushwhacker to a Methodist preacher. I've made millionaires and I don't want to be one myself. I got two fifty in my pocket right now that I can spend if I want to. I wouldn't change places

_____
° George Stuntz: surveyor; founder of Duluth.

with Rockefeller. I can eat and sleep in peace. Someday I'm gonna die and when I'm dead someone will say, Herbert is the man who started the production of tin in the Black Hills.

They went on looking for more iron. Visionaries, they still saw rich treasures; optimists, they still believed in the impossible. Always looking forward—Leonidas lived to the last in a little grimy house near the ore docks, the Mesabi Railroad running at his door; he died in 1928 and was buried on an iron-ore hill overlooking Kitchi Gammi. The earth of his grave trembles now from the loaded cars that run day and night down to the lake with the red dust that will go to the furnaces of the East to make guns. He left no debts, no will, some household goods, a hundred and fifty dollars in cash. His brothers now lie near him.

And the children and grandchildren aplenty have founded co-operative creameries, fought in wars, are aviators, geologists, dredgers, farmers.

I walked under the black frosty range sky; the villages squat desolately, old mines like graveyards of old machinery, tar-paper shacks in the cut-over of families thrown out by the introduction of machinery in the mines, or blacklisted from strikes and those who wait for death from silicosis of the lungs; the great open pits, lighted now, gleam at night and the ore cars move continuously down to the fiery furnaces past the graves of Stuntz, the Merritts, and the thousands of the unnamed workers who created this great empire.

DESCRIPTIVE ESSAY

JOHN MCPHEE

McPhee's essay, originally published in The New Yorker *and reprinted in his collection of essays,* Pieces of the Frame *(1975), demonstrates the unusual flexibility of the essay form. Although* The New Yorker, *a general-interest literary and cultural magazine, usually publishes substantial but somewhat traditionally structured profiles and essays on a wide range of subjects, more experimental work occasionally appears there as well. Here, McPhee undertakes both a journey and a game. Spinning round the place names of the Monopoly board—both at home and actually in Atlantic City—McPhee finds out a lot about modern urban life as he searches for that elusive "yellow" property known as "Marvin Gardens." If you have never played Monopoly, take a look at the board as you read this essay. Reducing our complicated capitalistic world to houses, hotels, utilities, and railroads may be understating the complexities of an economic system, but certainly the drive to monopolize and eventually to send your competitors into bankruptcy, if possible, has some of the authentic feel of corporate mergers and acquisitions about it. (Le Sueur's description of "Old Andy" and his friends, in the first paragraph of her essay, might make more sense when you look a greedy opponent in the eye after a particularly trying game.)*

McPhee has pushed the traditional essay beyond its usual boundaries here; it is closer in style to a piece of experimental fiction, as we follow the drama of search and discovery—will McPhee find Marvin Gardens?—interrupted periodically by the author's game-playing. There are two narrative journeys in this essay: In one the author is travelling around the Monopoly board in a series of contests with an unnamed opponent; in the other, he is traveling the "real" streets of the same names in Atlantic City, searching for Marvin Gardens on the surface, but finding urban America instead.

As it turns out, the correct spelling for "Marvin Gardens" is "Marven Gardens," the elusive "e" having originated in the first syllable of "Ventnor City" which, when elided with Margate, forms the correct spelling of the name. The two cities, Margate and Ventnor City, therefore make up the name—not just one, as McPhee writes. Both are suburban neighbors to Atlantic City proper. (See Ferretti in "Sources" for more about Marven Gardens.) Furthermore, in a twist which even McPhee could not have anticipated, the game of Monopoly may not have been invented by Darrow at all, but was originally a folk game played by such antimonopolists as the Quakers until its design was monopolized by Darrow and the game's manufacturers, Parker Brothers. (See Trillin in "Sources.") Regardless of these twists and turns, McPhee's essay remains an unusual mixture of autobiography and urban description.

The Search for Marvin Gardens

Go. I roll the dice—a six and a two. Through the air I move my token, the flatiron, to Vermont Avenue, where dog packs range.

———— • ————

The dogs are moving (some are limping) through ruins, rubble, fire damage, open garbage. Doorways are gone. Lath is visible in the crumbling walls of the buildings. The street sparkles with shattered glass. I have never seen, anywhere, so many broken windows. A sign —"Slow, Children at Play"—has been bent backward by an automobile. At the lighthouse, the dogs turn up Pacific and disappear. George Meade, Army engineer, built the lighthouse—brick upon brick, six hundred thousand bricks, to reach up high enough to throw a beam twenty miles over the sea. Meade, seven years later, saved the Union at Gettysburg.

I buy Vermont Avenue for $100. My opponent is a tall, shadowy figure, across from me, but I know him well, and I know his game like a favorite tune. If he can, he will always go for the quick kill. And when it is foolish to go for the quick kill he will be foolish. On the whole, though, he is a master assessor of percentages. It is a mistake to underestimate him. His eleven carries his top hat to St. Charles Place, which he buys for $140.

———————— • ————————

The sidewalks of St. Charles Place have been cracked to shards by through-growing weeds. There are no buildings. Mansions, hotels once stood here. A few street lamps now drop cones of light on broken glass and vacant space behind a chain-link fence that some great machine has in places bent to the ground. Five plane trees—in full summer leaf, flecking the light—are all that live on St. Charles Place.

———————— • ————————

Block upon block, gradually, we are cancelling each other out—in the blues, the lavenders, the oranges, the greens. My opponent follows a plan of his own devising. I use the Hornblower & Weeks opening and the Zuricher defense.° The first game draws tight, will soon finish. In 1971, a group of people in Racine, Wisconsin, played for seven hundred and sixty-eight hours. A game begun a month later in Danville, California, lasted eight hundred and twenty hours. These are official records, and they stun us. We have been playing for eight minutes. It amazes us that Monopoly is thought of as a long game. It is possible to play to a complete, absolute, and final conclusion in less than fifteen minutes, all within the rules as written. My opponent and I have done so thousands of times. No wonder we are sitting

° Hornblower & Weeks opening and the Zuricher defense: Parodies of chess maneuvers. McPhee's intention is to raise the status of Monopoly-playing to that of chess.

across from each other now in this best-of-seven series for the international singles championship of the world.

———————— • ————————

On Illinois Avenue, three men lean out from second-story windows. A girl is coming down the street. She wears dungarees and a bright-red shirt, has ample breasts and a Hadendoan Afro, a black halo, two feet in diameter. Ice rattles in the glasses in the hands of the men.
"Hey, sister!"
"Come on up!"
She looks up, looks from one to another to the other, looks them flat in the eye.
"What for?" she says, and she walks on.

———————— • ————————

I buy Illinois for $240. It solidifies my chances, for I already own Kentucky and Indiana. My opponent pales. If he had landed first on Illinois, the game would have been over then and there, for he has houses built on Boardwalk and Park Place, we share the railroads equally, and we have cancelled each other everywhere else. We never trade.

———————— • ————————

In 1852, R. B. Osborne, an immigrant Englishman, civil engineer, surveyed the route of a railroad line that would run from Camden to Absecon Island, in New Jersey, traversing the state from the Delaware River to the barrier beaches of the sea. He then sketched in the plan of a "bathing village" that would surround the eastern terminus of the line. His pen flew glibly, framing and naming spacious avenues parallel to the shore—Mediterranean, Baltic, Oriental, Ventnor—and narrower transsecting avenues: North Carolina, Pennsylvania, Vermont, Connecticut, States, Virginia, Tennessee, New York, Kentucky, Indiana, Illinois. The place as a whole had no name, so when he had completed the plan Osborne wrote in large letters over the ocean, "Atlantic City." No one ever challenged the name, or the names of Osborne's streets. Monopoly was invented in the early nineteen-thirties by Charles B. Darrow, but Darrow was only transliterating what Osborne had created. The railroads, crucial to any player, were the making of Atlantic City. After the rails were down, houses and hotels burgeoned from Mediterranean and Baltic to New

York and Kentucky. Properties—building lots—sold for as little as six dollars apiece and as much as a thousand dollars. The original investors in the railroads and the real estate called themselves the Camden & Atlantic Land Company. Reverently, I repeat their names: Dwight Bell, William Coffin, John DaCosta, Daniel Deal, William Fleming, Andrew Hay, Joseph Porter, Jonathan Pitney, Samuel Richards—founders, fathers, forerunners, archetypical masters of the quick kill.

———— • ————

My opponent and I are now in a deep situation of classical Monopoly. The torsion is almost perfect—Boardwalk and Park Place versus the brilliant reds. His cash position is weak, though, and if I escape him now he may fade. I land on Luxury Tax, contiguous to but in sanctuary from his power. I have four houses on Indiana. He lands there. He concedes.

———— • ————

Indiana Avenue was the address of the Brighton Hotel, gone now. The Brighton was exclusive—a word that no longer has retail value in the city. If you arrived by automobile and tried to register at the Brighton, you were sent away. Brighton-class people came in private railroad cars. Brighton-class people had other private railroad cars for their horses—dawn rides on the firm sand at water's edge, skirts flying. Colonel Anthony J. Drexel Biddle—the sort of name that would constrict throats in Philadelphia—lived, much of the year, in the Brighton.

———— • ————

Colonel Sanders' fried chicken is on Kentucky Avenue. So is Clifton's Club Harlem, with the Sepia Revue and the Sepia Follies, featuring the Honey Bees, the Fashions, and the Lords.

———— • ————

My opponent and I, many years ago, played 2,428 games of Monopoly in a single season. He was then a recent graduate of the Harvard Law School, and he was working for a downtown firm, looking up law. Two people we knew—one from Chase Manhattan, the other from Morgan, Stanley—tried to get into the game, but after a few rounds we found that they were not in the conversation and we sent them home. Monopoly should always be *mano a mano* anyway. My opponent won 1,199 games, and so did I. Thirty were ties. He was called into the Army, and we stopped just there. Now, in Game 2 of the series, I go immediately to jail, and again to jail while my opponent seines property. He is dumbfoundingly lucky. He wins in twelve minutes.

———————————— • ————————————

Visiting hours are daily, eleven to two; Sunday, eleven to one; evenings, six to nine. "NO MINORS, NO FOOD, Immediate Family Only Allowed in Jail." All this above a blue steel door in a blue cement wall in the windowless interior of the basement of the city hall. The desk sergeant sits opposite the door to the jail. In a cigar box in front of him are pills in every color, a banquet of fruit salad an inch and a half deep—leapers, co-pilots, footballs, truck drivers, peanuts, blue angels, yellow jackets, redbirds, rainbows. Near the desk are two soldiers, waiting to go through the blue door. They are about eighteen years old. One of them is trying hard to light a cigarette. His wrists are in steel cuffs. A military policeman waits, too. He is a year or so older than the soldiers, taller, studious in appearance, gentle, fat. On a bench against a wall sits a good-looking girl in slacks. The blue door rattles, swings heavily open. A turnkey stands in the doorway. "Don't you guys kill yourselves back there now," says the sergeant to the soldiers.

"One kid, he overdosed himself about ten and a half hours ago," says the M.P.

The M.P., the soldiers, the turnkey, and the girl on the bench are white. The sergeant is black. "If you take off the handcuffs, take off the belts," says the sergeant to the M.P. "I don't want them hanging themselves back there." The door shuts and its tumblers move. When it opens again, five minutes later, a young white man in sandals and dungarees and a blue polo shirt emerges. His hair is in a ponytail. He has no beard. He grins at the good-looking girl. She rises, joins him. The sergeant hands him a manila envelope. From it he removes his belt and a small notebook. He borrows a pencil, makes an entry in the notebook. He is out of jail, free. What did he do? He offended Atlantic City in some way. He spent a night in the jail. In the nineteen-thirties, men visiting Atlantic City went to jail, directly to jail, did not pass Go, for appearing in topless bathing suits on the beach. A city statute requiring all men to wear full-length bathing suits was not seriously challenged until

1937, and the first year in which a man could legally go bare-chested on the beach was 1940.

——————— • ———————

Game 3. After seventeen minutes, I am ready to begin construction on overpriced and sluggish Pacific, North Carolina, and Pennsylvania. Nothing else being open, opponent concedes.

——————— • ———————

The physical profile of streets perpendicular to the shore is something like a playground slide. It begins in the high skyline of Boardwalk hotels, plummets into warrens of "side-avenue" motels, crosses Pacific, slopes through church missions, convalescent homes, burlesque houses, rooming houses, and liquor stores, crosses Atlantic, and runs level through the bombed-out ghetto as far—Baltic, Mediterranean —as the eye can see. North Carolina Avenue, for example, is flanked at its beach end by the Chalfonte and the Haddon Hall (908 rooms, air-conditioned), where, according to one biographer, John Philip Sousa (1854–1932) first played when he was twenty-two, insisting, even then, that everyone call him by his entire name. Behind these big hotels, motels—Barbizon, Catalina—crouch. Between Pacific and Atlantic is an occasional house from 1910—wooden porch, wooden mullions, old yellow paint—and two churches, a package store, a strip show, a dealer in fruits and vegetables. Then, beyond Atlantic Avenue, North Carolina moves on into the vast ghetto, the bulk of the city, and it looks like Metz in 1919, Cologne in 1944. Nothing has actually exploded. It is not bomb damage. It is deep and complex decay. Roofs are off. Bricks are scattered in the street. People sit on porches, six deep, at nine on a Monday morning. When they go off to wait in unemployment lines, they wait sometimes two hours. Between Mediterranean and Baltic runs a chain-link fence, enclosing rubble. A patrol car sits idling by the curb. In the back seat is a German shepherd. A sign on the fence says, "Beware of Bad Dogs."

Mediterranean and Baltic are the principal avenues of the ghetto. Dogs are everywhere. A pack of seven passes me. Block after block, there are three-story brick row houses. Whole segments of them are abandoned, a thousand broken windows. Some parts are intact, occupied. A mattress lies in the street, soaking in a pool of water. Wet stuffing is coming out of the mattress. A postman is having a rye and a beer in the Plantation Bar at nine-fifteen in the morning. I ask him idly if he knows where Marvin Gardens is. He does not. "HOOKED AND NEED HELP? CONTACT N.A.R.C.O." "REVIVAL NOW GOING ON, CONDUCTED BY REVEREND H. HENDERSON OF TEXAS." These are signboards on Mediterranean and Baltic. The second one is upside down and leans against a boarded-up window of the Faith Temple Church of God in Christ. There is an old peeling poster on a warehouse wall showing a figure in an electric chair. "The Black Panther Manifesto" is the title of the poster, and its message is, or was, that "the fascists have already decided in advance to murder Chairman Bobby Seale in the electric chair." I pass an old woman who carries a bucket. She wears blue sneakers, worn through. Her feet spill out. She wears red socks, rolled at the knees. A white handkerchief, spread over her head, is knotted at the corners. Does she know where Marvin Gardens is? "I sure don't know," she says, setting down the bucket. "I sure don't know. I've heard of it somewhere, but I just can't say where." I walk on, through a block of shattered glass. The glass crunches underfoot like coarse sand. I remember when I first came here—a long train ride from Trenton, long ago, games of poker in the train—to play basketball against Atlantic City. We were half black, they were all black. We scored forty points, they scored eighty, or something like it. What I remember most is that they had glass backboards—glittering, pendent, expensive glass backboards, a rarity then in high schools, even in colleges, the only ones we played on all year.

I turn on Pennsylvania, and start back toward the sea. The windows of the Hotel Astoria, on Pennsylvania near Baltic, are boarded up. A sheet of unpainted plywood is the door, and in it is a triangular peephole that now frames an eye. The plywood door opens. A man answers my question. Rooms there are six, seven, and ten dollars a week. I thank him for the information and move on, emerging from the ghetto at the Catholic Daughters of America Women's Guest House, between Atlantic and Pacific. Between Pacific and the Boardwalk are the blinking vacancy signs of the Aristocrat and Colton Manor motels. Pennsylvania terminates at the Sheraton-Seaside—thirty-two dollars a day, ocean corner. I take a walk on the Boardwalk and into the Holiday Inn (twenty-three stories). A guest is registering. "You reserved for Wednesday, and this is Monday," the clerk tells him. "But that's all right. We have *plenty* of rooms." The clerk is very young, female, and has soft brown hair that hangs below her waist. Her superior kicks her.

He is a middle-aged man with red spiderwebs in his face. He

is jacketed and tied. He takes her aside. "Don't say 'plenty,' " he says. "Say 'You are fortunate, sir. We have rooms available.' "

The face of the young woman turns sour. "We have all the rooms you need," she says to the customer, and, to her superior, "How's that?"

———————— • ————————

Game 4. My opponent's luck has become abrasive. He has Boardwalk and Park Place, and has sealed the board.

———————— • ————————

Darrow was a plumber. He was, specifically, a radiator repairman who lived in Germantown, Pennsylvania. His first Monopoly board was a sheet of linoleum. On it he placed houses and hotels that he had carved from blocks of wood. The game he thus invented was brilliantly conceived, for it was an uncannily exact reflection of the business milieu at large. In its depth, range, and subtlety, in its luck-skill ratio, in its sense of infrastructure and socio-economic parameters, in its philosophical characteristics, it reached to the profundity of the financial community. It was as scientific as the stock market. It suggested the manner and means through which an under-developed world had been developed. It was chess at Wall Street level. "Advance token to the nearest Railroad and pay owner twice the rental to which he is otherwise entitled. If Railroad is unowned, you may buy it from the Bank. Get out of Jail, free. Advance token to nearest Utility. If unowned, you may buy it from Bank. If owned, throw dice and pay owner a total ten times the amount thrown. You are assessed for street repairs: $40 per house, $115 per hotel. Pay poor tax of $15. Go to Jail. Go directly to Jail. Do not pass Go. Do not collect $200."

———————— • ————————

The turnkey opens the blue door. The turnkey is known to the inmates as Sidney K. Above his desk are ten closed-circuit-TV screens—assorted viewpoints of the jail. There are three cellblocks—men, women, juvenile boys. Six days is the average stay. Showers twice a week. The steel doors and the equipment that operates them were made in San Antonio. The prisoners sleep on bunks of butcher block. There are no mattresses. There are three prisoners to a cell. In winter, it is cold in here. Prisoners burn newspapers to keep warm. Cell corners are black with smudge. The jail is three years old. The men's block echoes with chatter. The man in the cell nearest Sidney K. is pacing. His shirt is covered with broad stains of blood. The block for juvenile boys is, by contrast, utterly silent—empty corridor, empty cells. There is only one prisoner. He is small and black and appears to be thirteen. He says he is sixteen and that he has been alone in here for three days.

"Why are you here? What did you do?"

"I hit a jitney driver."

———————— • ————————

The series stands at three all. We have split the fifth and sixth games. We are scrambling for property. Around the board we fairly fly. We move so fast because we do our own banking and search our own deeds. My opponent grows tense.

———————— • ————————

Ventnor Avenue, a street of delicatessens and doctors' offices, is leafy with plane trees and hydrangeas, the city flower. Water Works is on the mainland. The water comes over in submarine pipes. Electric Company gets power from across the state, on the Delaware River, in Deepwater. States Avenue, now a wasteland like St. Charles, once had gardens running down the middle of the street, a horse-drawn trolley, private homes. States Avenue was as exclusive as the Brighton. Only an apartment house, a small motel, and the All Wars Memorial Building—monadnocks spaced widely apart—stand along States Avenue now. Pawnshops, convalescent homes, and the Paradise Soul Saving Station are on Virginia Avenue. The soul-saving station is pink, orange, and yellow. In the windows flanking the door of the Virginia Money Loan Office are Nikons, Polaroids, Yashicas, Sony TVs, Underwood typewriters, Singer sewing machines, and pictures of Christ. On the far side of town, beside a single track and locked up most of the time, is the new railroad station, a small hut made of glazed firebrick, all that is left of the lines that built the city. An authentic phrenologist works on New York Avenue close to Frank's Extra Dry Bar and a church where the sermon today is "Death in the Pot." The church is of pink brick, has blue and amber windows and two red doors. St. James Place, narrow and twisting, is lined with boarding houses that have wooden porches on each of three stories, suggesting a New Orleans made of salt-bleached pine. In a vacant lot on Tennessee is a white Ford station wagon stripped to the chassis. The windows are smashed. A plastic Clorox bottle sits on the driver's seat. The wind has pressed newspaper against the chain-link fence around the lot. Atlantic Avenue, the city's principal thoroughfare, could be seventeen American Main Streets placed end to end—discount vitamins and Vienna Corset shops, movie theatres, shoe stores, and funeral homes. The Boardwalk is made of yellow pine and Douglas fir, soaked in pentachlorophenol. Downbeach, it reaches far beyond the city. Signs everywhere—on windows, lampposts, trash baskets—proclaim "Bienvenue Canadiens!" The salt air is full of Canadian French. In the Claridge Hotel, on Park Place, I ask a clerk if she knows where Marvin Gardens is. She says, "Is it a floral shop?" I ask a cabdriver, parked outside. He says, "Never heard of it." Park Place is one block long, Pacific to Boardwalk. On the roof of the Claridge is the Solarium, the highest point in town—panoramic view of the ocean, the bay, the salt-water ghetto. I look down at the rooftops of the side-avenue motels and into swimming pools. There are hundreds of people around the rooftop pools, sunbathing, reading—many more people than are on the beach. Walls, windows, and a block of sky are all that is visible from these pools—no sand, no sea. The pools are craters, and with the people around them they are countersunk into the motels.

———————— • ————————

The seventh, and final, game is ten minutes old and I have hotels on Oriental, Vermont, and Connecticut. I have Tennessee and St. James. I have North Carolina and Pacific. I have Boardwalk, Atlantic, Ventnor, Illinois, Indiana. My fingers are forming a "V." I have mortgaged most of these properties in order to pay for others, and I have mortgaged the others to pay for the hotels. I have seven dollars. I will pay off the mortgages and build my reserves with income from the three hotels. My cash position may be low, but I feel like a rocket in an underground silo. Meanwhile, if I could just go to jail for a time I could pause there, wait there, until my opponent, in his inescapable rounds, pays the rates of my hotels. Jail, at times, is the strategic place to be. I roll boxcars from the Reading and move the flatiron to Community Chest. "Go to Jail. Go directly to Jail."

———————— • ————————

The prisoners, of course, have no pens and no pencils. They take paper napkins, roll them tight as crayons, char the ends with matches, and write on the walls. The things they write are not entirely idiomatic; for example, "In God We Trust." All is in carbon. Time is required in the writing. "Only humanity could know of such pain." "God So Loved the World." "There is no greater pain than life itself." In the women's block now, there are six blacks, giggling, and a white asleep in red shoes. She is drunk. The others are pushers, prostitutes, an auto thief, a burglar caught with pistol in purse. A sixteen-year-old accused of murder was in here last week. These words are written on the wall of a now empty cell: "Laying here I see two bunks about six inches thick, not counting the one I'm laying on, which is hard as brick. No cushion for my back. No pillow for my head. Just a couple scratchy blankets which is best to use it's said. I wake up in the morning so shivery and cold, waiting and waiting till I am told the food is coming. It's on its way. It's not worth waiting for, but I eat it anyway. I know one thing when they set me free I'm gonna be good if it kills me."

———————— • ————————

How many years must a game be played to produce an Anthony J. Drexel Biddle and chestnut geldings on the beach? About half a century was the original answer, from the first railroad to Biddle at his peak. Biddle, at his peak, hit an Atlantic City streetcar conductor with his fist, laid him out with one punch. This increased Biddle's legend. He did not go to jail. While John Philip Sousa led his band along the Boardwalk playing "The Stars and Stripes Forever" and Jack Dempsey ran up and down in training for his fight with Gene Tunney, the city crossed the high curve of its parabola. Al Capone held conventions here—upstairs with his sleeves rolled, apportioning among his lieutenant governors the states of the Eastern seaboard. The natural history of an American resort proceeds from Indians to French Canadians via Biddles and Capones. French Canadians, whatever they may be at home, are Visigoths here. Bienvenue Visigoths!

———————— • ————————

My opponent plods along incredibly well. He has got his fourth railroad, and patiently, unbelievably, he has picked up my potential winners until he has blocked me everywhere but Marvin Gardens. He has avoided, in the fifty-dollar zoning, my increasingly petty hotels. His cash flow swells. His railroads are costing me two hundred dollars a minute. He is building hotels on States, Virginia, and St. Charles. He has temporarily reversed the current. With the yellow monopolies and my blue monopolies, I could probably defeat his lavenders and his railroads. I have Atlantic and Ventnor. I need Marvin Gardens. My only hope is Marvin Gardens.

———————— • ————————

There is a plaque at Boardwalk and Park Place, and on it in relief is the leonine profile of a man who looks like an officer in a metropolitan bank—"Charles B. Darrow, 1889–1967, inventor of the game of Monopoly." "Darrow," I address him, aloud. "Where is Marvin Gardens?" There is, of course, no answer. Bronze, impassive, Darrow looks south down the Boardwalk. "Mr. Darrow, please, where is Marvin Gardens?" Nothing. Not a sign. He just looks south down the Boardwalk.

———————— • ————————

My opponent accepts the trophy with his natural ease, and I make, from notes, remarks that are even less graceful than his.

———————— • ————————

Marvin Gardens is the one color-block Monopoly property that is not in Atlantic City. It is a suburb within a suburb, secluded. It is a planned compound of seventy-two handsome houses set on curvilinear private streets under yews and cedars, poplars and willows. The compound was built around 1920, in Margate, New Jersey, and consists of solid buildings of stucco, brick, and wood, with slate roofs, tile roofs, multi-mullioned porches, Giraldic towers, and Spanish grilles. Marvin Gardens, the ultimate outwash of Monopoly, is a citadel and sanctuary of the middle class. "We're heavily patrolled by police here. We don't take no chances. Me? I'm living here nine years. I paid seventeen thousand dollars and I've been offered thirty. Number one, I don't want to move. Number two, I don't need the money. I have four bedrooms, two and a half baths, front den, back den. No basement. The Atlantic is down there. Six feet down and you float. A lot of people have a hard time finding this place. People that lived in Atlantic City all their life don't know how to find it. They don't know where the hell they're going. They just know it's south, down the Boardwalk."

DESCRIPTIVE ESSAY

CALVIN TRILLIN

This essay appeared in the "U.S. Journal" column of The New
Yorker, *an appropriate place for investigations into the "characters" and
characteristic places of America also celebrated by such radio and
television personalities as Garrison Keillor and Charles Kuralt. Trillin's
satirical humor captures both person and place in this essay on Newport,
Kentucky, a small city (population:21,000) facing Cincinnati on the
banks of the Ohio River. Newport once had a national reputation not too
different from that lingering odor which Trillin detected when he arrived:
It had been called "Sin Town, USA" by* Esquire *magazine in May,
1957. Trillin studies the city through the activities of Johnny TV Peluso,
a local hero (or character). The success of this essay depends in part on
its humor and in part on what seems to be the perfect marriage of a local
person and the spirit of a place.*

*Both McPhee's essay on Marvin Gardens and Trillin's essay on
Newport help to classify the type of essay I have labelled throughout this
text as "discursive." Such an essay explains, reveals, and captures the
spirit of its subject, without arguing for a "thesis" or single, main point.
Trillin's essay, more traditional in form than McPhee's, nonetheless uses
the buildup of details—from local contacts, interviews, and capsule items
about Newport's history—to give a unified impression of the city and its
culture. Trillin himself (perhaps not quite as much as McPhee) is present
in the essay, not only to visit a few places "across the river," but also to
comment on all of the assertions and folklike tales he hears.*

Newport, Ky.—Across the River

When I heard that the mayor of Newport, Kentucky, had a plan
to span the Ohio River, I naturally sought him out. Over the past
decade, I have heard so many civic boosters explain their plans for
what they often call "putting this place on the map" or "getting this
town moving again" that I have gradually become a fancier of Grand
Urban Schemes. I am attracted to a city that can offer a four-color
architect's rendering of a downtown marina-condominium-shop-
ping-mall-ice-skating-rink complex in the same way that devout

observers of bird life are drawn out of their way by wetlands said to be prime feeding grounds for the snowy egret. Collectors of Grand Urban Schemes, like spotters of snowy egrets, have their work cut out for them these days, the supply of big-scheme money having dried up faster than the supply of undeveloped wetlands. A few months ago, I read that the mayor of Utica, New York—who, it should be said, was considered somewhat eccentric even before he fired virtually the entire Department of Public Works—planned to transform the center of Utica into something he calls La Promenade, which would include not only the usual shops and the mandatory ice-skating rink but a reproduction of the Spanish Steps that presumably could, on days when the temperature was above zero, lead some romantic shoppers to believe that they had been transported from upstate New York to Roma. Except for La Promenade, though, a connoisseur of Grand Urban Schemes had little to talk about lately until it became known that a plan to span the Ohio had been hatched by the mayor of Newport—John Peluso, a television-repair-shop proprietor who has his own reputation for eccentricity and is known locally as Johnny TV.

The Ohio River has been spanned before, of course, but only conventionally—by bridges. In fact, Newport being directly across the river from downtown Cincinnati, there are several bridges within view of anyone standing on high ground—including a nineteenth-century suspension bridge built by the Roeblings as a sort of dress rehearsal for their heroic span between Brooklyn and the United States, as well as a recently completed bridge whose arch, painted bright yellow, is said by some locals to resemble the world's largest McDonald's sign. What Johnny TV Peluso has in mind is not another bridge but a system of huge aerial cable cars that would carry passengers high over the river between a hotel to be built on a Newport bluff and a landing pad somewhere near the stadium-and-colosseum complex that was constructed on the Cincinnati river front several years ago—a complex that itself qualifies as a Grand Urban Scheme, with a projected cost of just under one hundred million dollars. Someone unfamiliar with the attraction of such schemes might, of course, question the necessity of spending millions of dollars—twenty million, by the Mayor's latest estimate—on a cable-car system that would connect two riverbanks already connected by nine bridges. That is not the sort of question that leaps to Mayor Peluso's mind. What he asks instead, while standing on a bluff in Newport that he has arranged to buy, looking directly across the river at a hundred-million-dollar stadium-and-colosseum project, is how two such points can possibly remain unconnected by the country's longest urban aerial-cable-car system. Peluso has a number of selling points to make about the desirability of his scheme, but the remark he makes most often about it is "It's a natural!"

———————— • ————————

The person who told me about the cable-car scheme said something like "I hear the mayor of Newport, Kentucky, wants to put cable cars across the Ohio, so people can be brought over from Cincinnati to sin." So much for Mayor Peluso's notion that the cable cars would "change the image of the town and erase the stigma of being a sin city." Newport's reputation as a center of vice has been so strong for so many years that changing the city's image with a grand stroke of engineering would require considerably more than a twenty-million-dollar aerial-cable-car system. If some grand schemers in Newport managed to dismantle an Egyptian pyramid, transport it to Kentucky, and reconstruct it on the banks of the Ohio River, many people who had visited Newport over the years would assume that the purpose of the project was to provide an authentic setting for some particularly imaginative Egyptian belly dancing. As recently as the early sixties, Newport had open gambling, controlled by a syndicate from Cleveland, and some brothels that had operated long enough to have the reputation of old established firms. The elected officials of Newport tended to respond to any effort at reform by saying that gambling was good for business, which was at least true for many of them personally, since payoffs were thought to constitute a secondary industry of some importance. There was even a widespread theory that open gambling in Newport was good for business in Cincinnati, then known as a center for good-government advocates and respectable burghers, since part of the attraction Cincinnati held as a convention city was the opportunity it presented to be entertained in northern Kentucky—or, as that prospect has always been expressed in Cincinnati, to "go across the river."

The end of Newport's big-time gambling and prostitution industry came in a way that added more notoriety to the town than could have been accumulated in ten or fifteen more years of steady sinning. In 1961, George Ratterman, who had been a Notre Dame quarterback of national renown, announced that he planned to run for sheriff of Campbell County with the intention of closing the gambling casinos of Newport. Ratterman had some obvious advantages over previous reformers. As a Notre Dame football hero who was the father of eight children, he could hardly be dismissed—as some of the local ministers had been dismissed in Newport, a largely Catholic town—as another Protestant zealot whose teeth were set to gnashing at the thought of people having a good time this side of the hereafter. Running for a county rather than a city office, he could draw support from a higher-income suburb that was beginning to find Newport embarrassing. Not long after he announced his candidacy, Ratterman was arrested for assorted misdemeanors by some Newport policemen who said they had found him in a hotel room above the Tropicana Club in bed with a dancer who appeared at the club under the professional name of April Flowers.

Ratterman claimed that he had been drugged and set up, and, some dramatic testimony having been offered by others to that effect at his trial, the charges were dropped. Shortly before the election, six people were indicted by a federal grand jury for conspiring to frame Ratterman, and two were eventually convicted. April Flowers apparently decided to assist the prosecution, but even she did not remain unpunished, since the acting governor of Kentucky publicly revoked the Kentucky Colonel's° commission she had displayed to reporters while waiting to testify before the grand jury. The acting governor, in fact, seemed somewhat bewildered as to how Miss Flowers had come to be awarded a Kentucky colonelcy in the first place—particularly one whose official commission he had signed himself. A reporter I know in northern Kentucky says that April Flowers was at least able to continue her stripping career with the advantage of billing herself as "the only defrocked Kentucky colonel," but he offers no documentation. Ratterman, of course, was elected, winning a county-wide plurality in a three-man race. He did not, however, carry the city of Newport itself. Newport was carried by the Democratic candidate—Johnny TV Peluso. It should be noted that during the campaign Ratterman, who was not considered eccentric, proposed spanning the Ohio River with a seventy-

---

° Kentucky Colonel: an honorary title bestowed by the Governor's office on both natives and visitors alike as a gesture of hospitality.

thousand-seat stadium that would also include a six-hundred room hotel, inside parking for forty-five hundred cars, bowling alleys, covered gardens, and a boat dock. He reminded reporters that a similar project had been suggested for New York City by Governor Nelson A. Rockefeller.

———————— • ————————

During the campaign for sheriff, George Ratterman said that new industry would come to Newport just as soon as the unsavory characters associated with gambling departed. As it turns out, Newport's inventory of what a reformer would consider legitimate industries is more or less the same as it was fifteen years ago. There is still a brewery and a steel plant and a clothing factory; the main shopping street is still a grimy line of two-story brick buildings with tired-looking retail stores on the ground floors. The population has dropped almost twenty-five percent to twenty-three thousand, although—half of Newport's work force having traditionally worked elsewhere in the area—northern-Kentucky planners tend to attribute the population loss to normal suburbanization rather than to the sudden shortage of positions for blackjack dealers.

Newport's attempts to find a replacement for gambling seem to have concentrated on the field in which it has had the most experience—sinning. For a while, Newport was the scene of what the local papers sometimes referred to as "commercial-type charity bingo."° Through a legal loophole that a judge soon closed, night spots were allowed to attract customers with bingo as long as the game profits went to a designated charity. In the first five weeks of operation, it turned out, Newport's four bingo clubs took in three hundred and sixty-six thousand dollars, with the two clubs that filed reports on charitable contributions having distributed to the needy some seventeen hundred dollars—figures indicating that the appropriate name for the sport might have been "high-overhead bingo." Newport has had more success with the strip-joint industry. Conventioneers or respectable Cincinnati citizens who are, as the taxi-drivers say, "looking for a little excitement" still go across the river. Strip joints are hardly a replacement for a gambling industry whose annual gross

---

° commercial-type charity bingo: perhaps a unique local loophole in the law. Bingo games may be operated if their profits are turned over to a designated charity and if the operators are volunteers.

receipts were always estimated in the millions, although in a trial last year a Cincinnati insurance executive testified that in five and a half months of crossing the river to a place called the Pink Pussycat he personally managed to spend almost sixteen thousand dollars without placing a bet. When I first head that Saturday-night bridge traffic between Newport and Cincinnati was still brisk, it occurred to me, there being pretty much a buyer's market in public nudity these days, Cincinnati residents might merely be reacting to some atavistic twitch that associates northern Kentucky with sin. The strip-joint marquees seem the same as those in any other town. There is even a featured stripper named Trixie Delight, raising the possibility that the industry's copywriters may have run out of names and started over again, like a longtime dog breeder who finally gives up and names the new puppy Fido. Local connoisseurs agree, though, that Newport strip shows tend to be gamier than what is normally allowed in Cincinnati. In fact, a Cincinnati businessman I know who hadn't been across the river for a little excitement in some time volunteered to visit a couple of shows while I was in town, and pronounced himself shocked at the total nudity—precisely the reaction expressed by a friend he encountered outside one of the clubs, a man who said he had himself wandered over for the first time in several years, because he had been driven out of the house by his wife's Tupperware party. "They had open prostitution in the old days, of course," the businessman said, "But they would never have allowed this!"

Mayor Peluso says it's irritating to have Newport's past as Sin City dragged out over every little incident—most recently in accounts of a nude wedding held in one of the clubs—but Newport's past is remembered often because its present is constantly providing reminders. The reformers still have not carried Newport. The Pink Pussycat burned down last Christmas—with the help, fire investigators said, of some gasoline and a timing device. The proprietor was at the time appealing a conviction for promoting prostitution, and people were bound to be reminded that her late husband, a Newport "night-club figure" named Sammy Eisner, was murdered in 1971— and that he has not been the only night-club figure murdered in recent years, any more than the Pink Pussycat has been the only night club burned with the help of gasoline. They may even have been reminded that while working unsuccessfully to solve the Eisner murder state police brought indictments for various crimes against such Newport citizens as the chief of police, a former detective, a city commissioner, and the vice-mayor—Johnny TV Peluso.

————————— • —————————

The charge against Peluso was eventually dropped, and, being based on the origin of some bonds Peluso once used as collateral, it has no connection at all with the traditional Newport charge of bribery which was brought against many of the others indicted. ("Why they put me in with these other people I'll never know," the Mayor said. "It doesn't look good.") Like anyone who has served in a variety of Newport offices over the years, Peluso has had more experience than the average citizen in testifying before grand juries, but his style of politics has always been thought of as too personal and impetuous to suit the role of a syndicate patsy. ("I never took nothing from nobody," the Mayor often says, although he tries not to be puritanical about those who have.) Peluso tends to interpret political life as a series of personal battles—arguments with the police chief about the mayor's right to have a police radio, arguments with the city manager about whether the city is responsible for fixing a street that leads to some Peluso property, even arguments with the syndicate about flunkies from the gambling clubs feeding parking meters in front of his repair shop, Johnny's TV. He is the sort of public official who arrives quickly at an accident and drops everything to search for a lost pet. Those who have observed Johnny TV Peluso's career for some time believe that one of his most characteristic adventures was distributing eggs to the poor at Christmas, being sued some months later for failure to pay the bill for the eggs, and offering half payment on the grounds that the eggs were so small they looked as if they had been laid by pigeons.

Peluso says he always opposed syndicate gambling and bust-out joints—establishments where the odds on a player's going home a big winner were reduced by a rigged wheel or a large man in the parking lot. But he still calls himself a liberal—a term that in Newport refers strictly to one's views on gambling. He has occasionally called for a return of gambling ("It was helping the poor"), and, perhaps because one of his business flings was as the operator of a "commercial-type charity bingo," he still favors the return of bingo. During periods when he is in favor of blotting out the memory of gambling instead of reinstating gambling, he has been for the Grand Urban Scheme—putting a huge marina on the river front, building the Cincinnati Riverfront Stadium in Newport instead of in Cincinnati.

"You gotta think big," he told me as we drove to the bluff that would be the site of the cable-car hotel.

The Mayor's ideas about financing the scheme seem to be in flux. Sometimes he treats it as a private venture that will merely have the side effect of revitalizing Newport; sometimes he says he will donate the land, then try to raise funds through federal grants and local bond issues; sometimes he talks about selling stock in small lots, so people will feel that they have a piece of the project, "like a piece of the rock." Whatever the financing, Peluso is clear about the logic of the scheme. Like other people with Grand Urban Schemes, he finds the sheer size and novelty of the project compelling. Grand Urban Schemes are normally promoted with such enthusiasm for building the only or the largest that it seems almost superfluous to ask, "The only largest what?" Peluso, like other scheme promoters I have met, has a four-color architect's rendering and figures on how many jobs would result and, of course, a list of reasons why the scheme is a natural. "It's a link between Ohio and Kentucky," he told me as we gazed toward Cincinnati from the bluff, where Peluso already operated a sort of banquet hall. "What we're talking about is plugging into a ninety-six-million-dollar project. Twenty million dollars is chicken feed; you'd pay it off in five years. If I can strike on the right party, I'll get the job done."

One could ask why there needs to be a twenty-million-dollar link between Ohio and Kentucky, or why a ninety-six-million-dollar project has to be plugged into. But then why did there have to be a forty-seven-million-dollar arch in front of St. Louis? What did Nelson Rockefeller sound like when he first explained why it would be beneficial to construct what turned out to be a billion-dollar government mall in Albany? What makes Johnny TV Peluso's Grand Urban Scheme different from some others I've seen, I realized when the Mayor pointed out the sights cable-car riders would be able to take in, is not that his sales pitch is so much different but that nobody seems to have bought it. Newport is hardly in a position to ignore opportunities for revitalization, but there have been no statements by business leaders on how gross retail sales would be affected. There have been no angry letters from environmentalists opposed to further development of the river. The local papers have barely mentioned Peluso's project. Johnny TV's reputation for being rather erratic would limit the seriousness with which his scheme was taken, of course, but there is no rule that the man who thinks of a Grand Urban Scheme has to run it; the last time I saw the man who thought up the Louisiana Superdome, he was running a small antique shop in the French Quarter. It occurred to me that, after a decade or so of visionary projects all over the country, Johnny TV Peluso may have accomplished something of at least minor historical note—he may have thought of a Grand Urban Scheme so divorced from reality that even an American city paid no attention to it. "It would be a novelty," the Mayor was saying. "And here's the beauty part: it's above the smog area."

ESSAYS FROM THE DISCIPLINES

GEOGRAPHY

GEORGE R. STEWART

The three following selections from Stewart's "biography" of a road—
U.S. 40: Cross-section of the U.S.A. (1953)—capture, in both
photographs and prose, the relationship of place and history of selected
spots of our landscape. Although all three pieces focus on Ohio, each is
developed in a slightly different way: Cambridge is captured in a moment
of time (even down to "two sitters on the curbstone"); the S-Bridge is
presented as a monument to both past and present time and space; and
the mileposts represent how our very movements in place and time have
been variously orchestrated.

Stewart's pieces, especially with the photographs, have the quality
of a journal or travel log. Each prose piece is based on careful observation,
a touch of historical research, and some cultural analysis. They provide
an opportunity to overhear a cultural geographer at work, presenting his
perceptions and judgments somewhat informally.

Cambridge, Ohio

U.S. 40 passes through Cambridge along Wheeling Avenue, a street that like many others in the United States takes its name from the town to which it heads. This picture, looking west, taken at eight on a misty September morning, with the first autumn leaves fallen, displays much of the atmosphere of the smaller American town— even to the informality of the two sitters on the curbstone.

Cambridge, Ohio

Three eras in architecture are visible. The simple gable and plain lines of the painted brick building immediately across the street bespeak an early date. Actually it was built about 1842, and was intended as a tavern to serve traffic along the National Road.° Later it housed a large store known as the "Red Corner." By the enduring tradition of the small town the name still clings even though the building is no longer red. Now, with the old front cut away for display-windows, it houses a "grill," a shoe store, and the office of the power-company.

The heavily corniced building, just to the right, represents another period. Built in 1884, it is of the common style of that time, a period of extensive construction which has left its mark upon nearly all American towns and cities.

At the extreme right, the large five-story building is the Central National Bank. Built in 1906, it is an example of the early skyscraper period. Such baby skyscrapers have been erected in many small

---

° National Road: Once called the Cumberland Road, now known simply as U.S. 40. (See an atlas for its important path.) This road is often cited as a dialectal divider, between North and South Midlands dialects.

towns, in imitation of the larger cities, even though land values scarcely justified and certainly did not necessitate such height.

The Civil War memorial is also a mark of Middle Western towns. This one, like most of them, has little to recommend it artistically, but it at least leaves no doubt that the infantryman ruled the battlefields of that war. Wearing his characteristic cap, he holds the top of the column; a sailor faces us; a curiously paunchy cavalryman with slouch hat and short jacket presents his profile; an artilleryman is on the opposite side. In front of the column sit a woman and a child, allegorically representing: "Knowledge teaching Youth."

Around the octagonal base are chiseled the names of battles— Gettysburg, Atlanta, Winchester, Antietam, Chickamauga, Wilderness, Vicksburg, Shiloh. Except for Chickamauga, these can rate as Union victories. The almost equal division of Ohio troops between eastern and western armies is signalized by the inclusion of four eastern and four western battles.

Ironically, right in front of this War Memorial stands the sign "Wanted Volunteers."°

The gigantic elm tree shadowing the square suggests an age well over a century, and is recorded as having been a large tree as early as 1840. It must therefore antedate the arrival of the National Road at Cambridge in 1826, in all probability it was already well established in 1806 when the town was founded. Possibly the street was actually laid out to pass this tree.

The stone milepost at the curb is one of the original posts set along the National Road, and indicated a location 180 miles from Cumberland and 24 miles from Zanesville. It was moved and reset at its present location in 1929, and is no longer of practical value for mileage, being in addition almost illegible.

S-Bridge

Across little Fox Creek, just west of New Concord, Ohio, still stands one of the famous S-shaped bridges for which the National Road in Ohio was once famous. Many of these remained in use until

---

° "Wanted Volunteers": Given the date of Stewart's book (1953), this sign is most likely a recruitment notice for the Korean War.

S-Bridge

well on into the automobile period, although they represent almost the perfect visualization of a modern highway engineer's bad dream. Actually such bridges occur in other states also, for instance in Pennsylvania, but they seem to have been commonest in Ohio.

Although by-passed by the new highway, this particular bridge is still usable, and its S-shape appears as clearly from the marks of the tracks that cross it as from the lines of the parapet. This bridge was built in 1828, and its solid masonry still stands, although saplings are beginning to sprout along the parapet and will soon crack it.

Various folktales are told about the S-bridges. One is that they are really Z-shaped, and are thus a memorial for Ebenezer Zane.° Another inevitable one is that the designer was drunk at the time. One variant of this latter is that the designer was an Englishman and the builder an Irishman. The two met in a taproom, and the Irishman boasted that he could build any bridge an Englishman could design. After a few more drinks the Englishman retired and came forth with the plans for the S-bridge, which the Irishman thereupon constructed.

° Ebenezer Zane: From a family of pioneer settlers, Zane blazed the trail through the Northwest Territory (as authorized by Congress in 1796) which later became a part of the National Road.

In 1937 Mr. J. J. Swanson of the Ohio Highway Planning Survey investigated the S-bridges. One of them, near Hendryville, he found to be constructed on such completely irrational lines that he was inclined to favor the persistent Englishman-Irishman story. As far as the other bridges are concerned, his conclusions are wholly rationalistic, and are based upon the fact that the stone arches of the bridges are all so constructed as to cross the stream at a right angle to its course. The reasons for this procedure are obviously economic. A bridge thus built is the shortest one possible, and so uses the least material. It also demands only a simple arch, not a skew arch (angle of arch not at right angles to line of bridge), and a simple arch calls for simple stone-cutting and masonry. After the arch had been so constructed, the wingwalls could be angled off to the line of the highway at both ends. Since even the fastest moving traffic was hardly at more than ten miles an hour, there was no safety-factor involved, and the traveler was scarcely inconvenienced. The bridges of the National Road were a considerable financial problem to the straitened federal finances of the time, and the hard-pressed engineers entrusted with their construction had to save every possible penny.

At this point the new highway has been slightly shifted from the line of the National Road. In the distance, however, it angles back into the old route.

Construction is here so new that the four-lane highway has not actually been opened to traffic, as is evidenced by the road-block in the distance. The rather startling appearance of the large truck proceeding down the wrong lane is therefore fallacious.

The topography here shows the Allegheny Plateau beginning to flatten as it approaches the Central Lowland. The slopes are here gentler, the valleys wider, than in West Virginia and Pennsylvania. Oaks and elms dominate the tree growth.

Mileposts

Where the National Road still follows its original course, the motorist passes many old mileposts still standing. In Pennsylvania these are of cast iron, turned out by local foundries and hauled along with six-horse teams to the proper spot at the roadside. One of these

Mileposts

is still in place at the boundary line between Pennsylvania and West Virginia. Although apparently cast to resemble stone pillars and much resembling such pillars when painted, these mileposts consist only of the two sides that face the highway. From this milepost the total length of the National Road can readily be computed as 132 miles. In spite of modern relocations the mileage to Cumberland, as compiled from recent road-maps, is only one mile less than that given here. One may note that the state is Virginia, not West Virginia. This milepost was erected long before the separation of the two parts in 1863.

Stone mileposts occur along the road in Ohio. They are often much defaced, but are now tended by the highway commission. The one shown has been painted white, and the names filled in with black. The prominence of the name Cumberland on all the mileposts helped to make that the common name of the road.

The drivers of the Conestoga wagons, proceeding at their two or three miles an hour, would certainly have been mystified by the modern signpost appearing just to the east of the little town of Lafayette. It must be admitted that the modern automobilist, especially at night, is also sometimes mystified, and has been known to

turn up in the wrong lane and go in the wrong direction. This particular signboard, it must be admitted, is about as graphic as possible, and presents a minimum of reading.

Some of the western states have found it necessary to place plain signs upon the highway to indicate the direction in which the traveler is proceeding, thus indicating that the modern American tourist has gone a long way from Daniel Boone and Kit Carson. It is rather a humiliation to have to read: "You are now on U.S. 40, and proceeding west."

PHYSICS

W. H. LEHN

Lehn has taken on the challenge presented in Wilford's essay in the "Documentary Materials" section of this chapter: Does Lake Champlain have a sea monster (like Scotland's Loch Ness Monster)? Lehn's essay describes his scientific analysis of a phenomenon—atmospheric refraction over a lake which results in the distortion of images—which may result in sightings of "lake monsters." The essay appeared in a leading professional journal, Science, *indicating that it has passed the scrutiny*

of his professional peers. It does not, in itself, "debunk" the possibility of
lake monsters, but it does, in Lehn's words, aid in "weeding-out" reports
which would not rate as decisive pieces of evidence.

Lehn's hypothesis that "image distortion" may result in
"sightings" of lake monsters is supported by his research into the weather
conditions which create such images and which accompany monster
sightings. Furthermore, he provides photographs of actual distortions to
supplement his argument. He is careful not to deny the existence of
lake monsters; he is trying, he states, only to show that certain
observations may be due to atmospheric refraction instead.

Lehn follows traditional and solid scientific method: He reviews
what has already been written about "lake monsters" and then isolates
one factor which he finds missing from most accounts—that the "observed
or photographed evidence might have been optically distorted by the
atmosphere." He then proceeds to examine this omission by considering
both the observations made by others and his own photographic work.

Atmospheric Refraction and Lake Monsters

Lake monsters have been a part of legend among many peoples.
Modern sightings, too frequent to be ignored, have intrigued many
scientists, with the result that the subject of lake (and sea) monsters
has become the focus of some serious research. Gould (1) and Mackal
(2), and others have collected enough careful reports from reputable
eyewitnesses to dispel any doubt that the observers were indeed
seeing unusual phenomena.

The one element missing from all of these reports (with the
exception of Mackal's brief and somewhat incomplete appendix on
mirages) is any consideration that the observed or photographed
evidence might have been optically distorted by the atmosphere. It
may well be that many sightings of monsters can be explained as the
sighting of a distorted and hence unrecognized image of a familiar
creature or phenomenon.

In the same way that Mackal carefully weeds out much of the
"evidence" as representing standing waves, birds, otters, and so on,
it may be possible to accomplish some further weeding-out on the
basis of image distortion.

It is well known that approximately horizontal light rays are refracted slightly downward, toward the denser layers of the atmosphere (3). This refraction can become strong enough to cause visible distortions if a temperature inversion° is present to steepen the density gradient° near the earth's surface (4). Very interesting cases arise when the temperature gradient° is nonuniform with elevation. A single point on the object can then be the source for several rays, all entering the observer's eye at different vertical angles. The eye assumes that the rays entering it are straight; hence the observer perceives such a point as several different points at different elevations. When there is a continuum of many rays passing from the single object point to the eye, these image points appear to coalesce into a vertical line. The resulting vertical distension of features with this zone generally distorts them so much that they become unrecognizable (5).

A great many of the reports of monster sightings describe atmospheric conditions that are ideal for generating distorted images. Several relevant points are discussed in the following paragraphs.

According to Costello (6), monsters are frequently reported in Loch Ness, Scotland, as well as "in many other steep-shored lakes in the cold temperate regions of the Northern and Southern Hemispheres, roughly in a band on either side of 10° C isotherms."° The surface water temperature of such lakes is usually well below that of the air for the first half of the year, since the warming of the lake lags significantly behind the air temperature. Hence a temperature inversion near the water surface is virtually guaranteed for much of the time during the spring and summer months. Nighttime pooling of the cold air draining down the slopes will further strengthen this inversion. The notion that surface temperature inversions are correlated with monster sightings is supported by Mackal's analysis (2, appendix I) of Loch Ness data: of 249 sightings, only 31 were made at air

○ temperature inversion: a reversal of the usual situation; therefore, the temperature rises at higher levels instead of decreasing.
○ density gradient: The scale of density changes depending on the height at which the density is measured.
○ temperature gradient: The scale of temperature changes depending on the height at which the temperature is measured. In note 4, a gradient of 0.11 C/m would mean a change of $^{11}/_{100}$ of a degree Centigrade (C) per 1 meter (m) change in height.
○ isotherm: an imaginary line marking a region at a certain temperature.

temperatures below 13° C. Also, of a similar number of sightings, 77 percent were made in May through August—the months when the lake temperature lags behind the air temperature. Mackal states that the surface water temperature rarely reaches 15° C at the height of the warming; during spring and early summer the surface water is much colder.

The steep shores that Costello mentioned are not strictly necessary. The spring and summer inversions over prairie lakes (Lakes Manitoba and Winnipeg, for example) serve admirably for the generation of distorted images. Lake Manitoba is even reputed to have its own monster, Manipogo (7).

Another interesting correlation arises from Mackal's summary of lake surface conditions: 84 percent of the Loch Ness observations describe the lake as being calm or having only small ripples. Mackal is quite correct in stating that "disturbances at the surface are much easier to detect when the surface is otherwise calm" (2, p. 88). However, such conditions are also best for developing the strong shallow conduction inversion necessary for transmitting stable but distorted images.

Many of the sightings involve observer elevations close to the level of the lake itself—with the observer near the shore or in a boat. The distances along the line of sight are often of the order of 1 km or more (8). Either or both of these conditions require low, nearly horizontal light rays to pass from object to observer. Exactly these rays are most easily (and noticeably) deflected by refractive anomalies in the air.

Many different shapes are reported for the monsters seen in any particular lake. This is not surprising if some of the sightings are indeed distorted and unrecognizable objects of different though familiar objects. Conversely, similar objects distorted in different ways would also result in different descriptions.

The type of motion described in many of the sighting reports is consistent with observation of refractive effects. Within a stationary inversion layer, the nature of the transmitted image is quite sensitive to variations in the observer's elevation. The image can undergo a large vertical shift in response to small vertical movements of the observer. Further, under the right conditions, inanimate objects can appear mobile even if the observer himself is stationary. If the inversion layer is in slow motion, perhaps containing wavelike undulations, the image can grow, shrink, or move about. It can also appear and disappear without a sound or a ripple, as many of the observations describe. Such undulations can impart a sinuous appearance to an otherwise straight horizontal object (9). Possibly some of the reports of sinuous neck and body movements can be attributed to this effect.

Of the many hundreds of observations, only one will be summarized here (2, pp. 103–104; 10). The observation was made by H. L. Cockrell in the fall of 1958. Cockrell had spent several nights on Loch Ness in a kayak, hoping to photograph the monster at night. At dawn, at the end of his third night on the lake, the breeze suddenly dropped and left the lake surface mirror-smooth. As Dinsdale (10) quotes Cockrell, "Something appeared—or I noticed it for the first time—about 50 yards away on my port bow. It seemed to be swimming very steadily and converging on me. It looked like a very large flat head four or five feet long, and wide. About three feet astern of this I noticed another thin line. All very low in the water; just awash. I was convinced it was the head and back of a very large creature. It looked slightly whiskery and misshapen." Cockrell managed to take two photographs before a slight squall passed over the lake, and the object appeared to sink. After the squall had passed, he again saw something on the surface, but this time the object proved to be a floating stick, 4 feet long and 1 inch thick.

Mackal conjectures that the entire experience was the result of fatigue and "tremendous psychological bias," although this does not explain why the squall would interrupt the appearance. On the other hand, an explanation based on atmospheric refraction is quite consistent with the conditions described. The thickness of the stick could have been magnified by refraction due to a strong inversion over the lake. The refraction could even produce a second image vertically displaced from the first, to account for the second thin line seen slightly astern of the "head." These stable viewing conditions would be disrupted by the squall, causing the disappearance of the monster and the reappearance of the stick in its normal aspect.

An example of atmospheric distortion observed on Lake Winnipeg is provided by Figs. 1 to 3. The photographs were taken on the east shore of the lake on 25 April 1977. The air temperature was about 25° C, while the frozen lake surface was near 0° C. A very light east wind was moving warm air from the land to the lake. The calm air and extreme temperature differences permitted a very strong

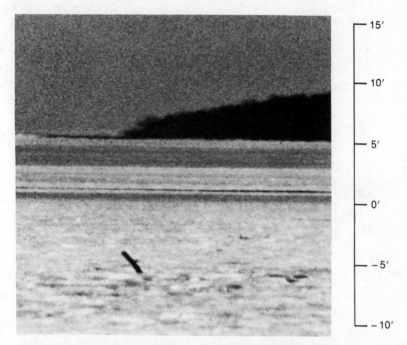

Figure 1. East side of Lake Winnipeg: view of Ironwood Point, 10 km away, from Grand Beach. The scale shows angles (in minutes of arc) subtended at the observer's eye.

Figure 2. The protruding stick of Fig. 1, vertically compressed by refraction (3:56 P.M. CDT).

Figure 3. The protruding stick of Figs. 1 and 2, vertically distended by refraction (3:59 P.M. CDT).

(nonuniform) conduction inversion° to develop over the lake. Observations were made by theodolite,° and photographs were taken from a fixed location with a Leitz 560-mm telephoto lens on Kodachrome 64 film. The lens elevation for all photographs was 1.4 mm above the lake surface.

Figure 1 shows a general view looking north over the lake to Ironwood Point, 10 km distant from the camera. The stick that protrudes from the ice in the foreground is estimated to be between 1 and 1 ½ km away from the camera. The vertical scale on the photograph is positioned to give the correct absolute elevation angle of the line of sight, as determined by the theodolite measurement at the time of the photograph. The calibration is in terms of angles subtended at the observer's eye. Because of the anomalous refraction, the horizon is elevated 6' above the level (11).

The photographs in Figs. 2 and 3 show different aspects taken on by the protruding stick at different times (12). The magnification is identical on both photographs, and the scale of subtended angles is provided along the edge of each (13). In Fig. 2 made at 3:56 P.M. central daylight time (CDT), the stick appears kinked and flattened,

---

° conduction inversion: a change in temperature conditions as a result of the movement of heat (in this case, "a very light east wind was moving warm air from the land to the lake").

° theodolite: precision instrument which gives readings of horizontal angles.

subtending an angle of only 1 ½'. In Fig. 3, made only 3 minutes later, the stick looks entirely different. Its height is now 6' and it appears to have developed a reverse curve. In this case, multiple ray paths originate from a point in the stick's "neck," causing vertical distension. Neither photograph looks very much like the real object itself. They are, however, not unlike some of the photographs given as evidence of the existence of lake monsters.

In summary, many of the conditions under which lake monsters have been sighted are ideal for the existence of strong atmospheric refraction. A critical analysis of sighting reports and photographs could likely explain many of them as distorted images of familiar objects.

It is to be hoped that all future reports of monster sightings will include sufficient meteorological data, such as general weather conditions, air temperature, temperature gradient if possible, and water temperature. Then a reasonable assessment can be made of whether the observation can, wholly or in part, be attributed to anomalous atmospheric refraction.

It is not the aim of this report to discredit the existence of yet unidentified animals or species, for there is impressive evidence to the contrary from sonar data and underwater photography. Rather, the objective is to sharpen optical observation techniques and to provide one more stage of evaluation before accepting such observations as unequivocal evidence (14).

REFERENCES AND NOTES

1. R. T. Gould, *The Case for the Sea Serpent* (Philip Allan, London, 1980).
2. R. P. Mackal, *The Monsters of Loch Ness* (Swallow, Chicago, 1976).
3. An extensive literature exists. On atmospheric refraction, see texts such as J. M. Pernter and F. M. Exner, *Meteorologische Optik* (Braumuller, Vienna, 1922); M. Minnaert, *Light and Colour in the Open Air* (Bell, London, 1940); W. J. Humphreys, *Physics of the Air* (Dover, New York, 1964); H. R. Reed and C. M. Russell, *Ultra High Frequency Propagation* (Boston Technical Publishers, Cambridge, 1966). On image distortion see, for example, A. B. Fraser, *Appl. Opt. 14*, A92 (1975); W. H. Lehn and H. L. Sawatzky, *Polarforschung 45*, 120 (1975); W. H. Lehn and M. B. El-Arini, *Appl. Opt. 17*, 3146 (1978); W. H. Lehn, *J. Opt. Soc. Am.*, in press.
4. The curvature of a nearly horizontal ray is approximately proportional to the temperature gradient. As an example, if the surface temperature is 0° C, an inversion with the relatively mild gradient of 0.11° C/m is sufficient to produce rays with the same curvature as the earth's.

5. See, for example, J. P. Koch, *Medd. Groenl. 46,* 191 (1917); J. P. Koch and A. Wegener, *ibid. 75,* 610 (1930). I have made frequent observations of such zones of vertical distension.

6. P. Costello, *In Search of Lake Monsters* (Garnstone, London, 1974), p. 290.

7. I have observed and photographed numerous mirages on Lakes Manitoba and Winnipeg. One of the observations was made by chance while swimming in Lake Manitoba on a hot day (7 August 1976); a thin horizontal black strip appeared on the surface of the lake for a few minutes, at an apparent distance of 1 or 2 km. Experience dictated that the observation be attributed to atmospheric refraction, but very little help from the imagination would have been required to interpret the shape as a long black serpent. For a brief history of the Manipogo case, see Costello (6, pp. 229–232).

8. To estimate distances of this magnitude by eye is difficult enough in a normal atmosphere; to do it in the presence of refractive anomalies is virtually impossible [for example, see W. H. Hobbs, *Ann. Assoc. Am. Geogr. 27,* 229 (1937)].

9. I have filmed such wavelike motion on Lake Winnipeg.

10. T. Dinsdale, *Loch Ness Monster* (Routledge & Kegan Paul, London, 1976), pp. 101–103.

11. For a camera height of 1.4 m, normal atmospheric conditions give a horizon elevation of about 2′ *below* the level.

12. Between 3:20 and 6:23 P.M., 22 exposures were made of this subject, each at a shutter speed of ¹⁄₂₅₀ second.

13. The photographs have been highly magnified, but not beyond the resolving ability of the unaided eye. Mackal (2, p. 250) gives the latter as ½′ of arc, and in a number of his cases the object observed subtended angles of this magnitude.

14. This work was supported in part by the University of Manitoba Northern Studies Committee, funded through the Federal Department of Indian and Northern Affairs, Ottawa, Canada.

DOCUMENTARY MATERIALS

FOLKLORE

WILLIAM T. COX

In these three sketches, Cox imitates scientific reports of the discovery of new species. (In keeping with the format of this section, perhaps only actual reports should be found here, but I am making an exception for folklore!) He includes all the important data: scientific name, habitat, and behavior. He also offers anecdotal material where appropriate.

In addition to imitating scientific reports, the author also uses the strategy of tall tales by providing the natural details ("wrecked forest . . . often ascribed to windstorms") to explain why the beast in question has for so long been undetected. As in the tall tales of folklore, Cox's creatures are always present—it's just that ordinary observers often miss them.

[Three Fearsome Creatures]

1. THE CACTUS CAT (*CATIFELINUS INEBRIUS*)

How many people have heard of the cactus cat? Thousands of people spend their winters in the great Southwest—the land of desert and mountain, of fruitful valleys, of flat-topped mesas, of Pueblos, Navajos, and Apaches, of sunshine, and the ruins of ancient cliff-dwellers. It is doubtful, however, if one in a hundred of these people ever heard of a cactus cat, to say nothing of seeing one sporting among the cholla and palo verde. Only the old-timers know of the beast and its queer habits.

The cactus cat, as its name signifies, lives in the great cactus districts, and is particularly abundant between Prescott and Tucson. It has been reported, also, from the valley of the lower Yaqui, in Old Mexico, and the cholla-covered hills of Yucatan. The cactus cat has thorny hair, the thorns being especially long and rigid on its ears. Its tail is branched and upon the forearms above its front feet are sharp, knifelike blades of bone. With these blades it slashes the base of giant cactus trees, causing the sap to exude. This is done systematically, many trees being slashed in the course of several nights as the cat makes a big circuit. By the time it is back to the place of beginning the sap of the first cactus has femented into a kind of mescal, sweet and very intoxicating. This is greedily lapped up by the thirsty beast, which soon becomes fiddling drunk, and goes waltzing off in the moonlight, rasping its bony forearms across each other and screaming with delight.

2. THE SQUONK (*LACRIMACORPUS DISSOLVENS*)

The range of the squonk is very limited. Few people outside of Pennsylvania have ever heard of the quaint beast, which is said to be fairly common in the hemlock forest of that state. The squonk is of a very retiring disposition, generally traveling about at twilight and dusk. Because of its misfitting skin, which is covered with warts and moles, it is always unhappy; in fact it is said, by people who are best able to judge, to be the most morbid of beasts. Hunters who are good at tracking are able to follow a squonk by its tear-stained trail, for the animal weeps constantly. When cornered and escape seems impossible, or when surprised and frightened, it may even dissolve itself in tears. Squonk hunters are most successful on frosty moonlight nights, when tears are shed slowly and the animal dislikes moving about; it may then be heard weeping under the boughs of dark hemlock trees. Mr. J. P. Wentling, formerly of Pennsylvania, but now at St. Anthony Park, Minnesota, had a disappointing experience with a squonk near Mont Alto. He made a clever capture by mimicking the squonk and inducing it to hop into a sack, in which he was carrying it home, when suddenly the burden lightened and the weeping ceased. Wentling unslung the sack and looked in it. There was nothing but tears and bubbles.

3. THE SPLINTER CAT (*FELYNX ARBODIFFISUS*)

A widely distributed and frightfully destructive animal is the splinter cat. It is found from the Great Lakes to the Gulf, and eastward to the Atlantic Ocean, but in the Rocky Mountains has been reported from only a few localities. Apparently the splinter cat inhabits that part of the country in which wild bees and raccoons abound. These are its natural food, and the animal puts in every dark and stormy night shattering trees in search of coons or honey. It doesn't use any judgment in selecting coon trees or bee trees, but just smashes one tree after another until a hollow one containing food is found. The method used by this animal in its destructive work is simple but effective. It climbs one tree, and from the uppermost branches bounds down and across toward the tree it wishes to destroy. Striking squarely with its hard face, the splinter cat passes right on, leaving the tree broken and shattered as though struck by lightening or snapped off by the wind. Appalling destruction has been wrought by this animal in the Gulf States, where its work in the shape of a wrecked forest is often ascribed to windstorms.

JOURNALISM

TOM LOFTIS

Probably many local reporters like Tom Loftis of Northern Kentucky's Kentucky Post *are assigned stories like this one: Three man-high birds have landed in rural Northern Kentucky—Quick, send out our new-species reporter! This is the stuff of local folklore, even if the education director at a nearby zoo says "They were probably Great Blue Herons."*

As a local "human interest" feature story, this newspaper piece includes the usual details of journalism. Loftis adds the anecdotes he picked up as he becomes part of an unofficial "investigating" team. These anecdotes and his participation reflect the homey touch of small-city journalism.

What? Three Man-high Birds

Glencoe, Kentucky: Jack Benny Courtney took his two daughters to the school bus stop and drove back the winding gravel road to his farm. He pulled up next to his white, two-story frame house, hopped out of his pick-up and walked down to the dirt path behind the house to the barn to feed his 80 Hereford and Angus cattle. Courtney loaded up the grain and hay troughs behind the barn and walked back past the house to the tobacco-stripping barn. It was a slightly overcast, normal Monday morning for the 37-year-old farmer, until he noticed three strange creatures about 1500 feet away in his cornfield.

Are those deer? he thought.

As he drew closer the creatures appeared bluish and were taller and thinner than deer. At 700 feet he recognized them: three giant purplish-gray birds, feeding in the plowed-under cornfield in front of the house.

"Quick, Mary, get out here and see this," he yelled to his wife as he ran into the house to get a camera. Fearful of scaring the creatures away, Jack and Mary Courtney quickly and quietly crept closer when Jack's mother, Lucille Courtney, Glencoe, drove up to the house. She saw the creatures in the field and thought they were giant blue flying monkeys. Courtney took a Polaroid snapshot of the big birds from 400 feet. When he tried to get closer, the three taxied down the cornfield, flapped up in the air and glided off toward the west. The photo was taken from too far a distance to be conclusive. It reveals only three grayish shapes of what could be birds.

Both Jack and Mary Courtney described the birds as about five feet tall, with long legs and necks and dark purple in color. They had about four-inch-long pointed beaks and a tuft of blue feathers at the back of their heads.

The incident which occurred March 7 reminded Jack Courtney of a similar large bird he saw two years ago on a small island on the lake behind his barn. Courtney got within 100 feet of that bird before it "flapped off making a whole lot of noise." Courtney said this bird was about six feet tall. "And I wasn't drinking either time," he volunteered.

Courtney told his sister's father-in-law, Clarence Vest of Verona, of both sightings. Vest, a retired ranger at Big Bone Lick State Park recalled that park Superintendent Jim Cleek had once told him of a similar incident near the park. Cleek recounted the most bizarre story of all. He said a man in his late 20's came into his office one morning two years ago and said a giant fanged bird was hovering over his house on Bender Road, the night before. "He said that it had jagged teeth, that it went 'Whoooosh, whoooosh, whooosh' when it flew . . . and it had no neck at all," Cleek said. "I thought at first the guy was drunk, full of pot or something, but his father also told us the same story. Two days later they moved out of the house because of it," Cleek said.

Cleek obtained Courtney's recent bird photo and asked Randy Cochran, *Kentucky Post* managing editor for graphics, to check into the great bird mystery. Cochran had the photo blown up, but still the shapes in the photo could not be distinguished.

This reporter, photographer Joe Ruh, and cartoonist Jack Gold went to the Courtneys' home Tuesday. We paged through the Court-neys' nature encyclopedia with the Courtneys who said the birds in the field looked somewhat like pictures of a Sandhill Crane or Great Blue Heron. But Sandhill Cranes are too small to fit the description and seldom found in this area, said Barry Wakeman, education coordinator at the Cincinnati Zoo.

Wakeman said the birds Courtney saw "probably were Great Blue Herons, although they are seldom seen in cornfields. They often grow to about five feet tall."

JOURNALISM

JOHN NOBLE WILFORD

When does a local monster become a national or even an international star? A simple answer may be when a national newspaper like the New York Times *picks up its story. Although "man-high" birds like those from Glencoe, Kentucky, have been sighted in other regions of the country, that particular set of birds would not necessarily receive national coverage. There are some similarities in this article by Wilford and the previous article from the* Kentucky Post, *but the* Times *has devoted considerably more space and energy to providing an extensive background to the usual details of a feature news story.*

Furthermore, to go national, the monster must attract scientists on both sides of the question. Here we meet J. Richard Greenwell and Roy Mackal, both leaders in the International Society of Cryptozoology, an organization of scientists which is committed to the belief that such animals exist (but are temporarily hidden or "cryptic"), and W. H. Lehn, whose more skeptical essay, based on the analysis of distortion in sightings because of atmospheric refraction, appeared in "Essays from the Disciplines" above. And, finally, a monster needs a strong fan club with a persistent leader, and Champ has one in Joe Zarzynski (see "Sources" for more information about his book, which reprints the Mansi photo discussed in Wilford's article).

In this feature story, Wilford is especially concerned about airing both sides of a controversial question. Loftis, as a local reporter, is mainly reporting what the farmers believe *they saw and only secondarily trying to find out what they* actually *saw.*

Is It Lake Champlain's Monster?

On July 5, 1977, Sandra Mansi was showing her husband-to-be the countryside around Lake Champlain where she had grown up. They talked and laughed about the legends of a large monster inhabiting the lake. While sitting on the shore, she recalled, they saw something move far out in the water. She thought it was a school of large fish, she said, until a head and then a long serpentine neck emerged from the water, growing bigger and bigger.

"I was scared to death," Mrs. Mansi said in an interview the other day. "I had a feeling I shouldn't be there."

Mrs. Mansi said she collected herself enough to snap a single color picture with a Kodak Instamatic, but decided to say nothing about it to anyone.

But as more and more people began reporting sightings of the so-called Lake Champlain monster, also known as Champ, Mrs. Mansi let it be known that she had what might be the only photograph of the creature.

For the scientists who would examine the picture in the ensuing months it would be one more of those tantalizing bits of evidence regarding the still tightly held secrets of nature. The evidence must be treated with the greatest skepticism, but it can't be rejected out of hand.

Dr. Roy P. Mackal, a University of Chicago biochemist who is an expert on the Loch Ness monster and other legendary animals, persuaded Mrs. Mansi to submit the photograph for analysis by scientists at the University of Arizona Optical Sciences Center.

The analysis has now been completed, and the Arizona optical scientists confirm that the picture has not been tampered with, though it was beyond their scope to determine whether the object in the picture was animate or inanimate, something ordinary or extraordinary. The believers can still believe that Lake Champlain, along with Loch Ness and other northern bodies of water, could harbor strange creatures from out of the past. The skeptics can still be skeptical, pointing out that observers can be deceived by atmospheric conditions or the giant sturgeon that sometimes break the surface of Champlain.

According to Dr. B. Roy Frieden, professor of optical sciences at Arizona, Mrs. Mansi's photograph was a high-quality print that "does not appear to be a montage or a superimposition of any kind" and that "the object appears to belong in the picture."

"We don't see any evidence of tampering with the photo," Dr. Frieden concluded.

To see if the object might have been superimposed on the

picture, Dr. Frieden examined the wave patterns through a microscope. There were no sharp lines of divergence in the waves.

The photograph was next examined through techniques developed for processing and enhancing images in military surveillance and planetary exploration by spacecraft. Called the Interactive Picture Processing System, the technique involves scanning the photograph by a densitometer, an array of light detectors that converts every point in the photograph into digital form and then records the digital codes on magnetic tape. More than one million numbers from the Champlain picture were stored on magnetic tape.

The tape was then played back and the picture displayed on a screen. By twisting dials, Dr. Frieden could change the light contrast and highlight certain features. He did this to determine if any objects—pulleys or ropes or anything suggesting a hoax—not readily visible in the photograph might be revealed. No such objects emerged.

J. Richard Greenwell, another member of the University of Arizona staff, who worked with Dr. Frieden during the analysis, said that all of the data from the photograph were stored on computer punch cards and used in further studies. Marine biologists who do research for the United States Navy are expected to conduct more detailed analyses of the object and the surrounding wave patterns.

Dr. Frieden observed one detail in the picture, a horizontal dark streak going from left to right, that "merits looking into." This, he suggested, could be a sandbar, which would make it easier for someone to have reached the site to perpetrate a hoax. Dr. Frieden emphasized, however, that he had no reason to believe that the object was indeed a hoax.

Mrs. Mansi said that she was sure it was no hoax. "I saw it move. I saw it at different angles. You know if something is living or not," she said.

Dr. Philip Reines, a professor of communications at the State University College at Plattsburgh, N.Y., who is considered an expert on nautical phenomena, said that two aspects of the Mansi photograph bothered him. One is that Mrs. Mansi says she cannot recall exactly where she took the picture. The other is that the negative of the picture is missing.

Dr. Reines said that having the negative would enable investigators to blow up and otherwise manipulate the picture with less distortion. Knowing the cove where the picture was taken, he added, would permit a more detailed examination of the water and the depths and thus determine the scale of the picture.

Mrs. Mansi, who now lives in Winchester, N.H., said that all she could remember is that the picture was taken from a secluded location north of St. Albans, Vt. She said that she was standing on a bank about six feet above the water line and about 100 to 150 feet from the object.

Dr. Reines said that the photograph was "very exciting," but he added, "I'm skeptical—the picture can very easily be misunderstood. People around here are very cautious in these matters. They want to make sure this isn't made into a farce and a circus."

In an article in the journal *Science* in 1979, Dr. W. H. Lehn of the University of Manitoba, raised the possibility that some of the reported sightings of lake monsters could be attributed to atmospheric distortions. Light refraction, caused by a temperature inversion that happens when cold lake water chills the lower layers of the air, could distort a stick or some other ordinary object so that it would take on a monstrous size or form.

Dr. Mackal of the University of Chicago, on the other hand, said that the picture tends to support his "working hypothesis" that the so-called monsters of Loch Ness, Lake Champlain and other lakes are "some kind of rare, elusive mammal, probably related to the zeuglodon, which was one episode in the evolution of the whale." The zeuglodon is thought to have been extinct for 20 million years.

"I've looked at the evidence and I'm convinced that the animals are there," Dr. Mackal said. "They are seagoing, but occasionally come into fresh water following fish, most often salmon. This picture is genuine in all respects and depicts one of these animals."

For the past seven years Joe Zarzynski, a schoolteacher from Saratoga Springs, N.Y., has been cataloguing reports of those who claim to have seen the monster of Lake Champlain with a view to convincing New York and Vermont authorities that the animals do exist and should be protected. He has a list of 132 sightings, some dating back to the 19th century, when P. T. Barnum advertised a $50,000 reward for a carcass, but most of them were reported in the last few years.

Mr. Zarzynski told of eight sightings since April. Two dark humps were seen in the water near Fort Ticonderoga. Something dark and 25 to 30 feet long was seen near Fort Henry, N.Y. On June 10

Marty Santos of Grand Isle, Vt., reported that while fishing he saw the monster and it seemed to be herding perch.

"I've never seen it myself," Mr. Zarzynski said. "I know there are theories that explain it away, the most common being that it is a large sturgeon. But some of these sightings are tough to shoot holes in. The Mansi picture is the first clear-cut photograph of Champ that I'm aware of. It really puts the cap on things."

STUDENT ESSAYS

Assignment 6. Write two reports like Cox's "Fearsome Creatures."

JILL BAKER

The Sewer Slug

The sewer slug is a snail-like creature which lives in the moist, dark pipelines of the sewer systems of large, metropolitan areas. This animal is rarely seen but can be heard splashing about the sewer, like an uncontrolled stingray, after particularly heavy rains. The sewer slug feeds primarily on leaves, dirt, and debris found in the water. Also, it enjoys an occasional synthetic dessert, such as a child's lost rubber ball or frisbee, which it can snatch into a pipe before an unsuspecting child can pry off the sewer lid to retrieve the toy.

The sewer slug resembles its taxonomic relative—the garden slug. It takes the shape of a gray, translucent frisbee, which is also one of its favorite delicacies. The slug can range from three to ten inches in diameter. If one was able to catch it, the slug would feel like the toy "Slime."

The sewer slug has a relatively short life span of fifty-three to fifty-five days. Exactly nine days before its death, the slug begins reducing its food intake. By the last night, the slug is dark brown in color, due to the depleted water intake, and is very weak. The night of its death, the sewer slug crawls out of the sewer to the gutter adjacent to its home and dies. As dawn breaks, an early riser may catch his first and final glimpse of the sewer slug disappearing into the morning mist as an evaporating puddle.

JENNIFER DIETRICH

The Cactus Animalia

The Cactus Animalia is of such diverse nature that taxonomists have not yet been able to classify it. As its name implies it has both plant and animal characteristics. At present our taxonomic system has it classified among the Animal Kingdom due to its ability to uproot and move about, a form of locomotion. The plant-like animal stands six to eight feet tall when fully uprooted and has sharp projectile and prickly arms or branches which extend from the center or pod of the stalk. The plant-animal grows only partially by photosynthesis and contains chlorophyll like most other green plants, but fleshy meat is its delicacy. When uprooted, its large root-like tentacles roam the ground in search of a snake or other desert life that is fleshy enough to satisfy the cactus's hunger. The creature settles for nothing less and therefore moves from place to place engulfing everything and spitting it back unless that piece of the desert satisfies its appetite.

Very few people have seen the creature due to the extreme heat of his Death Valley home where only night temperatures permit investigation of these cacti. When the sun sets and the moon creeps in, as the animal rests or sleeps, his root-like tentacles sink deep in the ground minimizing his body to three-fourths its size. This therefore makes the Cactus Animalia almost undistinguishable from other desert cacti. As far as scientists can tell the Cactus Animalia have always lived in the desert and have no intention of leaving. They can survive on photosynthesis and by other desert plant characteristics, even though they don't like to, and seem to have always managed to find meat somewhere in the Death Valley area. As records show, these cacti have been seen in the daylight moving at great speeds, but to get close enough to see distinct features resulted in the death of a few courageous but fleshy taxonomists.

QUESTIONS FOR DISCUSSION

WITHIN THIS CHAPTER:

1. What qualities of Hetty Fifield, in "A Church Mouse," do you consider distinctively American? How about Andrew Carnegie of "Old Andy Comes to the North Star Country"? or Johnny TV

Peluso of "Newport, Ky.—Across the River"? Do you detect one distinctive American "type," or set, of American characteristics?

2. Which author does a better job of conveying the sense of an American *place*: McPhee in "The Search for Marvin Gardens" or Trillin in "Newport, Ky.—Across the River"? Why?

3. What did George R. Stewart look for when considering a spot for his "biography" of a road, U.S. 40?

4. What characteristics do the sighting of unknown or fantastic creatures have in common?

5. What characteristics—based on your reading of *all* the selections in this chapter—would you require for a place or era to be considered an "American scene"?

Using Other Chapters:

6. How would the distinctions between "hallucination" and "perception" offered by Gibson in Chapter 3 help in the analysis of the unknown creatures discussed by Lehn, Loftis, and Wilford?

7. How does Roueché's "An Emotion of Weirdness" (Chapter 3) use the sense of place which is characteristic of many of the selections in this chapter?

8. What characteristics of the "American scene" do you find in the five *New York Times* cases in Chapter 4?

9. Could the events in seventeenth-century Salem (Chapter 5) or at Jonestown (Chapter 6) have happened anywhere? Would you argue instead that there is a distinctive sense of, or need for, a certain "place" for them?

10. Is there any similarity between the sightings of unknown creatures in this chapter and the sightings of "spectral images" or witches in Chapter 5?

ASSIGNMENTS

Within This Chapter:

1. Write an essay proposing a Grand Urban Scheme (like that of Trillin's Johnny TV Peluso)—some dramatic architectural or structural change in your area which would satisfy at least three of these conditions: (1) help business make money; (2) be unusual; (3) be visible at a fair distance; and (4) be safe.

2. After reading the three excerpts from Stewart, visit a square or intersection or some other spot in your area which lends itself to a compilation of observations and historical research like Stewart's. Write a journal entry or essay to capture a sense of the cultural history of this spot. (If convenient, include a snapshot or a Polaroid photo.)

3. In an essay, compare and contrast the interaction of the appearance and function of a local site as it was at least fifty years ago and as it is now. Be sure to include the site's exact location and the year or decade you have selected as a basis for comparison. If you are unsure about its past function, make an intelligent guess. It may be helpful to browse in local history sources first so that you are not in the position of admiring a spot which unfortunately has no recorded history. City atlases and business directories would also help.

4. Write a profile of a prominent or a controversial person in your community or region, emphasizing the relationship of this individual to the community or region. If possible, include quotations or incidents gathered from the local press or media, or even from interviews.

5. Write a folktale (perhaps a tall tale) based on the lives of the seven Merritt brothers depicted in Le Sueur's "Old Andy Comes to the North Star Country."

6. Write two reports like Cox's "Fearsome Creatures."

7. In the Ohio River (as in many other rivers) live giant catfish (five to seven feet long) that are only rarely spotted, and even more rarely captured. Write a news report based on your investigation of a giant catfish having been spotted by underwater construction workers at the site of a new bridge over the Ohio River. One of the workers has a fuzzy photograph taken with an underwater camera used at these sites to check the bridge's pilings.

8. In an essay, explain how you would apply Lehn's methods to any of the unknown creatures discussed by Loftis and Wilford.

9. Research the "discovery" of the coelacanth (a fish found only in fossil form until the 1930s) using the *New York Times Index* and *The Reader's Guide to Periodical Literature* for 1939. Survey and classify the different attitudes towards this "unknown animal." Sample a variety of types of reports—those in a newspaper, a popular magazine, a scientific journal, and a general or literary magazine.

10. Collect from friends, acquaintances, classmates, or children samples of folklore, such as jokes, jump-rope rhymes (or other games), tales,

graffiti, rituals (visiting a graveyard at night), etc. In an essay, describe and explain the samples you have collected and give a possible interpretation of the reasons for their popularity among the "subjects" you interviewed or listened to.

BEYOND THIS CHAPTER:

11. Using the selections by Le Sueur, Stewart, and Trillin in this chapter, and Chief Seattle's speech in Chapter 3, classify the different meanings "place" can have.

12. Using any of the selections in this chapter, or those in other chapters (such as Whittier, or others, in Chapter 5), define the differences between science and superstition, or science and folklore. Concentrate both on the objects of study and the methods.

SOURCES FOR FURTHER READING AND/OR RESEARCH

BONNER, JOHN TYLER. *Cellular Slime Molds.* Princeton: Princeton University Press, 1959. The standard book on the subject. Includes revealing photos of all aspects of a slime mold's life and loves. Excellent source for creating stories of unusual and/or fearsome creatures!

BRUNVAND, JAN HAROLD. *Folklore: A Study and Research Guide.* New York: St. Martin's Press, 1976. Short but thorough guide to the field of folklore —how to collect, how to do research, and how to write up the results; hints for beginning students plus a sample paper and a glossary.

————. *The Vanishing Hitchhiker: American Urban Legends and Their Meanings.* New York: Norton, 1981. Gathers together many contemporary urban folktales. Besides the title story, we encounter such other classics as "The Spider in the Hairdo" and the "Alligators in the Sewers."

COFFIN, TRISTRAM P., AND HENNIG COHEN, EDS. *Folklore in America.* New York: Doubleday, 1968. Small but nice collection of "tales, songs, superstitions, proverbs, riddles, games, folk drama and folk festivals," gathered from the *Journal of American Folklore.*

CONRON, JOHN. *The American Landscape: A Critical Anthology of Prose and Poetry.* New York: Oxford University Press, 1973. A textbook, chock full of excerpts from both famous and obscure writers from four centuries of writing about the landscape.

DORSON, RICHARD M. *America in Legend: Folklore from the Colonial Period to the Present.* New York: Pantheon, 1973. A rich collection of tales, songs, photos, and analysis surveying the "religious impulse" of the colonial period, the "democratic impulse" of the early national period, the "economic impulse" of the later national period, and the "humane impulse" of the contemporary period.

DOYLE, ARTHUR CONAN. *The Lost World* (1900). Various editions available. Doyle's novel almost created a genre of science fiction by itself. An expedition discovers a remote territory populated by animals from the age of dinosaurs. This book is one of the prime creators of such legends in the popular consciousness.

FERRETTI, FRED. "Marven Gardens: All Abloom Again." *New York Times,* August 7, 1977, Sec. II, p. 2. A clear explanation of the difficulties in the spelling of Marven Gardens. Also offers a history and contemporary description of this suburb's development.

FERRIS, WILLIAM. *Local Color: A Sense of Place in Folk Art.* New York: McGraw-Hill, 1983. Although only featuring folk-artists from Mississippi, the book is a model study of the relationship of place, folk art, and cultural voice in general.

GILES, JANICE HOLT. *The Believers* (1957). Various editions available. A novel set in a Shaker settlement in South Union, Kentucky, the home of an extremely influential sect of nineteenth-century worshipers and craftspeople.

GLASSIE, HENRY. *Pattern in the Material Folk Culture of the Eastern United States.* Philadelphia: University of Pennsylvania Press, 1968. The title is slightly deceiving, for this excellent book will guide students in the study of material culture (gravestones, houses, etc.) in any region of the United States. Also includes an extensive bibliography covering all regions.

GOULD, PETER, AND RODNEY WHITE. *Mental Maps.* Harmondsworth: Penguin, 1974. Illustrated with many examples of maps drawn by people whose perceptions of the same area differ because their classes, attitudes, etc. differ. A fascinating study.

HUMPHREYS, J. R. *The Lost Towns and Roads of America.* Garden City: Doubleday, 1961. Although this is a fine book, one should note that the towns were never "lost"—it just takes some time for people who live on the East Coast to find them. In any case, Humphreys travels east to west, stopping at small towns and out of the way places which retain a sense of their own past.

HURSTON, ZORA NEALE. *Mules and Men.* Philadelphia: Lippincott, 1935; various later editions. A collection of black folklore from an outstanding writer, anthropologist, and pioneer folklorist.

JEWETT, SARAH ORNE. "A White Heron," "The Town Poor," and other short stories. Various editions available. Tidy and powerful stories of nineteenth-century country people. Jewett does for Maine what Freeman did for Massachusetts. Great regional writing with universal truths.

KINGSTON, MAXINE HONG. *The Woman Warrior: Memoirs of a Survivor among Ghosts* (1976). Various editions available. Unique mixture of folktales, family stories, and autobiography from a Chinese-American writer.

KOUWENHOVEN, JOHN A. *The Arts in Modern American Civilization* (originally published in 1948 as *Made in America*). New York: Norton, 1967. A survey of the "vernacular" arts, crafts, and industries, emphasizing the American traditions of creating bridges, buildings, and many other objects. Very helpful for analyzing both local and national culture.

LEHN, W. H. "The Norse Merman as an Optical Phenomenon." *Nature,* 289 (Jan. 29, 1981), pp. 362–66. Similar in format to Lehn's article in "Essays from the Disciplines," this piece looks at a legendary Scandinavian animal. Lehn argues, once again, that the image seen does resemble a monster, but that the image seen was not the object there!

LESTER, JULIUS. *Black Folktales.* New York: Grove Press, 1969. Originally published as a collection of stories for the radical black civil-rights movement in the South in the 1960s, this collection now includes Lester's own versions of classic black tales.

LOWENTHAL, DAVID. "The American Scene." *Geographical Review,* 58 (1968), pp. 61–88. An excellent introduction to the idea that *how* we see our landscapes and townscapes is influenced by "idealized images and visual stereotypes."

MACKAL, ROY P. *Searching for Hidden Animals: An Inquiry into Zoological Mysteries.* Garden City: Doubleday, 1980. This probably is one of the fairest and best-written of the books about "the search for unknown animals" by a leading cryptozoologist of the University of Chicago. Includes sections on lake monsters, man-high birds, and other beings large and small, missing and found.

MOMADAY, N. SCOTT. "To the Singing, To the Drums." In Alan Ternes, ed. *Ants, Indians, and Little Dinosaurs.* New York: Scribner's, 1975. An essay by the Kiowan novelist who captures both past and present as he takes a return journey into his southwestern Indian culture.

NAIRN, IAN. *The American Landscape: A Critical View.* New York: Random House, 1965. A book of snapshots, both visual and verbal, of landscapes and townscapes with fine insights throughout; a book whose critical "snapshots" can be imitated by readers and writers anywhere.

RADNER, DAISIE, AND MICHAEL RADNER. *Science and Unreason.* Belmont, Calif.: Wadsworth, 1982. An excellent short textbook which dissects many pieces of pseudoscience (flat earth, ancient astronauts, etc.); an excellent guide to the methods and standards of skeptical science.

RIVERS OF AMERICA. A series of books edited by Hervey Allen and Carl Carmer and published by Rinehart and Company in the 1940s. Virtually every major American river is covered in this series of cultural histories, written by various hands. Consult the card catalog of your library under the name of the river in the region which interests you. The series is uniformly good and includes some notable writers as well: Edgar Lee Masters *(The Sangamon),* Thomas D. Clark *(The Kentucky),* and Frank Waters *(The Colorado).*

ROUECHÉ, BERTON. *Special Places: In Search of Small Town America.* Boston: Little, Brown, 1982. A collection of *New Yorker* magazine essays which capture the spirit and people of small cities and towns across the land. These essays have the same careful touch and sense of detail evident in the essays by Roueché in Chapters 3 and 5 of this text.

SMITH, HENRY NASH. *Virgin Land: The American West as Symbol and Myth* (1950). Cambridge: Harvard University Press, 1970. A cultural and historical study of the West as an image or symbol of a perfect place, an "agrarian utopia."

SOKOLOV, RAYMOND. *Fading Feast: A Compendium of Disappearing Regional Foods.* New York: Farrar, Straus, and Giroux, 1981. An unusually appetizing look at the culture of a number of places where the local folk eat extremely well because of the strength of their regional food traditions.

STEWART, GEORGE R. *Names on the Land: A Historical Account of Placenaming in the United States* (1945). San Francisco: Lexikos, 1982. An invaluable sourcebook.

TERKEL, STUDS. *American Dreams: Lost and Found.* New York: Pantheon, 1980. The bestselling author of *Working* here offers further examples of the twin arts of interviewing and oral history. Terkel attempts what he calls "a jazz work"—an "attempt, of theme and improvisation, to recount dreams, lost and found, and a recognition of possibility" among the one hundred Americans interviewed.

TRILLIN, CALVIN. "Berkeley, California—Monopoly and History." *The New Yorker,* February 13, 1978, pp. 90–96. The saga of Ralph Anspach, the inventor of a game called Anti-Monopoly, who tries to prove—eventually succeeding—that Parker Brothers monopolized the game of Monopoly.

WEBSTER, BAYARD. "Bowerbird of Myth Reported Seen." *New York Times,* November 11, 1981, pp. A1 and A15. A scientist photographs a bird of mythical status (this species of bowerbird not only builds a dramatic nest for its intended mate but lays out a selection of fruit), but his "boat capsized and the film was lost."

WHEELER, THOMAS C. *A Vanishing America: The Life and Times of the Small Town.* New York: Holt, Rinehart, and Winston, 1964. Twelve essays on towns typical of their regions (e.g., Thomas D. Clark on Harrodsburg, Kentucky; Conrad Richter on Pine Grove, Pennsylvania), with an introduction by novelist Wallace Stegner who argues that the "settled small towns of America" may have been "closer to [a] realization" of the American Dream than any comparable experience.

WPA (Works Progress Administration) State and City Guides. This ambitious publishing project in the 1930s covered every state and many cities. Look in the card catalog for specific titles. Many libraries have these books on their reference shelves and occasionally they are reissued by commercial publishers.

Wright, John K. *Human Nature in Geography: Fourteen Papers, 1925–1965.* Cambridge: Harvard University Press, 1966. Primarily a fine collection of essays mixing history and geography; also included are a number of essays which involve literary and religious themes. "From Kubla Khan to Florida" (about a poem by William Blake) and "What's 'American' about American Geography?" are especially recommended.

Zarzynski, Joseph W. *Champ: Beyond the Legend.* Wilton, N.Y.: Bannister Books/Lake Champlain Phenomena Investigation, 1984. A helpful collection of lore and photos about Champ and other cryptozoological phenomena (including the Mansi photo discussed in Wilford's article in "Documentary Materials").

Zelinsky, Wilbur. *The Cultural Geography of the United States.* Englewood Cliffs, N.J.: Prentice-Hall, 1973. A short but very readable text with a fine bibliography.

EXPLORATIONS

1. Ask a variety of people—your siblings, your children, senior citizens, etc.—to draw a map of a specific area (a downtown section or other area) in order to produce what Gould and White call "mental maps" (see "Sources"). How do the maps differ? How do the maps reveal these individuals' different perceptions of the same area?

2. Perhaps you live in an area where an "unknown animal" has been spotted. Visit the animal's supposed home, noting the features of landscape and climate (as Lehn does in "Essays from the Disciplines"). A visit to a local historical society may provide you with information about a legendary local animal or even a "human" creature.

3. Visit your local historical society, campus oral history project, black or ethnic studies center, or women's center. Most of these operate projects of various sorts, hold informational meetings, or present their goals in pamphlets. Find out how these institutions (or ones like them) use the past to understand the present or to influence the future.

CHAPTER TWO

Mechanisms of Mind

The title of this chapter is double-edged. The human mind thinks and solves problems, but by what means—what "mechanisms"—does it accomplish its ends? Although we now have numerous species of computers—"thinking machines"—can they think and solve problems as well as the human mind? Research into, and speculation about, thinking and artificial intelligence have become commonplace in the 1980s as scientists and philosophers attempt to answer two central questions: Can a machine "think"? And, is the human mind similar to a computer? The selections in this chapter approach both of these questions. However, many of the writers inevitably change the two questions into one: What do we mean by "think"?

Thinking and problem-solving are, of course, not identical processes, but trying to reach a solution to a problem does marvelous things to our concentration and makes us self-conscious enough to think about *how* we think. In the first essay, you may "listen" to Pye describe the process by which he came to design a draining rack. The "Documentary Materials" section offers a set of problems (by Duncker) and one strategy, pattern, or "algorithm," devised by Crovitz, to solve such problems. A third selection, by Gardner, describes a game you can play with friends or classmates to test and understand your powers of reasoning in an "inductive" fashion, that is, moving from particular facts to more generalized ideas or "patterns." Duncker and Crovitz come to problem-solving from psychology, while Sackson and Gardner approach the matter as game makers or mathematicians. The game makers are interested in how reality may or may not conform to "rules" or temporary interpretations of reality, while the psychologists are more interested in how the mind grapples with data. Gregory, who has done research in both psychology and artificial intelligence, offers still another viewpoint, in "Essays from the Disciplines," which suggests that we must go beyond psychological models of perception in order to understand how the mind works.

The other two essays from "Essays from the Disciplines," and Le Guin's story at the beginning of the chapter form a definite unit, since they all develop or test the ideas of British mathematician A. M. Turing, who not only helped to develop ideal and prototype computers but also posed what has become *the* most important philosophical question asked about them: How will we know when machines think? To answer this question, Turing devised what he called the "imitation game": Place yourself at a teletype console linked to another such console in a nearby room, where (unknown to you) either a human being or a computer "sits" posed to answer your questions or converse with you. If a machine can answer your questions or converse with you so that its human or mechanical status cannot be identified, then a machine *can* think. The essay by Bolter offers an intriguing discussion of this game, setting it in the context of the on-going debate about the possibility of "artificial intelligence."

Such an "imitation game" (now often called "Turing's Game") was portrayed by Ursula K. Le Guin in her startling short story, "Mazes." Here the consoles are gone and two intelligent (?) and rational (?) beings confront each other. In this story, the outcome is not encouraging: Will communications between rational species and machines eventually reach higher levels?

DISCURSIVE ESSAYS AND FICTIONS

PROCESS ESSAY

DAVID PYE

When you have finished reading this self-contained section from The Nature and Aesthetics of Design *(1964) by David Pye, who is professor of furniture design at England's Royal College of Art, you may well have the reaction that many other readers have had: Would I have thought of* that*? Pye explains the circumstances which led him to the invention of a portable draining rack: He turned to thinking about the "function" he wished to have carried out only after he rejected thinking of the "object" (a draining rack) itself.*

Pye's essay can be broken into three sections. In the first part, he offers some introductory remarks about creativity and invention. He then turns to an analysis of the process of thinking—how the rack was finally "envisaged." His concluding section offers some generalizations about design—how results may come about by concentrating on "function" and avoiding some traditional obstacles to finding solutions. In another section of his book, Pye insists that the usual definition of "function" (how a thing arrives at its results) is inadequate for an understanding of design. "Things," he writes, by themselves do not have "any actions or modes of action," but people do. And it is people who define the "function" of what they design or invent. A draining rack in this particular context (camping) must drain dishes; but it need not resemble other draining racks, even though they share the same "function."

[Designing a Draining Rack]

The poet invents new juxtapositions of words and phrases which convey new thoughts. The inventor makes new juxtapositions of things which give new results. Neither the poet's words nor the inventor's things have any remarkable properties of their own. They are everyday words and things. It is the juxtaposition of them which is new.

Before anything is made a desirable result is likely to have been envisaged. The man who envisages the result may already know of a system or several systems which are capable of giving rise to it, and in that case no further invention is needed. If you say, 'Invent me something which will result in these books and this alarm clock remaining at rest at this level which I indicate on the wall', I shall at once think of a shelf on brackets, which I remember to have seen giving the same sort of result with the same sort of things before. I shall not be hailed as a great inventor. I have simply had to determine the class to which the specified result belongs and to consider which devices of all those in my memory give rise to results of the same class. But have I really done even that? I doubt it. I have simply envisaged the books up there on the wall, compared the vision with various sights stored in my memory, found one which showed books half way up a wall, noticed that there was a shelf under the books, and concluded that a bookshelf would do now because it was suitable before.

That can be a bad procedure. There may be other systems which are better than the first which turns up in the memory.

The author once set about designing a draining rack. It was for the plates, pot-lids and so forth used by his family while living in a tent. It had therefore to be very small and very light. Because he started by thinking 'I must design a draining rack' instead of considering what kind of result was wanted, his train of thought was conditioned unprofitably. Racks act by supporting. Any instance of a rack which will support plates must have dimensions conformable with those of the plates, and there is a limit below which its size and therefore its weight cannot be reduced.

After prolonged thought the designer realized his mistake and started to consider what result he wanted, namely, a row of plastic plates edge-on in mid air. He then started to search his memory for results of the same class but not necessarily involving similar objects or, at any rate, objects which were closely similar. Doing this is not as easy as it sounds. Because it was not easy his mind ran to a result involving objects which, if not closely similar, at any rate were suggested by a very obvious association, namely a row of cups hanging on hooks. The unconscious association must have been plates—saucers: saucers—cups. Thus the thought of plates unearthed the memory of cups.

It was then easy to arrive at the required invention, a thin stick carrying a row of thin wire hooks like cup-hooks; for the desired result was by now well in mind, and the objects in it too, the flexible rather soft plastic plates, which being rather soft at once suggested that holes might be cut in their rims.

Designers and their clients seldom formulate their purposes in terms of the desired results, but on the contrary habitually do so in terms of the systems of things which give rise to them. As the example of the dish rack showed, this may be a bad habit; but it will only be bad if some new factor in the situation, such as plates made out of easily drilled plastic, is overlooked. Otherwise the designer's normal habit is mere common sense. If you want to enable someone to sit, it will be idiotic to proceed in the way that students of design are sometimes advised to do, and think out the whole problem from first principles, as though all the people who for the last four thousand years have been making and using chairs were half-wits. Where the problem is old, the old solutions will nearly always be best (unless a new technique has been introduced) because it is inconceivable that all the designers of ten or twenty generations will have been fools.

When a desirable result is envisaged and the memory, being searched, shows no immediate picture like the bookshelf, then the same procedure must be followed as was done with the dish rack. A similar result involving different objects must be sought, in the hope that the device which gave rise to it can be adapted to the objects which are now intended, or that these can be adapted to the device. It is here that our habit of refusing even to name results, and our habit of referring to them by way of mythical actions, and all the habits of mind associated with them and with the idea of 'function', all these help to make our task more difficult and to inhibit us from discerning analogies between different results; for we are averse from thinking of classes of results, as such, in any case, and have no proper tools to do the thinking with. Invention can only be done deliberately if the inventor can discern similarities between the particular result which he is envisaging and some other actual result which he has seen and stored in his memory (which must of course be well stored so as to give him a wide choice and therefore a better chance). The fact that we habitually visualise particular results is something of a stumbling block, too, in its way. We *envisage* or feel the desired result. We see it or feel it, objects and all. Our memories are visual or muscular memories of particular results, not conceptual memories of classes of results. We see or feel in our memories particular results each including a particular system with its particular components and above all with the particular objects which were involved. Out of that lot we have to abstract the class of result, averting our attention from the particular system and objects. This is not easy when one is reviewing the bloodless ghosts of memory.

If an exact classification of devices were made according to a close analysis of the characteristics of their results it would presumably be possible for computers to invent, provided that their memories were full-fed. For all I know they are doing it now. But it may be doubted whether the classification could be subtle enough or the feeding full enough to enable them to spot far-fetched similarities with the same genius which human inventors have sometimes shown. What association gave Watt his centrifugal governor? A merry-go-round? Who is going to feed a computer with merry-go-rounds?

SHORT STORY

URSULA K. LE GUIN

Anthropologists report the characteristics and behavior of a people; psychologists investigate how people and animals think. "Mazes" brings both anthropology and psychology together in a science-fiction "alien" story. In this story, the narrator, a maze-running animal of some kind, attempts to understand the anthropology of its keeper—either a lab technician or a psychologist—who is charged, in turn, with studying the maze-runner. Both fail miserably.

Species interaction and, of course, mutual suspicions have long been part of science fiction, and here Le Guin has added a new angle on the issue of interspecies communication: a "dance" to which the spectator— the lab technician or psychologist—is blind. This interaction between the narrator and its alien is a form of Turing's "imitation game" described in Turing's and Bolter's essays in "Essays from the Disciplines."

However, this story asks an even more radical question: What if one of the participants—a human one this time—does not even know of his or her involvement in the game?

Mazes

I have tried hard to use my wits and keep up my courage, but I know now that I will not be able to withstand the torture any longer. My perceptions of time are confused, but I think it has been several days since I realised I could no longer keep my emotions under aesthetic control, and now the physical breakdown is also nearly complete. I cannot accomplish any of the greater motions. I cannot speak. Breathing, in this heavy foreign air, grows more difficult. When the paralysis reaches my chest I shall die: probably tonight.

The alien's cruelty is refined, yet irrational. If it intended all along to starve me, why not simply withhold food? But instead of that it gave me plenty of food, mountains of food, all the greenbud leaves I could possibly want. Only they were not fresh. They had been picked; they were dead; the element that makes them digestible to us was gone, and one might as well eat gravel. Yet there they were, with all the scent and shape of greenbud, irresistible to my craving appetite. Not at first, of course. I told myself, I am not a child, to eat picked leaves! But the belly gets the better of the mind. After a while it seemed better to be chewing something, anything, that might still the pain and craving in the gut. So I ate, and ate, and starved. It is a relief, now, to be so weak I cannot eat.

The same elaborately perverse cruelty marks all its behavior. And the worst thing of all is just the one I welcomed with such relief and delight at first: the maze. I was badly disoriented at first, after the trapping, being handled by a giant, being dropped into a prison; and this place around the prison is disorienting, spatially disquieting. The strange, smooth, curved wall-ceiling is of an alien substance and its lines are meaningless to me. So when I was taken up and put down, amidst all this strangeness, in a maze, a recognisable, even familiar maze, it was a moment of strength and hope after great distress. It seemed pretty clear that I had been put in the maze as a kind of test or investigation, that a first approach toward communication was being attempted. I tried to cooperate in every way. But it was not possible to believe for very long that the creature's purpose was to achieve communication.

It is intelligent, highly intelligent, that is clear from a thousand evidences. We are both intelligent creatures, we are both maze-builders: surely it would be quite easy to learn to talk together! If that were what the alien wanted. But it is not. I do not know what kind of mazes it builds for itself. The ones it made for me were instruments of torture.

The mazes were, as I said, of basically familiar types, though the walls were of that foreign material colder and smoother than packed clay. The alien left a pile of picked leaves in one extremity of each maze, I do not know why; it may be a ritual or superstition. The first maze it put me in was babyishly short and simple. Nothing expressive or even interesting could be worked out from it. The second, however, was a kind of simple version of the Ungated Affirmation,° quite adequate for the reassuring, outreaching statement I wanted to make. And the last, the long maze, with seven corridors and nineteen connections, lent itself surprisingly well to the Maluvian mode, and indeed to almost all the New Expressionist techniques. Adaptations had to be made to the alien spatial understanding, but a certain quality of creativity arose precisely from the adaptations. I worked hard at the problem of that maze, planning all night long, re-imagining the links and spaces, the feints and pauses, the erratic, unfamiliar, and yet beautiful course of the True Run. Next day when I was placed in the long maze and the alien began to observe, I performed the Eighth Maluvian in its entirety.

It was not a polished performance. I was nervous, and the spatio-temporal parameters were only approximate. But the Eighth Maluvian survives the crudest performance in the poorest maze. The evolutions in the ninth encatenation,° where the "cloud" theme recurs so strangely transposed into the ancient spiralling motif, are indestructibly beautiful. I have seen them performed by a very old person, so old and stiff-jointed that he could only suggest the movements, hint at them, a shadow gesture, a dim reflection of the themes: and all who watched were inexpressibly moved. There is no nobler statement of our being. Performing, I myself was carried away by the power of the motions and forgot that I was a prisoner, forgot the alien eyes watching me; I transcended the errors of the maze and my own weakness, and danced the Eighth Maluvian as I have never danced it before.

When it was done, the alien picked me up and set me down in the first maze—the short one, the maze for little children who have not yet learned how to talk.

Was the humiliation deliberate? Now that it is all past, I see that there is no way to know. But it remains very hard to ascribe its behavior to ignorance.

After all, it is not blind. It has eyes, recognisable eyes. They are enough like our eyes that it must see somewhat as we do. It has a mouth, four legs, can move bipedally, has grasping hands, etc.; for

○ Ungated Affirmation, Eighth Maluvian, etc.: these are imaginary names of dance or "language" maneuvers, with echoes of both descriptions of mazes and expressions from ballet.

○ encatenation: a linked or connected series; in this case, a series of "dance" maneuvers.

all its gigantism and strange looks, it seems less fundamentally different from us, physically, than a fish. And yet, fish school and dance and, in their own stupid way, communicate!

The alien has never once attempted to talk with me. It has been with me, watched me, touched me, handled me, for days: but all its motions have been purposeful, not communicative. It is evidently a solitary creature, totally self-absorbed.

This would go far to explain its cruelty.

I noticed early that from time to time it would move its curious horizontal mouth in a series of fairly delicate, repetitive gestures, a little like someone eating. At first I thought it was jeering at me; then I wondered if it was trying to urge me to eat the indigestible fodder; then I wondered if it could be communicating *labially.* It seemed a limited and unhandy language for one so well provided with hands, feet, limbs, flexible spine, and all; but that would be like the creature's perversity, I thought. I studied its lip motions and tried hard to imitate them. It did not respond. It stared at me briefly and then went away.

In fact, the only indubitable *response* I ever got from it was on a pitifully low level of interpersonal aesthetics. It was tormenting me with knob-pushing, as it did once a day. I had endured this grotesque routine pretty patiently for the first several days. If I pushed one knob I got a nasty sensation in my feet, if I pushed a second I got a nasty pellet of dried-up food, if I pushed a third I got nothing whatever. Obviously, to demonstrate my intelligence I was to push the third knob. But it appeared that my intelligence irritated my captor, because it removed the neutral knob after the second day. I could not imagine what it was trying to establish or accomplish, except the fact that I was its prisoner and a great deal smaller than it. When I tried to leave the knobs, it forced me physically to return. I must sit there pushing knobs for it, receiving punishment from one and mockery from the other. The deliberate outrageousness of the situation, the insufferable heaviness and thickness of this air, the feeling of being forever watched yet never understood, all combined to drive me into a condition for which we have no description at all. The nearest thing I can suggest is the last interlude of the Ten Gate Dream, when all the feintways are closed and the dance narrows in and in until it bursts terribly into the vertical. I cannot say what I felt, but it was a little like that. If I got my feet stung once more, or got pelted once more with a lump of rotten food, I would go vertical forever. . . . I took the knobs off the wall (they came off with a sharp tug, like flower buds), laid them in the middle of the floor, and defecated on them.

The alien took me up at once and returned me to my prison. It had got the message, and had acted on it. But how unbelievably primitive the message had had to be! And the next day, it put me back in the knob room, and there were the knobs as good as new, and I was to choose alternate punishments for its amusement. . . . Until then I had told myself that the creature was alien, therefore incomprehensible and uncomprehending, perhaps not intelligent in the same *manner* as we, and so on. But since then I have known that, though all that may remain true, it is also unmistakably and grossly cruel.

When it put me into the baby maze yesterday, I could not move. The power of speech was all but gone (I am dancing this, of course, in my mind; "the best maze is the mind," the old proverb goes) and I simply crouched there, silent. After a while it took me out again, gently enough. There is the ultimate perversity of its behavior: it has never once touched me cruelly.

It set me down in the prison, locked the gate, and filled up the trough with inedible food. Then it stood two-legged, looking at me for a while.

Its face is very mobile, but if it speaks with its face I cannot understand it, that is too foreign a language. And its body is always covered with bulky, binding mats, like an old widower who has taken the Vow of Silence. But I had become accustomed to its great size, and to the angular character of its limb positions, which at first had seemed to be saying a steady stream of incoherent and mispronounced phrases, a horrible nonsense dance like the motions of an imbecile, until I realised that they were strictly purposive movements. Now I saw something a little beyond that, in its position. There were no words, yet there was communication. I saw, as it stood watching me, a clear signification of angry sadness—as clear as the Sembrian Stance. There was the same lax immobility, the bentness, the assertion of defeat. Never a word came clear, and yet it told me that it was filled with resentment, pity, impatience, and frustration. It told me it was sick of torturing me, and wanted me to help it. I am sure I understood it. I tried to answer. I tried to say, "What is it you want of me? Only tell me what it is you want." But

I was too weak to speak clearly, and it did not understand. It has never understood.

And now I have to die. No doubt it will come in to watch me die; but it will not understand the dance I dance in dying.

ESSAYS FROM THE DISCIPLINES

PHILOSOPHY / COMPUTER SCIENCE

A. M. TURING

This section is the first major part of Turing's classic investigation of machine intelligence. Here he is setting out, in his own terms, the "imitation game." While the ground rules of this game may appear simple, some of the particulars can be quite subtle. Bolter, in "Turing's Game," points out that if a computer is answering a math question during a round of the "imitation game," it cannot reply too quickly to the command, "Add 34957 to 70764." If it did not "pause about 30 seconds," the questioner would readily know that it was not a calculating human, but a calculator which answers such questions too easily. (Notice how well it avoids the request to write a sonnet. Wouldn't most humans respond similarly?)

Turing sets out to define his "imitation game" as a means of answering the question posed in the first paragraph: "Can machines think?" He proceeds to define his terms and offer various ways of studying the implications of his "game." American readers may be surprised by the English humor characteristically tucked into this essay ("We do not wish to penalize the machine for its inability to shine in beauty competitions. . . ."), for we have been conditioned to believe that philosophical questions, especially those involving mathematics, must lack humor. But Turing's ability to look at a complex problem in new ways may be said to have established a new field—artificial intelligence (AI).

Today this field extends in other directions as well: medical "expert systems" which can "diagnose" problems, scanning robots which can "see," or computers which understand spoken commands. But Turing's original goal—a reasoning or thinking machine—is still a priority of the AI researchers, and Turing's essay provides a look at one of the founding documents of a contemporary quest for new "mechanisms of mind."

Computing Machinery and Intelligence

1. THE IMITATION GAME

I propose to consider the question "Can machines think?" This should begin with definitions of the meaning of the terms "machine" and "think." The definitions might be framed so as to reflect so far as possible the normal use of the words, but this attitude is dangerous. If the meaning of the words "machine" and "think" are to be found by examining how they are commonly used it is difficult to escape the conclusion that the meaning and the answer to the question, "Can machines think?" is to be sought in a statistical survey such as a Gallup poll. But this is absurd. Instead of attempting such a definition I shall replace the question by another, which is closely related to it and is expressed in relatively unambiguous words.

The new form of the problem can be described in terms of a game which we call the "imitation game." It is played with three people, a man (A), a woman (B), and an interrogator (C) who may be of either sex. The interrogator stays in a room apart from the other two. The object of the game for the interrogator is to determine which of the other two is the man and which is the woman. He knows them by labels X and Y, and at the end of the game he says either "X is A and Y is B" or "X is B and Y is A." The interrogator is allowed to put questions to A and B thus:

c: Will X please tell me the length of his or her hair?

Now suppose X is actually A, then A must answer. It is A's object in the game to try to cause C to make the wrong identification. His answer might therefore be

"My hair is shingled, and the longest strands are about nine inches long."

In order that tones of voice may not help the interrogator the answers should be written, or better still, typewritten. The ideal arrangement is to have a teleprinter communicating between the two rooms. Alternatively the question and answers can be repeated by an intermediary. The object of the game for the third player (B) is to help the interrogator. The best strategy for her is probably to give truthful answers. She can add such things as "I am the woman, don't listen to him!" to her answers, but it will avail nothing as the man can make similar remarks.

We now ask the question, "What will happen when a machine takes the part of A in this game?" Will the interrogator decide wrongly as often when the game is played like this as he does when the game is played between a man and a woman? These questions replace our original, "Can machines think?"

2. CRITIQUE OF THE NEW PROBLEM

As well as asking "What is the answer to this new form of the question," one may ask, "Is this new question a worthy one to investigate?" This latter question we investigate without further ado, thereby cutting short an infinite regress.

The new problem has the advantage of drawing a fairly sharp line between the physical and the intellectual capacities of a man. No engineer or chemist claims to be able to produce a material which is indistinguishable from the human skin. It is possible that at some time this might be done, but even supposing this invention available we should feel there was little point in trying to make a "thinking machine" more human by dressing it up in such artificial flesh. The form in which we have set the problem reflects this fact in the condition which prevents the interrogator from seeing or touching the other competitors, or hearing their voices. Some other advantages of the proposed criterion may be shown up by specimen questions and answers. Thus:

Q: Please write me a sonnet on the subject of the Forth Bridge.

A: Count me out on this one. I never could write poetry.

Q: Add 34957 to 70764.

A: (Pause about 30 seconds and then give as answer) 105621.

Q: Do you play chess?

A: Yes.

Q: I have K at my K1, and no other pieces. You have only K at K6 and R at R1. It is your move. What do you play?

A: (After a pause of 15 seconds) R-R8 mate.

The question and answer method seems to be suitable for introducing almost any one of the fields of human endeavor that we wish to include. We do not wish to penalize the machine for its inability to shine in beauty competitions, nor to penalize a man for losing in a race against an airplane. The conditions of our game make these disabilities irrelevant. The "witnesses" can brag, if they consider it advisable, as much as they please about their charms, strength or heroism, but the interrogator cannot demand practical demonstrations.

The game may perhaps be criticized on the ground that the odds are weighted too heavily against the machine. If the man were to try and pretend to be the machine he would clearly make a very poor showing. He would be given away at once by slowness and inaccuracy in arithmetic. May not machines carry out something which ought to be described as thinking but which is very different from what a man does? This objection is a very strong one, but at least we can say that if, nevertheless, a machine can be constructed to play the imitation game satisfactorily, we need not be troubled by this objection.

It might be urged that when playing the "imitation game" the best strategy for the machine may possibly be something other than imitation of the behavior of a man. This may be, but I think it is unlikely that there is any great effect of this kind. In any case there is no intention to investigate here the theory of the game, and it will be assumed that the best strategy is to try to provide answers that would naturally be given by a man.

3. THE MACHINES CONCERNED IN THE GAME

The question which we put in section 1 will not be quite definite until we have specified what we mean by the word "machine." It is natural that we should wish to permit every kind of engineering technique to be used in our machines. We also wish to allow the possibility that an engineer or team of engineers may construct a machine which works, but whose manner of operation cannot be satisfactorily described by its constructors because they have applied a method which is largely experimental. Finally, we wish to exclude from the machines men born in the usual manner. It is difficult to frame the definitions so as to satisfy these three conditions. One might for instance insist that the team of engineers should be all of one sex, but this would not really be satisfactory, for it is probably possible to rear a complete individual from a single cell of the skin (say) of a man. To do so would be a feat of biological technique deserving of the very highest praise, but we would not be inclined to regard it as a case of "constructing a thinking machine." This prompts us to abandon the requirement that every kind of technique should be permitted. We are the more ready to do so in view of the fact that the present interest in "thinking machines" has been aroused by a particular kind of machine, usually called an "electronic computer" or "digital computer." Following this suggestion we only permit digital computers to take part in our game.

This restriction appears at first sight to be a very drastic one. I shall attempt to show that it is not so in reality. To do this necessitates a short account of the nature and properties of these computers.

It may also be said that this identification of machines with digital computers, like our criterion for "thinking," will only be unsatisfactory if (contrary to my belief), it turns out that digital computers are unable to give a good showing in the game.

There are already a number of digital computers in working order, and it may be asked, "Why not try the experiment straight away? It would be easy to satisfy the conditions of the game. A number of interrogators could be used, and statistics compiled to show how often the right identification was given." The short answer is that we are not asking whether all digital computers would do well in the game nor whether the computers at present available would do well, but whether there are imaginable computers which would do well.

PSYCHOLOGY

RICHARD GREGORY

As part of its review of current scholarship in various fields, London's Times Literary Supplement *ran this overview and critique of theories of perception in 1972. Gregory's distinction between "active" and "passive" theories of perception allows him to develop related critiques of behavioral and computer models of the mind. Although over a decade old, it nonetheless provides us with a revealing summation of the state of research in the field just at the moment when artificial intelligence began its challenge to established theories of perception.*

Gregory aims his review of the current status of various theories of perception at the educated reader who is not necessarily a psychologist or professional in the field. The Times Literary Supplement *provides authoritative reviews in a number of disciplines, although it tends to emphasize the humanities. Thus, Gregory was called on to cover the various theories with full, fairly nontechnical, explanations. Generally, the essay takes a strong stance against behaviorism—one of the orthodoxies of psychology which emphasizes the physiology of the mind— and instead offers some optimistic predictions about future developments based in part on understanding what "machine intelligence" (the British term for "artificial intelligence") can and cannot do.*

Seeing as Thinking: An Active Theory of Perception

Theories of perception—of what happens to bridge the extraordinary gap between sensory stimulation and our experience of external objects—have a long history of astonishing variety. Speculation goes back to the beginning of recorded philosophy—and scientific work on perception escapes the philosophical questions and dilemmas only when it narrows inquiry by over-blinkering specialization. How we see remains essentially mysterious after a century of intensive experiment, on animals and on men, by such a variety of scientists that aims and communication can be lost between them. An adequate theory should include not only the favoured sense of sight but also: hearing, touch, hot and cold, taste, smell, balance and position of the limbs, the various kinds of pain; and tickle, from its irritation to sensuous pleasure and delirious laugh-making.

To the philosopher and the experimental scientist, it is how we see that offers the most exciting questions, with hearing the runner-up, for sight dominates by its giving us immediate external reality. By simply looking we seem to understand what we see. This close association between seeing and knowing makes the sense of vision attractive not only to philosophers but also to experimental psychologists and physiologists who hope to discover in the brain mechanisms serving our experience and knowledge of the world. By coming to understand how we see, might we not at one stroke also discover how we think, remember, formulate hypotheses, appreciate beauty and—most mysterious—accept pictures and words as symbols, conveying not merely present reality but other realities distant in space and time? And if seeing involves all this, surely the net of understanding must be cast wide.

Perceptual theories form a spectrum—from passive to active theories. Passive theories suppose that perception is essentially camera-like, conveying selected aspects of objects quite directly, as though the eyes and brain are undistorting windows. The baby, it is supposed, comes to see not by using cues and hints to infer the world of objects from sensory data but by selecting useful features of objects available to it directly: without effort, information processing or inference. Active theories, taking a very different view, suppose that perceptions are constructed, by complex brain processes, from fleeting fragmentary scraps of data signalled by the senses and drawn from the brain's memory banks—themselves constructions from snippets from the past. In this view, normal everyday perceptions are not selections of reality but are rather imaginative constructions— fictions—based (as indeed is science fiction also) more on the stored past than on the present. In this view all perceptions are essentially fictions: fictions based on past experience selected by present sensory data. Here we should not equate "fiction" with "false." Even the most fanciful fiction as written is very largely true, or we would not understand it. Fictional characters in novels generally have the right number of heads, noses and even many of the opinions of people we know. Science-fiction characters may have green hair and an exoskeleton°—but is this novelty not a mere reshuffling of the pack of our experiences? It is doubtful if a new "card," suddenly introduced, could be meaningfully described or seen.

The passive paradigm° may, at least initially, seem more ac-

° exoskeleton: external hard covering of an insect or animal (the beetle's shell, for example).

° paradigm: the governing model or image of a science; a loose interpretation of the term popularized by Thomas Kuhn (see "Sources").

ceptable as a scientific theory. It fits well with—and indeed essentially is—the familiar "stimulus/response" notion in which behavior is described as controlled directly by prevailing conditions. This is also familiar in engineering: in most devices, input directly controls output, and much emphasis is put on measuring input and output, and relating them by transfer functions or something equivalent, to describe the system. B. F. Skinner in his behaviourism claims to do much the same—to give at least a statistical account of the relationship between stimulus (input) and behaviour (output) in animals and men. An engineer would go on to suggest "models," of what the internal mechanism might be, which transforms inputs into the outputs. But, rather curiously, Skinner does not attempt to make this further step, and apparently distrusts it. He says remarkably little about brains, and at times denies memory and indeed all internal processes. His description is purely in terms of input-output relations, with emphasis on how the probability of certain kinds of behaviour is changed by environmental changes, especially "reinforcers."°

Skinner himself has little interest specifically in perception, but passive theories of perception are in many ways similar. They have the same initial scientific credibility, but are (I believe) essentially incorrect. They deny that perception is an active combining of features stored from the past, building and selecting hypotheses of what is indicated by sensory data. On the active account we regard perceptions as essentially fictional. Though generally predictive, and so essentially correct, cognitive fictions may be wrong to drive us into error. On this active view, both veridical (correct-predictive) and illusory (false-predictive) perceptions are equally fictions. To perceive is to read the present in terms of the past to predict and control the future. This account is very different from the passive story implied by Skinner's behaviourism, and most ably propounded by James J. Gibson and Eleanor Gibson.

Why should one want to push all this stuff about "brain fictions" (as I do) when stimuli and responses are so easily observed, and so like the usual stuff of science? The essential reason is (I believe) very easily demonstrated, by common observation and by experiment. Current sensory data (or stimuli) are simply not ade-

---

° reinforcers: in behaviorism, those rewards which increase the likelihood of a given response to stimuli.

quate directly to control behavior in familiar situations. Behavior may continue through quite long gaps in sensory data, and remain appropriate though there is no sensory input. But how can "output" be controlled by "input" when there is no input? The fact is that sensory inputs are not continuously required or available, and so we cannot be dealing with a pure input-output system. Further, when we consider any common action, such as placing a book on a table (a favourite example of philosophers) we cannot test from retinal images the table's solidity and general book-supporting capabilities. In engineering terminology, we cannot monitor directly the most important characteristics of objects which must be known for behaviour to be appropriate. This implies that these characteristics are inferred, from the past. The other highly suggestive—indeed dominating—fact is that perception is predictive. In skills, there may be zero delay between sensory input and behaviour. But how could there be zero delay, except by acting upon a predictive hypothesis? (Surely J. J. Gibson's description of perceptions as selections from the available "ambient array" will not do. It would have to be a selection from a future "ambient array" for the passive account to work; but this evokes a metaphysics we cannot welcome. The significance of prediction in perception has been for too long almost totally ignored.)

It is the fact that behaviour does not need continuous, directly appropriate sensory data that forces upon us the notion of inference from available sensory and brain stored data. This account is very much in the tradition of the polymath nineteenth-century physicist and physiologist, Hermann von Helmholtz, who described perceptions as "unconscious inferences." This notion was unpalatable to later generations of psychologists, who were over-influenced by philosophers in their role—sometimes useful, but in this case disastrous—of guardians of semantic inertia: objecting to inference without consciousness. But with further data on animal perception, and computers capable of inference, this essentially semantic inhibition has gone. Curiously, though, the kinds of inference required for perception are remarkably difficult to compute.

The recent engineering-science of Machine Intelligence° is finding heavy weather designing computer programs to identify objects from television camera pictures. The reason seems to be (apart from the very large and fast computers required to perform

---

○ Machine Intelligence: British synonym for artificial intelligence.

the operations serially) that the computer requires a vast amount of stored data of common object properties, with ready and rapid access. It requires, in short, what we have called "fictions" to augment and make use of data monitored from the world by its camera eye, and—in machines dealing with real objects—its touch probes. In short: We may think of perception as an engineering problem, but it is a highly atypical problem even for advanced computer engineering, and it requires a special philosophy which is unfamiliar in science, because only brains and to a limited extent computers are cognitive.

The notion that interpreting objects from patterns is a "passive" business must strike the computer programmer engaged on this problem, in Machine Intelligence, as an extremely unfunny joke. His problem is to devise active programs adequate even for perceptual problems solved by simple creatures, long before man came on the scene.

The notion of perceptions as predictive hypotheses going beyond available data is alien and suspect to many physiologists. Cognitive concepts appear unnecessary—even metaphysical—to be explained away by physiological data. Certainly more physiological data are needed; but will they tell us by what mechanisms the brain's hypotheses are mediated, or will the "brain fiction" notion drop out as unnecessary? Prediction is dangerous, but there are surely strong reasons for believing cognitive concepts to be necessary. In the first place, it is not surprising that special concepts should be required for brain research, because the brain is unique, in nature, as an information-handling system. (Or at least it is on an active theory of brain function.) With the development of computers, we now have other information handling systems to consider. It is interesting to note that to describe computers, "software" concepts are adopted, similar to cognitive concepts. More basically, what are essentially cognitive concepts are very familiar in all sciences, but hidden under a different guise—the method of science.

Generalizations and hypotheses are vital to organized science, for the same reasons they are essential for brains handling data in terms of external objects. Science is itself not "passive" in our sense, but puts up hypotheses for testing, and acts on hypotheses rather than directly on available data. Scientific observations have little or no power without related generalization and hypotheses. Cognitive concepts are surely not alien to science, when seen as the brain's (relatively crude) strategies for discovering the world from limited data—which is very much the basic problem of all science. Scientific observations without hypotheses are surely as powerless as an eye without a brain's ability to relate data to possible realities—effectively blind.

The full power of human brain fiction is apparent when we consider how little current sensory information is needed, or is available, in typical situations. Here we do not need initially to consider particular experiments—and indeed the intentional simplifications and restrictions of the laboratory environment can make the point less obvious—that behaviour is generally appropriate to features of the world which are not continually available to the senses. When you trust your weight to the floor, or your mouth to the spoonful of food, you have not monitored the ground's strength or the food's palatability: you have acted on trust, on the basis of the past. You have acted according to probabilities, based on generalizations from past events—and neither generalization nor probabilities exist, except in your brain, for they are not properties of the world. Now suppose that you gave up acting on informed guesses and demanded continuously, direct selections of reality. How would you get on? Would you not avoid mistakes—never fall through rotten floor boards, never be upset by bad food—never be misled by going beyond the evidence? Yes, indeed, if there were sufficient evidence available. But the fact is that there is frequently no possibility, or time, for testing floorboards or food. They must be taken on trust— trust based on the past as stored in the brain.

We have arrived at questions which may be answered by experiment. We can measure performance in the partial or total absence of sensory data, and establish whether and how far perception and behaviour continue to remain appropriate. We find that we can continue to drive or walk, or perform laboratory eye-hand tracking experiments, through gaps in sensory data—and not merely inertially, for we can make decisions and change our actions appropriately during data gaps. We must then be relying on internal data. This requires an internal fiction of the world, which in unusual situations may be false. If the situation is unfamiliar, or changes in unpredictable ways, then we should expect systematic errors, generated by false predictions. Errors and illusions thus have great importance for active theorists; they become obsessively used tools for discovering the underlying assumptions and strategies of the perceptual "computer" by which we infer—not always correctly—external objects for sensory data.

Looking at books written by passive and active theorists, we find an amusing difference between their indexes. Passive books devote much space to stimulus patterns, but very little to the phenomena of perception: spontaneous reversals in depth, changes into other objects, distortions, perceptual paradoxes in which the mind reels by being apparently confronted by logically impossible objects. Active theorists fill their books with examples of such phenomena, interpreting them in various ways, while the passive theorist ignores them, or writes them off as too trivial to concern him. But neither uncertainty nor ambiguity, neither distortion nor paradox, can be properties of objects: so how can we *perceive* uncertainties, ambiguities, distortions or paradoxes if perception is but a passive acceptance of reality? This simple though surely powerful argument is not raised or answered by passive theorists. By playing down the obvious phenomena of perception (such as illusions, found as children's puzzles) passive books may look academically safe—but at the cost of leaving out what is most interesting.

We may now return to the point that, although we regard brain function as physical, physical and engineering concepts are not adequate for describing some aspects—especially perception of objects. This only appears to be a metaphysical statement if an extreme reductionist view of science is adopted. This matter is controversial; there are eminent scientists who hold that knowledge of a hydrogen atom and the laws of quantum mechanics are sufficient to describe, in principle, any physical situation. Others hold that even common effects such as friction, heat, inertia or gravity (let alone brain function) could not in principle be described in these elementary terms. They hold that with increased complexity and organization new properties arise requiring new concepts to describe them. It would certainly be difficult to ascribe the notion of "cognitive fictions" to a hydrogen atom! (But it would be equally difficult to ascribe such concepts as servo-control,° or even image-forming—so this is not a special objection to the "cognitive fiction" notion.)

There is a strong reason (apart from consciousness) why we wish to separate descriptions of aspects of brain function from phys-

° servo-control: British synonym for servomechanism, any mechanical and electronic system which carries out tasks.

ics. This is however a very tricky problem, easy to over-state and to misunderstand. Granted that brain activity is physical, we wish to hold that brain states representing information and problem-solving are not usefully described in terms of physical restraints. Consider the black marks (letters) on this page. They are physical (ink absorbed by paper), but their arrangement, surely, is not to be understood by the principles of physics. For this we must call upon English spelling and grammar, and upon the structure of what I am trying to say. In the vital respect of their order, they are free of the ink and paper of which they are made. If their order were determined directly by their material and its physical properties (as in crystal structure) then they could not serve as symbols. Being in this sense free of physical restraints, and given receptive brains (or computers), then they can serve as symbols, to represent objects in other time and space; or as abstractions which do not exist, in the sense that objects exist. This is true for all symbols: pictures, words, mathematical and musical notations, video and audio tapes, computer tapes. But symbols are powerless (or are just like any other objects) in the absence of brains or other information-handling systems. Evidently symbols must affect brains in some more or less lawful manner, but for this to be possible the relevant brain states must—like the typist's or compositor's characters—be free to adopt information-storing and representing orders. So they must in this rather limited sense be free of physical restraint, though not quite isolated from the rest of the physical world for learning and perceiving to be possible.

The celebrated (and I believe essentially misleading) Gestalt theory of perception postulated physiological restraints to explain many visual phenomena, such as preference for, and distortion towards, figures of "simple" and "closed" form. Visual forms were supposed to be represented in the brain by similarly shaped electrical brain fields—circles by circular brain traces, presumably houses by house-shaped brain traces. These brain traces were supposed to tend to form simple and closed shapes, because of their physical properties, much as bubbles tend to become spheres, as this form has minimum potential energy. Now this implies that visual "organizations" and distortions are due to physical restraints and forces which will not in general be relevant to the logical problems the brain must solve to infer objects from sensory patterns and stored data. This is quite different from a cognitive account of perceptual distortions, and other phenomena which may be supposed to arise from misapplication of strategies quite apart from the physiology involved. Using a slide-rule, an error may be due to physical errors in the rule itself, or to misapplication of the rule for the problem in hand. This is exactly the distinction involved here, between physiological and cognitive errors.

We should expect physiological restraints to produce the same effects for any object situation (for example after-images, due to retinal fatigue, to any bright light). Misplaced strategy errors should, on the other hand, be related to the kind of perceptual inference, from sensory pattern to object, being carried out. So the point is that the physiology should only produce errors when it is exerting general restraints. We should not expect this except in abnormal situations, such as when the physiological "components" are driven beyond their dynamic range. Considering phenomena of perception, such as ambiguous, distorting or paradoxical figures: Do these figures upset the physiology, or select inappropriate strategies, to generate errors? In these cases, it seems to be the object significance of the figures which is relevant. So these phenomena seem quite unlike after-images—here it is not so much the physiology as the cognitive strategies which we need to discover. This needs a different (but still a "scientific") way of thinking, and powerful experimental techniques, to discover cognitive strategies and how they can mislead.

To separate errors due to physiological restraints from errors due to misplaced strategies surely has importance beyond understanding perceptual errors. The same distinction (between physiological and cognitive processes, and how either can go wrong) might be important for understanding mental illness. If schizophrenia is errors in the brain's strategies for developing hypotheses of external states of affairs, this should be understood not only in terms of biochemistry and physiology but also in terms of the strategies by which we normally cope with things. Perhaps this matter of strategies is hidden by the apparent ease with which we continually solve problems of the utmost difficulty to computer programmers, who receive false answers when their programs are inappropriate. Seeing a table as something to support a book upon is to solve a problem so difficult it challenges the most advanced computer technology, and yet to us it is so simple that a passive theory of perception may seem plausible. This shows that passive theories may be so misleading as to hide aspects of brain function which we must see clearly to understand not only perception but all mental processes and how they can go wrong.

Recent discoveries by physiologists, especially by electrical recording from single brain cells during controlled stimuli to the eye, are so clearly important that they tend to dominate much current thinking about perception. The problem of how sensory patterns are interpreted in terms of objects tends to be ignored. The important physiological discovery is that certain stimulus patterns (lines of certain orientation, or movement, etc.) produce repeatable activity in specific brain cells. This discovery came as an unpalatable shock to passive theorists who tend to ignore brain function. To active theorists, it gives a kind of clue to the kinds of data accepted for building object-hypotheses. One might think from this that passive theories would drop out, leaving the field of physiologists and active cognitive psychologists to work together in blissful harmony. Actually things are not quite like this; the physiological advance is so concrete, and clearly important, that many physiologists and cognitive psycholgists feel that finding more feature analysers, and more abstract analysers, is the sole path we need to follow to understand vision. But is it? The physiological mechanisms being discovered relate to stimulus patterns only, and not recognition of objects as hypotheses. The physiological account thus remains passive, and so essentially inadequate, for the same reasons that cognitive passive accounts are inadequate.

The task ahead is to relate physiological processes not only to direct input-output links, as in reflexes, but also to the brain's logical and correlating activity, endowing it with the power to predict. This will require further physiological data, and current techniques are providing extremely important new information so this will surely be available. Experiments on the phenomena of perception itself, in animals and in men—essentially on how patterns are interpreted as objects—has confusions (or at least impeding disagreements) in its philosophy, and a lack of powerful research techniques. Some of the most interesting clues are at present coming from studies of development of perception in babies. Early changes of the nervous system as a result of experience are now being discovered, which will perhaps help to tie up, or relate, physiology and cognition. Possibly the most fundamental and rigorous ideas are coming not from biology but from attempts to program computers to see and handle object-relations. It proves necessary to make the computer develop hypotheses and select the most likely, given the data from its glass eye.

There is more to this, for some computer programs designed to give "scene analysis" (recognizing objects from pictures by computer) assign alternative object probabilities to selected features in the picture; and then change these probabilities, according to probabilities assigned to other features of the scene. For example, a given shape may be a box or a building. If what is taken to be a hand is above it, then the probability of the box hypothesis will be increased and the building hypothesis decreased—for hands are generally too small and too low to be above buildings, but not above boxes. Now this gives interactions, due to conditional probabilities, which may generate visual effects in computers or brains quite like the old Gestalt phenomena, but for an entirely different reason. The reason is to be understood in terms of cognitive strategies or procedures for making effective use of data for deciding what objects are present in the scene.

In Machine Intelligence only precisely formulated theories are adequate; any gaps or errors in the theory show up as errors in the machine. At present machines perform only the simplest tasks, and are easily confused by shadows or small changes we scarcely notice.

Although the difficulties in Machine Intelligence demonstrate all too well how little we know, it now seems that we are beginning to understand ourselves—the inference-mechanism of our humanity —by inventing adequate concepts for machines to infer objects from data, to perceive our world with their metal brains and human-devised programs. Is this science fiction? Yes—but like all fiction it may be largely true.

Philosophically, this is not the end of the matter. Behaviourism, with its related passive theories of perception, is unconcerned with what goes on between the senses and behaviour—and indeed denies that anything goes on. This may be a legitimate expedient for focusing attention upon certain questions in behavioural research, but as a philosophy it is a kind of nihilism with a built-in contradiction. We are supposed to accept the behaviourist's writings as expressing his observations, thoughts and judgments, which in these same writings he denies having. We are reminded of the poignant postcard received by Bertrand Russell saying, "I am a solipsist—why are there no other philosophers like me?"

PHILOSOPHY/COMPUTER SCIENCE

J. DAVID BOLTER

Bolter approaches the intriguing ground rules of Turing's "imitation game" from the disciplines of philosophy and computer science. His study, Turing's Man *(1984), from which this selection is taken, is subtitled* Western Culture in the Computer Age. *Bolter finds that the computer, as the dominant electronic technology of our age, helps to define, and even to control, how other disciplines regard humanness. For example, Bolter notes that Turing's "game" should be seen not only in the context of the behavioral sciences, but also that of philosophy (specifically logic). The computer in fact becomes a model for the mind as Turing's "man" searches for successful players of the "imitation game."*

As Bolter defines this phenomenon (Turing's "game"), he examines its implications, both in terms of its origins (behavioral science; logic) and its effects (the "computer model of the mind"). Turing's Man *has been one of the more successful cross-disciplinary books of the 1980s, for it sets out some of the new and complicated issues of artificial intelligence for a general intellectual audience which may not have a mathematical or computing background.*

Turing's Game

Let us look more closely at the claim, made in 1950, that by the year 2000 computing machines would be capable of imitating human intelligence perfectly. Turing envisioned a game in which a human player is seated at a teletype console, by which he can communicate with a teletype in another room. Controlling this second console would be either another human or a digital computer. The player could ask any questions he wished through his console in order to determine whether he was in contact with a man or a machine.

Suppose there were in fact a computer at the other console. If asked to write a sonnet, the machine could attempt one or refuse; after all, most humans are not poets. If given two numbers to add, the machine might wait thirty seconds and provide the answer or instead might prefer to make a mistake to imitate human fallibility. However, it would not produce the answer in less than a second, for that would be a clear indication of its electronic nature. Turing's game really demands a machine that is more than human, not merely equal to its biological counterpart, one capable of any intellectual feat a man or woman can perform and sly enough to mask any prowess that exceeds a human's abilities. It would be a machine that knew men and women better than they know themselves. Turing was optimistic about the prospect of this supercomputer: "I believe that in about fifty years' time it will be plausible to programme computers . . . to make them play the imitation game so well that an average interrogator will not have more than 70 per cent chance of making the right identification after five minutes of questioning" (Feigenbaum and Feldman, *Computers and Thought,* 19).

The appeal of Turing's test is easy to understand. It offers an operational definition of intelligence quite in the spirit of behavioral psychology in the postwar era. A programmer can measure success by statistics—the number of human subjects fooled by his machine. The test seems to require no subjective judgment; it says nothing about the machine writing a good poem or solving an important mathematical theorem. Every humanist, of course, is tempted to devise his own Turing test and so his own definition of humanity: a computer will never be fully human unless it can laugh, cry, feel sympathy, feel pain, and so on. Someone has suggested that a computer will pass for a human only when it begins to ask what are the differences between itself and a human being. Turing's own test is supposed to embrace any and all human qualities that can be communicated in writing. The player at the terminal may ask anything.

The test is cast in the form of a game, a duel of wits between man and machine. Games are in fact the form of intellectual activity that computers imitate most effectively. The Turing machine itself is a logical game, whose moves are governed by precise rules, and the computer plays a sort of game with every program it runs. Today, thirty years after Turning's proposal, a computer can play excellent chess, but no computer program could even attempt to play Turing's intelligence game. No computer could answer more than a question or two without revealing its mechanical nature.

The strategies for meeting Turing's proposal have varied. The most intriguing, if least successful, arose from the work of Norbert

Wiener, who in the 1940s devised the term "cybernetics"° for the "entire field of control and communication theory, whether in the machine or in the animal" (*Cybernetics,* 19). Wiener's work with servomechanisms° to aim antiaircraft guns and to do much else besides had convinced him that forms of life could be understood entirely in mechanical terms; they could not be understood as Cartesian clockwork, which was too crude and rigid, but rather as electromechanical or even electronic devices. Like others, Wiener compared the new electronic tubes to neurons and wanted to subsume the study of both under one discipline. Wiener's outlook was clearly as much influenced by pre-electronic control devices (feedback loops in various machines) as by the digital computers just being built. In *Cybernetics* he stressed direct contact with the world—experiments with the muscles of the cat, improved prostheses for amputees, sensing equipment, and so on. Current workers in artificial intelligence show less interest in such direct contact with the world and more interest in abstract thought.

Wiener was still only halfway along the line from Descartes to Turing. He wanted machines to imitate the man who acts in the world as well as the man who reasons, to explain muscle action in terms of feedback loops as well as chess in terms of a digital program. He relied on hardware devices for his metaphor of man and demanded a close correspondence between man and the machine made to imitate him. Vacuum tubes were meant to be a physical substitute for neurons, servomechanisms for nerves acting upon muscles. This line of thinking was forthright and compelling, and led to attempts to build a brain (in theory, seldom in practice) using simple electronic components. Those following Wiener's approach spoke of creating artificial brain cells and neural networks and allowing the machine to learn as a baby was presumed to do—presuming with Locke that the baby's mind was a tabula rasa at birth. But the theory of neural networks, which was developed mathematically, met with little or no practical success. In general, Wiener's preferences gave way to others in the 1950s, as computer hardware and especially programming languages became more sophisticated. Unfortunately, the elegant name of cybernetics, created from the Greek word for governor but

○ cybernetics: the study of mechanical and electronic substitutes for human processes.
○ servomechanism: a mechanical and electronic system which carries out tasks; e.g., a robot "arm" that caps a bottle.

smacking perhaps of the antiquated technology of the war years, also gave way to "artificial intelligence."

Specialists more or less gave up the idea of building a machine whose components would mirror the elements of the human brain; they no longer demanded a literal correspondence between man and machine. The new high-level languages led them to emphasize programs rather than hardware, and they turned to such tasks as computer chess and theorem proving, problems of "information processing," rather than Wiener's command and control. In fact, the Turing test is just such a problem; it requires the computer not to act in the world but to act a role by manipulating symbols on a teletype.

For some, direct simulation of human thought seemed the most appealing way to pass the Turing test. They sought to discover intuitively how humans solved mental problems and then to translate these intuitions into digital programs. They may also have expected that the human solution would be the most appropriate (most efficient) one for the computer. Others tried simply to make programs fast and effective, feeling no need to be faithful to some theory of human cognition. Marvin Minsky, a principal spokesman for this approach, defined artificial intelligence as "the science of making machines do things that would require intelligence if done by men" (*Semantic Information Processing,* ed. Marvin Minsky, v).

This new definition seemed to reassert the difference between men and computers. Men can solve problems in one way, machines in another. But in fact, the analogy remains firm in the minds of programmers. Computer programs are open to inspection, and human ways of thinking are not. When a programmer devises an algorithm° for playing chess or for analyzing English grammar, he can hardly avoid regarding human performance by analogy with his visible, intelligible algorithm. As one psychologist has put it, the computer model of the mind is the only working model available and even a bad model is better than none.

ANNOTATED BIBLIOGRAPHY [EXCERPT]

FEIGENBAUM, E. A., and FELDMAN, JULIAN. *Computers and Thought.* New York: McGraw Hill, 1963. An early collection by the artificial intelligence

---

° algorithm: a set of rules, or a model for solving problems (see Crovitz's use of Basic English as an algorithm in "Documentary Materials").

movement; contains Turing's paper on "Computing Machinery and Intelligence."

MINSKY, MARVIN, ed. *Semantic Information Processing.* Cambridge, Mass.: MIT Press, 1968. A collection by artificial language advocates.

WIENER, NORBERT. *Cybernetics.* New York: John Wiley and Sons, 1948. An elegant account of the identification of man and machine by the famous mathematician and student of technology. Wiener is in many ways a more civilized and sympathetic proponent of the making of electronic man than current writers.

DOCUMENTARY MATERIALS

LIST OF PROBLEMS

KARL DUNCKER

Psychologist Karl Duncker published On Problem-Solving—*one of the earliest attempts to isolate a pattern for problem-solving—in 1945. What follows is a selection of the problems he set for his subjects. Many of these questions were offered in the context of Duncker's essay, and I have therefore had to adjust them somewhat. (My adjustments are in square brackets.) Notice how the very phrases in the question ("flower stand or the like") can occasionally influence the direction of your problem-solving.*

[Problems]

1. Given a human being with an inoperable stomach tumor, and rays which destroy organic tissue at sufficient intensity, by what procedure can one free him of the tumor by these rays and at the same time avoid destroying the healthy tissue which surrounds it?

2. [Find] an absolutely unfailing signal to send down a river, i.e., one which cannot catch or be interrupted on the way.

3. In a large room, two ropes hang from the ceiling at a considerable distance from one another. One has a small ring on its free end, the other a small hook. A subject receives the task of fastening the two ropes together, but this is not possible directly. For the prob-

lem is just this: to begin with, how is he to get both ropes in his hands at once? The ropes hang inconveniently far apart.

4. Four equilateral triangles are to be constructed out of six matches.

5. A door is to be constructed so as to open toward both sides. How can this be attained?

6. Express (measure) the side of the square in terms of the radius r of the inscribed circle. [See Figure 1, below.]

7. A board (perhaps 8 inches broad) is to be made firm on two supports (as "flower stand or the like"). On the table lie two iron joints (for fastening bars and the like on stands), a wooden bar perhaps 8 inches long (as the one "support") and pliers. [How can the "stand" be made?]

8. A pendulum, consisting of a cord and a weight, is to be hung from a nail ("for experiments on motion"). To this end, the nail must be driven into the wall. On the table lies . . . [a cord and] a weight. [How is the pendulum to be constructed?]

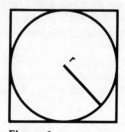

Figure 1.

PROCESS ESSAY

HERBERT CROVITZ

As a "heuristic," or problem-solving, approach, the psychologist Herbert Crovitz selected a set of relation-words from Basic English, an "invented" language of the 1930s designed by the Englishman C. K. Ogden as a "common language" for international activities like business and science, as well as a means of learning "regular" English more easily. (See "Assignment 7.")

"The Form of Logical Solutions" appeared in The American Journal of Psychology *in 1967 as a means of demonstrating how the Basic English algorithm (or pattern for problem-solving) could be used to solve problems similar to those in Duncker's list. In a later book,* Galton's Walk *(see "Sources"), Crovitz outlined how he would attack, let us say, Duncker's problem 4 (creating four equilateral triangles from six matches). He suggested, first of all, making a list of forty-two sentences with the relation-words, thereby creating a "set of all possible actions" from the key words of the problem. His algorithm looked like this:*

Take a _____ *about* a _____ .
Take a _____ *across* a _____ .
Take a _____ *after* a _____ .

And so forth, for all forty-two relational words in Table I at the end of his article. Selecting out one key word—"triangle"—from the problem, he substituted this key word for the blank space in all forty-two sentences. He therefore wrote:

Take a triangle *about* a triangle.
Take a triangle *across* a triangle.
Take a triangle *after* a triangle.

And so forth, again for all forty-two relational words. He then used two other key words and constructed another list of forty-two sentences:

Take matches *about* a triangle.
Take matches *across* a triangle.
Take matches *after* a triangle.

And so forth once more, until the end. Upon inspecting the lists, he saw that such sentences as "Take a triangle on *a triangle" or "Take matches* up *a triangle" helped to lead to a number of solutions.*

Crovitz's essay is really an extended scholarly note, as he is reporting mainly to his professional peers on research-in-progress. In this case, he suggests how the solutions to a number of famous problems could be translated back into the Basic English set of relation-words. By reversing the process, he concludes, some new problems could be solved by using the set of relation-words.

The Form of Logical Solutions

The aim of heuristic principles is to find methods and rules to assist discovery and invention.[1] Golann has reviewed the psychological study of creativity from four points of view: products, process, management, and personality.[2] The present analysis is restricted to *products* and consists of the result of a rather simple linguistic analysis of one formal characteristic of "creative" problem-solutions. Vygotsky has argued for the independence of thought and language, but he does not deny that people can think about words.[3] A heuristic question is whether there might be a set of words that are particularly worthy of thought, when the goal is to discover or invent. A well-known formal characteristic of many creative problems is that they often consist of taking two things in relation to each other. How many relations exist in which things may be taken? A potentially useful list of of such relations follows from a few successive simplifying assumptions. Assume that each such relation can be stated in an English sentence. It follows that a set of all randomly generated English sentences must include a subset of relational sentences. The vocabulary of normal English is, however, very large. Reduce the set of words to be considered to the 850 words of Ogden's *Basic English.*[4] Basic English is a short form of English in which the needs of everyday life can be conveyed: the recent publication of *The Basic Dictionary of Science* also shows that the normal words that describe scientific objects and concepts can be translated into Basic English without a loss of meaning and with a gain in clarity.[5] Assume that the set of all randomly generated Basic English sentences would include a subset of relational sentences. Such sentences can take a variety of forms but common to them all is that one thing is taken in some relation to another thing; the elementary form of such sentences is "Take A (one thing) in some relation to B (another thing)." The full set of allowable relations in such an elementary sentence is shown in Table 1.

The splendid variety of human inventions and discoveries is found in the products of men engaged in problem solving of the highest order; what cognitive steps that each made can not be known. But surely they were not equipped with a set of elementary sentences that could be used as templates to guide them to the form of solu-

Table 1.   The Relation-Words

about	for	round
across	from	still
after	if	so
against	in	then
among	near	though
and	not	through
as	now	till
at	of	to
because	off	under
before	on	up
between	opposite	when
but	or	where
by	out	while
down	over	with

tions. Whatever else the Periodic Table is, it is also the elementary sentences "Take A (one element) after B (another element)," on the basis of atomic number, and "Take A under B," on the basis of similar chemical properties. Similarly, the discovery of Neptune by Adams and Leverrier was also "Take A (the mass and orbit of an unknown body deforming the orbit of Uranus) from B (the orbit of Uranus)." And similarly, installing a fountain in one's garden to mask the noise of a nearby highway is also "Take A (the splashing of water) over B (the unwanted noise)."

The templates exist to be filled, and it may be possible to work backwards from them to problem-solutions. Even with them, much is required of a problem-solver: the choice of the goal, of the things to be related, and of the templates to be used. Nonetheless, the templates may have heuristic value in directing attention to the form of solutions.

NOTES

1. G. Polya, *How To Solve It,* 1957, 112.
2. S. E. Golann, Psychological Study of Creativity, *Psychol. Bull.*, 60, 1963, 548–565.
3. L. S. Vygotsky, *Thought and Language,* 1962, 51.
4. C. K. Ogden, *The System of Basic English,* 1934, 4.
5. E. C. Graham, *The Basic Dictionary of Science,* 1965, 1–54, *passim.*

DESCRIPTIVE ESSAY

MARTIN GARDNER

This selection brings together Gardner, a popular-science writer and connoisseur of games, and Sackson, an inventor of games. But the game here is one which is analogous to the crucial process of induction by which scientists and philosophers attempt to find patterns in the universe and test the validity of their hypotheses. Why not join them on a playful but revealing level? Draw up some sheets with 6 × 6 grids, follow Gardner's directions, and play!

As part of an ongoing column or feature ("Mathematical Games") in the general-science magazine Scientific American, *Gardner follows a somewhat regular pattern himself: He gives the background, historical or otherwise, to the problem or game he has selected, outlines the basic rules, and then draws some implications about contemporary science from the game. He uses some technical or scientific terminology, but he defines most of these terms for the nonprofessional.*

Sidney Sackson's Patterns

Many games and pastimes have flimsy analogies with induction, that strange procedure by which scientists observe that some ostriches have long necks and conclude that all unobserved ostriches also have long necks. In poker and bridge, for instance, players use observational clues to frame probable hypotheses about an opponent's hand. A cryptographer guesses that a certain "pattern word," say BRBQFBQF, is NONSENSE, then tests this inductive conjecture by trying the letters elsewhere in the message. An old parlor entertainment involves passing a pair of scissors around and around a circle of players. As each person transfers the scissors he says "Crossed" or "Uncrossed." Those acquainted with the secret rule tell a player when he says the wrong word, and the joke continues until everyone has guessed the rule inductively. The scissors' blades are a red herring; a player should say "Crossed" if and only if his *legs* are crossed.

Familiar games such as Battleship and Jotto have slightly stronger analogies with scientific method, but the first fullfledged induction game was Eleusis, a card game invented by Robert Abbott and first explained in my *Scientific American* column for June 1959. (Fuller details are in *Abbott's New Card Games*, a Stein and Day hard-cover book in 1963 and a Funk & Wagnalls paperback in 1969.) Eleusis intrigued many mathematicians—notably Martin D. Kruskal of Princeton University, who worked out an excellent variant that he described in 1962 in a privately issued booklet, *Delphi—a Game of Inductive Reasoning.*

In Eleusis and Delphi a secret rule, specifying the order in which single cards may be played, corresponds to a law of nature. Players try to guess the rule inductively and then (like scientists) test their conjectures. In this chapter I shall explain a new type of induc-tion game called Patterns, devised by Sidney Sackson and included in his delightful book *A Gamut of Games.*

Patterns is a pencil-and-paper game that can be played by any number of people, although preferably no more than six. It differs markedly from Eleusis and Delphi, but it shares with them such a striking similarity to scientific method that many thorny problems about induction, that have needled philosophers of science ever since David Hume showed induction has no logical justification, have pleasant analogues in the game.

Each player draws a square six-by-six grid on a sheet of paper. A player called the Designer (the role of Designer passes to another player with each new game) secretly fills in his 36 cells by drawing in each cell one of four different symbols. Sackson suggests the four shown in Figure 1, but any other four may be used. The Designer, who can be regarded as Nature, the Universe, or the Deity, is free to mark the cells as he likes; they may form a strong or a weakly ordered pattern, a partially ordered pattern, or no pattern at all. However (and here Sackson adopts the brilliant original idea of Abbott's), the method of scoring is such as to impel the Designer to create a pattern, or a regularity of nature, that is easy to discover for at least one player and yet difficult enough to be missed by at least one other player.

Four typical patterns given in Sackson's book are arranged roughly in order of difficulty [*see Figure 1*]. All have some type of visual symmetry, but nonsymmetrical forms of order can be used if the players are mathematically sophisticated. For example, a De-signer might take the cells in sequence, left to right and top to bot-tom, putting a plus sign in each cell whose number is prime and a star in all the remaining cells. The basis for ordering the Master Pattern

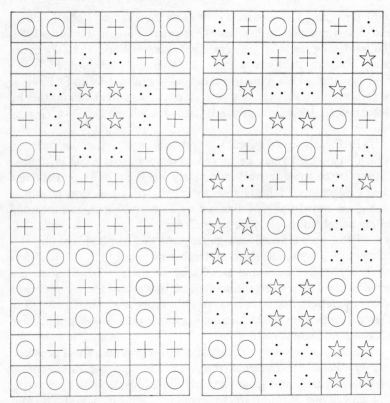

Figure 1. Patterns for Sidney Sackson's induction game, all showing forms of symmetry.

is intimately bound up with the Designer's estimate of the abilities of the other players because, as we shall see, he makes his highest score when one player does very well and another very poorly. Can the reader discern the simple basis for the nonsymmetrical ordering shown in Figure 2?

The Designer puts his sheet face down on the table. Any player may now make inquiries by drawing on his own grid a small slant line in the lower left-hand corner of any cell about which he seeks information. His sheet is passed face down to the Designer, who must enter the correct symbol in each cell in question. There are no turns. A player may ask for information whenever he wants, and there is no limit to the number of cells about which he may inquire. Each

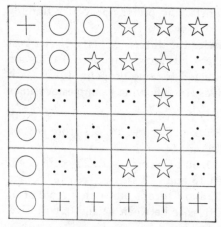

Figure 2.   How is this pattern ordered?

request represents an observation of nature—or an experiment, which is simply a controlled way of making special observations; cells filled in by the Designer correspond to the results of such observations. A player could ask for information about all 36 cells and obtain the entire pattern at once, but this is not to his advantage because, as we shall learn, it would give him a score of zero.

When a player believes he has guessed the Master Pattern, he draws symbols in all his untested cells. To make it easy to identify these inductions, guessed symbols are enclosed in parentheses. If a player decides he cannot guess the pattern, he may drop out of the game with a zero score. This is sometimes advisable because it prevents him from making a minus score and also because it inflicts a penalty on the Designer.

After all players have either filled in all 36 cells or dropped out of the game, the Designer turns his Master Pattern face up. Each player checks his guesses against the Master Pattern, scoring +1 for every correct symbol, −1 for every incorrect symbol. The sum is his final score. If he made a small number of inquiries and correctly guessed all or most of the entire pattern, his score will be high. If he has more wrong than right guesses, his score is negative. High scorers are the brilliant (or sometimes lucky) scientists; poor scorers are the mediocre, impulsive (or sometimes unlucky) scientists who rush poorly confirmed theories into print. Dropouts correspond to the mediocre or overcautious scientists who prefer not to risk framing any conjecture at all.

The Designer's score is twice the difference between the best and the worst scores of the others. His score is reduced if there are dropouts. Five points are subtracted for one dropout, 10 for each additional dropout. Sackson gives the following examples of games with a Designer (D) and players A, B, C:

If A scores 18, B scores 15, and C scores 14, D's score is 8, or twice the difference between 18 and 14.

If A scores 18, B scores 15, and C scores −2, D's score is 40, or twice the difference between 18 and −2.

If A scores 12, B scores 7, and C drops out with a score of 0, D's score is 19, or twice the difference between 12 and 0, with five points deducted for the single dropout.

If A scores 12 and B and C both give up, D scores 9. This is twice the difference between 12 and 0, with five points deducted for the first dropout, 10 for the second.

If all three players drop out, D's score is −25. His basic score is 0, with 25 points subtracted for the three dropouts.

An actual game played by Sackson suggests how a good player reasons [*see Figure 3*]. The five initial inquiries probe the grid for evidence of symmetry [*top*]. The sheet is returned with the five symbols filled in [*middle*]. A series of additional inquiries brings more information [*bottom*]. It looks as if the pattern is symmetrical around the diagonal axis from top left to bottom right. Since no stars have appeared, Sackson induces that they are absent from the pattern.

Now comes that crucial moment, so little understood, for the intuitive hunch or the enlightened guess, the step that symbolizes the framing of a hypothesis by an informed, creative scientist. Sackson guesses that the top left-hand corner cell contains a circle, that the three cells flanking it all have plus marks, and that, continuing down the diagonal, the pluses are flanked by three-spot symbols, the pattern repeating itself with larger borders of the same three symbols in the same order. To test this conjecture with as few new inquiries as possible, Sackson asks for information on only two more cells, the two cells shown empty but with slant lines on the grid at the bottom in Figure 3.

If those cells do not contain circles, his conjecture is false. As

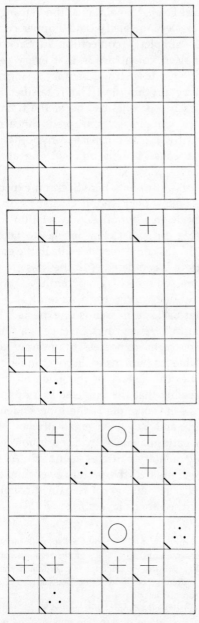

Figure 3. Three stages in probing for the Master Pattern.

the philosopher Karl Popper° maintains, the "strongest" conjecture is the one that is easiest to falsify, and Popper considers this the equivalent of the "simplest" conjecture. In Sackson's game the strongest (and simplest) conjecture is that every cell contains the same symbol, say a star. It is strong because a single inquiry about *any* cell, answered by anything but a star, falsifies it. The weakest conjecture is that each cell contains one of the four symbols. Such a hypothesis can be completely confirmed. Since no inquiry can falsify it, however, it is a true but useless hypothesis, empty of all empirical content because it tells one nothing about the Master Pattern.

The circles turn out to be where Sackson expected them. This increases what the philosopher Rudolf Carnap° calls the "degree of confirmation" of Sackson's hypothesis in relation to the total evidence he has bearing on it. Sackson decides to take the inductive plunge and "publish" his conjecture. He fills in the empty cells of his grid. When his pattern is compared with the Master Pattern [*see Figure 4*], a count of the guessed symbols (in parentheses) shows that Sackson has 20 right and one wrong, for a score of 19.

The single star Sackson missed is unexpected, but it is typical of the surprises Nature often springs. Science is a complicated game in which the universe seems to possess an uncanny kind of order, an order that it is possible for humans to discover in part, but not easily. The more one studies the history of the game of science, the more one has the eerie feeling that the universe is trying to maximize its score. A splended recent example is the independent discovery by Murray Gell-Mann° and Yuval Ne'eman of the "eightfold way." This is a symmetry pattern, defined by a continuous group structure, into which all the elementary particles seem to fit. As soon as enough information had accumulated the pattern was simple enough to be spotted by two physicists, and yet it remained complicated enough to be missed by all the other players.

○ Popper and Carnap: Karl Popper and Rudolf Carnap, philosophers of science who, among other things, disagreed on the validity of the term "induction"; Carnap accepted it as traditionally defined, while Popper maintained that a theory is not "confirmed" but resists attempts to "falsify" it. (See Gardner, *Order and Surprise*, in Sources, for a comparison of the positions.)

○ Gell-Mann and Ne'eman: Gell-Mann of the United States and Ne'eman of Israel both described in 1961 the pattern of quantum numbers and qualities which has become known as the "eightfold way" (originally a Buddhist religious term).

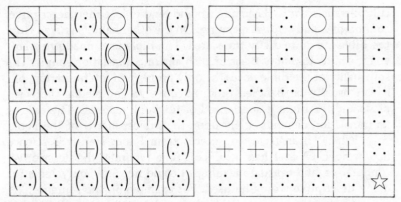

Figure 4. Player's grid (left) compared with Master Pattern (right).

STUDENT ESSAY

Assignment 7. "Translate" three passages into Basic English. In an essay, explain which kind of passage "translates" well and which does not. Include your passages and Basic English translations as an Appendix.

LORRIE BOX

A Plus and *A Minus for Basic English Translation*

Basic English is a simplistic language created for world-wide communication. Although it consists of a mere 850 words, one is able to manipulate the words to form many different combinations. Despite the fact that Basic English was not successful as an international language, it still offers us a good example of the difficulties involved in "translating" modern embellished English into an unadorned language.

The translations of diverse types of literature such as science fiction, the Bible, and specialized books vary significantly. The ease of translation depends upon the original content of the piece and its simplicity. Embellished prose and science fiction are extremely difficult to translate into Basic English and tend to lose their descriptive, connotative, and sensual meaning. On the other hand, passages from the Bible are quite easily translated. The Bible uses unadorned language similar to that of Basic English, making translation simple. The spirituality of the Bible poses the only problem of interpretation, but it can usually be handled quite effectively. The median between prose and the Bible is specialized or textbook material. The ease of its translation depends solely upon the subject matter of the book.

When I translated an excerpt from Frank Herbert's science fiction novel *Dune,* I had a difficult time retaining the descriptive, connotative, and sensual meanings. I could not find equivalents for many descriptive words he used. For example, in the sentence, "A mound-in-motion ran parallel to their rock island—moon-lit ripples, sand waves, a cresting burrow almost level with Paul's eyes at a distance of about a kilometer," the words "parallel," "burrow," and "cresting" did not translate well. Also, other words which dealt with the future and words which were coined by Mr. Herbert—such as "ornithopter"—were virtually impossible to translate. I also lost the connotative meaning and destroyed an entire level of interpretation. These factors, together with a lack of sensual stimulation, lessened the impact of the author's intended words. The initial force of the passage diminished and the sentence fell flat. The reading became dull.

The Bible passage I selected in contrast to the prose was quite easy to translate effectively. Thus, the original meaning of the passage was not difficult to discern from the translation. The Bible's old simplified English was very similar to Basic English. A good example of this was from Psalm 25: "Defeat does not come to those who trust in you, but to those who are quick to rebel against you." This passage was easily changed to: "Loss does not come to men and women who believe in you, but to men and women who are quick to fight against you." The sacrifice of divine meaning could usually be dealt with effectively by representing "God" as "Father," "He," or "Great Force," with minimal loss of meaning.

Falling between the prose and the Bible is specialized material. The subject matter of the book is responsible for the ease of translation. Biology texts, for example, use terms developed especially for a certain profession. These texts include words such as "phloem," "nematocyst," "cambium," and "basidiomycota," which have no equivalents in Basic English. Other texts which do not use many specific terms and which keep their language simple, such as speech or typing books, are easily and effectively translated. From a typing book, for example, the sentence, "I am sending you an example of my letter," can be "rewritten" into Basic English word for word with no loss of meaning. Even a psych book like *Self and World* can be translated without too much loss.

English translates best into Basic English when the original excerpt is plain and simple. With the imaginary words of science fiction and the technical terms of science, Basic English does not work well. With the simply worded Bible passages, the opposite is true. Selection is the key to which type of literature will retain its original meaning and be most effective after translation.

APPENDIX

1. PSALM 25:

To you, O Lord, I offer my prayer; in you, my God, I trust. Save me from the shame of defeat; don't let my enemies gloat over me.

Defeat does not come to those who trust in you, but to those who are quick to rebel against you.

Translation:

To you, Great Force, I give my thoughts; in you, my Great Father, I believe. Keep me from the shame of loss; do not let my bad competition laugh at me.

Loss does not come to men and women who believe in you, but to men and women who are quick to fight against you.

2. SPECIALIZED BOOK, *SELF AND WORLD:*

There is one reality, at least, which we all seize from within, by intuition and not by simple analysis. It is our own personality in its flowing through time—our self which endures. We may sympathize intellectually with nothing else, but we can certainly sympathize with our own selves.

Translation:

There is only one true thing we take from our self, by a belief and not by facts. It is the mind force in its going through time—the

self that lasts. We believe with knowledge no other thing, but we do
believe in self.

3. *DUNE:*

Paul stopped, pressed her into a gut of rock, turned and looked
onto the desert. A mound-in-motion ran parallel to their rock island
—moonlit ripples, sand waves, a cresting burrow almost level with
Paul's eyes at a distance of about a kilometer. The flattened dunes of
its track curved once—a short loop crossing the patch of desert where
they had abandoned their wrecked ornithopter.

Translation:

Paul stopped, forced her against a form of stone, turned and
looked across the sandy land. A mountain in motion went next to
their stone mass—moon light was on the sand waves. A tall round
mass about level to Paul's eye was a mile from him. The flat land
twisted from it only a time—a short curve across the part of sandy
land where they had left their broken plane.

QUESTIONS FOR DISCUSSION

WITHIN THIS CHAPTER:

1. Can you think of *another* solution to Pye's problem of designing a
   draining rack for a camping trip?

2. What thoughts do you imagine were running through the mind of
   the psychologist or lab technician (i.e., the person described by the
   narrator) in "Mazes"?

3. In your opinion, why are some people often suspicious of, or hostile
   to, computers or robots?

4. What qualities will a machine (computer) have to demonstrate to
   qualify as a genuine thinker?

5. Are some people "natural" (effortless) problem-solvers? Explain
   your answer. How would Crovitz answer that question?

6. Does luck play any role in discovering the "patterns" in Sackson's
   game?

Using Other Chapters:

7. In this text, dreams are in a separate chapter. Is this a mistake? Should dreams be considered a "mechanism of the mind," perhaps even another form of problem-solving technique? (If you wish, consult the essays by Melnechuk, Freud, Jung, and Kilton Stewart for various views on dreaming.)

8. In Melnechuk's essay in Chapter 3, the "mechanism of the mind" assumed by some researchers is based on a model of a computer. In what ways are a brain and a computer alike?

9. Look at Danto's essay on murderers in Chapter 4. What "mechanisms of mind" does he use to explain the behavior of various kinds of murderers?

10. What kind of problem-solving do the "medical detectives" (or epidemiologists) featured in Roueché's "Sandy" use (Chapter 5)?

ASSIGNMENTS

Within This Chapter:

1. Select three of Duncker's problems and try to solve them in any way that comes to mind. Then try to solve three others using the Crovitz/Basic English approach or algorithm (the forty-two relational sentences). Keep notes on your thinking as you go along. (Although it would be nice to solve the problems, *how* you try to solve them is of primary importance in this assignment.) Write an essay comparing the different approaches to problem-solving.

2. Make a batch of 6 × 6 grids and play a number of games of "Patterns" with classmates or friends. Again, keep notes on your approach(es) to solutions. Discuss with the other players how they attempted to discover the correct patterns. Write an essay in which you explain *induction* and the various ways this process was demonstrated by playing the game(s).

3. Use Pye's approach (the analysis of "function") to solve the remaining Duncker problems. In an essay, discuss this question: Are there significant differences in the approaches developed by Pye, Crovitz and, by implication, Sackson (originator of "Patterns"), or do all the approaches involve some common principle?

4. Write an essay on your own process of problem-solving. If you wish, use Crovitz/Basic English, "Patterns," or any other approach for comparison.

5. Write a dialogue, consisting of at least forty lines, between a person and a computer. The computer may be assuming a professional or business role such as that of a doctor or a banker, or it may "just" be imitating a human being. (Think of the various "money card" banking machines as one rudimentary model for your dialogue.) Then, analyze your dialogue as to whether it is a successful or unsuccessful example of the "imitation game." Your questioner (the human being) may be whomever or whatever you wish. Do not reveal the identities until the dialogue is "completed"; explain how or why your computer reacted to the human responses.

6. The philosopher A. J. Ayer, in a review of Bolter's *Turing's Man* ("Let Us Calculate," *New York Review of Books,* March 1, 1984, p. 16), stated that he found it difficult "not so much to include machines in the extension of my concept of intelligence as to allow them an inner life, to credit them with feelings and emotions, to treat them as moral agents." If machines could act in these ways, Ayer added, "then our only reason for denying them the full possession of consciousness would be on the score of their origin or their physical composition." Ayer concluded that the machines should *not* be denied such "full possession of consciousness . . . on either of those grounds." Write an essay, using any of the readings in this chapter, in which you agree or disagree with Ayer's critique.

BEYOND THIS CHAPTER:

7. Find a list of the complete 850-word Basic English vocabulary. Old dictionaries, such as the 1951 edition of *Webster's New World Dictionary of the American Language,* have it; or look up C. K. Ogden or Basic English in your library's card catalog. "Translate" three passages into Basic English (from such sources as the Bible, a course textbook, a short story, an American-heritage document like the Constitution, or a scientific report). In an essay, explain which kind of passage "translates" well and which does not. Include your passages and Basic English translations as an Appendix.

8. Philip Dick's novel *Do Androids Dream of Electric Sheep?* (retitled *Blade Runner—* see "Sources") is a comment on, or criticism of, the "imitation game." In an essay, compare/contrast Dick's version of the game with Turing's.

9. Using newspaper, magazine, or government sources (available in most Government Depository libraries), determine the latest advances in artificial intelligence. In an essay, explain to what extent the challenge of Turing's "imitation game" has been met.

10. Le Guin's science-fiction story in this chapter involves a version of the "imitation game." In an essay, argue either that (1) science fiction *by definition* always involves "imitation games"; or (2) a specific science-fiction story you have read carries out the "imitation game" successfully. (For the second choice, I would recommend stories by Asimov or Dick—see "Sources"—but stories by other authors would also work well.)

11. In 1983, Fusao Mori, the Senior Advisor of the Nikko Research Center (one of Japan's leading centers for computer research), predicted that in ten years artificial intelligence research will enable Japan's computers to "learn and infer and then solve problems," use "natural languages, voices, characters [Japanese ideograms], and figures," and translate foreign languages (see *Speaking of Japan,* Japan Institute for Social and Economic Affairs, Tokyo, vol. 5, July 1984). Interview someone on your campus or in industry who knows the current state of computer capabilities, then assess the accuracy and/or likelihood of Mori's predictions.

SOURCES FOR FURTHER READING AND/OR RESEARCH

ASIMOV, ISAAC. *The Robot Collection.* New York: Doubleday, 1982. A collection of all of Asimov's robot stories (many of them of uneven quality as fiction), these stories are among the most popular depictions of human–robot interaction and artificial intelligence.

BATESON, GREGORY. *Mind and Nature: A Necessary Unity.* New York: Dutton, 1979. A very speculative and inventive book which tries to discover the "pattern which connects" all living things and mental processes. Bateson argues for an identity between thinking and evolution.

BELLMAN, RICHARD, KENNETH L. COOKE, AND JO ANN LOCKETT. *Algorithms, Graphs, and Computers.* New York: Academic Press, 1970. Uses mathematical puzzles to teach the important subjects enumerated in the title of their book.

BERNSTEIN, JEREMY. *Science Observed: Essays out of My Mind.* New York: Basic Books, 1982. A fine collection of essays, mostly on contemporary issues in science, including a long and revealing look at Marvin Minsky, one of the leading scientists in the field of artificial intelligence.

BLACK, MAX. "Reasoning with Loose Concepts," in Black, *Margins of Precision: Essays in Logic and Language*. Ithaca, N.Y.: Cornell University Press, 1970. Challenges the idea that traditional logic would not be "applicable" to "reasoning with loose concepts" such as "short" and "rich." (See Zadeh below for a related formal and mathematical investigation of "fuzzy logic.")

BURNHAM, DAVID. *The Rise of the Computer State*. New York: Random House, 1983. Political and personal implications of all that record keeping by all those hungry computers who work for government and business.

CROVITZ, HERBERT. *Galton's Walk*. New York: Harper and Row, 1970. An extended analysis of the views of the influential nineteenth-century psychologist Francis Galton, who defined thinking as the "recurrence of the contents of consciousness"; also takes up algorithms other than Basic English.

DICK, PHILIP. *Blade Runner* (originally published in 1968 as *Do Androids Dream of Electric Sheep?*). Various editions available. An intriguing novel of the "imitation game" (played out on emotional rather than strictly rational grounds) by an undervalued science-fiction writer. Retitled when the 1982 film version (directed by Ridley Scott) was released.

FEIGENBAUM, EDWARD A., AND PAMELA MCCORDUCK. *The Fifth Generation: Artificial Intelligence and Japan's Computer Challenge to the World*. Reading, Mass.: Addison-Wesley, 1983. Popular and thorough account of Japanese "r and d" (research and development), whose goal is the "fifth" generation of KIPS (Knowledge Information Processing Systems) computers which will—using extensive knowledge banks and inference powers —be able to "reason."

GARDNER, HOWARD. *The Mind's New Science: A History of the Cognitive Revolution*. New York: Basic Books, 1985. This is an excellent cross-disciplinary study of "cognitive science"—a field which includes the latest insights into the function of the mind using psychology, artificial intelligence, linguistics, anthropology, and philosophy.

GARDNER, MARTIN. *Science: Good, Bad, and Bogus*. Buffalo, N.Y.: Prometheus Books, 1981. A collection of essays which find logical and scientific flaws in numerous subjects, like ESP and spoon-bending. (Spoon-bending?!)

————. *Order and Surprise*. Buffalo, N.Y.: Prometheus Books, 1983. Another collection of essays by Gardner, more inclusive than *Science: Good, Bad, and Bogus*, because here Gardner takes up a number of artistic, philosophical, and literary topics, and demonstrates their relationship to recent work in science.

————. *Sixth Book of Mathematical Games from* Scientific American. San Francisco: W.H. Freeman, n.d. One of Gardner's many books which develop games and problems (like Sackson's "Patterns," reprinted in another Gardner collection, *Mathematical Circus,* published in 1979); argues for the importance of using games and problems to teach mathematical and creative thinking.

GLEICK, JAMES. "Solving the Mathematical Riddle of Chaos." *New York Times Magazine,* June 10, 1984, pp. 31–32, 40, 44, 49, 66, 68, 70–71. An essay for the general reader on an extremely new field of research in physics nicknamed *chaos* (studying "the borderline between organized behavior and chaotic behavior" or how a dripping faucet "goes from a steady pattern to a random one").

HODGES, ANDREW. *Alan Turing: The Enigma.* New York: Simon and Schuster, 1983. The only complete and helpful biography of the man who is everywhere quoted but rarely appreciated; the subtitle is a pun: Turing's life has some mystery to it, including the wartime period when he helped crack the German code "ultra" with the "enigma machine."

KIDDER, TRACY. *The Soul of a New Machine.* Boston: Little, Brown, 1981. Popular, well-written account of the Eagle Project. The true story of a team of computer specialists in a race to design a fast personal computer; covers the technical, economic, and psychological realities of the computer industry.

KUHN, THOMAS. *The Structure of Scientific Revolutions.* Chicago: University of Chicago Press, 1962. Although in recent years some have challenged Kuhn's thesis that science proceeds by confronting and then disposing of paradigms, or models of reality, this is nonetheless an excellent book on the history of science.

MCCORDUCK, PAMELA. *Machines Who Think.* New York: Freeman, 1979. A very lively and thorough history of the artificial intelligence movement, from ancient times through Turing's era and the contemporary scene; many vignettes and reports of the various key figures in the field.

PAPERT, SEYMOUR. *Mindstorms: Children, Computers, and Powerful Ideas.* New York: Basic Books, 1980. An argument for understanding the education of children based on computers (especially a program called LOGOS, nicknamed TURTLE) and on the learning theories of the great Swiss psychologist, Piaget.

POE, EDGAR ALLAN. "Maelzel's Chess Player." Available in various editions of Poe's works. One of the first analyses of an "imitation game," as Poe demonstrates that Maelzel's invention was not a "pure machine," but a machine "regulated by mind."

POLYA, G. *How To Solve It: A New Aspect of Mathematical Method* (1945). Gar-

den City, N.Y.: Anchor Books, 1957. An early account of the importance of the heuristic (or questioning) approach to problem-solving.

PUTNAM, HILARY. "Robots: Machines or Artificially Created Life." *Journal of Philosophy,* 64 (November 1964), pp. 676–691. A closely-argued philosophical investigation into the question of a robot's "consciousness";
Putnam asks, among other questions, if Oscar—his pet name for a
robot—should have civil rights.

SACKSON, SIDNEY. *A Gamut of Games.* 2d ed. New York: Pantheon, 1982. Includes Sackson's version of "Patterns" and numerous other games.

SAGAN, CARL. *The Dragons of Eden: Speculations on the Evolution of Human Intelligence.*
New York: Ballantine Books, 1978. As his subtitle indicates, Sagan, in
an entertaining and convincing way, explains the relationship between
thinking and evolution.

SCIENTIFIC AMERICAN. "Computer Software." Vol. 251, No. 3 (September
1984). An entire issue of this magazine devoted to programs and
related topics, including Terry Winograd, "Computer Software for
Working with Language," and Douglas B. Lenat, "Computer Software
for Intelligent Systems," both of which are important summaries of
issues in artificial intelligence.

WATSON, JAMES D. *The Double Helix: A Personal Account of the Discovery of the
Structure of DNA.* New York: Atheneum, 1968. The co-discoverer (with
Francis Crick) of the structure of DNA offers his memoirs on the
solving of the DNA "problem," demonstrating that problem-solving,
luck, and nerve are all parts of scientific research.

WEIZENBAUM, JOSEPH. *Computer Power and Human Reason: From Judgment to Calcula-
tions.* San Francisco: Freeman, 1976. A critical account of the artificial
intelligence movement—Weizenbaum raises both moral and feasibil-
ity objections—and especially of ELIZA, the author's therapist–patient
program which had many people thinking that the "imitation game"
had finally been achieved.

WINOGRAD, TERRY. *Understanding Natural Language.* New York: Academic
Press, 1972. Not a general audience book—it requires a fairly high
level of programming knowledge—but the author's opening explanation and sample dialogue with his "robot" worker in the SHRDLU
program helps to illustrate why the program was important in the
study of language in artificial intelligence work.

ZADEH, L. A. "A Theory of Approximate Reasoning." *Machine Intelligence* 9
(1979), pp. 149–194. Explains "fuzzy" or "approximate" reasoning
as that process "by which a possibly imprecise conclusion is de-
duced from a collection of imprecise premises"; excellent bibliography.

EXPLORATIONS

1. Almost any experience with a computer will help you understand some of the issues in this chapter, but if you have the opportunity to try LOGOS, the TURTLE-using program designed by Papert (see "Sources"), you will be able to participate in one of the pioneering efforts to adapt artificial intelligence for teaching youngsters. In addition, ELIZA, one of the earliest artificial-intelligence programs, is available in commercial formats for home computers. ELIZA will attempt to help you with your personal "problems," like any good machine therapist would.

2. Find a children's puzzle or word game which is somewhere between easy and difficult to do. If it is a relatively unknown object or game, all the better. Ask as many people *of different ages* as you can to solve the puzzle while you observe them. Do children solve the puzzle or game in different ways than adults? At a different rate of speed?

3. Either in general magazines or in specialist computer magazines, monitor the accomplishments touted by the ads for computers and programs. Is artificial intelligence, or even a successful "imitation game," any closer?

CHAPTER THREE

Dreams and Visions

Although we all have dreams, we often have trouble remembering any except the most vivid or terrifying; and when we *do* remember them, we struggle to understand them. How often have we had other visual and subjective experiences—hallucinations, illusions, mirages, delirium, *déjà vu,* and daydreams—whose origins seem so hard to explain? This chapter surveys a wide range of human dreams and visions. We will take a look at the approaches to dream analysis of two of the most famous interpreters of dreams, Sigmund Freud and Carl Gustav Jung. Both of these psychiatrists were pioneers in exploring the concept of discovering clues to our conscious life and behavior from our unconscious moments. For Freud and Jung, *remembering* dreams was crucial. Now, however, there is some disagreement as to whether we *should* remember our dreams. "We dream," wrote Francis Crick and his collaborator, Graeme Mitchison, in 1983, "in order to forget."

Crick and Mitchison's controversial research is summarized in Theodore Melnechuk's popular exposition of dream theory, "The Dream Machine," the first selection in "Discursive Essays." If you are studying this topic for the first time, Melnechuk's essay, and those by Freud and Jung in "Essays from the Disciplines," will provide you with a thorough grounding in the subject. Because Freud's ideas in general, and his dream theory in particular, have a popular appeal even if his essays are not always as widely read as they should be, I have included a selection which summarizes his principal ideas in relation to dreams. Furthermore, Melnechuk's and Roueché's essays, which constitute the first section, also provide some helpful background on Freud's ideas. (Also, see Freud in "Sources.") Jung, who was originally a close follower of Freud, developed his own psychoanalytical practice and theory, emphasizing even more than Freud the importance of dream life, both for therapy and for exploring the hidden or subconscious aspects of all human behavior and culture. A third, possibly even more radical, account of dream life is recorded in the anthropological report by Kilton Stewart, whose study of the Senoi people of Malaya revealed their tremendous emphasis and reliance on dream life.

Roueché's essay in the first section, and the selections by Hitchcock in "Documentary Materials," Gibson in "Essays from the Disciplines," and Gregory in Chapter 2 offer various explanations for a number of other visual experiences. Roueché traces the curious history of *déjà vu,* an experience many people have had but few understand. Hitchcock records his own semiconscious images, ones which resemble the "spectral" figures raised in Chapter 5, "Perspectives on Salem." Gibson attempts to define the characteristics of both hallucinations and perceptions, reminding us that "subjectivity" in itself does not determine the status of one's visual life.

Dreams and visions, whether from within or without, may not always be explained by psychology. Chief Seattle, in "Documentary Materials," prophetically suggests that all that we see still may not be enough to comprehend *his* world of invisible and ever-present spirits. Nevertheless, the essays in this chapter offer numerous visual experiences and some convincing attempts at understanding them.

DISCURSIVE ESSAYS

REPORT

THEODORE MELNECHUK

Melnechuk's essay begins as a popular account from the magazine Psychology Today *of the controversial research of Francis Crick (Nobel Prize winner for his co-discovery of the structure of DNA) and*

*Graeme Mitchison. For centuries, dreams have been an important source
of psychological investigation. However, Crick and Mitchison's research
suggests, perhaps for the first time, that it may be better for the brain
not to have its dream life reawakened. It may be beneficial, even
necessary, for the brain to "erase certain false or nonsensical memories."
This idea certainly takes us a long way from Jung's or Freud's confidence
that psychological truths may be gained from dream analysis.*

*Melnechuk brings out for special mention two features of
contemporary science: First, Crick and Mitchison are using a model of the
brain which is dependent upon the essence of computer programming (the
analogy between the neural networks of the brain and electronic computer
components); second, the research of Crick and Mitchison is still in
process, its validity being hotly debated by other scientists. Both of these
points mean that you, as reader, can become witness to scientific history
as it unfolds.*

*The following essay is a report on current scientific research on a
specific topic. Melnechuk reviews the current state of knowledge in the
field, and then turns toward the latest research of Crick and Mitchison
as represented in their scientific essay "The Function of Dream Sleep,"
which appeared in the July 14, 1983, issue of* Nature, *the leading
British professional journal for scientists of all fields. Melnechuk is
careful to include the reactions of other scientists to the new research,
basing his essay in part on interviews with them. (He probably called
them up and asked them what they thought of Crick and Mitchison's
essay.) He concludes by discussing some implications of the new research.*

The Dream Machine

The vivid and often bizarre quality of dreams has prompted
many attempts to define their significance. In some societies, they
have been seen as experiences of a parallel reality; in others, as
sources of divine guidance. A number of modern theorists have suggested that dream activity accomplishes restorative or energy-saving
tasks. Freud considered dreams evidence of a "hidden" realm of
mental activity and called them "the royal road to the unconscious";
his book *The Interpretation of Dreams* (1900) is ancestral to entire schools
of psychotherapy based on dream symbolism.

A new era of dream research opened in 1953 with the discovery
of rapid eye movement (REM), the fitful shifting of the eyes beneath
closed eyelids that characterizes part of our sleep time. Researchers

soon correlated periods of REM sleep to dream activity and to patterns of electroencephalograph (EEG) waves that resembled those of an alert, awake person. REM sleep is widely considered to have great functional importance, occupying, as it does, roughly a quarter of each night's sleeping time. However, the function of REM sleep remains obscure and is still debated among sleep researchers three decades after its discovery.

One of the many mysterious features of dreaming is that despite its obvious impact on the dreamer, he or she at most can recall only a minute fraction of a night's dream. A new theory of dream sleep has now been formulated that accounts for the value of that unremembered dream activity: Francis Crick and Graeme Mitchison have proposed that REM sleep represents a needed process of "reverse learning" to erase certain false or nonsensical memories. This "damping-out" process, they suggest, is a natural product of evolution to eliminate modes of mental activity that might interfere with rational thought and memory. As the authors write in a recent article in *Nature,* "We dream in order to forget."

This novel theory, that dreams are part of a regular mental housecleaning system, has its origins in theoretical studies of how the brain works. Nobel laureate Crick, who helped delineate the spiral structure of DNA, is now a research professor with wide-ranging interests at The Salk Institute in La Jolla, California. In the 30 years since he co-wrote with James Watson the famous paper on DNA structure (about the same time as discovery of REM sleep), he has moved beyond molecular genetics to developmental biology and neuroscience. His work on dreams, with Mitchison of Cambridge University, emerges from both this new work and his training in physics.

REM dreams are not the only ones that occur. The four other stages of sleep, known collectively as non-REM sleep, occasionally produce dreams as well. But electroencephalograms made during non-REM sleep show brain waves unlike those in the fast, low-voltage EEG records of the awake brain. In addition, our infrequent non-REM dreams are usually thoughtlike in character, lacking the episodic, illogical, hallucinatory quality of REM dreams that, for example, Lewis Carroll featured to such striking effect in his two tales of Alice.

Every night, adults experience REM sleep for a total of 1½ to 2 hours, occurring in approximately four sessions that begin about

every 90 to 100 minutes. These sessions increase in length as the
night goes on, from about 10 minutes to perhaps 30 minutes or more.
The longest spell of dreaming usually precedes morning wake-up,
but the dreamer rapidly forgets its content, along with most of the
other dream episodes.

Despite our feeble ability to recall dreams, those few that break
into consciousness carry such power that people in all cultures have
assigned them great importance. In biblical and classical times,
dreams were considered prophetic. Some native Americans have paid
strict heed to dreams as visions of another reality, parallel to the
waking world.

Recently, dream theorists have become more specific and more
diverse. Psychologists often suppose that dreams either express unconscious impulses, as Freud suggested, or provide an avenue of
symbolic communication between the unconscious and the conscious, as Jung suggested. Others believe that dreams help consoli-
date memories—the opposite of the Crick-Mitchison idea. One researcher, Montague Ullman of Ardsley, New York, an investigator of
parapsychological phenomena, suggests that people who are dreaming may be unusually open to telepathic influences.

Neurobiological investigators, however, tend to regard dreams
as mere incidental by-products of the sleeping brain and therefore
without meaning. During the deepest stages of sleep, the neocortex,
the brain's largest and most recently evolved region, is isolated from
its normal input and output channels. Nonetheless, it remains as
active as in the waking state.

If the neocortex is isolated from sensory stimuli during sleep,
what prompts this automatic activity? J. Alan Hobson and Robert
W. McCarley of Harvard Medical School, following the pioneering
work of Michel Jouvet of Lyon, France, proposed that the neocortical activity in REM sleep is promoted by periodic excitations
from cell groups in the brain stem, a primitive part of the brain
between its higher regions and the spinal cord. According to Hobson and McCarley (see "Where Dreams Come From: A New Theory", *Psychology Today,* December 1978), these cell groups can be described as a "dream-state generator" that incites both the REM
and the episodic intrusion of apparently meaningless content into
the dreams of REM sleep. The neocortex then makes what sense it
can of the imagery resulting from spontaneous patterns of brain-
stem activity. Although the identity of the cell groups involved is

controversial, this general picture is accepted by many sleep researchers, including Crick and Mitchison.

While investigators debate the importance of dream content, they agree on the importance of REM sleep. People deprived of it for a few nights, by being awakened whenever their eyes move rapidly, will usually compensate by having greater-than-normal periods of REM sleep on succeeding nights of undisturbed sleep; a certain amount of REM sleep seems to be required.

Another argument for the importance of REM sleep lies in the fact that it is common to almost all mammals and birds. The exception is interesting—the spiny anteater, which, like the duck-billed platypus, is a primitive, egg-laying mammal. Although this anteater has normal non-REM sleep, it lacks the EEG sign of REM sleep, at least in young adults.

One feature of REM sleep of the greatest interest to Crick and Mitchison is that it is reserved for creatures with a neocortex—most mammals—or with brain structure analogous to the visual neocortex, called the wulst—birds. To these two researchers, this correlation is a clue that REM sleep serves a specific neocortical need.

The neocortex seems to be the seat of higher mental functions. It is relatively larger in primates than in most other mammals and larger in humans than in lower primates. Like other gray matter in the human brain, the neocortex consists of information-processing nerve cells, or neurons, estimated by Dr. Vernon B. Mountcastle of The Johns Hopkins University to number about 50 billion, and metabolically supportive cells called neuroglia, which may number 10 times that many. Each neocortical neuron can exchange information with thousands of other neurons at precise, one-way information-transfer points called synapses.

Unlike neurons in other areas of gray matter, the neocortical neurons communicate mainly with nearby neurons, and most of their synapses are capable of being excited, or excitatory. The dense neocortical web of mostly local connections is believed to store traces of remembered events and their associations. Each constellation of stimuli is thought to be represented by the activity of at least one subset of neocortical cells, called a cell assembly.

The increasing strength of an association between stimuli is thought to be reflected in an increased strength of the synaptic connections between the cells of its corresponding assembly, an idea put forth in 1958 by a Canadian psychologist, Donald O. Hebb. As a cell assembly is trained by a repeated stimulus—such as the sight of a familiar face—the synapses are strengthened. Moreover, the entire face can be recognized from only a part of its features, because the cells of an assembly, being mutually excitatory, can regenerate the activity of the entire assembly from the stimulated activity of only a few of its cells.

Since the publication of Hebb's idea, many neuroscientists have been working out the principles and mechanisms of interneuronal information storage and processing. However, they have been reluctant to tackle the awesome challenge of the neocortex as a whole, with its trillions of synapses between billions of neurons. They have begun instead with studies of far simpler systems, hoping to discover fundamentals that will also hold true for larger systems.

Important contributors to this enterprise include other ex-physicists who first applied their thinking to genetics and then to neuroscience. Marshall W. Nirenberg, who shared a Nobel for helping to translate the code by which DNA and RNA specify the assembly of amino acids into proteins, has since been studying the relationships of small numbers of brain cells in cell cultures. Similarly, Seymour Benzer, Sidney Brenner, and Cyrus Levinthal are studying the modest nervous systems of such tiny organisms as the fruitfly *Drosophila melanogaster*, nematode worms, and the crustacean *Daphnia*.

Crick is pursuing a somewhat different tack. Rather than study biological networks of a few hundred living neurons, he has joined the theoreticians who use artificial networks of a few hundred neuron-like components. In the early days of neural modeling, the networks were built of electronic components. Nowadays, the workings are more easily simulated by computer programs.

Most of these artificial neural "nets," or networks, use Hebb's idea that the storage of information increases in proportion to the strength of synapses between cells in an assembly. They also conform to two conclusions of the American neurophysiologist Karl S. Lashley, who wrote in 1950 that "Every instance of recall requires the activity of literally millions of neurons . . . and the same neurons which retain the memory traces of one experience must also participate in countless other activities."

Obviously, a simulated net of only several hundred cells cannot contain cell assemblies as large as those Lashley describes for the neocortex; on the other hand, modelers never make assemblies as small as only two connected cells. Instead, the information is distributed over enough synapses that the information is not lost if a few synapses are removed or added. Neural modelers call this quality "robustness." This quality is also possessed by the words spelled out at a college football game by a large bloc of students simultaneously flashing alphabet cards. The giant mosaic formed by the cards is sufficiently "robust" that a misplaced card or two makes little difference in the overall pattern.

In harmony with Lashley's second conclusion, the information in a neural model is also superimposed; that is, a given synapse will usually participate in storing more than one item of information. To help grasp this idea, visualize one child's "connect-the-dots" puzzle superimposed upon another so that some dots are shared by the two patterns.

Neural modelers have shown that nets possessing distributed, robust, and superimposed information storage can do many of the things that a neocortex is thought to do. For example, such a net can recognize a stimulus that it has been "trained" to remember when its "synaptic strengths" are set at appropriate levels. Indeed, the net can recognize a whole stimulus when presented with only a part of it. Just as you can recognize a friend from only a glimpse, a net with a computer-graphics attachment can convert with impressive accuracy a partial or blurry representation of a face into a complete portrait.

Such a net can simulate cognitive as well as perceptual functions of the neocortex. Suppose it is given an input pattern of stimulation that has common features with different cell assemblies. The net can produce an output that synthesizes many of the common features of stimuli.

Such nets can become overloaded if too many associations are stored at one time, or if the stored associations overlap too much. How the net will behave when overloaded depends on the structure of the net, according to Crick. But certain undesirable patterns of behavior are likely to emerge, ranging from inappropriate responses to outright instabilities. Crick and Mitchison call these unwanted patterns "parasitic modes of activity" and liken them to various psychopathological states in humans.

For example, an overloaded net may print out bizarre, farfetched associations, which the authors liken to abnormal fantasy. Or it may print multiple versions of the same memory, or it may become obsessive and produce one of only a small set of memories, no matter what stimulus it receives. It may even respond to input stimuli that normally would not evoke any response by printing an uncalled-for image, a "hallucination."

At first glance, "neurotic" and "psychotic" symptoms in simulated neuronal nets of only 100 cells may seem inconsequential. But such aberrations have been an important problem for neural modelers, the solution to which might cast light on the neuropathology of neurosis and psychosis in humans.

Is the human neocortex vulnerable to such parasitic modes of activity? Crick and Mitchison think it is, though not from overloading. Modelers have found that artificial nets cannot be overloaded if they are sufficiently enlarged; the neocortex has about a billion times more cells than the average artificial net.

But two characteristics of the neocortex render it susceptible to parasitic modes. First, the excitatory nature of most cortical synapses makes the neocortex prone to self-excitatory behavior. In migraine, epilepsy, and some drug-induced hallucinatory states, parts of the cortex become electrically unstable, their neurons firing together to produce large, slow, abnormal brain waves.

Second, the strengths of synapses between the various neocortical neurons are probably not determined in detail by genes. These strengths are likely refined by experience, especially in a species like ours that can learn vast amounts of unforeseen information. This semi-random process of making neocortical synapses presents great opportunities for the creation of cell assemblies whose activities imperfectly represent the real world.

How might the brain eliminate its own undesirable modes of activity? Crick and Mitchison suggest that it would have been advantageous for the brain to evolve in such a way that its major neocortical inputs would be turned off at regular intervals, isolating it from sensory stimuli. During isolation, the neocortex could be given a series of random stimuli by another part of the brain. These stimuli would serve to trigger latent parasitic modes of activity, especially in unwanted cell assemblies prone to be excited by nonsense stimuli. As each parasitic mode revealed itself, it would be damped out by some mechanism that would make it less likely to appear.

This is the point in their thinking about neural nets at which Crick and Mitchison had their clue to the possible function of dreaming. The self-corrective strategy that brains ought to have evolved to dissociate aberrant cell assemblies bears a striking resemblance to what happens neurobiologically in REM sleep. First, sensory stimulation is cut off by sleep. Then the neocortex is stimulated by non-specific signals from the brain stem. Meanwhile, the sleeper is having hallucinatory dreams that, for the most part, don't reach consciousness. Crick and Mitchison take these dreams to be the subjective representations of the parasitic modes of activity triggered in aberrant cell assemblies by signals from the brain stem.

To damp out the parasitic modes, it would seem that the brain only needs to decouple the neurons linked into a functional cell assembly by strengthened synapses. To accomplish this, Crick and Mitchison suggest, the brain may apply a process which is the reverse of the Hebbian synapse, strengthening thought to cement a learned association. That is, synapses may weaken between any cells that fire in a cell assembly during dreaming. "We dream in order to forget our dreams." In other words, their novel idea is that dreaming is a process of reverse learning, in which people unlearn their unconscious dreams. More precisely, dreaming is thought to weaken the synapses between neurons in assemblies that represent undesirable modes of neocortical activation.

Soon after conceiving of reverse learning, Crick and Mitchison found out that another group of neural net modelers, John J. Hopfield of the California Institute of Technology and his collaborators, had independently arrived at the same idea, although they had not connected it with REM sleep. The Hopfield group was able to show that reverse learning does indeed improve the behavior of the artificial neural network. In that net, the reverse learning suppresses most of the spurious memories—the ones Crick and Mitchison liken to fantasies, obsessions, and hallucinations—and improves the accessibility of stored realistic memories. Crick and Mitchison have since duplicated the Hopfield group's simulations and confirmed their findings. In brief, reverse learning improves some memory, at least in simulations of small artificial neural nets.

Crick and Mitchison insist that this disposal of spurious memories is different from the normally rapid forgetting of dreams that awaken the sleeper, end-of-the-night dreams. Reverse learning, they emphasize, is a positive mechanism to weaken the synaptic strengths of undesirable neuronal activity patterns, most of which are unremembered. This weakening reduces the chance that such a pattern will recur.

Why, then, do we have repeat dreams? The only repeat dreams we know about are those that awaken us, or that occur upon awakening. Crick and Mitchison think that if a dream awakens the dreamer for some reason, the dreamer then remembers it in the usual way; synapses between the participating neurons are strengthened instead of weakened. And because the spurious associations are strengthened, the dream is learned and is more likely to recur.

One of the strengths of the Crick-Mitchison theory is that it explains much of what is known about REM sleep. One of the strongest aspects of REM sleep is that all mammals, other than the spiny anteater, have more of it before and soon after birth than during adulthood. Newborn human beings, for example, may pass as much as one-third of their sleep time in dreams; human fetuses may experience even more REM sleep, especially during the last three months of gestation.

It seems unlikely that unborn fetuses, especially of animals, are dreaming about such things as memories and repressed desires. What then might be the function of their REM sleep? Some neurobiologists suggest that the neocortical activation enhances brain development by facilitating the formation of synapses. Other neuroscientists, concentrating on the eye movements themselves, suggest that activation of the visual system at a time when few or no visual stimuli are perceived benefits the organism by preparing the future brain mechanisms of stereoscopic vision.

Crick and Mitchison think that if this latter idea were true, all binocular animals would have REM sleep. Lower animals, however, have only non-REM sleep. Instead, Crick and Mitchison believe, unborn fetuses need extra REM sleep to purge their brains of undesirable connections between neurons.

However, the theory does not explain, as its authors point out, why people who are severely deprived of REM sleep in laboratory experiments do not all suffer from hallucinations, delusions, or obsessions. Only a few people seem to suffer in these ways, while others are irritable and unable to concentrate, have increased periods of fantasy while awake, or experience previously unconscious wishes and feelings. But these effects are rare in comparison with what the theory seems to call for.

The theory also fails to explain why some drugs that seem to prevent REM sleep do not also cause obvious psychological problems. Crick and Mitchison suspect that such drugs may have obscure side effects that distort this finding. Ernest L. Hartmann of Tufts University School of Medicine, an expert in sleep research, believes that these drugs do not deprive sleepers of their REM sleep in the same manner as artificial awakenings.

The Crick theory is being received unenthusiastically by some leading sleep scientists. Jouvet said, "The theory is interesting and worthy of publication and discussion, although I personally doubt that REM sleep evolved for reverse learning." Instead, Jouvet has thought for some time that, during paradoxical sleep, genetic programming of new synapse formation continues, of the sort that goes on in early brain development. Synapse formation is just about the opposite of the synapse-weakening that Crick and Mitchison propose. McCarley said, "This theory is the latest in a long line of ideas about the still unknown function of REM sleep. Even if it were true, it could be compatible with other suggested functions, such as Jouvet's neural development idea, or the exercise of the neural mechanisms of complex behaviors not often performed."

Daniel F. Kripke, founding director of the Sleep Disorders Clinic at the La Jolla VA Medical Center and professor of psychiatry at the University of California, San Diego, said, "Crick would be the first to admit that it will not be easy to marshal compelling evidence directly supportive of this hypothesis." Michael H. Chase of the University of California, Los Angeles, editor of many volumes of sleep symposia proceedings and a neurophysiologist, did not believe the theory was credible, because, he said, "It comprises a set of hypotheses founded on assumptions, some of which are either unsupported by facts or frankly counterfactual."

One difficulty stands above all others in proving this new idea. To test it directly, Crick and Mitchison would have to show that the occurrence of a given unremembered dream reduces the probability of dreaming it again. There is no way to do this. It may, however, be experimentally possible to demonstrate the weakening of synapses and to discover the microanatomical correlate or correlates of reverse learning. Presumably, this would be a variant of the way synapses strengthen during learning.

Re-enter the spiny anteater, the lowly exception to the rule that mammals have REM sleep. Happily for the Crick-Mitchison theory, this animal is exceptional in another way; it has a huge neocortex, which is inexplicable in so primitive an animal by any principles of neurophysiology. To Crick and Mitchison, the explanation is a simple one: Without REM sleep, and therefore without the reverse-learning mechanism for purging parasitic modes of neocortical activity, the spiny anteater evolved instead an enormous neocortex to escape hallucinations and other psychopathology. In the same way, artificial neural nets can avoid spurious memories if they are sufficiently increased in size. As mammals go, humans have relatively large neocortices, but if Crick and Mitchison are correct, ours are available full-time for mental activity because of our dreaming in REM sleep.

There is one logical consequence to the Crick-Mitchison theory that many people will find unpalatable. If the brain is trying to eradicate certain cortical patterns of activity in REM sleep, it follows that each dream retained by the neocortex would strengthen synaptic connections that should instead be weakened. The theory implies not only that dreams are meaningless, but also that their retention in memory could be harmful to our ability to learn, to reason, and to remember. Shakespeare notwithstanding, perhaps one should not want one's mind to be "such stuff as dreams are made on."

CAUSAL ANALYSIS

BERTON ROUECHÉ

Roueché's essay on déjà vu, the "emotion of weirdness," and his essay in Chapter 5 on "Sandy," a "hysterical" girl, are typical examples of his interest in "medical detection"—the pursuit of medical truths about human disease or experience. In this selection, he investigates the subjective experience of déjà vu—the feeling that we "have been here before," although we are reasonably sure we actually never have been "here"—and which, one report has estimated, one-third of us have experienced.

In this discursive and cross-disciplinary essay, Roueché ranges over many cultures and centuries for samples of the déjà vu experience. The structure he gives to his essay is in part personal: He remembers a particular moment of déjà vu from his youth, and his essay begins and ends with the setting of that original experience. (It is, by the way, the same U.S. 40 Stewart wrote of in Chapter 1.) The main body of the essay is organized in terms of various explanations of déjà vu and the literature Roueché brings to bear on these various explanations.

An Emotion of Weirdness

U.S. Highway 40, which links Kansas City and St. Louis by way of Columbia, the seat of the University of Missouri, crosses the Missouri River just east of Boonville, and for several miles below the town the highway follows the river through a lovely countryside of rolling fields and meadows. It has now been more than thirty years since I first saw that countryside, but I clearly recall the occasion. It was around eleven o'clock on a sunny September morning in 1928, and I was driving down to Columbia from my home in Kansas City with two Kansas City friends to begin my freshman year at the university. We came through Boonville and across the bridge and down along the river. Boonville is (or was in those days) a couple of hours from Kansas City, and we had begun to run out of talk. I was sitting slumped in my seat, vacantly watching the road ahead, when a patch of pasture caught my eye. There was nothing very remarkable about it—a slope of browning grass, a big, dusty elm, a dozen grazing sheep—but it jerked me erect in my seat. I had the feeling that I knew every foot and feature of it, that I had seen it all before. I turned and stared until it dropped away behind a bend. I was sure I had seen it before. And yet I knew I hadn't.

It was a strange and perplexing experience. It was even a little unsettling. But it was not (as I naturally thought at the time) a highly unusual one. The illusion I experienced that morning was a contrary form of amnesia that has come to be called the *déjà-vu* (literally, "already-seen") phenomenon, and it is probably the least uncommon of all temporary mental aberrations. Almost everyone has at one time or another felt its mystifying touch. A *déjà vu* much like my own is described in *Remembrance of Things Past.* Proust writes, "I had just seen, standing a little way back from the steep ridge over which we were passing, three trees, probably marking the entrance to a shady avenue, which made a pattern at which I was looking now not for the first time; I could not succeed in reconstructing the place from which they had been, as it were, detached, but I felt that it had been familiar to me once." Other writers are more explicit. "We all know the sensation of doing something or seeing something which is strangely familiar, as if we had done or seen it before," John Buchan notes in *Pilgrim's Way,* his autobiography. "I had one [such] experience in South Africa. . . . I was in the bushveld going from one native village to another by a road which was just passable, and which followed a sedgy stream. I was walking ahead, and my mules and boys were about two hundred yards behind. Suddenly I found myself in a glade where the brook opened into a wide, clear pool. The place was a little amphitheatre; on my left was a thicket of wild bananas, with beyond them a big baobab, and on my right a clump of tall stinkwood trees laced together with creepers. The floor was red earth with tufts of coarse grass, and on the edge of the pool was a mat of ferns. . . . I stopped in my tracks, for I had been here before. Something had happened to me here, and was about to happen again; something had come out of the banana thicket. I knew the place as well as I knew my own doorstep. I was not exactly frightened, only curious and excited, and I stood waiting with my heart in my mouth. And then the spell broke, for my mules clattered up behind me." Tolstoy, in his memoir *Childhood, Boyhood, and Youth,* relates an even more elaborate encounter with *déjà vu.* "And, suddenly," he writes, "I experienced a strange feeling: I recalled that precisely what was happening then was a repetition of something that had happened with me before; that just such a rain had pattered then, and the sun went down behind the birches, and I looked at *her,* and she read, and I magnetized her, and she looked around, and I recalled that it had happened before." A *déjà vu* of still greater complexity appears in *David Copperfield.* It would seem, in fact, to represent the ultimate refinement of such sensations. It involves a double illusion—a sense not only of total recognition but also of total anticipation. "We have all some experience," Dickens says for David, "of a feeling, that comes over us occasionally, of what we are saying and doing having been said and done before, in a remote time—of our having been surrounded, dim ages ago, by the same faces, objects, and circumstances—of our knowing perfectly what will be said next, as if we suddenly remembered it! I never had this mysterious impression more strongly in my life than before he uttered those words."

Familiarity has not done much to clarify the *déjà-vu* phenomenon. Neither has a century of quickening scientific interest. There is, to be sure, a certain amount of reliable statistical information on record. According to a comprehensive study by A. H. Chapman and Ivan N. Mensh—both members of the Department of Neuropsychiatry of the Washington University School of Medicine, in St. Louis—which appeared in the *Psychiatric Quarterly Supplement* in 1951, about one person in three has had (or can remember having) the experience at least once. A few of this group have had it many times. It chiefly occurs among young adults—those between the ages of twenty and thirty-five. Education and travel seem to be predisposing factors. *Déjà vu* also appears occasionally in mental illness and in psychomotor epilepsy (where it may form a part of the aura that classically heralds a seizure), but it is not a symptom of either. The people studied by Chapman and Mensh were sane and free of brain or central-nervous-system disease. From this study and others, it seems reasonably certain that *déjà vu,* as commonly experienced, is innocuous. Its basic nature, on the other hand, is a matter of some debate. Different investigators explain it very differently. Almost a dozen contradictory explanations are currently more or less in vogue. They range in character from the ruggedly commonsensical to the twilit transcendental. All, however, are rooted in one or the other of two fundamental assumptions. One of these supposes that the *déjà vu* is necessarily generated by the particular setting in which it occurs. The other takes the opposite position, considering the setting irrelevant.

The theories that stem from the latter assumption are essentially mechanistic. They attribute the *déjà vu* to a split-second disturbance in mental synthesis. The oldest attribution of this sort is based on the fact that the twin hemispheres of the cerebrum are capable of independent action. It was first proposed by a mid-nineteenth-century English neurologist named Arthur Ladbroke Wigan. "This delusion occurs only when the mind has been exhausted by excitement, or is from indisposition or any other cause languid, and only slightly attentive," he suggested in *The Duality of the Mind* in 1844. "The persuasion of the scene being a repetition comes on when the attention has been roused by some accidental circumstance, and we become, as the phrase is, wide awake. I believe the explanation to be this: only one brain has been used in the immediately preceding part of the scene—the other brain has been asleep, or in an analogous state nearly approaching it. When the attention of both brains is roused to the topic, there is the same vague consciousness that the ideas have passed through the mind before which takes place on re-perusing the page we had read while thinking on some other subject. The ideas *have* passed through the mind before, and as there was no sufficient consciousness to fix them in the memory without a renewal, we have no means of knowing the length of time that had elapsed between the *faint* impression received by the single brain, and the *distinct* impression received by the double brain. It may seem to have been many years."

A variation of this theory explains the cerebral confusion in more psychologically energetic terms. It substitutes for the briefly dozing brain a briefly heightened perception. Its basis—as was originally emphasized by Théodule Ribot, a leading French psychologist of the late nineteenth century— is the observation that in successful recollection the remembered object (person, place, or thing) returns for mental scrutiny as an image of the actual impression. In *déjà vu,* Ribot proposed in *Diseases of Memory,* the image follows so closely on the heels of perception that the mind somehow mistakes impression for reproduction. "The image is very intense and of the nature of a hallucination," he wrote. "It imposes itself upon the mind as a reality. Hence, the real impression is relegated to a secondary place as a recollection; it is localized in the past. . . . This illusory state does not efface the real impression, but, as it is detached from it [and] produced by it, it appears as a second experience. It appears to us more recent than the other, as indeed it is."

A less ingenious variation on the theme first sounded by Wigan dispenses with both the lagging hemisphere and the lightning image. It depicts *déjà vu* as a product simply of mental fatigue. The mind is for a moment too slack to distinguish between the new and the old, the present and the past. "It is inattention, failure of apperception, defective association of the mental contents which make [the phenomenon] possible," Havelock Ellis, an influential advocate of this interpretation, noted in *The World of Dreams.* "The mind has for the moment become flaccid and enfeebled; its loosened texture has, as it were, abnormally enlarged the meshes in which sensations are caught and sifted, so that they run through too easily. In other words, they are not properly *apperceived.* . . . The impressions of the world which are actual sensations as they strike the relaxed psychic meshwork are instantaneously passed through to become memories." Ellis goes on to summarize the views of the French psychologist Michael Léon-Kindberg as they appeared in a report on "Le Sentiment du Déjà Vu" in the *Revue de Psychiatrie* in 1903: "There is an absence of mental attention, of the effort of synthesis necessary to grasp an actual occurrence, which is, therefore, perceived with the same facility as a memory not requiring synthesis, with the resulting illusion that it is a memory."

———————— • ————————

Just why *déjà vu* should typically strike in an unfamiliar setting (my Missouri pasture, Proust's three distinctive trees, Buchan's

South African pool) has not yet been explained by those who lay the phenomenon to a fortuitous impairment of sensory correlation. Nor has the nature of the force that thus quiets or quickens or enfeebles the mind. Those who take the view that the setting produces the *déjà vu* are spared these awkward questions. The only question they must answer is why it looks familiar. They do so in a variety of ways, but on one point there is general agreement—that the familiarity of the setting springs from an actual memory. The plainest expression of this view asserts that the experience (or one much like it) has occurred before. No more is involved in *déjà vu* than a simple lapse of memory. The memory may be lightly blocked—a mere tip-of-the-tongue constriction. Or, as in a case described by the celebrated early-nineteenth-century Scottish physician John Abercrombie (in *Inquiries Concerning the Intellectual Powers*), it may lie deeply buried: "A lady in the last stage of a chronic disease was carried from London to a lodging in the country; there her infant daughter was taken to visit her, and, after a short interview, carried back to town. The lady died a few days after, and the daughter grew up without any recollection of her mother till she was of mature age. At this time, she happened to be taken into the room in which her mother died, without knowing it to have been so; she started on entering it, and, when a friend who was along with her asked the cause of her agitation, she replied, 'I have a distinct impression of having been in this room before, and that a lady, who lay in that corner and seemed very ill, leaned over me and wept.' " William James is one of those to whom *déjà vu* appears in this unambiguous light. His judgment, which he handed down in *The Principles of Psychology,* is characteristically direct. "There is a curious experience which everyone seems to have had," he wrote. "[It is] the feeling that the present moment in its completeness has been experienced before—we were saying just this thing, in just this place, to just these people, etc. This 'sense of pre-existence' has been treated as a great mystery and occasioned much speculation. . . . I must confess that the quality of mystery seems to me a little strained. I have over and over again in my own case succeeded in resolving the phenomenon into a case of memory, so indistinct that whilst some past circumstances are presented again, the others are not. The dissimilar portions of the past do not arise completely enough at first for the date to be identified. All we get is the present scene with a general suggestion of pastness about it. . . . It is noteworthy that just as soon as the past context grows complete and distinct, the emotion of weirdness fades from the experience."

James is not alone in noting that victims of *déjà vu* feel something more poignant than surprise and confusion. An emotion of weirdness is generally recognized as an almost invariable aftermath of a true *déjà-vu* experience. He is alone, however, in construing it as evidence in support of a pragmatic explanation of the phenomenon. It is usually considered a refutation of that theory. "In any case," Havelock Ellis concluded his review of the matter in *The World of Dreams*, "he [the victim] is liable to an emotion of distress which would scarcely be caused by the coincidence of resemblance with a real previous experience." Ellis's opinion is fully shared by the English neurologist Sir James Crichton-Browne. "The thought that is of the essence of the state is transient and vanishes before it can be grasped," he observed in a report in the *Lancet* in 1895. "It is often connected with circumstances of the most commonplace or trivial description—Oliver Wendell Holmes says it used to occur to a poor student when he was blacking his boots—and yet it startles as if it were a flash of revelation, and leaves behind it a sense of solemnity and doubt. Those who are visited by it know well that it is no ordinary reminiscence, no error of memory, no mere poetical fancy, but an absolute identification of the present with the past." And R. W. Pickford, professor of psychology at the University of Glasgow, writing in the *International Journal of Psycho-Analysis* in 1944, adds: *"Déjà vu* . . . involves a strange feeling of perplexity, a remainder, as it were, left over by the [victim's attempt at] rationalization."

The other theories of *déjà vu* that relate it to an actual memory accept the presence of a strong residual emotion as inherent in the nature of the experience. For in none of them is the memory involved a memory of ordinary quality. It is always a memory too darkly derived for an easy, unruffled acceptance. The darkest explanation is also the oldest of the many that man has contrived. It suggests that *déjà vu* is a memory of a memory—a glimpse of an earlier state of existence. The Greek metaphysician Pythagoras, of the sixth century B.C., who saw himself as the reincarnation of Euphorbus, a thirteenth-century physician and veteran of the Trojan War, was persuaded to do so by a shock of recognition involving Euphorbus's shield, and it is possible that this experience contributed to the belief in the transmigration of souls that lies at the heart of Pythagorean-ism. It is certain that other religious or philosophical systems embrac-ing the concept of metempsychosis° (Egyptian spiritism, Hinduism, Buddhism, Platonism, the cabalistic° interpretation of the Bible, Swedenborgianism,° theosophy°) have found in *déjà vu* an apparently conclusive demonstration of that conviction. So have many indepen-dent thinkers, among them Dante Gabriel Rossetti. In a poem called "Sudden Light," he concludes:

> *I have been here before,*
> *But when or how I cannot tell:*
> *I know the grass beyond the door,*
> *The sweet keen smell,*
> *The sighing sound, the lights around the shore.*
>
> *You have been mine before,—*
> *How long ago I may not know:*
> *But just when at that swallow's soar*
> *Your neck turned so,*
> *Some veil did fall,—I knew it all of yore.*

An interpretation of *déjà vu* that combines the supernatural with an uncanny anticipation of Lysenkoan genetics° is also on record. It was placed there by F. W. H. Myers, a founder of the London Society for Psychical Research, in 1903. "If it were found," he wrote in *Human Personality and Its Survival of Bodily Death*, "that a child that was de-scended from a line of seafaring ancestors, and that had never itself seen or heard of the dark-gleaming sea, manifested a feeling of recog-nition when first beholding it, we might be pretty sure that such a

○ metempsychosis: the belief that souls leave human or animal bodies at death and "travel" to new host humans and animals.
○ cabalistic: the belief that, through special interpretations, the Bible (or some other special text) may give up its secret messages.
○ Swedenborgian: the movement named after the eighteenth-century Swedish mystic Emanuel Swedenborg, who believed in such ideas as direct human contact with a spirit world.
○ theosophy: nineteenth-century movement which argued for direct mystical contact with divinity.
○ Lysenkoan genetics: a discredited Soviet approach to genetics during the Stalin era; promoted changes in heredity by means of changes in environment.

thing as recollection of prenatal events does take place." Or, in plainer words, that memories may be transmitted by heredity.

————————— • —————————

The memories that shape the other theories of *déjà vu,* though hidden and out of ordinary reach, are somewhat less remote. They at least reflect the rememberer's own experience. Three explanations involving such memories are in general circulation. One of these proposes that the memory is a dream memory—as in *The Trouble Makers,* a novel by Celia Fremlin: "For a moment her wits completely left her. Just as in her dream, the shabby fawn raincoat drooped from sloping shoulders." Another sees it as a daydream memory—the memory of a reverie, or, more particularly, the memory of some graphically imagined scene or setting, as in *Where Three Empires Meet,* an account of a journey through the western Himalayas, by E. F. Knight: "It all, in a way, seemed so familiar to me. Surely I had somewhere, long ago, lived amid this curious people and in such a weird land as this—but when and where? . . . [Then] I remembered that when a small boy I had read 'Gulliver's Travels,' and that the voyage to the flying island of Laputa had made a great impression on my imagination. I had conjured up that kingdom to my mind [as] just such a perspectiveless, artificial, unreal-looking land as this; and just such a people as these queer Ladakis had those no more queer people, the Laputans, appeared to my fancy."

The third concept of *déjà vu* sees it as a product of an unconscious memory. This is, of course, a psychoanalytic theory. It was first advanced by the French neuropathologist Joseph Grasset, in a contribution to the *Journal de Psychologie* entitled "La Sensation du 'Déjà Vu,' " in 1904. In the same year, in *The Psychopathology of Everyday Life,* Sigmund Freud, whose discovery of the unconscious had made the theory possible, came independently to a more comprehensive version of the same idea. Grasset traced *déjà vu* to the unconscious existence of a memory. The phenomenon occurs, he suggested, when the subterranean memory is jolted into consciousness by the impact of a new experience that closely resembles it. Freud fully agreed ("In such moments, something is really touched that we have already experienced, only we cannot consciously recall the latter because it never was conscious"), but he went further. It seemed to him that the presence of the memory in the unconscious needed explanation. The reason, he decided, was that it was too frightful for the conscious mind to bear. It had, in consequence, been firmly shackled by the mental-hygiene mechanism that he chose to call repression. He cited from his files an illustrative case: "A woman of thirty-seven years asserted that she most distinctly remembered that at the age of twelve and a half she paid her first visit to some school friends in the country, and as she entered the garden, she immediately had the feeling of having been there before. This feeling was repeated as she went through the living rooms, so that she believed she knew beforehand how big the next room was, what views one could have on looking out of it, etc. But the belief that this feeling of recognition might have its source in a previous visit to the house and garden, perhaps a visit paid in earliest childhood, was absolutely excluded and disproved by statements from her parents. The woman who related this sought no psychologic explanation, but saw in the appearance of this feeling a prophetic reference to the importance which these friends later assumed in her emotional life." A review of the circumstances surrounding the experience enabled Freud to see it differently: "When she decided on visiting her schoolmates, she knew that these girls had an only brother who was then seriously ill. . . . But it happened that her own only brother had had a serious attack of diphtheria some months before, and during his illness she had lived for weeks with relatives far from her parental home. . . . To the initiated, it will not be difficult to conclude from these indications that the expectation of her brother's death had played a great part in the girl's mind at that time, and that either it never became conscious or it was more energetically repressed after the favorable issue of the illness. . . . She found the analogous situation in her friends' home; their only brother was in danger of an early death. . . . She might have consciously remembered that she had lived through a similar situation a few months previous, but instead of recalling what was inhibited through repression, she transferred the memory feeling to the locality, to the garden and the house, and merged it into the *fausse reconnaissance*, ° namely, that she had already seen everything exactly as it was." But why did the memory of her brother's illness require repression? Freud considered the question, and then produced an answer: "From the fact of the repression, we may conclude that the former expectation of the death of her brother

___

° fausse reconnaissance: French, "false recognition."

was not far from evincing the character of a wish-phantasy. She would then have become the only child."

It was Freud's original impression that the unconscious memory projected in *déjà vu* could be only that of an unconscious fantasy. In time, however, he modified this assumption. He allowed himself to be persuaded (largely by the Hungarian neurologist Sandor Ferenczi) that buried memories of dream experiences, and even those of conscious fantasies, might reasonably be added to the list of precipitating factors.

The current psychoanalytic explanation of *déjà vu* differs from Freud's in one important respect. It has a more Freudian structure. Its scheme embodies the strictest possible interpretation of his doctrine of psychic determinism—that nothing in the life of the mind is arbitrary or accidental. Most contemporary psychoanalysts envision *déjà vu* as a doubly purposive phenomenon. It performs, they feel, both a defensive and a therapeutic role. The primary function of *déjà vu*, as psychoanalytically construed, is to prevent the emergence into consciousness of an intolerable memory. To this extent, it is merely a variation of the vigilant distorting mirror—known to Freud as screen, or substitute, memory—that always returns a flattering image of the past. But it also, and uniquely, has a secondary task. That is to simultaneously block a more immediate threat to emotional tranquillity. In addition, the psychoanalytic theory holds, this immediate threat—a more or less conscious anxiety engendered by some impending challenge—is an essential ingredient of *déjà vu*. It sets the phenomenon in motion. There is something about the new anxiety, some associational link or likeness, that recalls the old anxiety. The forbidden memory stirs, and drifts upward toward awareness. At this point, however, the ego intervenes. The defense it employs is an act of legerdemain that creates the *déjà vu* illusion. It searches the external world for a scene that bears a symbolic resemblance to the emerging memory. When one is found (or, if need be, fabricated), the ego artfully endows it with the memory's patina of age. It then thrusts it upon the expectant conscious mind as an innocuous counterfeit. Meanwhile, on another level, the associative link between the repressed memory and the currently threatening anxiety has the effect of blurring the reality of the latter. A new deception now occurs. The new anxiety, too, takes on the feeling of a past experience, and from this a sense of reassurance arises. "[*Déjà vu*] constitutes a defense reaction against future danger or unpleasantness, as well as against the anxiety associated with the memory of an undefined, unsolved experience which is originally responsible for the reaction," C. P. Oberndorf, clinical professor of psychiatry at the Columbia University College of Physicians and Surgeons, noted in a report in the *Psychiatric Quarterly* in 1941. "It serves to reassure the individual that he is not venturing into an entirely new field. . . . He now appreciates that the situation is not too greatly fraught with danger in the immediate future, since he has been in it, heard it, smelled it before, and has survived." A wartime observation by Louis Linn, an attending psychiatrist at Mount Sinai Hospital and a lecturer in community psychiatry at Columbia University, offers a certain clinical confirmation of this secondary function. Linn has reported that American soldiers in Italy frequently experienced *déjà vu* while passing through a strange town or village on the way to battle. Individual talks with the men led to the conclusion that they were unconsciously relating their present situation to some previous experience from which they had emerged unharmed. (The psychoanalytic explanation of *déjà vu* sensations in the aura of epilepsy stresses the reassuring aspect of the phenomenon. It may be, Jacob A. Arlow, a psychiatrist and a faculty member of the New York Psychoanalytic Institute, suggests in "The Structure of the *Déjà Vu* Experience," which appeared in the *Journal of the American Psychoanalytic Association* in 1959, that "such *déjà vu* phenomena represent the psychic response to the awareness of an imminent seizure, namely, the ego's attempt at reassurance in the face of the knowledge that the patient is about to experience a convulsion.") Nevertheless, psychoanalytic theory concedes that the mind's acceptance of these subliminal benefactions is not entirely painless. There is always a certain discomfort. Something of the repressed anxiety invariably breaks through the defensive labyrinth and strikes a glancing blow. It is this ambiguous wound that gives to *déjà vu* its prickly aftermath.

———————— • ————————

I spent four academic years and a late-summer session at the University of Missouri. In the course of my stay, I traveled Highway 40 at least a dozen times a year. My *déjà vu* pasture became a familiar sight. I saw it in all seasons and in every kind of weather, and it quickly lost its strange, unsettling quality. I came, in fact, to recognize it with an almost proprietary pleasure. And I think of it now with nostalgia.

ESSAYS FROM THE DISCIPLINES

PSYCHIATRY

SIGMUND FREUD

"The Interpretation of Dreams" comprises a section of an encyclopedia article entitled "Psychoanalysis," which Freud published in 1922. It has a number of advantages for readers who are new to Freud: It is his own introduction to the subject he pioneered, it is concise, and it defines most of its terms. One disadvantage, which it shares with many encyclopedia articles, is that it tends to be a bit dry and lacking in good examples. Nonetheless, it offers the essentials of Freud's dream theory.

Freud writes here in an expository way, introducing and defining a subject (dream interpretation) and some of its key features (for example, the manifest, or surface, content of a dream versus its latent or hidden meaning). The heart of Freud's approach may be found in his assertion in the fourth paragraph that "the dynamics of the formation of dreams are the same as those of the formation of symptoms." If this identity is accepted, then Freud's whole intellectual journey is justified, since "the same uniform law embraces both the normal and the abnormal"; research into troubled minds will therefore have dividends for "the understanding of the healthy mind."

Freud's theories—as well as Jung's—are often the subject of courses in psychology and even abnormal psychology. But you should be aware of some distinctions among the various disciplines at work here. Although Gibson's essay in this section has been reprinted from the cross-disciplinary journal Leonardo, *his research originates in the mainstream of psychology because he is interested in discovering how the processes of the mind work—especially those processes which are measurable or subject to experiment. In this regard, his discipline differs from psychiatry, which is a branch of medicine whose focus is the diagnosis and treatment of mental illness. Freud and Jung, both psychiatrists, practiced a form of diagnosis and treatment which has come to be called psychoanalysis, the process by which the trained therapist uses dreams, slips of the tongue, and other verbal behaviors to reveal the unconscious mind of a patient. The psychiatrist may be just as much a "scientist" as the psychologist, but the latter attempts a neutral, detached view of mental phenomena, to understand what is "going on"; the psychiatrist may wish to help the subjects alter what is "going on" in their minds.*

The Interpretation of Dreams

A new approach to the depths of mental life was opened when the technique of free association° was applied to dreams, whether one's own or those of patients in analysis. In fact, the greater and better part of what we know of the processes in the unconscious levels of the mind is derived from the interpretation of dreams. Psycho-analysis has restored to dreams the importance which was generally ascribed to them in ancient times, but it treats them differently. It does not rely upon the cleverness of the dream-interpreter but for the most part hands the task over to the dreamer himself by asking him for his associations to the separate elements of the dream. By pursuing these associations further we obtain knowledge of thoughts which coincide entirely with the dream but which can be recognized—up to a certain point—as genuine and completely intelligible portions of waking mental activity. Thus the recollected dream emerges as the *manifest dream-content,* in contrast to the *latent dream-thoughts* discovered by interpretation. The process which has transformed the latter into the former, that is to say into 'the dream', and which is undone by the work of interpretation, may be called *'dream-work'.*

We also describe the latent dream-thoughts, on account of their connection with waking life, as *'residues of the [previous] day'.* By the operation of the dream-work (to which it would be quite incorrect to ascribe any 'creative' character) the latent dream-thoughts are *condensed* in a remarkable way, they are *distorted* by the *displacement*° of psychical intensities, they are arranged with a view to being *represented in visual pictures;* and, besides all this, before the manifest dream is

○ free-association: Freud's method of allowing a person's unconscious ideas to "slip out." By having his patient respond, ideally without *conscious* monitoring, to certain ideas or images, Freud could "overhear" the unconscious speaking "in its own voice."
○ condensed . . . distorted . . . displacement: various terms to describe the tendencies of the dream's latent content to mask or disguise unpleasant experiences. In *condensation,* various experiences are combined into one; in *distortion,* certain experiences are radically changed; and in *displacement,* offensive objects or experiences are replaced by less disturbing images.

arrived at, they are submitted to a process of *secondary elaboration* which seeks to give the new product something in the nature of sense and coherence. But, strictly speaking, this last process does not form a part of dream-work.

The Dynamic Theory of Dream-Formation.— An understanding of the dynamics of dream-formation did not involve any very great difficulties. The motive power for the formation of dreams is not provided by the latent dream-thoughts or day's residues, but by an unconscious impulse, repressed during the day, with which the day's residues have been able to establish contact and which contrives to make a *wish-fulfilment* for itself out of the material of the latent thoughts. Thus every dream is on the one hand the fulfilment of a wish on the part of the unconscious and on the other hand (in so far as it succeeds in guarding the state of sleep against being disturbed) the fulfilment of the normal wish to sleep which set the sleep going. If we disregard the unconscious contribution to the formation of the dream and limit the dream to its latent thoughts, it can represent anything with which waking life has been concerned—a reflection, a warning, an intention, a preparation for the immediate future or, once again, the satisfaction of an unfulfilled wish. The unrecognizability, strangeness and absurdity of the manifest dream are partly the result of the translation of the thoughts into a different, so to say *archaic,* method of expression, but partly the effect of a restrictive, critically disapproving agency in the mind, which does not entirely cease to function during sleep. It is plausible to suppose that the *'dream-censorship',* which we regard as being responsible in the first instance for the distortion of the dream-thoughts into the manifest dream, is a manifestation of the same mental forces which during the day-time had held back or *repressed* the unconscious wishful impulse.

It has been worth while to enter in some detail into the explanation of dreams, since analytical work has shown that the dynamics of the formation of dreams are the same as those of the formation of symptoms. In both cases we find a struggle between two trends, of which one is unconscious and ordinarily repressed and strives towards satisfaction—that is, wish-fulfilment—while the other, belonging probably to the conscious ego, is disapproving and repressive. The outcome of this conflict is a *compromise-formation* (the dream or the symptom) in which both trends have found an incomplete expression. The theoretical importance of this conformity between dreams and symptoms is illuminating. Since dreams are not pathological phenomena, the fact shows that the mental mechanisms which produce the symptoms of illness are equally present in normal mental life, that the same uniform law embraces both the normal and the abnormal and that the findings of research into neurotics or psychotics cannot be without significance for our understanding of the healthy mind.

Symbolism.—In the course of investigating the form of expression brought about by dream-work, the surprising fact emerged that certain objects, arrangements and relations are represented, in a sense indirectly, by 'symbols', which are used by the dreamer without his understanding them and to which as a rule he offers no associations. Their translation has to be provided by the analyst, who can himself only discover it empirically by experimentally fitting it into the context. It was later found that linguistic usage, mythology and folklore afford the most ample analogies to dream-symbols. Symbols, which raise the most interesting and hitherto unsolved problems, seem to be a fragment of extremely ancient inherited mental equipment. The use of a common symbolism extends far beyond the use of a common language.

PSYCHIATRY

C. G. JUNG

In this excerpt from a longer essay, Jung outlines his own theory of dream interpretation as distinct from Freud's. He acknowledges Freud's pioneering efforts in involving the dreamer in interpreting dreams, but disagrees with Freud's emphasis on dreams as mainly a look into the "repressed wishes" of the dreamer. For Jung, as this essay makes clear, entry into dream life provides a privileged look into the world of the "collective unconscious," a psychic pool of mental phenomena which we all share by virtue of being human. Because so many of the dream experiences we have are shared by other cultures, Jung categorized these recurring images as "archetypes" common to all humans.

Jung's approach to dream analysis has always been a model of cross-disciplinary study, for he believed that it was necessary to have a knowledge of mythology, folklore, psychology, and comparative religion in order to understand the archetypes of our dream life. These fields of study

*provided an analyst like Jung with the background to consider dreams to
be "universally human" experiences primarily, and "personal"
experiences secondarily. "The dream," he states (in a section of the essay
not reprinted), "uses collective figures because it has to express an eternal
human problem that repeats itself endlessly, and not just a disturbance of
personal balance."*

*Both Jung's and Freud's essays have become more than
psychoanalytical documents: They have become classic statements for
readers of all disciplines. Jung (again, like Freud) often tried in his essays
to range more freely over his topic than most specialists would dare. He
includes in this essay, therefore, an introduction to dreams as psychic
phenomena as well as a guide toward interpreting dreams. At the same
time, he explains his more "generous"—compared to Freud's—system of
dream interpretation. Finally, he has a mixed audience in mind. The
essay will be heavy going for many of us "lay" (non-psychoanalytical)
readers, but Jung also intended the essay to communicate with professional
psychologists and psychoanalysts who probably leaned toward Freud's
more popular theory of dreams as "repressed wishes."*

*Jung's style is usually clear, but there is more than a touch of
psychoanalytical jargon. You may appreciate his essay better by first
reading quickly through the glosses at the foot of each page. Despite some
difficulties you may encounter, the essay should give you an important
way of appreciating and studying dreams.*

On the Nature of Dreams [1]

Medical psychology differs from all other scientific disciplines
in that it has to deal with the most complex problems without being
able to rely on tested rules of procedure, on a series of verifiable
experiments and logically explicable facts. On the contrary, it is
confronted with a mass of shifting irrational happenings, for the
psyche is perhaps the most baffling and unapproachable phenomenon with which the scientific mind has ever had to deal. Although
we must assume that all psychic phenomena are somehow, in the
broadest sense, causally dependent, it is advisable to remember at
this point that causality is in the last analysis no more than a statisti-

[1]First published as "Vom Wesen der Traume," *Ciba-Zeitschrift* (Basel), IX: 99 (July 1945).

cal truth. Therefore we should perhaps do well in certain cases to make allowance for absolute irrationality even if, on heuristic° grounds, we approach each particular case by inquiring into its causality. Even then, it is advisable to bear in mind at least one of the classical distinctions, namely that between *causa efficiens*° and *causa finalis.*° In psychological matters, the question "Why does it happen?" is not necessarily more productive of results than the other question "To what purpose does it happen?"

Among the many puzzles of medical psychology there is one problem-child, the dream. It would be an interesting, as well as difficult, task to examine the dream exclusively in its medical aspects, that is, with regard to the diagnosis and prognosis of pathological conditions. The dream does in fact concern itself with both health and sickness, and since, by virtue of its source in the unconscious, it draws upon a wealth of subliminal perceptions, it can sometimes produce things that are very well worth knowing. This has often proved helpful to me in cases where the differential diagnosis between organic and psychogenic symptoms presented difficulties. For prognosis, too, certain dreams are important.[2] In this field, however, the necessary preliminary studies, such as careful records of case histories and the like, are still lacking. Doctors with psychological training do not as yet make a practice of recording dreams systematically, so as to preserve material which would have a bearing on a subsequent outbreak of severe illness or a lethal issue—in other words, on events which could not be foreseen at the beginning of the record. The investigation of dreams in general is a life-work in itself, and their detailed study requires the co-operation of many workers. I have therefore preferred, in this short review, to deal with the fundamental aspects of dream psychology and interpretation in such a way that those who have no experience in this field can at least get some idea of the problem and the method of inquiry. Anyone who is familiar with the material will probably agree with me that a

---

[2] Cf. "The Practical Use of Dream-Analysis," pars. 343ff.

○ heuristic: using a pattern or series of questions for discovery or investigation (compare the similar term, "algorithm," in Chapter 2).

○ *causa efficiens:* Latin, "effective cause": how, or by what means, something happens.

○ *causa finalis:* Latin, "final cause": purpose or goal.

knowledge of fundamentals is more important than an accumulation of case histories, which still cannot make up for lack of experience.

The dream is a fragment of involuntary psychic activity, just conscious enough to be reproducible in the waking state. Of all psychic phenomena the dream presents perhaps the largest number of "irrational" factors. It seems to possess a minimum of that logical coherence and that hierarchy of values shown by the other contents of consciousness, and is therefore less transparent and understandable. Dreams that form logically, morally, or aesthetically satisfying wholes are exceptional. Usually a dream is a strange and disconcerting product distinguished by many "bad qualities," such as lack of logic, questionable morality, uncouth form, and apparent absurdity or nonsense. People are therefore only too glad to dismiss it as stupid, meaningless, and worthless.

Every interpretation of a dream is a psychological statement about certain of its contents. This is not without danger, as the dreamer, like most people, usually displays an astonishing sensitiveness to critical remarks, not only if they are wrong, but even more if they are right. Since it is not possible, except under very special conditions, to work out the meaning of a dream without the collaboration of the dreamer, an extraordinary amount of tact is required not to violate his self-respect unnecessarily. For instance, what is one to say when a patient tells a number of indecent dreams and then asks: "Why should *I* have such disgusting dreams?" To this sort of question it is better to give no answer, since an answer is difficult for several reasons, especially for the beginner, and one is very apt under such circumstances to say something clumsy, above all when one thinks one knows what the answer is. So difficult is it to understand a dream that for a long time I have made it a rule, when someone tells me a dream and asks for my opinion, to say first of all to myself: "I have no idea what this dream means." After that I can begin to examine the dream.

It is Freud's great achievement to have put dream-interpretation on the right track. Above all, he recognized that no interpretation can be undertaken without the dreamer. The words composing a dream-narrative have not just *one* meaning, but many meanings. If, for instance, someone dreams of a table, we are still far from knowing what the "table" of the dreamer signifies, although the word "table" sounds unambiguous enough. For the thing we do not know is that this "table" is the very one at which his father sat when he refused the dreamer all further financial help and threw him out of the house as a good-for-nothing. The polished surface of this table stares at him as a symbol of his lamentable worthlessness in his daytime consciousness as well as in his dreams at night. This is what our dreamer understands by "table." Therefore we need the dreamer's help in order to limit the multiple meanings of words to those that are essential and convincing. That the "table" stands as a mortifying landmark in the dreamer's life may be doubted by anyone who was not present. But the dreamer does not doubt it, nor do I. Clearly, dream-interpretation is in the first place an experience which has immediate validity for only two persons.

If, therefore, we establish that the "table" in the dream means just that fatal table, with all that this implies, then, although we have not explained the dream, we have at least interpreted one important motif of it; that is, we have recognized the subjective context in which the word "table" is embedded.

We arrived at this conclusion by a methodical questioning of the dreamer's own associations. The further procedures to which Freud subjects the dream-contents I have had to reject, for they are too much influenced by the preconceived opinion that dreams are the fulfilment of "repressed wishes."° Although there are such dreams, this is far from proving that all dreams are wish-fulfilments, any more than are the thoughts of our conscious psychic life. There is no ground for the assumption that the unconscious processes underlying the dream are more limited and one-sided, in form and content, than conscious processes. One would rather expect that the latter could be limited to known categories, since they usually reflect the regularity or even monotony of the conscious way of life.

On the basis of these conclusions and for the purpose of ascertaining the meaning of the dream, I have developed a procedure which I call "taking up the context." This consists in making sure that every shade of meaning which each salient feature of the dream has for the dreamer is determined by the associations of the dreamer himself. I therefore proceed in the same way as I would in deciphering a difficult text. This method does not always produce an immediately understandable result; often the only thing that emerges, at

___

° repressed wishes: in Freud's system, that which our unconscious might urge us to do, but which we keep within, or "repressed."

first, is a hint that looks significant. To give an example: I was working once with a young man who mentioned in his anamnesis° that he was happily engaged, and to a girl of "good" family. In his dreams she frequently appeared in very unflattering guise. The context showed that the dreamer's unconscious connected the figure of his bride with all kinds of scandalous stories from quite another source —which was incomprehensible to him and naturally also to me. But, from the constant repetition of such combinations, I had to conclude that, despite his conscious resistance, there existed in him an unconscious tendency to show his bride in this ambiguous light. He told me that if such a thing were true it would be a catastrophe. His acute neurosis° had set in a short time after his engagement. Although it was something he could not bear to think about, this suspicion of his bride seemed to me a point of such capital importance that I advised him to instigate some inquiries. These showed the suspicion to be well founded, and the shock of the unpleasant discovery did not kill the patient but, on the contrary, cured him of his neurosis and also of his bride. Thus, although the taking up of the context resulted in an "unthinkable" meaning and hence in an apparently nonsensical interpretation, it proved correct in the light of facts which were subsequently disclosed. This case is of exemplary simplicity, and it is superfluous to point out that only rarely do dreams have so simple a solution.

The examination of the context is, to be sure, a simple, almost mechanical piece of work which has only a preparatory significance. But the subsequent production of a readable text, i.e., the actual interpretation of the dream, is as a rule a very exacting task. It needs psychological empathy, ability to coordinate, intuition, knowledge of the world and of men, and above all a special "canniness" which depends on wide understanding as well as on a certain "intelligence du cœur."° All these presupposed qualifications, including even the last, are valuable for the art of medical diagnosis in general. No sixth sense is needed to understand dreams. But more is required than routine recipes such as are found in vulgar little dream-books, or

○ anamnesis: Greek, "remembrance"; a patient's recollections.
○ neurosis: a psychological and emotional condition marked by anxiety and obsessional behavior.
○ intelligence du coeur: French, literally, "knowledge of the heart," meaning to have sympathy, to be understanding, in terms of emotional life.

which invariably develop under the influence of preconceived notions. Stereotyped interpretation of dream-motifs is to be avoided; the only justifiable interpretations are those reached through a painstaking examination of the context. Even if one has great experience in these matters, one is again and again obliged, before each dream, to admit one's ignorance and, renouncing all preconceived ideas, to prepare for something entirely unexpected.

Even though dreams refer to a definite attitude of consciousness and a definite psychic situation, their roots lie deep in the unfathomably dark recesses of the conscious mind. For want of a more descriptive term we call this unknown background the unconscious. We do not know its nature in and for itself, but we observe certain effects from whose qualities we venture certain conclusions in regard to the nature of the unconscious psyche. Because dreams are the most common and most normal expression of the unconscious psyche, they provide the bulk of the material for its investigation.

PSYCHOLOGY

J. J. GIBSON

Gibson's stated attempt in this essay from the cross-disciplinary journal Leonardo *is to distinguish hallucinations from perceptions. He proposes three criteria for differentiating between the two experiences: A hallucinatory image is not "explorable, or investigable, or susceptible to increased clarity by sense-organ adjustment." Perhaps equally important is Gibson's insistence on defining the activity of visual perception as taking in an "ambient" array of stimuli, because such an "active" theory—one might even call it a "natural" theory—concentrates on how the eye actually behaves rather than on certain laboratory-controlled behavior (for example, that measured by the tachistoscope). Gibson's distinctions, although important in themselves, will also prove helpful in studying the "spectral images" explored in Chapter 5, "Perspectives on Salem." Gibson's ideas are, in part, challenged by Gregory in "Seeing as Thinking" in Chapter 2.*

The readers of Leonardo, *a journal which encourages the cross-fertilization of ideas and images between scientists and artists, would be interested in the precision of Gibson's criteria as well as the information which he provides on how the eye perceives. Although clearly relying on the assumptions of the professional psychologist—he concentrates on categorizing and defending his criteria for distinguishing between hallucinations and perceptions—Gibson writes here clearly and distinctly for the general reader.*

On the Relation between Hallucination and Perception

All discussions of hallucination that I have been able to find assume, first, that it is a false perception and second, that it is nevertheless indistinguishable to the perceiver from a true perception. This indistinguishability is sometimes expressed by saying that a hallucination is accompanied by the same "feeling of reality" as is a perception. To the subject it is seemingly a genuine percept.

This assumption rests on a deeper assumption, going back at least to John Locke, asserting that a memory image differs from a sense impression or sense-percept only in being fainter or less vivid. If the image is taken to be a replica or representation of the original impression, it would have to be the same as the original unless it were somehow "weaker." It follows that if an image can become less faint or more vivid, for any reason, it will become indistinguishable from a sense impression.

The importance of hallucinations for the theory of perception, therefore, is that they seem to confirm this old assumption that in certain circumstances *a person cannot tell the difference between a mental image and a percept.* Someone who is hallucinating *behaves* as if he were perceiving a fact of the environment, not imagining it. At least he is sometimes said to give this report. The other evidence in favor of this old assumption is the Perky experiment (1) showing that a faint optical picture secretly projected from behind on a translucent screen is often not identified as a real picture when the observer is imagining an object on the screen of the same kind. The psychologist Titchener believed, on grounds of this sort, that an image is easily "confused with a sensation" (2, p. 198) and he asserted that "in certain pathological states the image may become what is called an hallucination" (2, p. 199).

This assumption that images, whether of memory, imagination, dreams or those occurring in hallucinations, are made of the same stuff as percepts can and should be challenged. It is contradicted by the theory of perceptual systems I have proposed (3, chap. 3). An implication of this theory is that *a person can always tell the difference between a mental image and a percept when a perceptual system is active over time.* When the information for perception is obtained by the system, as contrasted with information supposedly imposed on the receptors, a percept should *never* be confused with an image, since the activities of orienting, exploring and optimizing will always distinguish the two cases (3, chap. 2).

According to this theory, the essential difference between a memory image and a percept is not that of being *fainter* or *weaker* or *less vivid;* the difference is essentially that the image is not *explorable,* or *investigable* or *susceptible to increased clarity by sense-organ adjustment.* The supposed criterion of faintness or low intensity has always been debatable as in McDougall's article on hallucination (4) and some thinkers have suggested that *liveliness* or being *lifelike* is a better indication of a percept. This suggests to me that the so-called *feeling of reality* that accompanies a percept is actually a result of the *tests for reality* that go along with active perception. Actually, they are tests for the existence of an external source of stimulation.

It is fair to ask at this point how the theory of perceptual systems would explain the occurrence of hallucinations. I would argue, first, that under conditions of disease or drugs an observer may remain passive and thus fail to apply these tests for the existence of an external object, tests that would betray the spontaneous images he is experiencing for what they are. I am saying, in other words, that although an image may not be *distinguished* from a percept, this does not mean it has become *indistinguishable* from a percept. One can suppose, second, that some observers tend to believe in the existence of a world that is different from the environment they usually perceive, that they either want to experience it or are fascinated by the possibility and that hence they are not inclined to apply these tests for the existence of a real object. Seekers of "psychedelic experience" seem to be persons of this sort (5).

The theory of perceptual systems emphasizes the external loops that permit orientation, exploration and adjustment but it also admits the existence of internal loops, more or less contained within the central nervous system. Only in this way could the facts of dreaming be explained. In the waking state, the internal loops are driven or modulated by the external ones but in sleep they may become active spontaneously, the internal component of a perceptual system running free as it were, like a motor without a load. In the case of daydreams and waking fantasies, one can suppose that internal experiencing of a similar sort occurs in parallel with ordinary perceiving; the former being split off from the latter, and the latter being reduced.

There is no doubt but what the brain alone can generate experience of a sort. What it *cannot* do is to generate *perceptual* experience. In a daydream, the brain can seemingly generate imaginings even while the retina-brain-eye-retina system is still registering the surrounding world. But in a night dream the inputs of the optic nerves are missing and ocular adjustments, if they occurred, would have no effect on the inputs of the optic nerves. Note that, on this theory, the rapid eye-movements that accompany night dreams are frustrated efforts of the perceptual system to explore an ambient optic array° that cannot be sampled because the eyes are closed, or an optic array that does not even exist because of darkness. Rapid eye-movements are a good index of having a dream because ocular exploration is an expression of an effort to perceive. The dreamer is *trying to look,* as it were. But since there is no feedback from these eye-movements, since they have no consequences, the dream wanders on uncontrolled.

An observer can orient his head and eyes to some component of an optic array. This is the same as *fixating* the object of interest and, along with this, goes accommodating for it and converging on it. An observer can *explore* or *scan* the optic array. This is to look at its parts in succession by saccadic° eye-movements or to examine a sector of the environment. But an observer *cannot* orient his head and eyes to an afterimage° or a memory image. An observer cannot *accommodate* and *converge* on an image of any sort. He cannot *scan,*

○ ambient or optic array: Gibson's definition of the eye-in-process: It looks around —is "ambient"—as it perceives; see Gibson, *Ecological Approach to Visual Perception,* in "Sources."

○ saccadic: describing the movement of the eye as it jumps from fixed point to fixed point; during the act of reading, for example.

○ afterimage: a faint replica (retained for a very short time) of something seen. (For extended descriptions of this and "eidetic image," below, see Haber in "Sources.")

or *inspect* or *examine* a subjective image in the sense that one can apply the fovea of the eye to any detail of an optic array. (It is sometimes said that a person can fixate on and scan a so-called "eidetic" image° or a hallucination but this is unproved and I have grave doubts about it.)

A tentative rule seems to emerge from the above considerations. Whenever adjustment of the perceptual organs yields a corresponding change of stimulation there exists an external source of stimulation and one is *perceiving.* Whenever adjustment of the perceptual organs yields *no* corresponding change of stimulation there exists *no* external source of stimulation and one is imagining, dreaming or hallucinating. For example, whenever a body-movement, hand-movement, head-movement or eye-movement yields a change in visual stimulation that *can be reversed by a reversal of that movement,* then there is a source of visual stimulation in the environment outside the observer. Otherwise not. As a corollary, it may be added that if nothing one does has any effect on a persisting stimulus, the source is within the body itself. Such is the case with an intense afterimage or a pain caused by tissue-damage. The psychologist should note the difference between this rule and the formula proposed by von Holst (6) and being elaborated by Held and others.

What does the theory of perceptual systems have to say about the kind of perception induced in the psychological laboratory with a *tachistoscope,* that is, with momentary exposure of some display? The purpose of this instrument is to prevent the occurrence of exploratory eye movement and, by limiting the input of the optic nerves to that from a single fixation, supposedly to simplify the problem of perception or to isolate a pure form of perception. In this case, the taking of successive samples is blocked, as are accommodation and convergence, and the completion of what I called an *external loop* of visual activity is cut short. The system is held down to the completion of its internal loops of activity, to that component of perception confined within the central nervous system, that is, the arousal of images. The tachistoscope thus forces perception to be a process of supplementing a momentary input. It becomes a matter of "enrichment" instead of "differentiation" as I once put it (7). This kind of

° eidetic image: a sharply defined image retained for a relatively long period—about 30 seconds or more.

visual perception is very interesting but there is some question as to whether it is not a mere laboratory curiosity, unrepresentative of day-to-day activity.

According to the theory of perceptual systems, the act of perceiving is essentially different from the act of imagining. The perceptual systems are modes of overt attention, not channels of a sense. According to the theory of sensory channels, however, the act of perceiving is a *mixture* of sensing and imagining. If the inputs of the sensory nerves are taken as the point of departure, perceiving has to be essentially similar to having images. Memories have to be combinable with sense impressions and are perhaps confusable with them. There is a genuine theoretical issue between these two positions. Is it empirically true or not that a person can always tell the difference between an image and a percept when his perceptual system is active over time?

There is an interesting analogy between the above question and this question: Can a person always tell the difference between a faithful perspective picture and the scene pictured when the visual system is active over time? Artists have long known that a painting (or transparency) viewed under just the right conditions can "fool the eye," that is, can be almost indistinguishable from the object or scene represented if viewed through a window similar to the frame of the painting. But the use of two eyes instead of one and the moving of the head instead of keeping it stationary will always reveal the existence of the flat surface of the picture. One can fool a stationary eye but not an active visual system.

REFERENCES

1. C. W. Perky, An Experimental Study of Imagination, *Am. J. Psychol.* 21, 422 (1910).
2. E. B. Titchener, *A Textbook of Psychology* (New York: Macmillan, 1924).
3. J. J. Gibson, *The Senses Considered as Perceptual Systems* (Boston: Houghton Mifflin, 1966).
4. W. McDougall, Hallucination. In: *Encyclopedia Britannica*, Vol. 11, 1929.
5. R. E. L. Masters, and J. Houston, *The Varieties of Psychedelic Experience* (New York: Dell, 1966).
6. E. von Holst, Relations between the Central Nervous System and the Perceptual Organs, *Br. J. Anim. Behav.* 2, 89 (1954).

7. J. J. Gibson and E. J. Gibson, Perceptual Learning: Differentiation or Enrichment? *Psychol. Rev.* 62, 32 (1955).

DOCUMENTARY MATERIALS

AUTOBIOGRAPHICAL LETTER

EDWARD HITCHCOCK

Hitchcock wrote this "case" about himself in the form of an "open," or public, letter to a scientific colleague in 1845. Such a self-examination during illness is an extraordinary early document of psychology, especially notable because of its thoroughness. John Greenleaf Whittier (see "Documentary Materials" for Chapter 5) used Hitchcock as a point of reference, as the illusions here resembled "spectral evidence." Hitchcock was professor of geology at Amherst College at the time of the letter, and later became president of the college, thus giving credence to the evidence which comes from an eminent and respectable source.

> *The form of this selection is that of extended personal testimony in letter form, an approach not uncommon in nineteenth-century science. Published with this letter was a scientific reply by N. W. Fiske, also of Amherst, but it is not reprinted below. Fiske offered the standard contemporary interpretation of what Hitchcock "saw": "There is a great tendency in the mind so to combine with its real perceptions the mere conceptions and imaginations which are awakened in immediate connection with them, as to invest the blended whole with an illusive appearance of reality."*

> *Although this is a letter, it was probably intended more for public than personal reading, and it therefore omits the usual bits of friendliness we associate with letters. In order to safeguard his reputation, Hitchcock states in a section of the letter not reprinted that he was "apparently free from any tendency to mental derangement." In addition, a testimonial from his doctor supporting his sanity was forwarded with this account and, throughout Hitchcock's letter, numerous references to other parties recording his accounts of visions are found. In all of these ways, Hitchcock attempts to build a strong case for his accuracy and objectivity.*

Case of Optical Illusion in Sickness

The first peculiarity in the state of my vision that I noticed, was precisely the same as that observed in my former sickness, viz. a disposition to connect almost every irregular object, on which my eye rested, into a delineation of the human countenance. This effect of course ceased as soon as the eyes were shut, and it was increased by the indistinctness of objects. Thus, a phrenological bust,° about as large as life, stood upon a cupboard before me, as much as eight feet from the floor. A white flannel gown having been thrown over the foot bed-post, between me and the cupboard, the whole was converted, in the evening, into a beautiful bust, of colossal height, with the folds of the drapery arranged as gracefully as if done by the chisel of Canova.° The only want of proportion appeared in the too small size of the head.

The most perfect examples of the vision that floated before me, I can hardly doubt should be referred to genuine dreams, in which waking consciousness was more or less entirely gone. And had they been confined to such a state, I should not trouble you with any further descriptions. But they occurred in every state, up to the fullest and most wakeful consciousness, in which there could have been nothing like what we call sleep; indeed, I strove in vain to excite the least tendency to sleep.

In regard to my dreams, those which occurred in the early part of the night were of a much duller and grosser kind than those which closed my slumbers usually about the dawning of the day. The two great elements of these dreams were motion and crowded masses of people, most of whom were also in motion. They seemed apparently to interfere with one another, and yet no actual interference occurred. I seemed to join one of the moving masses, and though the area around me was all crowded with human beings, or blocked up by rocks, trees, and mountains, yet no actual obstruction seemed ever to be in my way; but with a quiet and delightful motion, and with no

○ phrenological bust: in phrenology, a nineteenth-century pseudo-science, one's character could be interpreted by the shape of the head (and, sometimes, literally by the bumps on the head).
○ Canova: eighteenth-century Italian sculptor.

jarring or collision, I seemed to be brought to the spot to which I was destined. Yet I never could see exactly how I moved; nor did I ever get sight of a steamboat, a rail car, a carriage, or, except in one or two instances, of a horse, and scarcely saw any water, and yet, the splendid landscapes frequently presented before me appeared to be situated upon the coast. In no case but once, do I recollect to have parted from terra firma. In this case, a party of us in a barouche° seemed to come in sudden proximity with a barouche of ladies dressed in white, whom I understood to be from Saturn, and my impression is that we met somewhere near the orbit of Jupiter. In making our mutual *salam*° we came near overturning our barouches, and the alarm of seeing the ladies from that distant planet, who were very large, about being tossed into our vehicle, awakened me. I ought to confess that on the afternoon previous to that night, I had been persuaded to do what I had not done for ten or twelve years, viz. to take a cup of weak black tea; and I presume that had I taken only water, as usual, imagination could not have got me farther off than the orbit of the moon.

I have been surprised at the pleasantness of nearly all the images that passed before me, and the absence of almost every thing disgusting. It is true that during the early part of the night they were often rather coarse; such sights for instance as a man often sees as he passes along the outer parts of a city when the tide is out, and dirty timber, old hulks, and often dirty sailors may be seen. Still it did not revolt the feelings merely to pass in my strange vehicle along such places, when in the next moment elegant houses, columns and temples, with rocks, trees and mountains in the distance, appeared. In one instance the physician had administered assafœtida,° in order to put a stop to these flights of fancy, and I went to sleep in the expectation that if my visions occurred, they must be of a disgusting kind. But instead of this, I fancied myself in some oriental land (probably from the known origin of the drug) in a sunny day, on the shores of an indented bay, reposing upon a sofa as in feeble health, while all around there stood in respectful silence, many well dressed in Turk-

○ barouche: four-wheeled carriage with separate seat for driver and facing seats for passengers.
○ *salam:* often spelled "salaam"; a greeting in Islamic countries meaning "peace"; usually accompanied by a bow.
○ assafoetida: now spelled "asafetida"; a bitter, smelly drug/chemical derived from the roots of a Middle Eastern plant.

ish costume, as well as some Franks, and at a little distance I saw the French servant of some man of distinction coming to me with a message, who proved however to be Mrs. H. with a cup of medicine, and all my oriental magnificence vanished.

I had fallen into a slumber more deep than any during the severer part of my sickness. Mrs. H. made slight efforts to awaken me. She also applied a sponge to my parched mouth. The first thing I was conscious of, was a sudden commotion extending through all nature around me, which produced a cry, "the greatest *discovery of the age.*" It seemed as if all nature had been bound together immovably, and the discovery consisted in a fluid which loosed her bands. It was the water applied to my mouth which gave a start to the wheels in my system, which had almost stopped; and this gave the idea of nature being bound together.

——————— • ———————

In order to render the remaining cases more intelligible, I must make some preliminary statements.

At that stage of my complaint, when irregular objects began to assume regular forms upon the retina, I noticed that both by day and by night the images which surrounding objects made upon the eye, remained for a considerable time after closing the eyelid. Presently, I perceived that those images began to change their figures into objects and scenes as unlike the original as possible. This was especially the case when I directed the attention of the mind to the light that seemed directly before me. So long as the mind concentrated its attention upon the objects, the changes went on; and I know not but I might have followed the succession of images for hours, had I dared to do it. From the particular image before me, I could form no idea of that which would succeed. And yet one scene would graduate into another in the easiest and most natural manner.

I soon found that after my eyes were closed, the more entirely the external light was excluded, the more distinct would be the images, and the more rapid the changes of scene. Hence I usually placed my hand or a handkerchief over my eyes. If questions were put to me while examining the images, it seemed to produce some confusion, but simply by withdrawing the attention. Rolling my eye-balls in their sockets did not increase the power of vision at all.

I went about the examination of these objects with as entire freedom from drowsiness, and with as perfect a command of all my powers, as ever I possessed in my life. In a few instances, after closing the eyes for some time, I began to feel slightly drowsy, and this I think rendered the vision more distinct. Withdrawing the attention from the object would usually end the illusion, even though the eyes continued shut; but sometimes, especially at night, it would continue as long as the eyes were closed. An examination of these images produced no more fatigue than it would to look over a collection of pictures in a gallery—probably not as much.

The chief agent in producing the changes of objects before my mind, appeared to be internal motion among the particles. The figures, say of the paper hangings of the wall, or of the landscape abroad, usually at first became smaller and smaller, until the surface appeared granulated, very much like what I have frequently seen upon the screen of the solar microscope, when a menstruum° was in the focus, containing a salt which was just beginning to crystallize. The next step in the process was usually a rising of the particles and rolling round an axis, just as I have seen a whirlwind raise the dust and leaves, and sweep the whole, while thus revolving, along the surface: or sometimes the whole body before me would pass away in a continuous current, and another succeed. After these motions, objects would usually begin to assume more regular forms, and there came before me mountains and valleys, cities and temples, and human beings. They were almost always however in motion, scarcely lingering long enough for me to get a distinct conception of them, especially, as in almost all cases the light seemed more like that of twilight than like that of midday. Frequently, vast rocks and even huge mountains came moving towards me, and I seemed to pass under them. They came apparently within a few inches of my eyes; and had I believed them real, I should have trembled as I saw myself about to be ground to powder. But so perfectly conscious was I of the illusion, that it merely amused me to see them approaching, because I loved to see how, by their curious convolutions, they would pass me unharmed. Sometimes the rolling together of these vast masses of rocks, exactly resembled that which we witness among the clouds when a thunder storm is rising and contrary winds are curling the vapor in every direction.

Though such was the usual mode in which a change of images was effected, yet sometimes the change took place without

° menstruum: liquid or solvent.

any visible intestine motion among the particles, and no less perfectly.

The only thing approaching the apparent motions above described, which I witnessed with my eyes open, was this: In the evening the ceiling of the room sometimes appeared as if numerous threads of white silk were suspended at various points and hung in festoons; appearing indeed exactly as if numerous cobwebs hung in the usual manner from the ceiling, and were strongly illuminated. There was, however, among them no apparent motion.

Finding myself possessed of the extraordinary power above described, I could not resist the temptation to make a few experiments, partly to relieve the tedium of those who were watching at my bed-side. I told them that if they would record my descriptions, I would close my eyes and give myself up to the control of fancy. I did not dare to prolong my excursions much; but such facts as were thus recorded I will now present, as recorded by the individuals who acted as amanuenses. I will only say, that never in my life am I aware of having been more perfectly awake, and of possessing more entire control over the faculties of attention and observation than during these examinations, although all my powers were weakened by disease.

The following notes were made on Tuesday evening by Mrs. Hitchcock, and did not constitute a continuous series of examinations, but are the record of a few striking facts as I mentioned them from time to time. And the same indeed is more or less true of all the cases subsequently described.

Tuesday evening, Feb. 1.—"I see beautiful clouds that appear to be produced by the glimmering of the candle in the room, falling upon my eyelids."

"I am in a room hung round by fine paintings." (Interrupted.)

"I seem to be in a parlor in the city of New York richly furnished."

"I am looking into a cedar swamp during a snow storm. I see also a deep rail road cut in granite; and the whole scene appears to me to be on the Boston and Worcester rail road a little east of Westborough."

"I stand at the east end of a large hall filled with a great variety of articles. The whole reminds me somewhat of a fair in Boston last December, which I attended for a few moments."

Wednesday morning, Feb. 2.—"I stand now in the piazza of a large circular house, with a circular fence before it and brick walks."

"I am upon the sea coast, examining some large masses and walls of granite. The rock resembles that in southeastern Massachusetts. On one of the walls which does not face the ocean, but forms the bank between a small creek and the ocean, I see four colossal carved figures represented as wrestling, two and two."

Afternoon. —"I have been looking out the window towards the college until, upon closing my eyes, a strong impression of objects remains upon the retina. This has slowly changed into a long room, with pillars on one side indistinctly seen; and now it opens on one side and at the end, and appears to be a piazza. Till this moment I had not covered my eyes; but on placing a thick handkerchief over them, objects become much more distinct. I now stand at the east end of the piazza, and before me is a landscape: on my right a hill, apparently pasture ground, partially covered with snow, and its top more or less with trees. Towards the left is a valley partially wooded, and down this valley the strongest light seems to conduct me. I have now come to an enclosure, where I see indistinctly large masses of timber laid up with a good deal of regularity. I now see them more distinctly, and they are two ships upon the stocks. I now withdraw my attention and open my eyes."

HISTORICAL DOCUMENT

CHIEF SEATTLE

This speech is reprinted from W. C. Vanderwerth's collection of Indian speeches, Indian Oratory *(1971). Vanderwerth characterized Chief Seattle, leader of both the Suquamish and Duwamish tribes in what is now the state of Washington, as a convert to Catholicism by missionaries who was quite reponsive to the pressures of the white settlers. After the organization of the Washington Territory in 1853, the new governor made a speech in the town that is now Seattle. A white translator, Dr. Henry Smith, recorded the chief's tragic reply which accepted his tribe's removal to a reservation. Chief Seattle's sense of place as the overlap of past, present, and future was certainly undervalued by the white settlers. Today, in an age of pollution and overcrowding, it has the ring of prophecy; especially poignant is his comment that the "memory" of his tribe will become a "myth among the White Man."*

American Indian oratory, sometimes regardless of tribe, often takes the form of bold prophetic statements. In a historical irony which we are only beginning to understand, the Indians' understanding of their exploitation by the white settlers and their government was incredibly sharp. Despite his conversion to Catholicism, Chief Seattle's speech constantly evokes the presence of an invisible world of Indian spirits who serve, for him at least, as the final court of appeal.

The Indians' Night Promises to Be Dark

Yonder sky that has wept tears of compassion upon my people for centuries untold, and which to us appears changeless and eternal, may change. Today is fair. Tomorrow it may be overcast with clouds. My words are like the stars that never change. Whatever Seattle says the great chief at Washington can rely upon with as much certainty as he can upon the return of the sun or the seasons. The White Chief says that Big Chief at Washington sends us greetings of friendship and goodwill. This is kind of him for we know he has little need of our friendship in return. His people are many. They are like the grass that covers vast prairies. My people are few. They resemble the scattering trees of a storm-swept plain. The great—and I presume—good White Chief sends us word that he wishes to buy our lands but is willing to allow us enough to live comfortably. This indeed appears just, even generous, for the Red Man no longer has rights that he need respect, and the offer may be wise also, as we are no longer in need of an extensive country.

There was a time when our people covered the land as the waves of a wind-ruffled sea cover its shell paved floor, but that time long since passed away with the greatness of tribes that are now but a mournful memory. I will not dwell on, nor mourn over, our untimely decay, nor reproach my paleface brothers with hastening it as we too may have been somewhat to blame.

Youth is impulsive. When our young men grow angry at some real or imaginary wrong, and disfigure their faces with black paint, it denotes that their hearts are black, and that they are often cruel and relentless, and our old men and old women are unable to restrain them. Thus it has ever been. Thus it was when the white man first began to push our forefathers westward. But let us hope that the hostilities between us may never return. We would have everything to lose and nothing to gain. Revenge by young men is considered gain, even at the cost of their own lives, but old men who stay at home in times of war, and mothers who have sons to lose, know better.

Our good father at Washington—for I presume he is now our father as well as yours, since King George has moved his boundaries further north—our great and good father, I say, sends us word that if we do as he desires he will protect us. His brave warriors will be to us a bristling wall of strength, and his wonderful ships of war will fill our harbors so that our ancient enemies far to the northward— the Hydas and Tsimpsians—will cease to frighten our women, children and old men. Then in reality will he be our father and we his children. But can that ever be? Your God is not our God! Your God loves your people and hates mine. He folds his strong protecting arms lovingly about the pale face and leads him by the hand as a father leads his infant son—but He has forsaken His red children—if they really are His. Our God, the Great Spirit, seems also to have forsaken us. Your God makes your people wax strong every day. Soon they will fill all the land. Our people are ebbing away like a rapidly receding tide that will never return. The white man's God cannot love our people or He would protect them. They seem to be orphans who can look nowhere for help. How then can we be brothers? How can your God become our God and renew our prosperity and awaken in us dreams of returning greatness. If we have a common heavenly father He must be partial—for He came to His paleface children. We never saw Him. He gave you laws but had no word for his red children whose teeming multitudes once filled this vast continent as stars fill the firmament. No; we are two distinct races with separate origins and separate destinies. There is little in common between us.

To us the ashes of our ancestors are sacred and their resting place is hallowed ground. You wander far from the graves of your ancestors and seemingly without regret. Your religion was written upon tables of stone by the iron finger of your God so that you could not forget. The Red Man could never comprehend nor remember it. Our religion is the traditions of our ancestors—the dreams of our old men, given them in the solemn hours of night by the Great Spirit; and the visions of our sachems, and is written in the hearts of our people.

Your dead cease to love you and the land of their nativity as soon as they pass the portals of the tomb and wander way beyond the stars. They are soon forgotten and never return. Our dead never forget the beautiful world that gave them being. They still love its verdant valleys, its murmuring rivers, its magnificent mountains, sequestered vales and verdant lined lakes and bays, and ever yearn in tender, fond affection over the lonely hearted living, and often return from the Happy Hunting Ground to visit, guide, console and comfort them.

Day and night cannot dwell together. The Red Man has ever fled the approach of the White Man, as the morning mist flees before the morning sun.

However, your proposition seems fair and I think that my people will accept it and will retire to the reservation you offer them. Then we will dwell in peace, for the words of the Great White Chief seem to be the words of nature speaking to my people out of dense darkness.

It matters little where we pass the remnant of our days. They will not be many. The Indians' night promises to be dark. Not a single star of hope hovers above his horizon. Sad-voiced winds moan in the distance. Grim fate seems to be on the Red Man's trail, and wherever he goes he will hear the approaching footsteps of his fell destroyer and prepare stolidly to meet his doom, as does the wounded doe that hears the approaching footsteps of the hunter.

A few more moons. A few more winters—and not one of the descendants of the mighty hosts that once moved over this broad land or lived in happy homes, protected by the Great Spirit, will remain to mourn over the graves of a people—once more powerful and hopeful than yours. But why should I mourn at the untimely fate of my people? Tribe follows tribe, and nation follows nation, like the waves of the sea. It is the order of nature, and regret is useless. Your time of decay may be distant, but it will surely come, for even the White Man whose God walked and talked with him as friend with friend, cannot be exempt from the common destiny. We may be brothers after all. We will see.

We will ponder your proposition and when we decide we will let you know. But should we accept it, I here and now make this condition that we will not be denied the privilege without molestation of visiting at any time the tombs of our ancestors, friends and children. Every part of this soil is sacred in the estimation of my people. Every hillside, every valley, every plain and grove, has been

hallowed by some sad or happy event in days long vanished. Even
the rocks, which seem to be dumb and dead as they swelter in the
sun along the silent shore, thrill with memories of stirring events
connected with the lives of my people, and the very dust upon which
you now stand responds more lovingly to their footsteps than to
yours, because it is rich with the blood of our ancestors and our bare
feet are conscious of the sympathetic touch. Our departed braves,
fond mothers, glad, happy-hearted maidens, and even our little children who lived here and rejoiced here for a brief season, will love
these somber solitudes and at eventide they greet shadowy returning
spirits. And when the last Red Man shall have perished, and the
memory of my tribe shall have become a myth among the White
Men, these shores will swarm with the invisible dead of my tribe, and
when your children's children think themselves alone in the field, the
store, the shop, upon the highway, or in the silence of the pathless
woods, they will not be alone. In all the earth there is no place
dedicated to solitude. At night when the streets of your cities and
villages are silent and you think them deserted, they will throng with
the returning hosts that once filled them and still love this beautiful
land. The White Man will never be alone.

Let him be just and deal kindly with my people, for the dead
are not powerless. Dead, did I say? There is no death, only a change
of worlds.

ANTHROPOLOGICAL REPORT

KILTON STEWART

Although anthropologists' reports of isolated, even "lost," tribes often
make fascinating reading, Stewart's stories of the Senoi have been
particularly popular, especially among many "hip" 1960s commentators
who agreed with the great Senoi emphasis on the importance of dreams
and supposed extrasensory powers of the mind. In fact, the Senoi may be
said to live almost two lives, their waking lives and their dream lives.
But these do not constitute two worlds. As Stewart points out, the forces
which influence the Senoi easily move between waking and dream states.
Perhaps Stewart saw his research as a confirmation of Jung's emphasis on
archetypes. ("Dream beings," Stewart writes below, "are only facets of

*one's own spiritual and psychical makeup.") In any case, his essay sets
out the "principles of Senoi psychology," a psychology which Stewart
finds on a creative level with the development of "television and nuclear
physics."*

*Stewart's essay combines three aspects of an anthropologist's report
of his research, although the essay is organized somewhat informally: He
gives a brief description of the tribe, sets out their "principles" of
psychology, and offers a "collection of dreams."*

Dream Theory in Malaya

If you should hear that a flying saucer from another planet had
landed on Gulangra, a lonely mountain peak in the Central Mountain
Range of the Malay Peninsula a hundred years ago, you would want
to know how the space ship was constructed and what kind of power
propelled it, but most of all you would want to know about the
people who navigated it and the society from which they came. If
they lived in a world without crime and war and destructive conflict,
and if they were comparatively free from chronic mental and physical ailments, you would want to know about their methods of healing
and education, and whether these methods would work as well with
the inhabitants of the earth. If you heard further that the navigators
of the ship had found a group of 12,000 people living as an isolated
community among the mountains, and had demonstrated that these
preliterate people could utilize their methods of healing and education, and reproduce the society from which the celestial navigators
came, you would probably be more curious about these psychological
and social methods that conquered space inside the individual, than
you would about the mechanics of the ship which conquered outside
space.

As a member of a scientific expedition travelling through the
unexplored equatorial rain forest of the Central Range of the Malay
Peninsula in 1935, I was introduced to an isolated tribe of jungle folk,
who employed methods of psychology and inter-personal relations
so astonishing that they might have come from another planet. These
people, the Senoi, lived in long community houses, skillfully constructed of bamboo, rattan, and thatch, and held away from the
ground on poles. They maintained themselves by practising dry-

land, shifting agriculture, and by hunting and fishing. Their language, partly Indonesian and partly Non-Kamian, relates them to the peoples of Indonesia to the south and west, and to the Highlanders of Indo-China and Burma, as do their physical characteristics.

Study of their political and social organization indicates that the political authority in their communities was originally in the hands of the oldest members of patrilineal° clans, somewhat as in the social structure of China and other parts of the world. But the major authority in all their communities is now held by their primitive psychologists whom they call *halaks.* The only honorary title in the society is that of *Tohat,* which is equivalent to a doctor who is both a healer and an educator, in our terms.

The Senoi claim there has not been a violent crime or an inter-communal conflict for a space of two or three hundred years because of the insight and inventiveness of the *Tohats* of their various communities. The foothill tribes which surround the Central Mountain Range have such a firm belief in the magical powers of this Highland group that they give the territory a wide berth. From all we could learn, their psychological knowledge of strangers in their territory, the Senoi said they could very easily devise means of scaring them off. They did not practise black magic, but allowed the nomadic hill-folk surrounding them to think that they did if strangers invaded their territory.

This fear of Senoi magic accounts for the fact that they have not, over a long period, had to fight with outsiders. But the absence of violent crime, armed conflict, and mental and physical diseases in their own society can only be explained on the basis of institutions which produce a high state of psychological integration and emotional maturity, along with social skills and attitudes which promote creative, rather than destructive, inter-personal relations. They are, perhaps, the most democratic group reported in anthropological literature. In the realms of family, economics, and politics, their society operates smoothly on the principle of contract, agreement, and democratic consensus, with no need of police force, jail, psychiatric hospital to reinforce the agreements or to confine those who are not willing or able to reach consensus.

Study of their society seems to indicate that they have arrived at this high state of social and physical cooperation and integration

○ patrilineal: descent and kinship in a family traced through the father.

through the system of psychology which they discovered, invented, and developed, and that the principles of this system of psychology are understandable in terms of Western scientific thinking.

It was the late H. D. Noone, the Government Ethnologist of the Federated Malay States, who introduced me to this astonishing group. He agreed with me that they have built a system of interpersonal relations which, in the field of psychology, is perhaps on a level with our attainments in such areas as television and nuclear physics. From a year's experience with these people working as a research psychologist, and another year with Noone in England integrating his seven years of anthropological research with my own findings, I am able to make the following formulations of the principles of Senoi psychology.

Being a pre-literate group, the principles of their psychology are simple and easy to learn, understand, and even employ. Fifteen years of experimentation with these Senoi principles have convinced me that all men, regardless of their actual cultural development, might profit by studying them.

Senoi psychology falls into two categories. The first deals with dream interpretation; the second with dream expression in the agreement trance or cooperative reverie. The cooperative reverie is not participated in until adolescence and serves to initiate the child into the states of adulthood. After adolescence, if he spends a great deal of time in the trance state, a Senoi is considered a specialist in healing or in the use of extra-sensory powers.

Dream interpretation, however, is a feature of child education and is the common knowledge of all Senoi adults. The average Senoi layman practises the psychotherapy of dream interpretation of his family and associates as a regular feature of education and daily social intercourse. Breakfast in the Senoi house is like a dream clinic, with the father and older brothers listening to and analyzing the dreams of all the children. At the end of the family clinic the male population gathers in the council, at which the dreams of the older children and all the men in the community are reported, discussed, and analyzed.

While the Senoi do not of course employ our system of terminology, their psychology of dream interpretation might be summed up as follows: man creates features or images of the outside world in his own mind as part of the adaptive process. Some of these features are in conflict with him and with each other. Once internalized, these hostile images turn man against himself and against his fellows. In dreams man has the power to see these facts of his psyche, which have been disguised in external forms, associated with his own fearful emotions, and turned against him and the internal images of other people. If the individual does not receive social aid through education and therapy, these hostile images, built up by man's normal receptiveness to the outside world, get tied together and associated with one another in a way which makes him physically, socially, and psychologically abnormal.

Unaided, these dream beings, which man creates to reproduce inside himself the external socio-physical environment, tend to remain against him the way the environment was against him, or to become disassociated from his major personality and tied up in wasteful psychic, organic, and muscular tensions. With the help of dream interpretations, these psychological replicas of the socio-physical environment can be redirected and reorganized and again become useful to the major personality.

The Senoi believes that any human being, with the aid of his fellows, can outface, master, and actually utilize all beings and forces in the dream universe. His experience leads him to believe that, if you cooperate with your fellows or oppose them with good will in the day time, their images will help you in your dreams, and that every person should be the supreme ruler and master of his own dream or spiritual universe, and can demand and receive the help and cooperation of all the forces there.

In order to evaluate these principles of dream interpretation and social action, I made a collection of the dreams of younger and older Senoi children, adolescents, and adults, and compared them with similar collections made in other societies where they had different social attitudes towards the dream and different methods of dream interpretation. I found through this larger study that the dream process evolved differently in the various societies, and that the evolution of the dream process seemed to be related to the adaptability and individual creative output of the various societies. It may be of interest to the reader to examine in detail the methods of Senoi dream interpretation:

The simplest anxiety or terror dream I found among the Senoi was the falling dream. When the Senoi child reports a falling dream, the adult answers with enthusiasm, "That is a wonderful dream, one of the best dreams a man can have. Where did you fall to, and what did you discover?" He makes the same comment when the child reports a climbing, travelling, flying, or soaring dream. The child at first answers, as he would in our society, that it did not seem so wonderful, and that he was so frightened that he awoke before he had fallen anywhere.

"That was a mistake," answers the adult-authority. "Everything you do in a dream has a purpose, beyond your understanding while you are asleep. You must relax and enjoy yourself when you fall in a dream. Falling is the quickest way to get in contact with the powers of the spirit world, the powers laid open to you through your dreams. Soon, when you have a falling dream, you will remember what I am saying, and as you do, you will feel that you are travelling to the source of the power which has caused you to fall.

"The falling spirits love you. They are attracting you to their land, and you have but to relax and remain asleep in order to come to grips with them. When you meet them, you may be frightened of their terrific power, but go on. When you think you are dying in a dream, you are only receiving the powers of the other world, your own spiritual power which has been turned against you, and which now wishes to become one with you if you will accept it."

The astonishing thing is that over a period of time, with this type of social interaction, praise, or criticism, imperatives, and advice, the dream which starts out with fear of falling changes into the joy of flying. This happens to everyone in the Senoi society. That which was an indwelling fear or anxiety, becomes an indwelling joy or act of will; that which was ill esteem toward the forces which caused the child to fall in his dream, becomes good will towards the denizens of the dream world, because he relaxes in his dream and finds pleasurable adventures, rather than waking up with a clammy skin and a crawling scalp.

The Senoi believe and teach that the dreamer—the "I" of the dream—should always advance and attack in the teeth of danger, calling on the dream images of his fellows if necessary, but fighting by himself until they arrive. In bad dreams the Senoi believe real friends will never attack the dreamer or refuse help. If any dream character who looks like a friend is hostile or uncooperative in a dream, he is only wearing the mask of a friend.

If the dreamer attacks and kills the hostile dream character, the spirit or essence of this dream character will always emerge as a servant or ally. Dream characters are bad only as long as one is afraid and retreating from them, and will continue to seem bad and fearful as long as one refuses to come to grips with them.

According to the Senoi, pleasurable dreams, such as of flying or sexual love, should be continued until they arrive at a resolution which, on awakening, leaves one with something of beauty or use to the group. For example, one should arrive somewhere when he flies, meet the beings there, hear their music, see their designs, their dances, and learn their useful knowledge.

Dreams of sexual love should always move through orgasm, and the dreamer should then demand from his dream lover the poem, the song, the dance, the useful knowledge which will express the beauty of his spiritual lover to a group. If this is done, no dream man or woman can take the love which belongs to human beings. If the dream character demanding love looks like a brother or sister, with whom love would be abnormal or incestuous in reality, one need have no fear of expressing love in the dream, since these dream beings are not, in fact, brother or sister, but have only chosen these taboo images as a disguise. Such dream beings are only facets of one's own spiritual or psychic makeup, disguised as brother or sister, and useless until they are reclaimed or possessed through the free expression of love in the dream universe.

If the dreamer demands and receives from his love partners a contribution which he can express to the group on awakening, he cannot express or receive too much love in dreams. A rich love life in dreams indicates the favor of the beings of the spiritual or emotional universe. If the dreamer injures the dream images of his fellows or refuses to cooperate with them in dreams, he should go out of his way to express friendship and cooperation on awakening, since hostile dream characters can only use the image of people for whom his good will is running low. If the image of a friend hurts him in a dream, the friend should be advised of the fact, so he can repair his damaged or negative dream image by friendly social intercourse.

Let us examine some of the elements of the social and psychological processes involved in this type of dream interpretation:

First, the child receives social recognition and esteem for discovering and relating what might be called an anxiety-motivated psychic reaction. This is the first step among the Senoi toward convincing the child that he is acceptable to authority even when he reveals how he is inside.

Second, it describes the working of his mind as rational, even when he is asleep. To the Senoi it is just as reasonable for the child to adjust his inner tension states for himself as it is for a Western child to do his homework for the teacher.

Third, the interpretation characterizes the force which the child feels in the dream as a power which he can control through a process of relaxation and mental set, a force which is his as soon as he can reclaim it and learn to direct it.

Fourth, the Senoi education indicates that anxiety is not only important in itself, but that it blocks the free play of imaginative thinking and creative activity to which dreams could otherwise give rise.

Fifth, it establishes the principle that the child should make decisions and arrive at resolutions in his night-time thinking as well as in that of the day, and should assume a responsible attitude toward all his psychic reactions and forces.

Sixth, it acquaints the child with the fact that he can better control his psychic reactions by expressing them and taking thought upon them, than by concealing and repressing them.

Seventh, it initiates the Senoi child into a way of thinking which will be strengthened and developed throughout the rest of his life, and which assumes that a human being who retains good will for his fellows and communicates his psychic reactions to them for approval and criticism, is the supreme ruler of all the individual forces of the spirit—subjective—world whatsoever.

———————— • ————————

Man discovers his deepest self and reveals his greatest creative power at times when his psychic processes are most free from immediate involvement with the environment and most under the control of his indwelling balancing or homeostatic power. The freest type of psychic play occurs in sleep, and the social acceptance of the dream would, therefore, constitute the deepest possible acceptance of the individual.

Among the Senoi one accumulates good will for people because they encourage on every hand the free exercise and expression of that which is most basically himself, either directly or indirectly, through the acceptance of the dream process. At the same time, the child is told that he must refuse to settle with the denizens of the dream world unless they make some contribution which is socially mean-ingful and constructive as determined by social consensus on awakening. Thus his dream reorganization is guided in a way which makes his adult aggressive action socially constructive.

Among the Senoi where the authority tells the child that every dream force and character is real and important, and in essence permanent, that it can and must be outfaced, subdued, and forced to make a socially meaningful contribution, the wisdom of the body operating in sleep, seems in fact to reorganize the accumulating experience of the child in such a way that the natural tendency of the higher nervous system to perpetuate unpleasant experiences is first neutralized and then reversed.

We could call this simple type of interpretation dream analysis. It says to the child that there is a manifest content of the dream, the root he stubbed his toe on, or the fire that burned him, or the composite individual that disciplined him. But there is also a latent content of the dream, a force which is potentially useful, but which will plague him until he outfaces the manifest content in a future dream, and either persuades or forces it to make a contribution which will be judged useful or beautiful by the group, after he awakes.

We could call this type of interpretation *suggestion.* The tendency to perpetuate in sleep the negative image of a personified evil, is neutralized in the dream by a similar tendency to perpetuate the positive image of a sympathetic social authority. Thus accumulating social experience supports the organizing wisdom of the body in the dream, making the dreamer first unafraid of the negative image and its accompanying painful tension states, and later enabling him to break up that tension state and transmute the accumulated energy from anxiety into a poem, a song, a dance, a new type of trap, or some other creative product, to which an individual or the whole group will react with approval (or criticize) the following day.

The following further example from the Senoi will show how this process operates:

A child dreams that he is attacked by a friend and, on awakening, is advised by his father to inform his friend of this fact. The friend's father tells his child that it is possible that he has offended the dreamer without wishing to do so, and allowed a malignant character to use his image as a disguise in the dream. Therefore, he should give a present to the dreamer and go out of his way to be friendly toward him, to prevent such an occurrence in the future.

The aggression building up around the image of the friend in the dreamer's mind thereby becomes the basis of a friendly exchange.

The dreamer is also told to fight back in the future dreams, and to conquer any dream character using the friend's image as a disguise.

Another example of what is probably a less direct tension state in the dreamer toward another person is dealt with in an equally skillful manner. The dreamer reports seeing a tiger attack another boy of the long house. Again, he is advised to tell the boy about the dream, to describe the place where the attack occurred and, if possible, to show it to him so that he can be on his guard, and in future dreams kill the tiger before it has a chance to attack him. The parents of the boy in the dream again tell the child to give the dreamer a present, and to consider him a special friend.

Even a tendency toward unproductive fantasy is effectively dealt with in the Senoi dream education. If the child reports floating dreams, or a dream of finding food, he is told that he must float somewhere in his next dream and find something of value to his fellows, or that he must share the food he is eating; and if he has a dream of attacking someone he must apologize to them, share a delicacy with them, or make them some sort of toy. Thus, before aggression, selfishness, and jealousy can influence social behavior, the tensions expressed in the permissive dream state become the hub of social action in which they are discharged without being destructive.

My data on the dream life of the various Senoi age groups would indicate that dreaming can and does become the deepest type of creative thought. Observing the lives of the Senoi it occurred to me that modern civilization may be sick because people have sloughed off, or failed to develop, half their power to think. Perhaps the most important half. Certainly, the Senoi suffer little by intellectual comparison with ourselves. They have equal power for logical thinking while awake, considering their environmental data, whereas our capacity to solve problems in dreams is inferior compared to theirs.

In the adult Senoi a dream may start with a waking problem which has failed solution, with an accident, or a social debacle. A young man brings in some wild gourd seeds and shares them with his group. They have a purgative effect and give everyone diarrhea. The young man feels guilty and ashamed and suspects that they are poisonous. That night he has a dream, and the spirit of the gourd seeds appears, makes him vomit up the seeds, and explains that they have value only as a medicine, when a person is ill. Then the gourd spirit gives him a song and teaches him a dance which he can show his group on awakening, thereby gaining recognition and winning back his self-esteem.

Or, a falling tree which wounds a man appears in his dreams to take away the pain, and explains that it wishes to make friends with him. Then the tree spirit gives him a new and unknown rhythm which he can play on his drums. Or, the jilted lover is visited in his dreams by the woman who rejected him, who explains that she is sick when she is awake and not good enough for him. As a token of her true feeling, she gives him a poem.

The Senoi does not exhaust the power to think while asleep with these simple social and environmental situations. The bearers who carried out our equipment under very trying conditions became dissatisfied and were ready to desert. Their leader, a Senoi shaman, had a dream in which he was visited by the spirit of the empty boxes. The song and music this dream character gave him so inspired the bearers, and the dance he directed so relaxed and rested them, that they claimed the boxes had lost their weight and finished the expedition in the best of spirits.

Even this solution of a difficult social situation, involving people who were not all members of the dreamer's group, is trivial compared with the dream solutions which occur now that the Senoi territory has been opened up to alien culture contacts.

Datu Bintung at Jelong had a dream which succeeded in breaking down the major social barriers in clothing and food habits between his group and the surrounding Chinese and Mohammedan colonies. This was accomplished chiefly through a dance which his dream prescribed. Only those who did his dance were required to change their food habits and wear the new clothing, but the dance was so good that nearly all the Senoi along the border chose to do it. In this way, the dream created social change in a democratic manner.

Another feature of Datu Bintung's dream involved the ceremonial status of women, making them more nearly the equals of men, although equality is not a feature of either Chinese or Mohammedan societies. So far as could be determined this was a pure creative action which introduced greater equality in the culture, just as reflective thought has produced more equality in our society.

In the West the thinking we do while asleep usually remains on a muddled, childish, or psychotic level because we do not respond to dreams as socially important and include dreaming in the educative process. This social neglect of the side of man's reflective thinking, when the creative process is most free, seems poor education.

STUDENT ESSAY

Assignment 2. Write an essay, selecting one or more dreams for analysis, and try to discover any meaning or pattern in your dreaming.

MICHELLE CARR

But Is It Only a Nightmare?

"All aboard," yelled the aged captain. Deb, my best friend, and I walked aboard the U.S. Liberty. We were on our way to the Bahama Islands for our summer vacation. We were bubbling over with excitement, and we couldn't wait to sunbathe on the tropic beaches in the hot sun. The liner was rather crowded, and the noisy voices of anxious passengers blended with the sound of the waves hitting the side of the metal ship. After traveling for a couple of hours, we finally reached the Atlantic Ocean. The ocean's waters were very calm, and the sky was clear with no chance of a storm showing. Suddenly, a turbulent wind caused a wave to rise out of the water and engulf our ship. We were knocked out because of the tremendous force of the wind, but when we woke up, the ship was on the shore of a strange island. However, Deb and I were the only ones left on the ship, and the ocean was calm again. We were filled with fear along with a sense of adventure. This was the first of a series of mental scenes. The nightmare was a mixture of unreal and real events along with many strong emotions which all combined to create this fantasy.

My dream continued. Deb and I had landed in a new world. How did we get there? Where were the others? These were the questions crossing our minds. The island itself was very fascinating; all its vegetation and soil were a dark blue. The lavender mountain in the background was the only thing that contrasted in color and size to the rest of the island. There were no trees, just overgrown cactus plants of fifteen feet or more in height, covered with thorns. A few bushes also covered with thorns were scattered around. The only sign of animal life was the orange birds flying over the island. They looked like normal penguins, except they flew and were orange. In this portion of the dream the island looked real except for the coloring of its contents. Blue, lavender, and orange are my favorite colors, and penguins are my favorite type of bird. It is possible that these things were mixed in my dream. The planning of my vacation and my reading of *The Bermuda Triangle* might have also mixed to form this fascinating part of the dream.

The third part of my dream occurred when Deb and I were observing the island, and we were absorbed in its scenery. Because of our concentration, we didn't notice the natives who sneaked behind us. Hearing the shuffling of feet, we quickly turned around and saw five green natives of human form dressed in straw skirts. Shocked by their appearance, Deb almost fainted, and I had to hold her up until she regained her balance. We stood there; no muscles in our body would let us move. Surprisingly, one of the natives asked in English why we were here. Stuttering while I talked, I told him about the wreck. He nodded and asked us to feast with them. I was surprised by their hospitality, but I had an uneasy feeling inside. The feast was a roasted orange penguin and some fruits. After we had eaten, we asked how to get off the island. The natives stared at us, and a shiver ran up my spine. I knew there was trouble. The same native who spoke before told us we'd have to play a game if we wanted to leave the island. We had no choice; we had to say yes. The game was that they'd give us an hour head start, and then they'd hunt us with spears. If we could get to the purple mountain before they caught us, we could leave. If they caught us, they'd spear us. This portion of the dream was rather unbelievable, but the realness of the scene made it seem as if it was happening. Before I went to bed, I had watched a Tarzan movie. It is possible that the natives and their hunting game resulted from watching it.

My dream continued. We were running through the bushes. The thorns were scratching and cutting our skin as we ran. Sweat and blood mixed as they ran down our foreheads. Our hearts were pounding inside us with a rapid rate. The sun's rays beat down, and no shade could be found. The jungle never stopped. It seemed the more we ran, the farther we got from the mountain. Our legs were weakening, but we had to go on. Later, when I woke up, I was really sweating, and my legs ached. This made the dream seem even more realistic.

Finally Deb and I were standing over a cliff, and the natives were behind us. There was no escape. Should we jump? Terror and confusion set in. But the dream ended; I woke up. This was the last of the series of this nightmare. The combination of all the events happening in my real life and ideas already in my brain seemed somehow to form an almost realistic dream. This nightmare caused me to think twice about my summer vacation. But what could have made the dream so real? Could the dream have been a warning about my summer vacation? As a result, I decided not to go. The nightmare had that realistic effect which made me change my mind. I wondered if it was just a nightmare.

QUESTIONS FOR DISCUSSION

WITHIN THIS CHAPTER:

1. Why is the Crick–Mitchison approach to dreams so different from virtually *all* other dream theories? Is it a convincing approach?

2. Why is computer theory essential to the Crick–Mitchison approach?

3. Of the different explanations Rouiché offers to explain *déjà vu*, which one do you find the most convincing? Why?

4. Why does Gregory, in Chapter 2, criticize the Gibsons' approach to perception? How does Gregory's approach differ from theirs? Why does he end up talking about artificial (machine) intelligence?

5. What are the major differences between the Freudian and the Jungian approaches to dream interpretation?

6. Why is Kilton Stewart's explanation of the Senoi dreamers closer to Jung's ideas than to Freud's approach to dream interpretation?

7. In what ways is Chief Seattle's vision similar to a dream? Different?

USING OTHER CHAPTERS:

8. Compare Hitchcock's "optical illusions" with the "spectral images" described in several of the essays in Chapter 5, "Perspectives on Salem."

9. Apply the three key "tests" outlined by Gibson in the fifth paragraph of his essay for a discussion of the difference between hallucination and perception and Hitchcock's "optical illusions" in this chapter, or the "spectral images" found in Chapter 5.

10. After reading a number of the selections about Jim Jones and Jonestown in Chapter 6, would you say that Jones had a "vision"?

ASSIGNMENTS

WITHIN THIS CHAPTER:

1. Compare and contrast any two of the four different approaches to dream interpretation found in this chapter—Freud's, Jung's, Stewart's, and Crick–Mitchison's.

2. Record at least three of your dreams. (Keep a paper and pencil next to your bed for quick notetaking when you wake up. If you *think* you don't dream, set your alarm for the middle of the night and reach for your pencil!) Selecting one or more of these dreams for analysis, write an essay in which you try to discover any meanings or patterns in your dreaming. (It may be helpful to refer to one of the "Sources.")

3. Analyze any of your dreams in the context of Jung's or Freud's essays, or—although Jung called them "vulgar"—in the context of any popular "dream interpretation" book.

4. Interview five or six people, asking them to tell you their most vivid, terrifying, or memorable dreams and why they think the dreams were significant. Using either Jung's, Freud's, or Stewart's approaches, analyze the importance of these dreams to your interviewees.

BEYOND THIS CHAPTER:

5. Using Gibson's criteria for distinguishing hallucinations from perceptions, analyze Hitchcock's "Case of Optical Illusion in Sickness," and any of the pieces in Chapter 5 which describe "spectral evidence."

6. In an essay, offer your own interpretation of visual perception based on what might be called a synthesis or compromise between the interpretations of Gregory (Chapter 2) and Gibson (this chapter).

7. Using Melnechuk and one or more authorities from this chapter's "Sources" (such as McCarley and Hobson; Cartwright, et al.; Evans), report on the latest controversies in dream research.

8. Compare and contrast the special use of dream knowledge in Stewart with that in Ursula K. Le Guin's novel *The Word for World Is Forest* (see "Sources").

9. There are many famous dreams and dreamlike passages in literature: Coleridge's poem "Kubla Khan"; Lewis Carroll's Alice books; Kafka's short stories and novels; Thurber's short story "The Secret Life of Walter Mitty"; as well as many others which your instructor should be able to suggest. Read one such work and explain the importance of the dream to the selection.

SOURCES FOR FURTHER READING AND/OR RESEARCH

CARTWRIGHT, ROSALIND D. *Nightlife: Explorations in Dreaming.* Englewood Cliffs, N.J.: Prentice–Hall, 1977. A good overview of all aspects of dream life.
———, et al. "Broken Dreams: A Study of the Effects of Divorce and Depression on Dream Content." *Psychiatry,* 47 (August 1984), pp. 251–259. Presents an approach to dream research which attempts to directly link "dream characteristics" and "major life changes."

CRICK, FRANCIS, AND GRAEME MITCHISON. "The Function of Dream Sleep." *Nature,* 304 (14 July 1983), pp. 111–114. The authors "propose . . . a new explanation for the function of REM sleep"; discussed in Melnechuk's essay in "Discursive Essays."

DOOB, LEONARD W. "Eidetic Imagery: A Cross-Cultural Will-O'-The-Wisp?" *Journal of Psychology,* 63 (1966), pp. 13–34. Despite the author's wistful title, he offers his intriguing cross-cultural research (in America and Africa) which substantiates his conclusion that eidetic imagery "transcends" culture and is "spontaneously reported in similar terms everywhere."

EVANS, CHRISTOPHER. *Landscapes of the Night: How and Why We Dream.* New York: Viking, 1983. Another good overview of dream research; especially important for its author's presentation of the computer model to dreaming which suggests that our mind, while asleep, sifts through our mental experience to update its "programs."

FARADAY, ANN, AND JOHN WREN–LEWIS. "A Report from the Senoi." *Dreamworks,* 3 (1983–1984), pp. 278–280. A brief but intriguing challenge to Stewart's views on the Senoi. The authors found the Senoi to be dreamers, but not manipulators of dreams.

FREUD, SIGMUND. *The Interpretation of Dreams.* Various editions available. Not the same essay as the one in this chapter, but a longer, complete outline of Freud's theory of dreams.

GIBSON, J. J. "What Is a Form?" *Psychological Review,* 58 (Nov. 1951), pp. 403–412. Although this essay appeared in a journal of psychology, it nonetheless offers excellent distinctions for the study of mathematics and art as well.

————. *The Ecological Approach to Visual Perception.* Boston: Houghton Mifflin, 1979. Important concepts of perception offered in the context of the author's "ecological approach" of the "moving eye." He distinguishes among three kinds of vision: ambient (looking around), ambulatory (walking and encountering the world), and aperture ("snapshots" with the static eye acting as a camera).

GIBSON, J. J., AND ELEANOR GIBSON. "The Senses as Information-Seeking Systems." *Times Literary Supplement,* June 23, 1972, p. 711. A reply to Gregory's essay in "Essays from the Disciplines." The Gibsons find that Gregory places too much emphasis on the mind's use of "previous knowledge" to interpret visual sensations. (See also, in the same issue of the *Times Literary Supplement,* "Commentary," p. 718, which compares the two positions.)

GREGORY, RICHARD L. *The Intelligent Eye.* New York: McGraw-Hill, 1971. An excellent history of, and guide to, visual perception, the book comes equipped with 3-D stereo illustrations, and glasses to use with the author's diagrams and mini-experiments.

HABER, RALPH NORMAN. "Eidetic Images." *Scientific American,* 220 (April 1969), pp. 36–44. Using drawings, explains the results of experiments with children which support the existence of eidetic imagery.

JUNG, C. G. "Psychological Aspects of the Mother Archetype." Available in various editions of Jung's work as well as in the definitive *Collected Works* (published by Princeton University Press). A very good introduction to Jung's system, both generally ("On the Concept of the Archetype" is especially helpful) and specifically concerning the mother archetype.

LE GUIN, URSULA K. *The Word for World Is Forest.* New York: Berkley Books, 1976. Although the author has stated that she did not know of Stewart's account of the Senoi, this anthropological science-fiction novel portrays a remarkable people of another world whose dream and waking lives constitute one continuous web.

McCARLEY, ROBERT W., AND J. ALLAN HOBSON. "The Neurobiological Origins of Psychoanalytical Dream Theory," *American Journal of Psychiatry,* 134 (November 1977), pp. 1211–1221.

————. "The Brain as a Dream State Generator: An Activation-Synthesis Hypothesis of the Dream Process," *American Journal of Psychiatry,* 134 (December 1977), pp. 1335–1348. A pair of related articles by the leading revisionists of Freud's dream-theory. Somewhat technical but important articles, the second one offers a model of the brain which suggests that "dreaming sleep is physiologically determined," while the first critiques Freud's inaccurate "neurobiological assumptions."

NOONE, RICHARD, AND DENNIS HOLMAN.   *In Search of the Dream People.* New York: William Morrow, 1972. A fascinating, if somewhat sensational, account of H. D. Noone, brother of one of the authors, who "discovered" the Senoi of Malaya. Stewart's essay in "Documentary Materials" is a distillation of his experiences under H. D. Noone's tutelege.

STEWART, KILTON.   "The Dream Comes of Age." *Mental Hygiene,* 46 (1962), pp. 230–237. Cross-cultural comparisons of dreaming among such diverse peoples as the Senoi of Malaya, the Yami of Botel Tobago, and the Negritos of Luzon, with Stewart's brief conclusion suggesting practical applications of dream education.

————.   *Pygmies and Dream Giants.* New York: Norton, 1954; reprint, New York: Harper and Row, 1975. An autobiographical account of the author's experiences and research among tribes in Luzon in the Philippines; Many passages on the importance of studying "primitive" dreaming.

TART, CHARLES T., ED.   *Altered States of Consciousness.* New York: Wiley, 1969. In addition to Stewart's essay on the Senoi, Tart reprints numerous essays on such "altered states" as hypnosis, meditation, and psychedelic experimentation; excellent bibliography.

EXPLORATIONS

1. Spend the night with a friend, designating one of you as the sleeper and the other as the observer. Every two hours the observer should wake the subject and interview him or her in depth about his or her dreams. On another night, switch roles.

2. Many campuses have psychology labs or clinics which conduct perceptual tests, and even sleep/dream experiments. Apply for permission to visit such a facility or, if you are feeling daring or broke, apply to be a subject.

3. If, unfortunately, you are taken ill with flu or a similar disease while your classmates are studying this chapter, turn misfortune into advantage by monitoring your own delirium, hallucinations, or fevered dreams.

CHAPTER FOUR

Investigating Murder

"A good murder sells newspapers." To this old saying, we would probably add nowadays: ". . . and attracts viewers to TV shows." Why? Probably because a murder is shocking, sensational, at once a personal and public event. Murder, as a human problem, simply never goes away. It raises both practical and philosophical questions. The practical questions are usually criminological or legal: Who did it? Why? How should the guilty be punished? But the philosophical questions are equally persistent and unsettling: Why do people kill? Are there social or psychological patterns in murder? Are all accused parties equal in the eyes of the law?

This chapter presents materials for the study of both sets of questions. In very practical terms, a number of cases are opened here for your inspection: Susanna of the Apocryphal scriptures and the nineteenth-century "Case of an Apprentice" represent the dangerously thin line between circumstantial evidence and certainty. A second group—five cases culled from a century of the *New York Times*—reveals the wide variety of murder cases which become public record. The *Times* is not a sensationalist newspaper, but as you read the excerpts from this century, you will see how styles of murder *and* reporting have changed. After some immersion in these two groups of cases, you may elect to try a case yourself—either to check up on the official verdict or to offer a solution to an unsolved crime. (See "Assignment 6.") The final essay in this chapter, by Patricia Parr, shows how one student went about reconstructing a crime and pointing a finger at those who went unpunished for it.

The philosophical questions dominate in the first selections in this chapter. Susan Glaspell's play and Janet Rifkin's essay ask feminist questions about murder and the law, challenging us to ask if justice really is—or *should be*—blind. Jorge Luis Borges's retelling of the Billy the Kid story may serve as a way of explaining newspapers' success with murder stories: Sometimes, in the hands of a skillful writer, they are the stuff of legends.

Somewhere between the practical and the philosophical lies the psychological, and here Bruce L. Danto's essay offers a recent gathering of information on murder victims and their murderers, as well as the interpretations of murder of some psychologists and psychiatrists.

A look at today's newspaper or the evening news on television will convince us that murder is not simply an academic topic. Nevertheless, in order to try to comprehend its dramatic impact, we begin with some literary interpretations.

DISCURSIVE ESSAYS AND FICTIONS

PLAY

SUSAN GLASPELL

The play Trifles *is a very unusual look at a murder, since both the murder victim, John Wright, and the suspected murderer, his wife, Minnie Foster Wright, are never actually present on stage. The sad nature of their relationship becomes apparent, nonetheless, as we listen to representatives of the law and the community discuss a shocking crime. Glaspell only glances at some aspects of a traditional crime story—details such as the* means *(how it was done) or* opportunity *(who was present)—although they are important parts of the story. Glaspell concentrates instead on the social and personal drama of Minnie Wright, placing Minnie's motive in the context of the role of women in society.*

Susan Glaspell was the playwright-founder of the famous Provincetown Players of Cape Cod, Massachusetts, a group which helped launch Eugene O'Neill's climb to fame. In the first production of Trifles, *at Provincetown's Wharf Theatre on August 8, 1916, Glaspell herself played Mrs. Hale; her husband, George Cram Cook (the co-author of a number of other plays), played Lewis Hale. She based the play on her own short story which also had a revealing title—"A Jury of Her Peers." The half-century which has passed since the play's first performance may have dimmed its popularity but not the controversial questions it asks. Like the "Case of an Apprentice" which follows it,* Trifles *raises questions about circumstantial evidence, but it goes beyond looking at the methods of obtaining justice to ask a more fundamental question about the nature of justice itself.*

Trifles

SCENE

The kitchen in the now abandoned farm-house of John Wright, a gloomy kitchen, and left without having been put in order—unwashed pans under the sink, a loaf of bread outside the bread-box, a dish-towel on the table—other signs of incompleted work. At the rear the outer door opens and the SHERIFF *comes in followed by the* COUNTY ATTORNEY *and* HALE. *The* SHERIFF *and* HALE *are men in middle life, the* COUNTY ATTORNEY *is a young man; all are much bundled up and go at once to the stove. They are followed by the two women—the Sheriff's wife first; she is a slight wiry woman, with a thin nervous face.* MRS. HALE *is larger and would ordinarily be called more comfortable looking, but she is disturbed now and looks fearfully about as she enters. The women have come in slowly, and stand close together near the door.*

COUNTY ATTORNEY: *(rubbing his hands)* This feels good. Come up to the fire, ladies.

MRS. PETERS: *(after taking a step forward)* I'm not—cold.

SHERIFF: *(unbuttoning his overcoat and stepping away from the stove as if to mark the beginning of official business)* Now, Mr. Hale, before we move things about, you explain to Mr. Henderson just what you saw when you came here yesterday morning.

COUNTY ATTORNEY: By the way, has anything been moved? Are things just as you left them yesterday?

SHERIFF: *(looking about)* It's just the same. When it dropped below zero last night I thought I'd better send Frank out this morning to make a fire for us—no use getting pneumonia with a big case on, but

I told him not to touch anything except the stove—and you know Frank.

COUNTY ATTORNEY: Somebody should have been left here yesterday.

SHERIFF: Oh—yesterday. When I had to send Frank to Morris Center for that man who went crazy—I want you to know I had my hands full yesterday. I knew you could get back from Omaha by to-day and as long as I went over everything here myself—

COUNTY ATTORNEY: Well, Mr. Hale, tell just what happened when you came here yesterday morning.

HALE: Harry and I had started to town with a load of potatoes. We came along the road from my place and as I got here I said, "I'm going to see if I can't get John Wright to go in with me on a party telephone." I spoke to Wright about it once before and he put me off, saying folks talked too much anyway, and all he asked was peace and quiet—I guess you know about how much he talked himself; but I thought maybe if I went to the house and talked about it before his wife, though I said to Harry that I didn't know as what his wife wanted made much difference to John—

COUNTY ATTORNEY: Let's talk about that later, Mr. Hale. I do want to talk about that, but tell now just what happened when you got to the house.

HALE: I didn't hear or see anything; I knocked at the door, and still it was all quiet inside. I knew they must be up, it was past eight o'clock. So I knocked again, and I thought I heard somebody say "Come in." I wasn't sure, I'm not sure yet, but I opened the door— this door *(indicating the door by which the two women are still standing)* and there in that rocker—*(pointing to it)* sat Mrs. Wright.
(They all look at the rocker.)

COUNTY ATTORNEY: What—was she doing?

HALE: She was rockin' back and forth. She had her apron in her hand and was kind of—pleating it.

COUNTY ATTORNEY: And how did she—look?

HALE: Well, she looked queer.

COUNTY ATTORNEY: How do you mean—queer?

HALE: Well, as if she didn't know what she was going to do next. And kind of done up.

COUNTY ATTORNEY: How did she seem to feel about your coming?

HALE: Why, I don't think she minded—one way or other. She didn't pay much attention. I said, "How do, Mrs. Wright, it's cold, ain't it?" And she said "Is it?"—and went on kind of pleating at her apron. Well, I was surprised; she didn't ask me to come up to the stove, or to set down, but just sat there, not even looking at me, so I said, "I want to see John." And then she—laughed. I guess you would call it a laugh. I thought of Harry and the team outside, so I said a little sharp: "Can't I see John?" "No," she says, kind o' dull like. "Ain't he home?" says I. "Yes," says she, "he's home." "Then why can't I see him?" I asked her out of patience. " 'Cause he's dead," says she. *"Dead?"* says I. She just nodded her head, not getting a bit excited, but rockin' back and forth. "Why—where is he?" says I, not knowing what to say. She just pointed upstairs—like that *(himself pointing to the room above).* I got up, with the idea of going up there. I walked from there to here—then I says, "Why, what did he die of?" "He died of a rope round his neck," says she, and just went on pleatin' at her apron. Well, I went out and called Harry. I thought I might—need help. We went upstairs and there he was lyin'—

COUNTY ATTORNEY: I think I'd rather have you go into that upstairs, where you can point it all out. Just go on now with the rest of the story.

HALE: Well, my first thought was to get that rope off. It looked... *(Stops, his face twitches.)* ... but Harry, he went up to him, and he said, "No, he's dead all right, and we'd better not touch anything." So we went back down stairs. She was still sitting that same way. "Has anybody been notified?" I asked. "No," says she, unconcerned. "Who did this, Mrs. Wright?" said Harry. He said it business-like—and she stopped pleatin' of her apron. "I don't know," she says. "You don't *know?"* says Harry. "No," says she. "Weren't you sleepin' in the bed with him?" says Harry. "Yes," says she, "but I was on the inside." "Somebody slipped a rope round his neck and strangled him and you didn't wake up?" says Harry. "I didn't wake up," she said after him. We must 'a looked as if we didn't see how that could be, for after a minute she said, "I sleep sound." Harry was going to ask her more questions, but I said maybe we ought to let her tell her story first to the coroner, or the sheriff, so Harry went fast as he could to Rivers' place, where there's a telephone.

COUNTY ATTORNEY: And what did Mrs. Wright do when she knew that you had gone for the coroner?

HALE: She moved from that chair to this over here . . . *(Pointing to a small chair in the corner.)* . . . and just sat there with her hands held together and looking down. I got a feeling that I ought to make some conversation, so I said I had come in to see if John wanted to put in a telephone, and at that she started to laugh, and then she stopped and looked at me—scared. *(The* COUNTY ATTORNEY, *who has had his notebook out, makes a note.)* I dunno, maybe it wasn't scared. I wouldn't like to say it was. Soon Harry got back, and then Dr. Lloyd came, and you, Mr. Peters, and so I guess that's all I know that you don't.

COUNTY ATTORNEY: *(looking around)* I guess we'll go upstairs first— and then out to the barn and around there. *(To the* SHERIFF.) You're convinced that there was nothing important here—nothing that would point to any motive?

SHERIFF: Nothing here but kitchen things.

(The COUNTY ATTORNEY, *after again looking around the kitchen, opens the door of a cupboard closet. He gets up on a chair and looks on a shelf. Pulls his hand away, sticky.)*

COUNTY ATTORNEY: Here's a nice mess.

(The women draw nearer.)

MRS. PETERS: *(to the other woman)* Oh, her fruit; it did freeze. *(To the* COUNTY ATTORNEY.) She worried about that when it turned so cold. She said the fire'd go out and her jars would break.

SHERIFF: Well, can you beat the women! Held for murder and worryin' about her preserves.

COUNTY ATTORNEY: I guess before we're through she may have something more serious than preserves to worry about.

HALE: Well, women are used to worrying over trifles.

(The two women move a little closer together.)

COUNTY ATTORNEY: *(with the gallantry of a young politician)* And yet, for all their worries, what would we do without the ladies? *(The women do not unbend. He goes to the sink, takes a dipperful of water from the pail and, pouring it into a basin, washes his hands. Starts to wipe them on the roller-towel, turns it for a cleaner place.)* Dirty towels! *(Kicks his foot against the pans under the sink.)* Not much of a housekeeper, would you say, ladies?

MRS. HALE: *(stiffly)* There's a great deal of work to be done on a farm.

COUNTY ATTORNEY: To be sure. And yet . . . *(With a little bow to her.)* . . . I know there are some Dickson county farmhouses which do not have such roller towels.

(He gives it a pull to expose its full length again.)

MRS. HALE: Those towels get dirty awful quick. Men's hands aren't always as clean as they might be.

COUNTY ATTORNEY: Ah, loyal to your sex, I see. But you and Mrs. Wright were neighbors. I suppose you were friends, too.

MRS. HALE: *(shaking her head)* I've not seen much of her of late years. I've not been in this house—it's more than a year.

COUNTY ATTORNEY: And why was that? You didn't like her?

MRS. HALE: I like her all well enough. Farmers' wives have their hands full, Mr. Henderson. And then—

COUNTY ATTORNEY: Yes—?

MRS. HALE: *(looking about)* It never seemed a very cheerful place.

COUNTY ATTORNEY: No—it's not cheerful. I shouldn't say she had the homemaking instinct.

MRS. HALE: Well, I don't know as Wright had, either.

COUNTY ATTORNEY: You mean that they didn't get on very well?

MRS. HALE: No, I don't mean anything. But I don't think a place'd be any cheerful for John Wright's being in it.

COUNTY ATTORNEY: I'd like to talk more of that a little later. I want to get the lay of things upstairs now.

(He goes to the left, where three steps lead to a stair door.)

SHERIFF: I suppose anything Mrs. Peters does'll be all right. She was to take in some clothes for her, you know, and a few little things. We left in such a hurry yesterday.

COUNTY ATTORNEY: Yes, but I would like to see what you take, Mrs. Peters, and keep an eye out for anything that might be of use to us.

MRS. PETERS: Yes, Mr. Henderson.

(The women listen to the men's steps on the stairs, then look about the kitchen.)

MRS. HALE: I'd hate to have men coming into my kitchen, snooping around and criticizing.

(She arranges the pans under the sink which the COUNTY ATTORNEY *had shoved out of place.)*

MRS. PETERS: Of course it's no more than their duty.

MRS. HALE: Duty's all right, but I guess that deputy sheriff that came out to make the fire might have got a little of this on. *(Gives the roller towel a pull.)* Wish I'd thought of that sooner. Seems mean to talk about her for not having things slicked up when she had to come away in such a hurry.

MRS. PETERS: *(who has gone to a small table in the left rear corner of the room, and lifted one end of a towel that covers a pan)* She had bread set. *(Stands still.)*

MRS. HALE: *(eyes fixed on a loaf of bread beside the bread-box, which is on a low shelf at the other side of the room. Moves slowly toward it.)* She was going to put this in there. *(Picks up a loaf, then abruptly drops it. In a manner of returning to familiar things.)* It's a shame about her fruit. I wonder if it's all gone. *(Gets up on the chair and looks.)* I think there's some here that's all right, Mrs. Peters. Yes—here; *(Holding it toward the window.)* this is cherries, too. *(Looking again.)* I declare I believe that's the only one. *(Gets down, bottle in her hand. Goes to the sink and wipes it off on the outside.)* She'll feel awful bad after all her hard work in the hot weather. I remember the afternoon I put up my cherries last summer.

(She puts the bottle on the big kitchen table, center of the room, front table. With a sigh, is about to sit down in the rocking-chair. Before she is seated realizes what chair it is: with a slow look at it, steps back. The chair which she has touched rocks back and forth.)

MRS. PETERS: Well, I must get those things from the front room closet.

(She goes to the door at the right, but after looking into the other room, steps back.) You coming with me, Mrs. Hale? You could help me carry them.

(They go in the other room: reappear, MRS. PETERS *carrying a dress and skirt,* MRS. HALE *following with a pair of shoes.)*

MRS. PETERS: My, it's cold in there.

(She puts the clothes on the big table, and hurries to the stove.)

MRS. HALE: *(examining the skirt)* Wright was close. I think maybe that's why she kept so much to herself. She didn't even belong to the Ladies' Aid. I suppose she felt she couldn't do her part, and then you don't enjoy things when you feel shabby. She used to wear pretty clothes and be lively, when she was Minnie Foster, one of the town girls singing in the choir. But that—oh, that was thirty years ago. This all you was to take in?

MRS. PETERS: She said she wanted an apron. Funny thing to want, for there isn't much to get you dirty in jail, goodness knows. But I suppose just to make her feel more natural. She said they was in the top drawer in this cupboard. Yes, here. And then her little shawl that always hung behind the door. *(Opens stair door and looks.)* Yes, here it is.

(Quickly shuts door leading upstairs.)

MRS. HALE: *(abruptly moving toward her)* Mrs. Peters?

MRS. PETERS: Yes, Mrs. Hale?

MRS. HALE: Do you think she did it?

MRS. PETERS: *(in a frightened voice)* Oh, I don't know.

MRS. HALE: Well, I don't think she did. Asking for an apron and her little shawl. Worrying about her fruit.

MRS. PETERS: *(starts to speak, glances up, where footsteps are heard in the room above. In a low voice)* Mr. Peters says it looks bad for her. Mr. Henderson is awful sarcastic in a speech and he'll make fun of her sayin' she didn't wake up.

MRS. HALE: Well, I guess John Wright didn't wake when they was slipping that rope under his neck.

MRS. PETERS: No, it's strange. It must have been done awful crafty and still. They say it was such a—funny way to kill a man, rigging it all up like that.

MRS. HALE: That's just what Mr. Hale said. There was a gun in the house. He says that's what he can't understand.

MRS. PETERS: Mr. Henderson said coming out that what was needed for the case was a motive; something to show anger, or—sudden feeling.

MRS. HALE: *(who is standing by the table)* Well, I don't see any signs of anger around here. *(She puts her hand on the dish towel which lies on the table, stands looking down at the table, one half of which is clean, the other half messy.)* It's wiped here. *(Makes a move as if to finish work, then turns and looks at loaf of bread outside the bread-box. Drops towel. In that voice of coming back to familiar things.)* Wonder how they are finding things upstairs? I hope she had it a little more red-up up there. You know, it seems kind of *sneaking.* Locking her up in town and then coming out here and trying to get her own house to turn against her!

MRS. PETERS: But, Mrs. Hale, the law is the law.

MRS. HALE: I s'pose 'tis. *(Unbuttoning her coat.)* Better loosen up your things, Mrs. Peters. You won't feel them when you go out.

(MRS. PETERS *takes off her fur tippet, goes to hang it on hook at back of room, stands looking at the under part of the small corner table.)*

MRS. PETERS: She was piecing a quilt. *(She brings the large sewing basket and they look at the bright pieces.)*

MRS. HALE: It's log cabin pattern. Pretty, isn't it? I wonder if she was goin' to quilt it or just knot it?°
(Footsteps have been heard coming down the stairs. The SHERIFF *enters, followed by* HALE *and the* COUNTY ATTORNEY.)

SHERIFF: They wonder if she was going to quilt it or just knot it.
(The men laugh, the women look abashed.)

COUNTY ATTORNEY: *(rubbing his hands over the stove)* Frank's fire didn't do much up there, did it? Well, let's go out to the barn and get that cleared up.
(The men go outside.)

MRS. HALE: *(resentfully)* I don't know as there's anything so strange, our takin' up our time with little things while we're waiting for them to get the evidence. *(She sits down at the big table smoothing out a block with decision.)* I don't see as it's anything to laugh about.

° to quilt or to knot: To quilt is to stitch layers of fabric together (using the shape or the color of the pieces to form a design, like the "log cabin" of folk-art quilts). To knot refers to a different technique in quilting by which pieces are joined by string which is knotted after it is passed through the layers of fabric.

MRS. PETERS: *(apologetically)* Of course they've got awful important things on their minds.

(Pulls up a chair and joins MRS. HALE *at the table.)*

MRS. HALE: *(examining another block)* Mrs. Peters, look at this one. Here, this is the one she was working on, and look at the sewing! All the rest of it has been so nice and even. And look at this! It's all over the place! Why, it looks as if she didn't know what she was about!

(After she has said this they look at each other, then start to glance back at the door. After an instant MRS. HALE *has pulled at a knot and ripped the sewing.)*

MRS. PETERS: Oh, what are you doing, Mrs. Hale?

MRS. HALE: *(mildly)* Just pulling out a stitch or two that's not sewed very good. *(Threading a needle.)* Bad sewing always made me fidgety.

MRS. PETERS: *(nervously)* I don't think we ought to touch things.

MRS. HALE: I'll just finish up this end. *(Suddenly stopping and leaning forward.)* Mrs. Peters?

MRS. PETERS: Yes, Mrs. Hale?

MRS. HALE: What do you suppose she was so nervous about?

MRS. PETERS: Oh—I don't know. I don't know as she was nervous. I sometimes sew awful queer when I'm just tired. *(*MRS. HALE *starts to say something, looks at* MRS. PETERS, *then goes on sewing.)* Well, I must get these things wrapped up. They may be through sooner than we think.

(Putting apron and other things together.) I wonder where I can find a piece of paper, and string.

MRS. HALE: In that cupboard, maybe.

MRS. PETERS: *(looking in cupboard)* Why, here's a bird-cage. *(Holds it up.)* Did she have a bird, Mrs. Hale?

MRS. HALE: Why, I don't know whether she did or not—I've not been here for so long. There was a man around last year selling canaries cheap, but I don't know as she took one; maybe she did. She used to sing real pretty herself.

MRS. PETERS: *(glancing around)* Seems funny to think of a bird here. But she must have had one, or why should she have a cage? I wonder what happened to it?

MRS. HALE: I s'pose maybe the cat got it.

MRS. PETERS: No, she didn't have a cat. She's got that feeling some people have about cats—being afraid of them. My cat got in her room and she was real upset and asked me to take it out.

MRS. HALE: My sister Bessie was like that. Queer, ain't it?

MRS. PETERS: *(examining the cage)* Why, look at this door. It's broke. One hinge is pulled apart.

MRS. HALE: *(looking too)* Looks as if some one must have been rough with it.

MRS. PETERS: Why, yes.
(She brings the cage forward and puts it on the table.)

MRS. HALE: I wish if they're going to find any evidence they'd be about it. I don't like this place.

MRS. PETERS: But I'm awful glad you came with me, Mrs. Hale. It would be lonesome for me sitting here alone.

MRS. HALE: It would, wouldn't it? *(Dropping her sewing.)* But I tell you what I do wish, Mrs. Peters. I wish I had come over some times when *she* was here. I—*(Looking around the room.)*—wish I had.

MRS. PETERS: But of course you were awful busy, Mrs. Hale— your house and your children.

MRS. HALE: I could've come. I stayed away because it weren't cheerful—and that's why I ought to have come. I—I've never liked this place. Maybe because it's down in a hollow and you don't see the road. I dunno what it is, but it's a lonesome place and always was. I wish I had come over to see Minnie Foster sometimes. I can see now—
(Shakes her head.)

MRS. PETERS: Well, you mustn't reproach yourself, Mrs. Hale. Somehow we just don't see how it is with other folks until—something comes up.

MRS. HALE: Not having children makes less work—but it makes a quiet house, and Wright out to work all day, and no company when he did come in. Did you know John Wright, Mrs. Peters?

MRS. PETERS: Not to know him; I've seen him in town. They say he was a good man.

MRS. HALE: Yes—good; he didn't drink, and kept his word as well as most, I guess, and paid his debts. But he was a hard man, Mrs. Peters. Just to pass the time of day with him. *(Shivers.)* Like a raw wind that gets to the bone. *(Pauses, her eye falling on the cage.)* I should think she would 'a wanted a bird. But what do you suppose went with it?

MRS. PETERS: I don't know, unless it got sick and died.

(She reaches over and swings the broken door, swings it again, both women watch it.)

MRS. HALE: You weren't raised round here, were you? *(*MRS. PETERS *shakes her head.)* You didn't know—her?

MRS. PETERS: Not till they brought her yesterday.

MRS. HALE: She—come to think of it, she was kind of like a bird herself—real sweet and pretty, but kind of timid and—fluttery. How—she—did—change. *(Silence; then as if struck by a happy thought and relieved to get back to everyday things.)* Tell you what, Mrs. Peters, why don't you take the quilt in with you? It might take up her mind.

MRS. PETERS: Why, I think that's a real nice idea, Mrs. Hale. There couldn't possibly be any objection to it, could there? Now, just what would I take? I wonder if her patches are in here—and her things.

(They look in the sewing basket.)

MRS. HALE: Here's some red. I expect this has got sewing things in it. *(Brings out a fancy box.)* What a pretty box. Looks like something somebody would give you. Maybe her scissors are in here. *(Opens box. Suddenly puts her hand to her nose.)* Why—(*MRS. PETERS *bends nearer, then turns her face away.)* There's something wrapped up in this piece of silk.

MRS. PETERS: Why, this isn't her scissors.

MRS. HALE: *(lifting the silk)* Oh, Mrs. Peters—it's—
*(*MRS. PETERS *bends closer.)*

MRS. PETERS: It's the bird.

MRS. HALE: *(jumping up)* But, Mrs. Peters—look at it. Its neck! Look at its neck! It's all—other side *to.*

MRS. PETERS: Somebody—wrung—its neck.

*(Their eyes meet. A look of growing comprehension, of horror. Steps are heard outside. *MRS. HALE *slips box under quilt pieces, and sinks into her chair. Enter *SHERIFF *and *COUNTY ATTORNEY. MRS. PETERS *rises.)*

COUNTY ATTORNEY: *(as one turning from serious things to little pleasantries)* Well, ladies, have you decided whether she was going to quilt it or knot it?

MRS. PETERS: We think she was going to—knot it.

COUNTY ATTORNEY: Well, that's interesting, I'm sure. *(Seeing the bird-cage.)* Has the bird flown?

MRS. HALE: *(putting more quilt pieces over the box)* We think the—cat got it.

COUNTY ATTORNEY: *(preoccupied)* Is there a cat?

*(*MRS. HALE *glances in a quick covert way at* MRS. PETERS.*)*

MRS. PETERS: Well, not now. They're superstitious, you know. They leave.

COUNTY ATTORNEY: *(to* SHERIFF PETERS, *continuing an interrupted conversation)* No sign at all of any one having come from the outside. Their own rope. Now let's go up again and go over it piece by piece. *(They start upstairs.)* It would have to have been some one who knew just the—(*MRS. PETERS *sits down. The two women sit there not looking at one another, but as if peering into something and at the same time holding back. When they talk now it is in the manner of feeling their way over strange ground, as if afraid of what they are saying, but as if they can not help saying it.)*

MRS. HALE: She liked the bird. She was going to bury it in that pretty box.

MRS. PETERS: *(in a whisper)* When I was a girl—my kitten—there was a boy took a hatchet, and before my eyes—and before I could get there—*(Covers her face an instant.)* If they hadn't held me back I would have—*(Catches herself, looks upstairs where steps are heard, falters weakly)*—hurt him.

MRS. HALE: *(with a slow look around her)* I wonder how it would seem never to have had any children around. *(Pause.)* No, Wright wouldn't like the bird—a thing that sang. She used to sing. He killed that, too.

MRS. PETERS: *(moving uneasily)* We don't know who killed the bird.

MRS. HALE: I knew John Wright.

MRS. PETERS: It was an awful thing was done in this house that night, Mrs. Hale. Killing a man while he slept, slipping a rope around his neck that choked the life out of him.

MRS. HALE: His neck. Choked the life out of him.
(Her hand goes out and rests on the bird-cage.)

MRS. PETERS: *(with rising voice)* We don't know who killed him. We don't *know.*

MRS. HALE: *(her own feeling not interrupted)* If there'd been years and years of nothing, then a bird to sing to you, it would be awful—still, after the bird was still.

MRS. PETERS: *(something within her speaking)* I know what stillness is. When we homesteaded in Dakota, and my first baby died—after he was two years old, and me with no other then—

MRS. HALE: *(moving)* How soon do you suppose they'll be through, looking for the evidence?

MRS. PETERS: I know what stillness is. *(Pulling herself back.)* The law has got to punish a crime, Mrs. Hale.

MRS. HALE: *(not as if answering that)* I wish you'd seen Minnie Foster when she wore a white dress with blue ribbons and stood up there in the choir and sang. *(A look around the room.)* Oh, I *wish* I'd come over here once in a while. That was a crime! That was a crime! Who's going to punish that?

MRS. PETERS: *(looking upstairs)* We mustn't—take on.

MRS. HALE: I might have known she needed help! I know how things can be—for women. I tell you, it's queer, Mrs. Peters. We live close together and we live far apart. We all go through the same things—it's all just a different kind of the same thing. *(Brushes her eyes, noticing the bottle of fruit, reaches out for it.)* If I was you I wouldn't tell her her fruit was gone. Tell her it *ain't.* Tell her it's all right. Take this in to prove it to her. She—she may never know whether it was broke or not.

MRS. PETERS: *(takes the bottle, looks about for something to wrap it in; takes petticoat from the clothes brought from the other room, very nervously begins winding this around the bottle. In a false voice)* My, it's a good thing the men couldn't hear us. Wouldn't they just laugh. Getting all stirred up over a little thing like a—dead canary. As if that could have anything to do with—with—wouldn't they *laugh!*
(The men are heard coming down stairs.)

MRS. HALE: *(under her breath)* Maybe they would—maybe they wouldn't.

COUNTY ATTORNEY: No, Peters, it's all perfectly clear except a reason for doing it. But you know juries when it comes to women. If there was some definite thing. Something to show—something to make a story about—a thing that would connect up with this strange way of doing it.

(The women's eyes meet for an instant. Enter HALE *from outer door.)*

HALE: Well, I've got the team around. Pretty cold out there.

COUNTY ATTORNEY: I'm going to stay here a while by myself. *(To the* SHERIFF.*)* You can send Frank out for me, can't you? I want to go over everything. I'm not satisfied that we can't do better.

SHERIFF: Do you want to see what Mrs. Peters is going to take in?

(The COUNTY ATTORNEY *goes to the table, picks up the apron, laughs.)*

COUNTY ATTORNEY: Oh, I guess they're not very dangerous things the ladies have picked out. *(Moves a few things about, disturbing the quilt pieces which cover the box. Steps back.)* No, Mrs. Peters doesn't need supervising. For that matter, a sheriff's wife is married to the law. Ever think of it that way, Mrs. Peters?

MRS. PETERS: Not—just that way.

SHERIFF: *(chuckling)* Married to the law. *(Moves toward the other room.)* I just want you to come in here a minute, George. We ought to take a look at these windows.

COUNTY ATTORNEY: *(scoffingly)* Oh, windows!

SHERIFF: We'll be right out, Mr. Hale.

*(*HALE *goes outside. The* SHERIFF *follows the* COUNTY ATTORNEY *into the other room. Then* MRS. HALE *rises, hands tight together, looking intensely at* MRS. PETERS, *whose eyes make a slow turn, finally meeting* MRS. HALE'S.*

A moment MRS. HALE *holds her, then her own eyes point the way to where the box is concealed. Suddenly* MRS. PETERS *throws back quilt pieces and tries to put the box in the bag she is wearing. It is too big. She opens the box, starts to take bird out, cannot touch it, goes to pieces, stands there helpless. Sound of a knob turning in the other room.* MRS. HALE *snatches the box and puts it in the pocket of her big coat. Enter* COUNTY ATTORNEY *and* SHERIFF.*)*

COUNTY ATTORNEY: *(facetiously)* Well, Henry, at least we found out that she was not going to quilt it. She was going to—what is it you call it, ladies?

MRS. HALE: *(her hand against her pocket)* We call it—knot it, Mr. Henderson.

(Curtain)

NARRATIVE ESSAY

SAMUEL PHILLIPPS

In nineteenth-century England, the jurist Samuel Phillipps gathered and published his Famous Cases of Circumstantial Evidence, *from which this "Case of an Apprentice" has been reprinted. Phillipps actually presented two quite different kinds of cases of circumstantial evidence: (1) those faked by the truly guilty party in order to throw the blame for a crime on someone else, or for revenge; and (2) those in which the circumstantial evidence simply traps an innocent party. The selection below, representing the second type, tells of a young sailmaker who is an innocent victim of a convincing and damning chain of events.*

Today, the expression "circumstantial evidence" often takes on the popular meaning of somehow inadequate evidence, such as is seen in popular TV programs and films which refer to the evidence as "only" circumstantial. It actually refers to "indirect" evidence from which a fact must be inferred; "direct" evidence, on the other hand, is an object or eyewitness's statement directly related to the commission of the alleged crime. In his introduction to Famous Cases of Circumstantial Evidence, *Phillipps states that he is retelling these stories to diminish the reliance on circumstantial evidence (what he calls "that conclusion which the jury draw for themselves, from circumstances or minor facts as sworn to by witnesses"). Instead, he argues for greater reliance on what we now call "direct" evidence (whereby "the witness swears distinctly to the commission of the act or crime which forms the subject of the trial"). The story of the young sailmaker shows all too well how presumptions often can come "to aid" other presumptions, and a fatal chain of circumstantial evidence is established.*

Case of an Apprentice

In the year 1723, a young man who was serving his apprentice-ship in London to a master sailmaker, got leave to visit his mother, to spend the Christmas holidays. She lived a few miles beyond Deal, in Kent. He walked the journey, and on his arrival at Deal, in the evening, being much fatigued, and also troubled with a bowel complaint, he applied to the landlady of a public house, who was acquainted with his mother, for a night's lodging. Her house was full, and every bed occupied; but she told him that if he would sleep with her uncle, who had lately come ashore, and was boatswain of an Indiaman, he should be welcome. He was glad to accept the offer, and after spending the evening with his new comrade, they retired to rest. In the middle of the night he was attacked with his complaint, and wakening his bedfellow, he asked him the way to the garden. The boatswain told him to go through the kitchen; but, as he would find it difficult to open the door into the yard, the latch being out of order, he desired him to take a knife out of his pocket, with which he could raise the latch. The young man did as he was directed, and after remaining near half an hour in the yard, he returned to his bed, but was much surprised to find his companion had risen and gone. Being impatient to visit his mother and friends, he also arose before day, and pursued his journey, and arrived home at noon.

The landlady, who had been told of his intention to depart early, was not surprised; but not seeing her uncle in the morning, she went to call him. She was dreadfully shocked to find the bed stained with blood, and every inquiry after her uncle was in vain. The alarm now became general, and on further examination, marks of blood were traced from the bedroom into the street, and at intervals, down to the edge of the pier-head. Rumor was immediately busy, and suspicion fell, of course, on the young man who slept with him, that he had committed the murder, and thrown the body over the pier into the sea. A warrant was issued against him, and he was taken that evening at his mother's house. On his being examined and searched, marks of blood were discovered on his shirt and trousers, and in his pocket were a knife and a remarkable silver coin, both of which the landlady swore positively were her uncle's property, and that she saw them in his possession on the evening he retired to rest with the young man. On these strong circumstances the unfortunate youth was found guilty. He related all the above circumstances in his defence; but as he could not account for the marks of blood on his person, unless that he got them when he returned to the bed, nor for the silver coin being in his possession, his story was not credited. The certainty of the boatswain's disappearance, and the blood at the pier, traced from his bedroom, were two evident signs of his being murdered; and even the judge was so convinced of his guilt, that he ordered the execution to take place in three days. At the fatal tree the youth declared his innocence, and persisted in it with such affecting asseverations, that many pitied him, though none doubted the justness of his sentence.

The executioners of those days were not so expert at their trade as modern ones, nor were drops and platforms invented. The young man was very tall; his feet sometimes touched the ground, and some of his friends who surrounded the gallows contrived to give the body some support as it was suspended. After being cut down, those friends bore it speedily away in a coffin, and in the course of a few hours animation was restored, and the innocent saved. When he was able to move, his friends insisted on his quitting the country and never returning. He accordingly travelled by night to Portsmouth, where he entered on board a man-of-war, on the point of sailing for a distant part of the world; and as he changed his name, and disguised his person, his melancholy story never was discovered. After a few years of service, during which his exemplary conduct was the cause of his promotion through the lower grades, he was at last made a master's mate, and his ship being paid off in the West Indies, he, with a few more of the crew, were transferred to another man-of-war, which had just arrived short of hands from a different station. What were his feelings of astonishment, and then of delight and ecstasy, when almost the first person he saw on board his new ship was the identical boatswain for whose murder he had been tried, condemned, and executed, five years before! Nor was the surprise of the old boatswain much less when he heard the story.

An explanation of all the mysterious circumstances then took place. It appeared the boatswain had been bled for a pain in his side by the barber, unknown to his niece, on the day of the young man's arrival at Deal; that when the young man wakened him, and retired to the yard, he found the bandage had come off his arm during the night, and that the blood was flowing afresh. Being alarmed, he rose to go to the barber, who lived across the street, but a press-gang laid hold of him just as he left the public house. They hurried him to the pier, where their boat was waiting: a few minutes brought them on board a frigate, then underway for the East Indies, and he omitted ever writing home to account for his sudden disappearance. Thus were the chief circumstances explained by the two friends, thus strangely met. The silver coin being found in the possession of the young man, could only be explained by the conjecture, that when the boatswain gave him the knife in the dark, it is probable that as the coin was in the same pocket, it stuck between the blades of the knife, and in this manner became the strongest proof against him.

NARRATIVE ESSAY

JORGE LUIS BORGES

Borges was an Argentine writer of fantasies, parodies, detective stories, and unlikely tales. His imaginative reconstruction of the life and death of Billy the Kid is found in his collection of essays about bad characters called A Universal History of Infamy *(1974). I do not know why Borges changed Billy's surname from Bonney to Harrigan, but it does happen to be true that Billy the Kid grew up in a tenement in New York City (a fact which seems to be among the most unlikely of all!).*

This Billy the Kid is the result of Borges's mixture of the plausible and the unlikely. We see a figure through the eyes of a teller of tall tales who knows his audience realizes that he is putting them on, but both still enjoy an outrageous treatment of an outrageous character. Some kind of truth, if not poetic justice, is the outcome.

Borges's essay takes the form of a mini-biography, but still he uses a number of techniques from fiction such as scene-setting, anecdotes, dialogue, and refrains or recurring words (e.g., "not counting Mexicans") which give the piece a tone closer to that of myth or legend. So much of this story "sounds" like it may be true that we are tempted to forget that it is an artful retelling of many of the Billy the Kid legends passed down by the "folk" for the last hundred years.

The Disinterested Killer Bill Harrigan

An image of the desert wilds of Arizona, first and foremost, an image of the desert wilds of Arizona and New Mexico—a country famous for its silver and gold camps, a country of breathtaking open spaces, a country of monumental mesas and soft colors, a country of bleached skeletons picked clean by buzzards. Over this whole country, another image—that of Billy the Kid, the hard rider firm on his horse, the young man with the relentless six-shooters, sending out invisible bullets which (like magic) kill at a distance.

The desert veined with precious metals, arid and blinding-bright. The near child who on dying at the age of twenty-one owed to the justice of grown men twenty-one deaths—"not counting Mexicans."

THE LARVAL STAGE

Along about 1859, the man who would become known to terror and glory as Billy the Kid was born in a cellar room of a New York City tenement. It is said that he was spawned by a tired-out Irish womb but was brought up among Negroes. In this tumult of lowly smells and woolly heads, he enjoyed a superiority that stemmed from having freckles and a mop of red hair. He took pride in being white; he was also scrawny, wild, and coarse. At the age of twelve, he fought in the gang of the Swamp Angels, that branch of divinities who operated among the neighborhood sewers. On nights redolent of burnt fog, they would clamber out of that foul-smelling labyrinth, trail some German sailor, do him in with a knock on the head, strip him to his underwear, and afterward sneak back to the filth of their starting place. Their leader was a gray-haired Negro, Gas House Jonas, who was also celebrated as a poisoner of horses.

Sometimes, from the upper window of a waterfront dive, a woman would dump a bucket of ashes upon the head of a prospective victim. As he gasped and choked, Swamp Angels would swarm him, rush him into a cellar, and plunder him.

Such were the apprentice years of Billy Harrigan, the future Billy the Kid. Nor did he scorn the offerings of Bowery playhouses, enjoying in particular (perhaps without an inkling that they were the signs and symbols of his destiny) cowboy melodramas.

GO WEST!

If the jammed Bowery theaters (whose top-gallery riffraff shouted "Hoist that rag!" when the curtain failed to rise promptly on schedule) abounded in these blood and thunder productions, the simple explanation is that America was then experiencing the lure of the Far West. Beyond the sunset lay the goldfields of Nevada and California. Beyond the sunset were the redwoods, going down before the ax; the buffalo's huge Babylonian face; Brigham Young's beaver hat and plural bed; the red man's ceremonies and his rampages; the clear air of the deserts; endless-stretching range land; and the earth itself, whose nearness quickens the heart like the nearness of the sea. The West beckoned. A slow, steady rumor populated those years— that of thousands of Americans taking possession of the West. On that march, around 1872, was Bill Harrigan, treacherous as a bull rattler, in flight from a rectangular cell.

THE DEMOLITION OF A MEXICAN

History (which, like certain film directors, proceeds by a series of abrupt images) now puts forward the image of a danger-filled saloon, located—as if on the high seas—out in the heart of the all-powerful desert. The time, a blustery night of the year 1873; the place, the Staked Plains of New Mexico. All around, the land is almost uncannily flat and bare, but the sky, with its storm-piled clouds and moon, is full of fissured cavities and mountains. There are a cow's skull, the howl and the eyes of coyotes in the shadows, trim horses, and from the saloon an elongated patch of light. Inside, leaning over the bar, a group of strapping but tired men drink a liquor that warms them for a fight; at the same time, they make a great show of large silver coins bearing a serpent and an eagle. A drunk croons to himself, poker-faced. Among the men are several who speak a language with many s's, which must be Spanish, for those who speak it are looked down on. Bill Harrigan, the red-topped tenement rat, stands among the drinkers. He has downed a couple of *aguardientes*° and thinks of asking for one more, maybe because he hasn't a cent left. He is somewhat overwhelmed by these men of the desert. He sees them as imposing, boisterous, happy, and hatefully wise in the handling of wild cattle and big horses. All at once there is dead silence, ignored only by the voice of the drunk, singing out of tune. Someone has come in—a big, burly Mexican, with the face of an old

° aguardientes: Spanish, "fiery water"; generic term for various alcoholic drinks.

Indian squaw. He is endowed with an immense sombrero and with a pair of six-guns at his side. In awkward English, he wishes a good evening to all the gringo sons of bitches who are drinking. Nobody takes up the challenge. Bill asks who he is, and they whisper to him, in fear, that the Dago—that is, the Diego—is Belisario Villagrán, from Chihuahua. At once, there is a resounding blast. Sheltered by that wall of tall men, Bill has fired at the intruder. The glass drops from Villagrán's hand; then the man himself drops. He does not need another bullet. Without deigning to glance at the showy dead man, Bill picks up his end of the conversation. "Is that so?" he drawled. "Well, I'm Billy the Kid, from New York." The drunk goes on singing, unheeded.

One may easily guess the apotheosis. Bill gives out handshakes all around and accepts praises, cheers, and whiskeys. Someone notices that there are no notches on the handle of his revolver and offers to cut one to stand for Villagrán's death. Billy the Kid keeps this someone's razor, though he says that "It's hardly worthwhile noting down Mexicans." This, perhaps, is not quite enough. That night, Bill lays out his blanket beside the corpse and—with great show—sleeps till daybreak.

DEATHS FOR DEATHS' SAKE

Out of that lucky blast (at the age of fourteen), Billy the Kid the hero was born, and the furtive Bill Harrigan died. The boy of the sewer and the knock on the head rose to become a man of the frontier. He made a horseman of himself, learning to ride straight in the saddle—Wyoming- or Texas-style—and not with his body thrown back, the way they rode in Oregon and California. He never completely matched his legend, but he kept getting closer and closer to it. Something of the New York hoodlum lived on in the cowboy; he transferred to Mexicans the hate that had previously been inspired in him by Negroes, but the last words he ever spoke were (swear) words in Spanish. He learned the art of the cowpuncher's maverick life. He learned another, more difficult art—how to lead men. Both helped to make him a good cattle rustler. From time to time, Old Mexico's guitars and whorehouses pulled on him.

With the haunting lucidity of insomnia, he organized populous orgies that often lasted four days and four nights. In the end, glutted, he settled accounts with bullets. While his trigger finger was unfailing, he was the most feared man (and perhaps the most anonymous and most lonely) of that whole frontier. Pat Garrett, his friend, the sheriff who later killed him, once told him, "I've had a lot of practice with the rifle shooting buffalo."

"I've had plenty with the six-shooter," Billy replied modestly. "Shooting tin cans and men."

The details can never be recovered, but it is known that he was credited with up to twenty-one killings—"not counting Mexicans." For seven desperate years, he practiced the extravagance of utter recklessness.

The night of the twenty-fifth of July, 1880, Billy the Kid came galloping on his piebald down the main, or only, street of Fort Sumner. The heat was oppressive and the lamps had not been lighted; Sheriff Garrett, seated on a porch in a rocking chair, drew his revolver and sent a bullet through the Kid's belly. The horse kept on; the rider tumbled into the dust of the road. Garrett got off a second shot. The townspeople (knowing the wounded man was Billy the Kid) locked their window shutters tight. The agony was long and blasphemous. In the morning, the sun by then high overhead, they began drawing near, and they disarmed him. The man was gone. They could see in his face that used-up look of the dead.

He was shaved, sheathed in ready-made clothes, and displayed to awe and ridicule in the window of Fort Sumner's biggest store. Men on horseback and in buckboards gathered for miles and miles around. On the third day, they had to use make-up on him. On the fourth day, he was buried with rejoicing.

ESSAYS FROM THE DISCIPLINES

PSYCHIATRY

BRUCE L. DANTO

Danto's essay offers a social-psychological framework for examining the patterns of murder in America. Although it would seem from the title that he might stress a purely psychiatric or psychoanalytic approach, his survey of the research on murder reveals patterns which also result from

*the impact of economic and social factors on an individual's psychology.
Danto offers a number of controversial arguments early on in his essay:
He cites research which suggests that "victims may be as strongly
motivated to be killed as their killers are to kill"; furthermore, he
suggests that "all societies and cultures seem to hold homicide as a value
and preserve its various functions." The first of these two controversial
arguments may be called psychological or psychoanalytical; the second,
sociological (or perhaps, anthropological). His essay offers numerous
examples of research which, in his opinion, support these arguments.*

*Since Danto sets out to survey all the major conclusions of
numerous researchers on murder, his essay tends primarily to be a
classification. But, as noted above, he also offers two controversial
arguments which he supports with psychoanalytical profiles. His essay,
therefore, is both a classification and an argument. In summing up others'
research, he often uses lists and synopses—two effective ways of
summarizing large amounts of data. The essay is predominantly objective
in intention, although Danto does include some snippets of personal
experience to support the points he is making. The essay relies on a large
number of terms peculiar to psychology and psychoanalysis and, to a
certain extent, the author assumes that the reader knows these terms well.
Readers outside Danto's disciplines may call such a reliance on terms a
matter of "jargon" (relying on language specific to an in-group), but in a
number of instances he is careful to explain these terms. Nevertheless it
might be helpful to look first through some of the terms glossed at the foot
of each page.*

A Psychiatric View of Those Who Kill

This article reviews some of the known facts about homicide
and killers and some of the research on the psychological aspects of
murderers. However, before this material is presented, note should be
taken of the fact that victims may also play a role in their homicide.
Studies in Baltimore (Van Keuren 1977) and other places point out
that in about 55 percent of all homicide cases the victim and killer
knew one another, and the homicide often arose out of conflicts in
their relationship. Lester and Lester (1975) point out that victims may
be as strongly motivated to be killed as their killers are to kill. Viewed
in this light a homicide may not be an isolated event; it may be an
expression of an integral pattern of a relationship. An additional

feature of the victim-precipitated homicide is the fact that in this type of homicide one can see a close relationship between suicide and murder. Certainly, if the victim seeks his own death, then his behavior toward the killer is provocative and clearly self-destructive.

In our efforts to understand the behavior of murderers, it is important to relate this behavior to aggression. Aggression, an expression or act of attack or hostility, may be defensive or offensive. The former serves the function of enhancing survival; the latter is destructive, unprovoked, and rooted in a person's character.

Aggression serves other purposes as well. For some, it relieves boredom, represents a mode of verbal communication, and can also provide a means for the nonverbal motor discharge of hostile feeling. Aggression develops last in the order of feelings, with love feelings developing first, fear of the world next at about three months of age and finally aggression at age one. For most people, when aggression assumes the form of violence, it provides the final solution to events connected with a conflictual relationship, imagined or real.

Violence and murder have always been prominent in people's minds, while today the news media, toymakers, television, and moviemakers exploit it. Classic tragedy established a tradition for the theater and literature. Even, or especially, in opera, homicide provides excitement and suspense for the entertainment of the audience.

All societies and cultures seem to hold homicide as a value and preserve its various functions by attaching it to cultural practices. Some people do not accept homicide as a part of our life. They protest its existence and try to end its prevalence by moving to ban firearms, capital punishment, life imprisonment, hunting, and the eating of meat. Although common in all societies, these efforts represent ineffective approaches to control a type of behavior and social problem which has deeply rooted origins and feelings, and has not resulted from access to gadgets. An attempt is being made to stop a type of coping behavior which has been time-honored as a way for people to resolve conflicts, yet until we have a better grasp on what causes it and why some people chose to handle their problems and impulses by killing people, we shall find ourselves forever involved in an exercise of futility.

Surprisingly little has been written about the characteristics of murderers and their victims. Wille (1974), Lunde (1976), and Wolfgang (1958) have collected and analyzed some data. A summary of their information follows.

CHARACTERISTICS OF MURDER

Murder occurs more frequently in the heavy business districts of large cities and in the low-grade residential areas around those business centers. The rate is higher during times of prosperity (except for lynchings, which occurred more commonly during the Depression). Henry and Short (1954) held this view and felt that this relationship to economic conditions supported the notion that suicide and homicide are ways people have of coping with frustration.

In his study of about 500 murderers Wolfgang (1958) observed that most murders occurred within a small population subgroup. A subculture of violence° existed in this group; members reacted with violence to insults or slurs (even so-called trivial slights) and carried weapons in anticipation of violence or attacks. They were more likely to interpret daily neutral situations and challenges as threatening. Because weapons were carried, the use of force had the potential for producing serious injury of death. Those deviating from this value system were either ostracized from the subculture or became its victims.

Alcohol plays an important role in homicide whether it occurs in the subculture or the general murderer group. However, this does *not* mean that murderers are necessarily alcoholics. It *does* mean that judgment and control of aggression might be compromised when a person is drinking. Studies have revealed that persons arrested for most violent crimes, generally have, if they were drinking, a urine level of alcohol between .2 and .29 percent—about twice the level required to prove a drunk-driving charge.

RESULTS OF RESEARCH ABOUT MURDERERS

1. Estimates report that from 25 to 67 percent of murderers have a childhood history of violence, that is, they either witnessed it or were victims of it.

° subculture of violence: a situation in which socioeconomic factors (such as poverty, ghettoization, etc.) contribute to the use of force as an escape valve or as a means of settling disputes (see M. E. Wolfgang in Danto's "References" and in "Sources" at the end of this chapter).

2. Results of psychological tests, such as the Thematic Apperception Tests (TAT),° show that murderers have less anger, less fear, less aggression, less awareness of the outcome of an event, and they are less inclined to see control as being due to chance, and more due to power. Surprisingly, there is no difference in the responses of psychotic and nonpsychotic murderers in these tests.

3. Murderers fantasize less about anger, fear, and aggression. It shows in their behavior. They do not express or show much feeling. It might be said that many murderers are emotionally inhibited.

4. Murderers have two distinct methods of coping with emotional tension: they either push back into the unconscious all elements of intense thought or feeling (repression), or they display a behavioral set or expectancy in which they are ready to fight whenever they feel an inner sense of danger arising from their contact with others.

5. Murderers rarely verbalize feelings and, in general, maintain shallow or superficial interpersonal relationships.

6. Many male murderers struggle with deep, inner guilt feelings about sex; they see women as being dangerously seductive. Some attempt to deal with or relieve such sexual guilt feelings by killing a woman. Once she is dead, the killer does not have to feel guilty, have fear of her, or worry about being less powerful than she.

7. Most murderers are between 20 and 40 years of age; today, most are closer to 20.

8. A quarter of all murderers today are women; their victims are usually someone close. In order of greatest frequency, the victims are a husband, a lover, or an older child of the woman.

° Thematic Apperception Test (TAT): a personality analysis test which attempts to probe an individual's unconscious tendencies, desires, etc., by observing the subject's reactions to ambiguous pictures (e.g., two persons, one lying down, the other standing over the first with hands out).

9. From a racial standpoint, a murderer is more likely to be black; ten times more black men than black women are murderers. The black female murder rate is five times higher than the murder rate of white females.

10. It has been observed that fewer than 30 percent of the victims are strangers to the murderer.

11. About 30 percent of all homicides are committed during the process of a felony.

12. Firearms are the chosen murder weapon of either the very young or old. In other cases, 20 percent use knives; for black murderers, the use of knives jumps to about 50 percent.

13. At least 50 percent of the time, the provocative incident which causes the murder is a quarrel, which has occurred within three days of the death.

14. The presence of a classic mental illness is rare among murderers at the time they kill. When present, psychosis° occurs in about 7 percent of the cases. Dissociative reaction,° a type of anxiety state in which the mind becomes explosively overwhelmed or flooded by anxiety, occurs in about 10 percent of the cases in which mental illness exists.

15. About 50 percent of all murders are premeditated. The killer is provoked by a disturbing event which causes him to lose self-esteem or feel less of a man: his wife has sex with another partner, a boss fires him from a job, a neighbor puts him down, and so forth.

16. About 70 percent of the murderers have defective super egos, that is, they have defective consciences. They are insensitive to the wrongness of violence, the importance of another person's life, and the importance of maintaining control and finding the right channels for expressing

○ psychosis: an extremely serious mental disorder in which a *psychotic* person has lost contact with reality.
○ dissociative reaction: a sudden or temporary flight from one's own usual identity.

aggression. These factors are related to the murderer's lack of love and caring experiences.

17. About 13 percent of all murderers become psychotic after killing.

18. Most murderers kill on weekends. July and December are peak months for murders, which commonly occur between 8:00 P.M. and 2:00 A.M.

19. Murderers have higher rates of killing in certain parts of the United States. The South accounts for 31 percent of the population but 44 percent of all the murders committed in this country. The South is followed by the West, then the North Central States, with the lowest rate being in the Northeastern states.

20. Murderers chose men as their victims three times more often than they chose women. Of the men killed by their wives or girlfriends, alcohol has been imbibed by the killer in about 50 percent of the cases.

21. Of the victims, about 25 percent resemble the murderer in that they have a criminal record and are from the lower socioeconomic areas.

22. In terms of what happens after the murder, about two-thirds (66 percent) are in custody within 24 hours; if the murder is not solved within 48 hours, the chance of solving the crime and apprehending the murderer drops remarkably.

23. Following court trial and disposition, 60 percent of the murderers are convicted; the median time served by those convicted of first degree murder is 10.5 years, and for second degree murder, five years.

———————— • ————————

Wille (1974) classified murderers into 10 different types. The first type he called the *depressive killer.* This murderer seldom has a criminal record and does not display antisocial behavior. He may commit suicide, murder, or murder-suicide. He feels that life is hopeless, and he wants to end the suffering of others. In this class of murderer, murder followed by suicide is very common.

The next type of murderer has a psychotic disease, such as schizophrenic reaction, paranoid type. In this disorder, the murderer may be hearing voices that threaten to kill him or that tell him to kill in order to protect himself. He may feel he is aiding the Lord in a mission to rid the world of sin. He feels others are against him and may be following or plotting against him. He kills to prove some type of world or global idea—ridding the world of sin, or protecting himself from imagined enemies.

The third kind of murderer has some type of organic brain damage or condition that may be the result of head trauma caused by an auto accident, epilepsy, brain deterioration from senile brain disease, or from some type of hereditary organic disease which destroys normal brain function.

The fourth type of murderer has a psychopathic personality and displays a history of social maladjustment. He is nonfeeling and insensitive about the needs and rights of others, has a defective conscience and a callous and cynical outlook on the world. Despite his defective conscience, his behavior is confessional; he often leaves telltale evidence and clues to his homicidal act. From the standpoint of ego structure, he has a defective integrative function and does not seem to profit from experience, repeating the same basic mistakes in judgment and control.

The fifth type of murderer has a passive aggressive personality. His life history reveals countless instances in which he expressed great violence when a victim threatened to cut off or reject his dependency needs. A common example of this is seen when a murderer's wife cannot tolerate her marriage to this demanding and violent person and either files for divorce or threatens to do so. Instead of trying to get help to change his way of handling the relationship, he kills the person whom he drove away.

The alcoholic character makes up the sixth type of murderer. In this person, inner aggression is unleashed when the expression-enhancing effect of alcohol is combined with its intoxicating effects (which act on the brain itself). Furthermore, brain damage from chronic alcoholism may occur and produce a rage which is seen with organic brain disease.

The seventh type of murderer has a hysterical personality—and is more likely to be a woman. She is more likely to threaten murder than actually commit it, yet such threats should not be taken lightly. Such persons do not bind anxiety well and may become flooded and overwhelmed by it; they may even appear to be psychotic. The usual diagnosis for such a mental state is *dissociative reaction*, a neurotic disorder which is frequently associated with amnesia about the murder.

The eighth type of murderer in Willie's classification is the child who is a killer. In New York, a two-year-old child killed another child by cutting, and in Finestere, France, a two-year-old killed another child by bashing in his skull with a statue. Such child murderers use methods such as cutting, beating, pushing the victim from a height, drowning, and shooting. When a child is the murderer, his act may be precipitated by an intensification of rivalry in the family, feelings of rejection (resulting, for instance, from being placed in a foster home), some organic or medical problem that may make a child feel intensely inferior (such as growth problems, congenital anomalies, or low IQ), the existence of a learning disorder, or exposure to parental violence with an unconscious identification with it.

On the other hand, Bender (1959) found that children who kill are very impulsive, and all but 3 out of 33 children studied were suffering from schizophrenia, brain disease, or epilepsy. In their background, antecedent events like contact with violent death within the family or close neighborhood residents, pyromania, unfavorable home conditions, learning disorders, or retardation existed.

Suggesting a different factor was Sargent (1962), who found that the child who kills is a person who acts as an agent for an adult, almost as if he acts out the lethal wish of that adult. He may have felt hostility toward the victim but would not have acted on it in a lethal manner without unconscious prompting by the involved adult. When this happens, the murdering child is surprised that the victim is dead, as he really did not mean to kill him.

The ninth type of murderer might be a mentally retarded person. Murder by such persons is rare; but when they do kill, often it is to cover up some abnormal sexual contact they have had with a child. Mass murder by this type of killer is unheard of.

Finally, the tenth type of killer is known as a sex killer. He gains some type of sexual excitement from the act of killing, which may involve mutilation of the body before or after death of the victim. Intercourse as well as acts of cannibalism may be involved—i.e., eating the flesh of the victim or drinking his blood. This type of person is usually psychotic and is not usually a rapist. Sometimes he kills a woman in order to relieve sexual jealousy or to deprive another man; the murder can be also a vehicle to reach the man. He may express latent homosexual impulses by being more concerned about the man's action than the woman's.

Murder by minor sexual offenders, such as window peepers and exhibitionists, is rare. Rare also is murder by one suffering from necrophilia. The necrophilic person is sexually attracted by the putrefactive stench and the coldness of the cadaver.

The adult who kills a child has become a more common type of murderer and constitutes a special area of interest for the Oakland County Child Murders Task Force. What is known about such killers merits examination. Kaplund and Reich (1976) studied 112 cases of child homicide in New York in 1968–69. They found that the victims were predominantly boys and were under five years of age. Two-thirds of the victims were born out of wedlock. The assailants were primarily the mothers. Paramours rarely murdered their own children but did kill the children of their predecessors. The assailants displayed histories of prehomicidal deviant behavior in terms of alcoholism, drug abuse, and criminal behavior. Severe mental illness and suicide attempts were rare. They murdered by means of kicking and beating, primarily, and such behavior was consistent with impulsive and explosive rage rather than with premeditation.

Resnick (1969) studied parents who kill their children. About 30 percent of the victims were under six months of age, which led him to conclude that the homicidal parents were women who suffered either a post partum depression or psychosis after delivery. If the children were older, it was found that their parental killers perceived them as being defective for some reason, real or imagined. Although the victims were evenly divided between the sexes, there were twice as many mothers who killed as fathers, a wider range in age, from 20–50 years, in contrast to men who fell between 25–35 years, and about 60 percent of all murdering parents were psychotic by psychiatric diagnosis. As a method of murder, fathers used striking, squeezing, and stabbing; mothers used drowning, suffocation, and gassing.

He felt they killed for specific reasons. *Altruistic Filicide* ° occurred when the parent wanted to spare the child from suffering from a real or imagined condition or from abandonment when the parent

○ filicide: killing one's child.

committed suicide. This was consistent with observations made by D. J. West (1966). The next type of filicide was *Unwanted Child*. In this type, the parent wanted to eliminate a child who was either illegitimate, a product of an extramarital affair, or was viewed by the parent as being in the way of some future aspiration. In *Spouse Revenge Filicide* the child was killed to deprive the spouse and cause suffering through the loss of a favorite child. *Accidental Filicide* is an inevitable consequence of a battered child syndrome. Frequently, it occurs as a result of intense rage when physical discipline is being administered. The final type he classified was *Acutely Psychotic Filicide*, one in which the parent is severely mentally disturbed. Running throughout all of these parent murders of children is a common denominator—anger and rage directed toward a child who is an object upon which anger felt toward the murderer's parents, spouse, or sibling has been displaced.

Among murderers who kill children none seem to be more feared than sexual molesters of children who are strangers to them. In my experience, child molesters rarely kill. In fact, they show violence toward their child victims in less than 3 percent of all reported molestings. However, the murder of a molested child generates tremendous anxiety in the community. The molester who kills is a person whose homicidal direction involves some interesting background. Many who become psychotic and subsequently kill are individuals who have been reared in a home atmosphere in which they have been a victim of homosexual assault by their fathers. Frequently, they commit a burglary before they abduct, molest, and kill a child. Not infrequently, they harbor deep resentment toward children because of sibling rivalry and competitive resentment they felt toward a sister or brother. In other cases, they kill a child as a way of striking back at the adult world. In this way, they deprive another parent, who represents a transference object, of a child to satisfy resentment they felt for being deprived of parents. Thus, the unconscious target is one or more parents who are survivor victims of homicide.

Guttmacher (1973) studied 175 murderers and classified them in terms of psychiatric diagnoses. Forty percent of his group suffered from a psychosis involving a number of serious conditions or illnesses that impaired mental functioning to the degree that the person could not handle the ordinary demands of daily living. Although paranoid schizophrenia is the most common of these diagnoses, mental patients, on the whole, have no greater incidence of homicidal behavior than the general population. Guttmacher's classification was not based on sane vs. insane. Rather, he attempted to classify murderers by psychiatric diagnosis so that he could apply psychological theory to explain their murderous behavior and see if treatment was possible. One-third of his group of psychotic patients had been hospitalized in the past because of their psychoses.

Guttmacher utilized psychoanalytic theory to develop a classification system based on psychodynamic concepts rather than the traditional descriptive psychiatric diagnoses with which he had initiated his studies. He concluded that the average murderer was free of any prominent psychopathology or mental illness, but has not identified with parental social values and conscience, and for that reason has a defective conscience. He comes from a socially disadvantaged family and, as a child, experienced emotional deprivation or inadequate nurturing. Such experiences cause the killer to fail to appreciate the deprivation caused when he kills. His own experience of deprivation causes him extreme frustration, and this can lead to murder.

Guttmacher's second type of murderer is sociopathic.° His background involves a physically abusive father who was rejecting to a seductive, hysterical mother. Parental marital disharmony is usually found. The experience of childhood cruelty from his father makes the murderer behave cruelly toward others as an adult in order to achieve the feeling of revenge. His childhood cruelty to animals points to his future unconscionable violent aggression toward others as an adult. His adolescent history reveals delinquency, truancy, and running away from home. As he grows into adulthood, he will have a history of criminal offenses.

The alcoholic murderer according to Guttmacher is one who, when sober, is able to control his aggressive feelings. However, alcohol unleashes his violent aggression as controls are either removed or dangerously compromised. Prior to his act of murder, he has lost sexual potency, employment, or chances for advancement because of his drinking; and he imagines that he is losing his wife or love interest to another, worthier, man. Convinced of his woman's infidelity, his jealousy becomes pathological. While intoxicated, he kills her.

Guttmacher's next type is called the avenging murderer. This person kills in response to the sudden withdrawal of sexual interest

○ sociopathic: showing hatred of society.

by a spouse or lover. The relationship with the victim has been ambivalent. When sex is withdrawn, the hatred grows to the point that the killer directs his aggression to the destruction of the love object.

Guttmacher described the schizophrenic murderer and the sadistic murderer. The schizophrenic murderer kills his victims in accordance with his paranoid delusions and hallucinations. The sadistic murderer kills to achieve sexual pleasure and chooses victims with specific occupations or qualities (prostitutes, teachers, elderly women, children, or those who are chronically ill). He sees his victims as being objects for his pleasure—not as fellow human beings. His pleasure may come from abusing, mutilating, or killing his victims. He has been a loner and unable to break strong emotional ties to his mother. His daydreams and fantasies are rich and ever-flowing; usually, there have been no normal sexual experiences. For the sadistic murderer, there is no history of identified mental illness.

According to Lunde, (1976) there is a difference between a mass murderer and a serial murderer. The mass murderer is almost always psychotic from a legal standpoint (legally insane). He kills a number of victims in a single episode and chooses victims he does not know well. However, they may have symbolic significance to him.

The serial murderer, on the other hand, kills one person at a time over a long period of time. He may know the victim quite well, or at least know a particular type of victim he is seeking (spouse, child, certain type of worker, blonde-haired person, etc.). Lunde considered the serial murderer to be one who might know his victim and does not have a history of diagnosed mental illness.

I would add to this discussion that the serial murderer usually has an obsessive-compulsive pattern to his killing; he needs to repeat the style and pattern of killing, as well as his choice of victim. His homicidal behavior is repetitive and frequently tells a story of his conflicts. For example, in the Oakland County (Michigan) child killings, the murderer selected children in the same age range, sodomized the boys and forced the girls into oral sexual acts, was gentle in his method of killing, washed the bodies and dressed the victims, and always left the body where it was sure to be found. He acted out a story in which he replaced the natural parents of the child he abducted, committed a sexually perverse act on the child, then murdered him or her; in so doing, he showed the parents how poorly they protected their child and how great their loss could be. The parents are his victims. He kills children to avenge some childhood hurt induced by his own parents toward whom he is now venting angry feelings. He checks on the parental loss by attending the child's funeral or following it on television. We know this because he dropped a funeral visitor's card where the body of the first murdered child was found.

Tanay (1976) offers other observations about murderers, and sees three types. When a person kills against his conscious wishes and the murder is carried out during an altered state of consciousness, it is *ego dystonic* murder. When this occurs, part of the psychic structure is split off from the rest of the personality. This process, called dissociation, may be induced by psychological, physiological, or pharmacological factors. A second type of murderer, one remarkably less common, he calls *ego syntonic.* In this type of murder, the killer deliberately chooses homicide as his method of coping with the important psychological issue. He accepts violence as a method of resolving conflict. Finally, the third type of murderer Tanay calls *psychotic;* his description is consistent with what Guttmacher and Lunde described as murder by a schizophrenic person.

Tanay's approach to murder focuses on ego states or impairment of the rational part of the mind and on the act itself, and does not deal with other personality features of either the murderer, the significance of his victim, or the social forces which might produce the murder.

Abrahamsen (1973) observed that murderers have certain psychological characteristics. They cannot spell correctly and do so by the way the word sounds. They display deep feelings of revenge and fantasize grandiose accomplishments. They feel extreme loneliness, withdrawal, distress, helplessness, fears, loss of self-esteem, and feelings of insignificance. As children, they were sexually overstimulated because they witnessed parental intercourse or slept with parents. They reflect a blurred self-image and are suggestible and impressionable. They cannot handle frustration or withstand it; this causes a need to release hostility. They are powerless to change their self-centeredness into healthy ideals and conscience. Because of this impairment, they fall into dependency states and develop a contempt for authority. They display suicidal tendencies with depression and see the victim as a composite image of themselves. There is also a history of antisocial behavior and threats of violence.

Both Tanay and Abrahamsen feel that the murderer is a particular type of person, with each type having certain well-defined characteristics; neither examines the role of the victim or the social forces that have acted on the killer. There is no room for interaction between killer and victim in such theories, and no vehicle for explaining the different motives and needs of murderers, as well as the dramas their murderous behavior reveals. Furthermore, Dr. Abrahamsen sees misspelling as being important, whereas most observers of criminals in general would agree that factors such as sound educational achievement is sorely lacking in their backgrounds, and would not set murderers apart from other criminals.

There have been efforts to correlate electroencephalogram (e.e.g.)° findings and psychiatric conditions or criminal activities like homicide. The most widely discussed finding on e.e.g. has been the 6–14 per second positive spike pattern° in the temporal area. Gibbs feels this is a correlate of thalamic and hypothalamic° epilepsy, one found in adolescents during sleep. When such cases have been reviewed it has been shown that psychodynamic° factors were responsible for the crimes, not organic factors. Any other than coincidental factor relationship between e.e.g. finding and psychiatric condition as it relates to criminal behavior or homicide is either purely statistical or inferential and is not consistent with a real causal relationship (Lester and Lester, 1975).

Kutash et al. (1978) discussed results of psychological tests and concluded that information from them has been less than significant, as the results have not been correlated with clinical data. This has been especially true for studies of Rorschach° responses by murderers. The latter test had been used to study movement responses, color shading responses, external restraints, body, family murder, murderers in comparison to suicides, and prediction of murder.

○ electroencephalogram (e.e.g.): test which traces electric charges in the brain, and has diagnostic value for some physical and mental disorders.

○ spike pattern: the peak or variation in the wave pattern on an e.e.g.

○ thalamic and hypothalamic: refer to sections of the brain involved in emotional life; the former is involved in sensing pain or pleasure, while the latter may be considered a control center.

○ psychodynamic: relating human behavior and motivation to responses to the environment.

○ Rorschach Test: a psychoanalytical test in which a subject reacts to a set of standard inkblot patterns. A psychiatrist studies these reactions as a means of discerning personality traits or attitudes.

Kahn (1967) studied Rorschach responses by murderers in terms of reality testing. These responses correlated to findings of legal insanity as determined by forensic specialists. However, it threw no more light on the murderer as a person or phenomenon than did studies on intelligence factors (Deiker, 1973).

Some studies have linked clinical material along with raw data from the protocols° (Resnick, 1969). In this way better insight is available regarding the psychodynamics of the murderer. In the study by Satten et al. (1960) ten murderers displayed impairment in dealing with color. This means that patients studied expressed their trouble in making clearcut boundaries between fantasy and reality. In their responses to the TAT, there was striking evidence of primitive and murderous hostility even though their stories were brief and constricted. Tested murderers rationalized murder in their themes on the basis that the killer had been provoked into it. As they related their stories and responses, there was little accompanying affect. Significantly, although those patients tested denied conscious fantasy of homicide or ideas of murder, such material was clearly seen on their responses to test items and stimuli.

In a similar study, Miller and Looney (1974) studied murderers who seem to dehumanize others. Their findings indicate that such killers fail to see people as humans. They had trouble seeing if the figure was alive or dead in the TAT drawings. They failed to demonstrate an awareness of either life or death or that people are seen as being immortal and godlike and incapable of being dead.

Kutash et al. (1978) revealed that for the catathymic type killer, one who suddenly experiences an overwhelming intense type of emotional reaction like rage, the F column° is tall and brittle on Rorschach responses. This result means that there is little intrapsychic° or emotional stimulation. For this person there is a rigid ego which is prone to sudden disintegration under meaningful or significant stress. This sudden breakdown is seen in many murders where there is psychosis or significant psychopathology, schizophrenic reaction, or a schizo-affective or paranoid type.

These writers (Kutash et al., 1978) feel secure in the knowledge that the Rorschach test offers the psychological investigator

○ protocols: the procedures or profiles connected with case studies.
○ F column: one of the measures of the responses to a Rorschach Test.
○ intrapsychic: within the mind.

the opportunity to record such responses of aggressive feeling as killing, explosions, blood, death, or fighting. "Integration of specific content with the specific stimulus pull of the various cards further clarifies the in-depth conflicts. Both the ability to empathize and the press of primitive impulses are extremely relevant findings brought out with clarity by the Rorschach." Despite the absolute merit of this test, it does not reveal the significant surface factors or psychodynamics. The latter information can be obtained from the TAT or Blackie Test.° Among tests they found to be of little value were the MMPI° and other personality inventory type tests. However, they felt figure drawings tests were often helpful. Kutash and his group cautioned that all psychological tests are beneficial to throw light on why people kill providing that the test results are integrated with the psychopathology of the crime.

Another way of classifying murderers was provided by Miller and Looney (1974). As a base for their system, they focused on the degree to which the killer dehumanizes his victim. They divided homicides into (1) high risk with total and permanent victim dehumanization, (2) high risk with partial and transient dehumanization, and (3) low risk with transient and partial dehumanization. Although this system could not be applied to forensic diagnostic problems, it could offer a judge psychological factors and issues in regard to pre-sentence psychiatric evaluations. It does offer a view of the killer in terms of how he sees his victim and how he relates to that victim. Over the years as a police officer and psychiatrist who regularly faces dangerous and violent persons, I can attest to the importance of looking for clinical signs in a person who gives me the feeling I am being dehumanized. I look for blank expressions, gazes which pass through or at me as if I were a lamp or wall or clear glass window pane. If that appearance is accompanied by little or no affect and an ice-cold emotional remoteness, then I know I am either in trouble or must exercise great caution and care not to act provocatively or in any threatening manner.

○ Blackie Test: psychoanalytical test for the study of sexual development. Its full title, usually with a different spelling for the key word, is "The Blacky Pictures: A Technique for the Exploration of Personality Dynamics."
○ MMPI Test: the Minnesota Multiphasic Personality Inventory. It consists of 560 true/false questions; the analysis of the individual's responses offers an assessment of personality adjustment. (Sample: "At times I see things that other people do not see.")

Revitch (1975, 1977) has developed a classification system which is easy to follow and quite helpful. He saw *Environmentally Stimulated Homicides* as resulting from social pressures and a weakening of authority and social controls. Examples of these in terms of military events like the massacres in Vietnam and strife in Iran and other Middle Eastern countries appear daily in the newspapers. Under social disintegration of this order, violence flourishes on a broad social basis. Similarly, when violence constantly occurs on the streets, values about the importance of a life diminish and the aged and others who are otherwise helpless become targets on a broad scale.

Revitch defines as *Situational Homicides* those which occur in a stressful situation or relationship. They may occur impulsively or with premeditation and may be adaptive or maladaptive. They may even serve a logical purpose. Usually, interactional conflicts are involved in this type of homicide.

Impulsive Homicides are defined by Revitch as those which involve poor impulse control, possibly a multiplicity of antisocial acts; they can also involve homicides that are diffuse, poorly structured, and are either premeditated or unpremeditated. The offenders display a lifestyle which is unstructured and lacking in direction and predictability. Psychologically, they show looseness of personality integration. Certainly Richard Speck, who murdered several nurses in Chicago, is an excellent example of this type of killer.

Under *Catathymic Homicides* ° Revitch and others included those killers who kill under the influence or stimulation of ideas that are charged with intense feelings based on a strong wish, fear, or ambivalent striving. One example of this type of psychiatric state is schizophrenic reaction, schizoaffective° type. Some hysterical personalities would fall into this category as well.

Another interesting feature associated with killers, according to psychiatrist Irwin Finkelstein (in a personal conversation) is that many of them act out a rescuer fantasy before the homicide. A girl

○ catathymic: an emotional reaction directed against persons who symbolize a disturbing element in the patient's life. For example, a suppressed hatred of the father may come out as rebellion against a teacher.

○ schizoaffective: a mixture of schizophrenic and affective (manic-depressive) symptoms. Schizophrenia is a severe psychotic condition, marked by delusions, hallucinations, loss of contact with reality, and extreme disturbance of emotional balance.

who knew a boy who killed a rabbi right after morning Sabbath services reported that the killer had been firing into a couch in her apartment the night before. At that time he told her and others of his plan to kill the rabbi. No one stopped him or heard his pleas for control to be brought in from some outside resource. In another case in which I was involved a very disturbed man, when angry, would blow up appliances in his home with a military rifle. It had been taken away from him by his father, but he found where it was hidden and brought it back home. When violent at work he would become involved in fights. As a draftsman he had held 12 jobs in seven years and had been involved in 27 fights in that period of time. One night after his wife failed to serve him dinner first, he began shooting up his home. She left with the children, and the police were called. He saw this as sport and began firing at them. He killed two officers, wounded two others, an innocent bystander, and a boy who was watching television in his own home nearby. He surrendered, was acquitted subsequently due to insanity, and committed suicide in the Forensic Center.

This material clearly illustrates the fact that many violent and homicidal persons give early warning signs through their behavior. In my experience, these individuals are psychotic and usually suffering from either a schizophrenic reaction or paranoid type of personality trait disturbance. They are asking for help from others and communicating their need for control. When a homicide occurs, it is because that help and control has not been forthcoming and their cry for help has been unheard and unmet.

From my discussion, it is apparent that there have been many approaches to studying the psychological and psychodynamic factors in those who kill. Among those of us who deal with killers, study them, and treat them there has been a considerable move away from classical and traditional medical, psychiatric, and sociological models. Despite many insights that have developed from such research, there has been precious little money, talent or time devoted to this growing problem concerning the killer in our society. The incidence keeps rising and the number of victims are countless, yet there has been little governmental interest to turn to the places where killers can be found for volunteer studies, namely, the prisons. Our country has the greatest number available but the least amount of interest in turning to them for answers as to cause and solution.

REFERENCES

ABRAHAMSEN, D. 1973. *The Murdering Mind.* New York: Harper.

BENDER, L. 1959. "Children and Adolescents who Kill." *American Journal of Psychiatry* 116:510–13.

DEIKER, T. E. 1973. "Wais Characteristics of Indicted Male Murderers." *Psychological Reports* 32:1066.

GUTTMACHER, M. 1973. *The Mind of the Murderer.* Selected Libraries Reprint Series. New York: Arno Press.

HENRY, A. AND J. SHORT. 1954. *Suicide and Homicide.* Glencoe, Illinois: The Free Press.

KAHN, M. W. 1967. "Correlates of Rorschach Reality Adherence in the Assessment of Murderers who Plead Insanity." *Journal of Protective Techniques and Personality Assessment* 31:44–47.

KAPLUND, D. AND R. REICH. 1976. "The Murdered Child and his Killers." *American Journal of Psychiatry* 133(7):809–813.

KUTASH, I. L., B. SAMUEL, AND L. S. SCHLESINGER & ASSOCIATES. 1978. *Violence: Perspectives on Murder and Aggression.* San Francisco: Jossey-Bass Publishers.

LESTER, D. AND G. LESTER. 1975. *Crimes of Passion: Murder and the Murderer.* Chicago: Nelson Hall.

LUNDE, D. T. 1976. *Murder and Madness.* San Francisco: San Francisco Book Co.

MILLER, D. AND J. LOONEY. 1974. "The Prediction of Adolescent Homicide; Episodic Dyscontrol and Dehumanization." *American Journal of Psychoanalysis* 34(3):187–98.

RESNICK, P. 1969. "Child Murder by Parents." *American Journal of Psychiatry* 126:325–34.

REVITCH, E. 1975. "Psychiatric Evaluation and Classification of Antisocial Activities." *Disturbance of Nervous System* 36:419–21.

REVITCH, E. 1977. "Classification of Offenders for Prognostic and Dispositional Evaluation." *Bulletin of Academy Law & Psychiatry* 8:1–11.

SARGENT, D. 1962. "Children Who Kill." *Social Work* 7(1):35–42.

SATTEN, J., K. A. MENNINGER, AND M. MAYMAN. 1960. "Murder Without Apparent Motive: A Study in Personality Disorganization." *American Journal of Psychiatry* 117:48–53.

TANAY, E. 1976. *The Murderers.* Indianapolis: Bobbs-Merrill.

VAN KEUREN, R. T. 1977. "Victim-Precipitated Homicide." *Vita* 4(2):19–21.

WEST, D. J. 1966. *Murder Followed by Suicide.* Cambridge: Harvard University Press.

WILLE, W. 1974. *Citizens Who Commit Murder.* St. Louis: Warren Greene.

WOLFGANG, M. E. 1958. *Patterns in Criminal Homicide.* Philadelphia: University of Pennsylvania Press.

LAW

JANET RIFKIN

This selection is taken from the author's longer essay, "Toward a Theory of Law and Patriarchy," which appeared in the Harvard Women's Law Journal *in 1980. To a certain extent, its appearance in a "new" law journal devoted to studies of women and the law reflects Rifkin's general argument in her essay: that American society is partriarchal— "any kind of group organization in which males hold dominant power and determine what part females shall and shall not play"—and that the law has evolved to support that patriarchy.*

In this excerpt, her specific approach is to demonstrate how the law evolved in order to separate the "realms" of men and women—men in the marketplaces of history, and women at home. Rifkin uses selected quotations and examples, primarily from historical texts, to demonstrate her argument that the law evolved as a specific response to the competition of men and women in the marketplace. In addition, she glances at another important argument, that law in a patriarchy has usually been defined as something entirely "natural," i.e., the way things are and must be. In that way, the status quo seems inevitable and unchangeable.

Patriarchy, Law and Capitalism

In *Law and the Rise of Capitalism,* Michael Tigar and Madeline Levy show that the Thirteenth Century in England and in continental Europe "saw the creation and application of specific rules about contracts, property and procedure which strengthened the power of the rising bourgeoisie."[1] They show that these "rules were fashioned in the context of a legal ideology which identified freedom of action for businessmen with natural law and natural reason."[2]

In their study, however, Tigar and Levy do not examine the emerging law in relation to women. They do not discuss, for example, how the rise of capitalism profoundly changed the nature of work, the family, and the role of women. I maintain that law, which emerged "as a form of rationality appropriate to the social relations generated by the emergence of entrepreneurial capitalism,"[3] retained the pre-existing hierarchy of masculine authority and made more explicit the subordination of women to men by increasingly excluding women from working in trades and relegating them to the private world of the home, which itself also became more and more nonproductive.

The feudal world, which was organized for war, was essentially a masculine world.[4] Although laws and custom put wives under the power of their husbands,[5] records indicate, nonetheless, participation by some noble women in social, political and legal activities.[6] Women also demonstrated great productive capacity when society was organized on the basis of family and domestic industry.[7] At the end of the Fourteenth Century, one-fourth of the cloth woven in York was produced by women.[8] Laws, restrictive in some spheres, there encouraged women's economic participation. The Act of 1363, for example, declared that:

> [T]he intent of the king and of his council is that women, that is to say brewers, bakers, carders and spinners, and workers as well of wool as of linen-clothing . . . . and all other that do use and work all handiworks, may freely use and work as they have done before this time.[9]

This attitude began to change, however, during the next century as legal regulations promulgated by various guilds became increasingly restrictive of women's participation. Many of these laws reflected the blatant threat of competition to the male workers. In Bristol in 1461, it was complained that weavers employed their wives, daughters, and maidens "by the which many and divers of the king's liege people, likely men to do the king service in his wars and in the defence of this his land, and sufficiently learned in the said craft, goeth vagrant and unoccupied, and may not have their labour to their living."[10]

Sometimes a guild prohibited employment of women, though generally widows could work in their husband's craft. As late as 1726, the Baker's craft in Aberdeen which was distressed by the competition of women who used their own ovens and sold the produce themselves passed a law which mandated a severe fine to any freeman in the baking trade who allowed a woman to use his oven.[11] Other craft guilds were equally restrictive of women working in trades. Rachel Baxter, for example, was admitted to the tailor's craft provided "that she shall . . . have only the privilege of mantua-making,° and no ways make stays, or import the same to sell from any other place . . . and it is hereby declared that thi [sic] presents to be no precedent to any woman in tyme coming."[12]

Thus, with the emergence of capitalism and through the power of legal regulation, women were affected in several fundamental ways: individual wages were substituted for family earnings, enabling men to organize themselves in the competition of the labor market without sharing with the women of their families all the benefits derived through their combination;[13] the withdrawal of wage-earners from home life to work upon the premises of the masters and the prevention of the employment of the wage-earner's wife in her husband's occupation,[14] and the rapid increase of wealth which allowed the upper class women to withdraw altogether from business.[15]

Whereas the system of family industry united labor and capital in one person or family group, capitalism brought them into conflict and competition; men and women struggled with each other to secure work and wages.[16] The keystone of the male journeymen's superior economic position in capitalism lay in their ability to restrict their own numbers by promulgating and enforcing laws which specifically limited numbers, imposed long apprenticeship programs and limited the number of apprentices.[17]

The pre-existing patriarchal culture supported historically by kinship bonds and custom was transformed in capitalism through law in the service of new economic interest.

> [C]ustomary and traditional modes of conceptualizing bonds of obligation and duty were of diminishing relevance in bourgeois society, where people experienced a growing and radical separation between public life and private life. . . . [F]amily, and personal dependence begin to dissolve and crumble under the corrosive impact of the single universalist principles of social solidarity underlying capitalist social relations—*exchange.*[18]

The role of law in early capitalism was to help create a climate in which production for exchange could thrive. To accomplish this, law, always a symbol of male authority, fostered competition between women and men and severely limited female participation in the world of market production. Law became a primary and powerful tool of the rising bourgeoisie. Legal regulations were enacted which

---

○ mantua: woman's cloak or gown.

symbolized a continuation of the male authority of the past and which transformed and updated patriarchal society to serve new capitalistic interests. Laws were used increasingly to restrict women from working in trades, relegating them to the private world of the home. Thus, legal rules helped to create a social order where women were excluded from the public world of production exchange. And these new laws, justified in the name of the natural order, were accepted as an accurate vision of the world.

NOTES

1. M. TIGAR & M. LEVY, *Law and the Rise of Capitalism* 6 (1978).
2. *Id.*
3. FRASER, "The Legal Theory We Need Now," 37 *Socialist Rev.* 147, 154 (1978).
4. D. STENTON, *The English Woman In History* 29 (1957).
5. 2 F. POLLOCK & F. MAITLAND, *The History of English Law* 399–436 (2d ed., 1898).
6. D. STENTON, *supra* note 4, at 29–38.
7. A. CLARK, *Working Life of Women in the Seventeenth Century* 290 (1919).
8. E. LIPSON, 1 *The Economic History of England* 359 (7th ed. 1937).
9. *Id.* at 361.
10. *Id.*
11. E. BAIN, *Merchant and Craft Guilds* 228 (1887).
12. *Id.* at 257.
13. A. CLARK, *supra* note 7, at 296.
14. *Id.*
15. *Id.*
16. *Id.* at 297–98.
17. *Id.* at 298.
18. Fraser, *supra* note 3, at 154–55 (emphasis in original).

DOCUMENTARY MATERIALS

THE BIBLE

THE APOCRYPHAL SCRIPTURES

The phrase "Susanna and the Elders" has evolved into a shorthand expression in literature and art for a situation in which a woman is the victim of unjust accusation. (There are dramatic and fascinating portrayals of Susanna's story in paintings by the Italian Tintoretto and the American Thomas Hart Benton, as well as in a poem by Wallace Stevens). The anonymous author skillfully creates a trap for Susanna with both circumstantial and direct evidence. Such evidence "works" because it meshes with social expectations about men's and women's roles. Obviously, there should be no male present, except perhaps her husband, when Susanna bathes, but when the elders spy on her, they rely on their social standing and power to protect them from accusation. The elders give direct *but false eyewitness evidence (they wrestled with the "young man") as well as* indirect, *or circumstantial, evidence (the garden door was open). Their case against Susanna is therefore of a wider scope than against Phillipps's apprentice, who was convicted solely on circumstantial evidence.*

Susanna's story appears in the Apocryphal Scriptures, the ancient Semitic books which lack the authoritative covers of the Old Testament. Disagreements among religious scholars and leaders over many centuries have relegated a number of stories like Susanna's to such unofficial status. But as Nicholas Lange points out (see "Sources"), this story has always been popular with both Christian and Jewish readers, as well as writers and painters.

The History of Susanna

There dwelt a man in Babylon, called Joacim. And he took a wife, whose name was Susanna, the daughter of Chelcias, a very fair woman, and one that feared the Lord. Her parents also were righteous, and taught their daughter according to the law of Moses.

Now Joacim was a great, rich man, and had a fair garden joining unto his house, and to him resorted the Jews, because he was more honourable than all others.

The same year were appointed two of the ancients of the people to be judges, such as the Lord spake of, that wickedness came from Babylon from ancient judges, who seemed to govern the people. These kept much at Joacim's house; and all that had any suits in law came unto them.

Now, when the people departed away at noon, Susanna went into her husband's garden to walk. And the two elders saw her going in every day and walking, so that their lust was inflamed toward her.

And they perverted their own mind, and turned away their eyes, that they might not look unto heaven, nor remember just judgments. And albeit they both were wounded with her love; yet durst not one show another his grief. For they were ashamed to declare their lust, that they desired to have to do with her. Yet they watched diligently from day to day to see her.

And the one said to the other: "Let us now go home, for it is dinner-time."

So when they were gone out, they parted the one from the other, and, turning back again, they came to the same place, and, after they had asked one another the cause, they acknowledged their lust; then appointed they a time both together when they might find her alone.

And it fell out as they watched a fit time, she went in as before, with two maids only, and she was desirous to wash herself in the garden, for it was hot. And there was nobody there save the two elders that had hid themselves, and watched her.

Then she said to her maids: "Bring me oil and washing-balls, and shut the garden doors, that I may wash me." And they did as she bade them, and shut the garden doors, and went out themselves at privy doors to fetch the things that she had commanded them; but they saw not the elders, because they were hid.

Now, when the maids were gone forth, the two elders rose up, and ran unto her, saying: "Behold the garden doors are shut, that no man can see us, and we are in love with thee; therefore consent unto us, and lie with us. If thou wilt not, we will bear witness against thee, that a young man was with thee, and therefore thou didst send away thy maids from thee."

Then Susanna sighed, and said: "I am straitened on every side; for if I do this thing, it is death unto me, and if I do it not, I cannot escape your hands. It is better for me to fall into your hands, and not to do it, than to sin in the sight of the Lord."

With that Susanna cried with a loud voice; and the two elders cried out against her.

Then ran the one and opened the garden door.

So when the servants of the house heard the cry in the garden, they rushed in at a privy door, to see what was done unto her. But when the elders had declared their matter, the servants were greatly ashamed, for there never was such a report made of Susanna.

And it came to pass the next day, when the people were assembled to her husband Joacim, the two elders came also full of mischievous imagination against Susanna to put her to death, and said before the people: "Send for Susanna, the daughter of Chelcias, Joacim's wife." And so they sent.

So she came with her father and mother, her children, and all her kindred.

Now Susanna was a very delicate woman, and beauteous to behold. And these wicked men commanded to uncover her face (for she was covered) that they might be filled with her beauty. Therefore her friends, and all that saw her, wept.

Then the two elders stood up in the midst of the people, and laid their hands upon her head. And she, weeping, looked up towards heaven, for her heart trusted in the Lord.

And the elders said: "As we walked in the garden alone, this woman came in with two maids, and shut the garden doors, and sent the maids away. Then a young man, who there was hid, came unto her, and lay with her. Then we that stood in a corner of the garden, seeing this wickedness, ran unto them. And when we saw them together, the man we could not hold, for he was stronger than we, and opened the door, and leaped out. But having taken this woman, we asked who the young man was, but she would not tell us. These things do we testify."

Then the assembly believed them, as those that were the elders and judges of the people; so they condemned her to death.

Then Susanna cried out with a loud voice, and said: "O everlasting God, that knowest the secrets, and knowest all things before they be; thou knowest that they have borne false witness against me, and, behold, I must die; whereas I never did such things as these men have maliciously invented against me."

And the Lord heard her voice.

Therefore when she was led to be put to death, the Lord raised up the holy spirit of a young youth, whose name was Daniel, who cried with a loud voice: "I am clear from the blood of this woman!"

Then all the people turned them towards him, and said: "What mean these words that thou hast spoken?"

So he, standing in the midst of them, said: "Are ye such fools, ye sons of Israel, that, without examination or knowledge of the truth, ye have condemned a daughter of Israel? Return again to the place of judgment, for they have borne false witness against her."

Wherefore all the people turned again in haste, and the elders said unto him: "Come, sit down among us, and show it us, seeing God hath given thee the honour of an elder."

Then said Daniel unto them: "Put these two aside one far from another, and I will examine them."

So when they were put asunder one from another, he called one of them, and said unto him: "O thou that art waxen old in wickedness, now thy sins, which thou hast committed aforetime, are come to light. For thou hast pronounced false judgment and hast condemned the innocent, and hast let the guilty go free, albeit the Lord saith: 'The innocent and righteous shalt thou not slay.' Now, then, if thou hast seen her, tell me, under what tree sawest thou them companying together?" Who answered: "Under a mastick-tree."°

And Daniel said: "Very well; thou hast lied against thine own head, for even now the angel of God hath received the sentence of God to cut thee in two."

So he put him aside, and commanded to bring the other, and said unto him: "O thou seed of Chanaan, and not of Juda, beauty hath deceived thee, and lust hath perverted thine heart. Thus have ye dealt with the daughters of Israel, and they for fear companied with you; but the daughter of Juda would not abide your wickedness. Now therefore tell me, under what tree didst thou take them companying together?" Who answered: "Under a holm-tree."°

Then said Daniel unto him: "Well, thou hast also lied against thine own head, for the angel of God waiteth with the sword to cut thee in two, that he may destroy you."

With that all the assembly cried out with a loud voice, and praised God, who saveth them that trust in him. And they arose against the two elders (for Daniel had convicted them of false witness by their own mouth), and according to the law of Moses, they did unto them in such sort as they maliciously intended to do to their neighbor: and they put them to death. Thus the innocent blood was saved the same day.

Therefore Chelcias and his wife praised God for their daughter Susanna, with Joacim her husband, and all the kindred, because there was no dishonesty found in her.

From that day forth was Daniel had in great reputation in the sight of the people.

° mastick-tree: Mediterranean evergreen of the cashew family.
° holm-tree: a holly.

JOURNALISM

CASES FROM THE *NEW YORK TIMES*

This section consists of five newspaper articles drawn from the list of cases compiled by Keith Krause to facilitate studying and writing about historical murder cases (see "Assignment 6"). The articles demonstrate that there are at least as many ways of writing about murders as committing them, a sobering conclusion with which you may agree after reading these pieces which span a century of the New York Times. *Among the five is one of the editorials on the "Kelsey Tar and Feather Outrage," the subject of the "Student Essay" which closes this chapter.*

The murders represented here have psychological, sociological, and even folkloric implications. In the Kelsey Case, a young man's poetry and courtship are rejected by a woman whose boyfriend and accomplices then turn to vicious revenge. (For the full details of the case, see the "Student Essay.") The "Staten Island Mystery" involves love and competition as well, but in this instance bigamy also plays a dangerous role. (Note the Times'*s use of euphemism: When the article states that there were "evidences of malpractice," it is using nineteenth-century shorthand for abortion.) Both the "Philadelphia Poisoning Ring" and the "Joseph Aronowitz Case" focus on organized crime, although the trial testimonies for both indicate a great deal of disorganization and in-fighting. The "Luther Boddy Case" concentrates on an individual's crime, but this article from the* Times *demonstrates how the "outlaw" can generate a "folk" status amid tremendous public and official interest. For instance, were there really, as this and other articles about the case insist, 40,000 police officers and deputies looking for Boddy? (Could Boddy have become a "Billy the Kid" in another era?)*

The last three selections rely on a journalistic approach, one in which the reporter gets down who–what–where–when as soon as possible. The Kelsey selection is an editorial, recording not only facts and events but also opinions, inferences, and interpretations. The selection on the Staten Island incident comes closest to what we today would call a feature article since it traces the "history" of the case. Although we expect more subjective writing in editorials, notice that attitudes toward the subject and cultural stereotypes form an important part of all five pieces. The Times'*s assessment of what constitutes a "fact," and the extent of its own reporters' involvement in a case, also change over the years.*

Kelsey Tar and Feather Outrage

New York Times, *October 17, 1875*

THE KELSEY TRAGEDY

The trial of Banks and Sammis for assault and battery upon Charles G. Kelsey, at Huntington, Long Island, has resulted in their acquittal. There is strong reason to believe that after the mob had tarred and feathered the unfortunate Kelsey, he was subsequently foully murdered. Probably the murder was committed not by the men who were prominent in the tar and feather outrage, but by still more brutal ruffians, who were stimulated by the success with which a mob had assaulted a single man, to the commission of the graver crime. The evidence at the recent trial, including the admissions of Banks, was so strong that it is difficult to understand how any jury could have returned a verdict of acquittal. If, however, these two men cannot be punished for the assault upon Kelsey, it is evidently improbable that his unknown murderers can be brought to justice.

The impunity which has thus far followed the crimes committed in Huntington is thoroughly disgraceful. There is little doubt that Kelsey was a very objectionable person. If he really wrote the letters which he is accused of having sent to Miss Smith, he deserved a severe, but legal, punishment. The fact that a young woman did not think it at all indelicate to come out of her house to gaze on a half-naked wretch struggling with his tormentors, was not very credible to her. But, however infamous and unprovoked may have been his conduct, it afforded no possible excuse for the cowardly assault made upon him by the mob, and still less for his subsequent murder. If respectable Huntington men can unite to tar and feather a defenseless wretch, if Huntington ladies can assemble to witness the pleasing spectacle, and if Huntington brutes can commit an atrocious murder, and neither local public sentiment nor local juries can find anything to be condemned in these humane amusements, Huntington must be a peculiarly desirable residence for decent and civilized beings. It is to be hoped that one more effort will be made to discover and punish the perpetrators of the murder, before the memory of the murdered man is forgotten. Skillful detectives ought in time to be able to find the guilty men, and the reward for their apprehension ought to be increased, and the offer of it continued until the last hope of redeeming Huntington justice from the stain which now remains upon it has vanished.

The Staten Island Mystery

New York Times, *January 15, 1881*

HISTORY OF THE CRIME—FINDING THE BARREL AT SILVER LAKE—SOLVING THE MYSTERY

Three boys employed in herding cattle in the woods near Silver Lake, a short distance south of Tompkinsville, Staten Island, on Sunday, Sept. 15, 1878, noticed a portion of a barrel protruding from the soft ground a few feet from a wagon-track known as the "Little Serpentine Road." From boyish curiosity they began to excavate around the barrel, and soon saw that a piece of old carpet was nailed over its top. Removing this they were horrified at finding the contents to be the nude body of a woman in an advanced stage of decomposition. The body was bent double, the arms being folded across the breast, and as the height of the barrel had been reduced to 18 inches, it was evident that much difficulty had been experienced in fitting the body into it. A preliminary post-mortem examination disclosed what were regarded as unmistakable evidences of malpractice. There was also found a well-defined fracture on the temporal bone of the head. More than a month was exhausted in futile efforts to trace the identity of the body. On Sept. 18 the remains were buried among the unidentified dead in the Potter's Field of the island. Three days later a report was circulated that the body was that of Annie Hommell, a young girl who, having been betrayed by her employer, a merchant of Saugerties, N.Y., had disappeared. The body was exhumed with a view to ascertaining whether or not it was hers. It was found to be not hers. The testimony which led to the arrest of Edward Reinhardt for the murder of his wife was given by August Keymer, an old German, known on the island as the "Watercress Man." He testified that about eight weeks previous to that date he had seen a young man digging a hole near the road-side above the valley in which Silver Lake lies. A barrel similar to that found by the cow-boys stood near by, and the young man said he was burying a dog. On the day following, Keymer accompanied Coroner Dempsey and a *Times* reporter to a marble-yard at No. 125 Attorney-street, in this City, and pointed out Reinhardt as the young man whom he had seen digging the hole near the lake. In reply to questions, Reinhardt admitted that he had lived in Gore-street, Stapleton, Staten Island, and was then residing at No. 132 Broome-street with Pauline Dithmar, his reputed wife. He appeared at the inquest and in his testimony acknowledged that he had lived in Gore-street with Mary Ann Degnan, the victim of the murder, but denied that she was his wife. He was arrested the next day. His trial for murder was begun on May 2, and during its progress it was shown that the body found in the barrel was that of Mary Ann Degnan, his first wife, whom he alleged he had been forced to marry. A few days before her death Reinhardt married Pauline Dithmar. After Mary Ann Degnan's disappearance, Reinhardt informed the neighbors that she had gone to visit an aunt in Newark. At the trial, however, he acknowledged that he had buried her body near the lake, but insisted that her death, on July 19, was due to the effects of medicine she had taken and that he had disposed of the body to avoid the possibility of suspicion resting on himself.

The Luther Boddy Case

New York Times, *September 5, 1922*

CROWDS OF NEGROES AT BODDY FUNERAL

Women in Hysterics During Services for Slayer of Two Detectives

Hear Message from Dead

Pastor Tells of Last Words to Relatives: "I Will Meet You in the Kingdom"

Thousands of negroes lined the streets of Harlem yesterday as the hearse containing the remains of Luther Boddy, 19-year-old murderer, motored slowly down Seventh Avenue past the corner of 135th Street, where, on the night of Jan. 5, he killed Detectives Francis J. Buckley and William A. Miller.

Boddy was put to death in Sing-Sing Prison Thursday night. Since Friday his body has been lying in the funeral parlors of H. Adolph Howell, at 107 West 136th Street, where some 30,000 persons have filed in to view the man whose crime, escape, capture and sentence form one of the most sensational chapters in the record of the New York police.

The services for Boddy, held in the Colored Methodist Episcopal Church in West 130th Street, were punctuated by the cries of hysterical women. The church, formerly a synagogue, was packed to the doors, and a detail of thirty policemen, under Deputy Inspector William McGrath and Captain Patrick Gargan, was sent there.

When the Rev. R. R. Wilson, who visited the condemned man in the death house, told how Boddy had accepted religion and passed serenely to the death chair, exclamations rang through the church. The minister described how Boddy dismissed his relatives on the afternoon of his death with the words, "Go home, I will meet you in the kingdom."

In his sermon, the Rev. W. Y. Bell, pastor of the church from which Boddy was buried, took as his theme, "Shun Evil Companions." Three hymns, requested by Boddy, were sung during the services. The deadman's parents-in-law, his brothers and sisters and his four-year-old son, Luther Boddy, Jr., accompanied the body to Cedar Grove Cemetery, Flushing, Long Island.

At the height of the crime wave last Winter, Boddy, on his way to the West 135th Street station house, whipped out a concealed pistol from his sleeve, shot his captors, Detectives Miller and Buckley, then eluded for several days the efforts of 40,000 police officers in the metropolitan district to find him. He finally was captured in Philadelphia by a negro magistrate.

Within twenty-five days of his crime, Boddy was indicted, tried and convicted. His wife, who is serving a term for larceny in Auburn Prison, was allowed to bid him farewell in the death house on Aug. 22.

Philadelphia Poisoning Ring

New York Times, *September 23, 1939*

SIX SLAYINGS TOLD BY "FAITH HEALER"

Confessed Murderer Links Paul Petrillo to Three Killings of Philadelphia "Ring"

Witness Tried "Evil Eye"

Defendant Flings Up Hand as an Antidote
While Counsel and Judge Are Conferring

Morris Bolber, "faith healer," appeared as a Commonwealth witness in the arsenic murder trials today and electrified a courtroom crowd with a detailed account of six slayings.

He not only linked Paul Petrillo, alleged "witch doctor" who now is on trial, with three of the killings, but threw the room into an uproar with an attempt to "put the evil eye" on the defendant.

Petrillo appeared unnerved when the "faith healer" took the chair. Bolber for awhile ignored him, then, with eyes wide open, seemed to be trying to "work on" Petrillo, who returned the stare for a moment and then glanced wildly about the room. When he turned again to look at Bolber the witness was still staring at him.

Petrillo opened the first and fourth fingers of his hand, with the three other fingers closed, and pointed the hand at Bolber, trying to ward off "the evil eye." The incident ended with the return of the opposing lawyers, who had been conferring with Judge Albert S. O'Millar.

Bolber, who had expressed contempt for Petrillo as merely a "fortune teller" and who has pleaded guilty to the murder of Romain Manduik, an arsenic victim, said that he knew of "seventy murders" in Philadelphia and that seventeen arrests had been made on the basis of his information. He told Lemuel B. Schofield, attorney for Petrillo, that he himself was really innocent, and had "only told what I know for the benefit of the people of Philadelphia."

Bolber testified that Petrillo admitted killing Luigi La Vecchio, for whose death he (Petrillo) now is on trial. Moreover, he said, Petrillo gave him $800 out of $2,000 insurance to "keep quiet."

He said that Petrillo killed Antonio Giacobbe and plotted the murder of Joseph Arena, who was drowned at a New Jersey beach. He charged that Petrillo killed Giacobbe not so much for the insurance money but because he was in love with the victim's wife, Millie.

The jurors, who had been restless as Mr. Schofield and Vincent P. McDevitt, assistant district attorney, wrangled over testimony, followed Bolber's testimony with renewed interest.

After he had told of patching up domestic quarrels by use of his "Chinese love powder," Mr. Schofield shouted at him.

"You know that you're guilty of murder, don't you? You know you're going to the electric chair?"

"Yes, I know, but I don't care," was the reply.

In another court room further testimony was heard in the trial of Emedio Mucelli, accused of the murder of Giuseppe di Martino.

The Joseph Aronowitz Case

New York Times, *March 3, 1955*

2 ARE HELD HERE IN "RIDE" MURDER

Robles' Nephew is Detained with Ex-Convict in Killing of Aronowitz Last Month

Two new figures in the murder of Joseph Aronowitz on Feb. 15 were held in Brooklyn last night as material witnesses. Bail was set at $50,000 each. They had been questioned all day after their arrest by State Troopers Tuesday night near Catskill, N.Y.

The two men are Joseph McKeon, 34 years old, a former convict with no known address, and Salvadore Perez, 23, of 1040 Rosedale Avenue, the Bronx. Perez is a nephew of August Robles, who was shot dead Feb. 20 when he battled a small army of policemen trying to arrest him.

Aronowitz, a 40-year-old ex-convict of 25 West Eighty-third Street, was "taken for a ride" just before he was to testify for the state in a Baltimore hold-up case. His body was found in an abandoned automobile in Brooklyn.

Meanwhile it was understood that the police had a clear idea of the identity of the mysterious "Blackie." Mrs. Aronowitz said he reputedly was one of two men hired to kill her husband. "Blackie" and an "Augie," who may have been Robles, visited the Aronowitz home about a month before the murder while Aronowitz was out. They said they were policemen, but Aronowitz, on his return home, identified them as his pursuers.

According to District Attorney Edward S. Silver of Kings County, McKeon and Perez know who killed Aronowitz and who hired the killer. Last December, Mr. Silver said, Rosario Lococo, 44, a truck driver of 160 West Eighty-seventh Street, visited McKeon to try to hire him to kill Aronowitz. Lococo is now being held without bail as a material witness and parole violator. He was paid to have disclosed at the time of the visit the identity of the man who wanted the shooting done. McKeon turned down the proposition.

Several weeks later, however, McKeon arranged with Lococo to meet the principal in a Manhattan restaurant. Robles was present at that conference, Mr. Silver said. The District Attorney declared that Robles and Perez had spoken to Aronowitz in January and, through promises and threats, sought to keep him from testifying.

"These circumstances and others," asserted Mr. Silver, "indicate that Perez has intimate and actual knowledge of the person or persons who shot and killed Aronowitz."

McKeon and Perez were arraigned before County Judge Nathan R. Sobel, who approved a request for high bail.

Martin J. Yamin, 32, of 24 Riverside Drive, a former Baltimore magistrate accused in the hold-up and now under $25,000 bail as a material witness in the Aronowitz murder, was also in the District Attorney's office yesterday.

STUDENT ESSAY

Assignment 6: In an essay, provide a narrative and full analysis of one historical murder case from the "List of Cases" in the Appendix to these "Assignments."

PATRICIA PARR

The Murder of Kelsey:
A Crime That Escaped Punishment

It was a night in 1872, when some of the citizens of Huntington, Long Island, decided to enforce their own brand of justice. It was a cold night in November, a night that later was described differently by almost everyone involved. It was the night a rejected lover lost his life. Much later, the people of Huntington again took on the responsibility of the law, this time in indignation over the outrage of the tarring and feathering, and ultimate murder of Charles G. Kelsey that had occurred nearly ten months earlier. The *New York Times* described the "vigorous efforts of citizens determined to discover the murderers."[1] Yet, when the tangled and sordid affair was finally sifted through and sorted out, not one of those men implicated in the murder actually received a prison term. How could the perpetrators of the horrible crime escape the fury of a community-wide investigation, leaving the case forever labeled: "unsolved"?

The night of the murder climaxed a long stretch of bad luck for the ill-fated Kelsey. His "crimes," punished by public humiliation and death, stemmed from his defective personality and his love for a popular, vain, and irresponsible young woman named Julia Smith. Although Kelsey, according to the August 31, 1873, edition of the *New York Times,* was "young and ambitious"[2] and had a "turn for literature,"[3] he was later acknowledged by an editorial dated October 17, 1875, to be "a very objectional person."[4] The entrance of objection into the character sketch of Kelsey is the result of the ways he expressed his literary and poetic skills in relationship to Miss Smith. He had fallen in love with her, despite the fact that she was already engaged to a young man named Royal Sammis. Kelsey pursued his feelings, undaunted by threats from Sammis and the fact that Miss Smith "declined his attentions,"[5] (according to the September 1, 1873, article in the *New York Times*). Kelsey allegedly wrote "indecent letters" to Miss Smith that shocked her delicate modesty and sparked her fiance's jealous anger. It can be concluded that neither Kelsey's over-dramatic poetry nor his stubborn quest for the love of Miss Smith was appreciated. In fact, these conclusions can be labeled as the factors that incited in Royal Sammis and his friends a bloodthirsty determination to teach him a lesson on that night in November.

Ten months later, on August 31, 1873, the *New York Times* reported the discovery of the "trunkless" (legs only) remains of a man by two fishermen off the coast of Oyster Bay, not far from Huntington.[6] The body was linked to the disappearance of Charles G. Kelsey, and the whole scandalous story was unfolded for the public in the pages of the *Times.* On November 4, 1872, a group of Huntington young people had "amused themselves at the expense of Kelsey" by subjecting him to the pain and humiliation of being tarred and feathered. Several young men had masked themselves and ambushed

Kelsey as he made his way towards Mrs. Oakley's house, where Miss Julia Smith resided.[7] Kelsey's younger sister, Charlotte, was later able to force Miss Smith to admit she had lured Charles there by placing a lamp in her window that night.[8] In the hands of the brutal mob, Kelsey was stripped, his body exposed to the chill of early November. His "long, poetic curls" were cut off, and his head was "gashed" in the process. Then he was coated from head to foot with hot smelly tar and chicken feathers. At the height of his misery, a lantern was held up to him so that "a party of ladies, his love included, could inspect his agony." At this point, Kelsey hurled a boot at his tormentors, which hit and broke the lantern. He then "broke from his captors" and was never seen again.[9]

The next morning, Kelsey's family reported hearing Charles in the house and yard late that night. His bed was undisturbed, but on the floor lay a crumpled, blood-spotted woolen jacket and a few feathers.[10] Out in the yard near the well was a bucket, and it was assumed that Kelsey had been attempting to rid himself of his sticky coating. There were signs of a "desperate struggle" in the yard and a trail of hooves and wagon wheels leading off in the direction of Lloyd's Beach at Oyster Bay, five miles from Huntington. At the beach were discovered a bloody shirt, one boot, two lemons, and a necktie. The only other evidence at this point was the sinister testimony of a resident of Oyster Bay. James Hood reported seeing two men, laden with a heavy-looking bundle, embark in a small boat late that night at Lloyd's Beach. Hood testified that, when the two men returned to shore, their burden was absent.[11]

The revealed details of the events that took place on November 4, 1872, and the gory sensationalism of the discovery of the mutilated body attracted a large crowd to Coroner Bayliss' inquest on August 30, 1873, at Oyster Bay. The *New York Times* reported that they listened in "intrigued silence" as the fishermen described how they had come upon the remains while dragging for oysters in the bay. There were bits of tar and a few feathers clinging to the flesh, and the pants had been "working with the tide." They also heard Kelsey's brothers and sisters acknowledge that these remains, which consisted of a man's hips and legs but no feet, were indeed those of their missing brother. In a pocket of the trousers which had covered the "trunkless" body had been found a thin chain with a small hook and crossbar. The family identified it as belonging to Kelsey. The bloody clothes found at the beach were his too, they stated, and the two blood-saturated lemons had been bought by him soon before he disappeared.[12]

After the inquest medical reports, during which doctors attributed the cause of death to hemorrhaging, came a long session of conflicting descriptions of the night of November 4.[13] The ladies that had willingly witnessed Kelsey's predicament claimed they would never have come to watch had they known what it was they were invited to observe.[14] Miss Smith claimed that Kelsey had broken into the basement of Mrs. Oakley's house.[15] One of the suspects, John Hurd, claimed that the tarring and feathering had never even occurred, later perjuring himself by admitting it had.[16] John Prime, another suspect, refused to give any information at all, "on the advice of certain parties."[17]

Extremely vital testimony was given at the inquest by Titus Conkling, a servant in the Sammis household. He reinforced the claim that others had made: that Royal Sammis had frequently threatened Kelsey with violence, if he did not renounce his love for Miss Smith. Titus stated that he had seen his employer with a club and a mask leave the house on the night of the fourth of November. When he returned, Titus testified that Royal Sammis informed him that he had participated in the tarring and feathering of Kelsey.[18]

The public's reaction, described by several *New York Times* articles, was sympathy towards Kelsey and anger toward the men involved in the tragedy. Kelsey's funeral reportedly drew the largest crowd ever in Long Island, New York, and there were many a "moistened eye" and "quivering lip."[19] The people of Huntington objected strongly to the "blackening" of the good name of their community. They held town meetings and discussed plans to raise enough money to hire the very best lawyers, who would then solve the Kelsey mystery.[20] The town even offered a reward for any important information regarding the case, so great was its unified determination to clear up the matter.[21]

The momentum created by the arousal of public feeling resulted in the arrest, on November 2, 1873, at Oyster Bay, of seven of the men implicated in the assault and murder of Kelsey. The *New York Times* lists Dr. George Banks and Royal Sammis among those indicated.[22] This headway in the case, however, was soon bogged down by jurisdictional and legal conflicts. It seems that the murder had taken place in Huntington, Suffolk County, while the grisly body itself had been recovered in Oyster Bay, Queens County. The defense lawyer for the prisoners argued that they could not be held in Queens County since they had committed no "punishable acts" within its jurisdiction.[23] So, on November 12, 1873, all seven prisoners were discharged.[24]

The Kelsey case, however, was not over yet. The dedicated efforts of friends of Kelsey were rewarded at last, when Dr. Banks and Royal Sammis were brought to trial, according to the October 17, 1873, *Times* article, on charges of assault and battery. Unfortunately, this small victory for those loyal to the memory of Kelsey was short-lived and incomplete. The conclusions drawn at Banks and Sammis's trial were the conclusions officially accepted for the whole affair. Banks and Sammis were *not* responsible for the death of Charles Kelsey. They were promptly acquitted. Who, then, *was* responsible for the inhuman torture and murder? The official answer to this question was that a band of "ruffians" motivated by the success of the party of respectable, eminent citizens of Huntington, had tarred and feathered Kelsey with apparent impunity. Thus, the case joined the list of unsolved murders, since these murderers were not expected to be "brought to justice."[25]

There was no *real* justice in the Kelsey case. The red tape and technicalities of a complex legal system, coupled with a waning public interest in the scandal, produced its quiet demise. Shrewd lawyers, with an eye for legal loopholes, gained freedom for their guilty clients. By manipulating the law, they managed to transfer the suspicion of guilt to some theoretical band of roughnecks who had no credible motives. The treatment of the case by the *New York Times* illustrates the gradually declining concern by the general population for the event. As the story progressed, the *Times* articles shrank considerably and dropped obscurely to the bottoms of pages and the last few columns. Their headings changed from the dramatic "Kelsey Outrage," to simply "The Kelsey Case," and then disappeared altogether under a listing of Long Island news briefs. A few editorials referred to the people of Huntington as "savages"[26] and sarcastically pointed out that their brutal idea of sport was shamefully above the law,[27] but no action was taken against the men known to have been involved. Those zealous citizens of Huntington who had vowed to solve the tragic case must have found it easier than they had first believed to accept the mysterious death of their neighbor, as the grass grew tall on his grave and his memory faded. The case was as dead as Kelsey himself, when, as a further insult, the very last article appeared in the *Times* on August 2, 1877. This short piece described a detective who was certain that Kelsey was still alive and would be made to pay for the anguish he had inflicted on Royal Sammis and his wife, Julia Smith Sammis. The detective reported that the couple, living in a tenement house, were "broken in mind and body" because of the affair.[28] The victim had become the criminal. If many people even noticed the small article on that late summer day, probably few remembered the man it claimed to be alive or realized the final outrage it represented against him, the poet and lover, Charles G. Kelsey.

NOTES

1. "Funeral," *New York Times,* 6 Sept. 1873, p. 5, col. 1.
2. "Body Found Near Cold Spring Harbor, Long Island," *New York Times,* 31 Aug. 1873, p. 5, col. 2.
3. "Body Found . . . ," p. 5, col. 2.
4. "Kelsey Tragedy at Huntington; Acquittal of Banks and Sammis," *New York Times,* 17 Oct. 1875, p. 6, col. 3.
5. "Disgrace to Community," *New York Times* editorial, 1 Sept. 1873, p. 4, col. 2
6. "Body Found . . . ," p. 5, col. 2.
7. "Body Found . . . ," p. 5, col. 2.
8. "Verdict of Coroner's Jury," *New York Times,* 26 Oct. 1873, p. 5, col. 3.
9. "Body Found . . . ," p. 5, col. 2.
10. "Disgrace to Community," p. 4, col. 2.
11. "Body Found . . . ," p. 5, col. 2.
12. "Body Found . . . ," p. 5, col. 2.
13. "Morse's Testimony," *New York Times,* 3 Sept. 1873, p. 8 col. 3.
14. "Course in Regard to Downing, District Attorney," *New York Times,* 5 Sept. 1873, p. 5, col. 2.
15. "Testing," *New York Times,* 19 Sept. 1873, p. 8, col. 2.
16. "District Attorney Downing Withdraws from Case," *New York Times,* 10 Sept. 1873, p. 5, col. 1.
17. "Testing," p. 8, col. 2.
18. "Testing," p. 8, col. 2.
19. "Funeral," p. 5, col. 1.
20. "Course . . . ," p. 5, col. 2.
21. "Reward Offered by Governor Dix," *New York Times,* 30 Oct. 1873, p. 8, col. 2.
22. "Arrests," *New York Times,* 29 Oct. 1873, p. 7 col. 3.
23. "Conflicting Jurisdiction," *New York Times,* 2 Nov. 1873, p. 3, col. 2.

24. "Banks, Sammis, McKay, Burgess, Hurd, Prime, and Wood Discharged From Arrest," *New York Times,* 12 Nov. 1873, p. 5, col. 5.
25. "Kelsey Tragedy at Huntington; Acquittal of Banks and Sammis," *New York Times,* 17 Oct. 1875, p. 6, col. 3.
26. "Kelsey Case in Huntington, Long Island," *New York Times* editorial, 11 Jan. 1877, p. 4, col. 4.
27. "Kelsey Murder in Huntington, Long Island: A Practical Joke," *New York Times,* 15 Aug. 1876, p. 4, col. 5.
28. "Kelsey Rumored to be Still Living," *New York Times,* 2 Aug. 1877, p. 8, col. 2.

BIBLIOGRAPHY

"Arrests," *New York Times,* 29 Oct. 1873, p. 7, col. 3.

"Banks, Sammis, McKay, Burgess, Hurd, Prime, and Wood Discharged from Arrest," *New York Times,* 12 Nov. 1873, p. 5, col. 5.

"Body Found Near Cold Spring Harbor, Long Island," *New York Times,* 31 Aug. 1873, p. 5, col. 2.

"Change Asked," *New York Times;* 16 May 1874, p. 2, col. 6.

"Conflicting Jurisdiction," *New York Times,* 2 Nov. 1873, p. 3, col. 2.

"Course in Regard to Downing, District Attorney," *New York Times,* 5 Sept. 1873, p. 5, col. 2.

"Disgrace to Community," *New York Times,* 1 Sept. 1873, p. 4, col. 2.

"District Attorney Downing Withdraws from Case," *New York Times,* 10 Sept. 1873, p. 5, col. 1.

"Doctor Banks Misled by Saint Louis Man," *New York Times,* 5 Nov. 1873, p. 12, col. 4.

"Funeral," *New York Times,* 6 Sept. 1873, p. 5, col. 1.

"Halving of Reward for Recovery of the Remains," *New York Times,* 25 Nov. 1873, p. 5, col. 6.

"Kelsey Case in Huntington, Long Island," *New York Times* editorial, 11 Jan. 1877, p. 4, col. 4.

"Kelsey Murder Case in Huntington, Long Island: A Practical Joke," *New York Times,* 15 Aug. 1876, p. 4, col. 5.

"Kelsey Rumored to be Still Living," *New York Times,* 2 Aug. 1877, p. 8, col. 2.

"Kelsey Tragedy at Huntington; Acquittal of Banks and Sammis," *New York Times,* 17 Oct. 1875, p. 6, col. 3.

"Morse's Testimony," *New York Times,* 3 Sept. 1873, p. 8, col. 3.

"Outrage in Huntington," *New York Times,* 1 Sept. 1873, p. 5, col. 2.

"Payment of Huntington Town Reward Refused," *New York Times,* 23 Dec. 1873, p. 8, col. 3.

"Persons Indicted," *New York Times,* 8 Nov. 1873, p. 7, col. 3.

"Reward Offered by Governor Dix," *New York Times,* 30 Oct. 1873, p. 8, col. 2.

"Reward Paid to Finders of Remains," *New York Times,* 2 Dec. 1873, p. 5 col. 3.

"Rumors of New Evidence in the Kelsey Case," *New York Times,* 12 March 1876, p. 12, col. 1.

"Sammis Brothers Discharge on their Own Recognizance," *New York Times,* 6 Nov. 1876, p. 8, col. 4.

"Sammis Taken to Brooklyn," *New York Times,* 9 Nov. 1873, p. 8, col. 2.

"Seen by John Gonaud," *New York Times,* 25 Feb. 1874, p. 8, col. 4.

"Story of Sanford Brown: He Saw Kelsey," *New York Times,* 31 Dec. 1873, p. 8, col. 2.

"Testing," *New York Times,* 19 Sept. 1873, p. 8, col. 2.

"Town Auditors of Huntington Restrained from Paying Reward," *New York Times,* 4 Dec. 1873, p. 5, col. 2.

"Verdict of Coroner's Jury," *New York Times,* 26 Oct. 1873, p. 5, col. 3.

"What the Trial is to Reveal," *New York Times,* 10 Jan. 1874, p. 8, col. 1.

"Work of Comstock Detective," *New York Times,* 5 Nov. 1873, p. 5, col. 5.

QUESTIONS FOR DISCUSSION

WITHIN THIS CHAPTER:

1. In *Trifles,* how was John Wright killed?

2. Who killed John Wright? What evidence supports your conclusion?

3. After reading *Trifles,* "Case of an Apprentice," and "The History of Susanna," explain the concept of circumstantial evidence.

4. According to Janet Rifkin, in what ways are legal systems "patriarchal" institutions? Do her ideas provide a means for analysis of "The History of Susanna"?

5. Which of the five *New York Times* accounts of murders seems to you to be the most objective? The most subjective or opinionated? Why?

6. Which of the five *New York Times* cases would attract you as a researcher? Why?

USING OTHER CHAPTERS:

7. Which of the four figures featured in the Kelsey, Boddy, and Philadelphia cases from the *New York Times* do you think could have

become legendary (like Billy the Kid in the Borges essay in this chapter, or like some of the characters in the "Discursive Essays and Fictions" of Chapter 1)? Why?

8. In what ways were the "witches" of Salem convicted by circumstantial evidence (see Chapter 5)? Was there any other kind of evidence used to convict them?

9. How does Jonestown support Rifkin's idea of a patriarchal society? (See Chapter 6.)

10. Using Danto's essay, with its profiles of different kinds of murderers, classify Jim Jones (Chapter 6).

ASSIGNMENTS

WITHIN THIS CHAPTER:

1. Reread *Trifles,* but this time pay close attention to the ways Mrs. Peters and Mrs. Hale act to protect Minnie Wright from suspicion of murder. Write an essay which lists and explains their protective actions.

2. One of Rifkin's main points, in "Patriarchy, Law, and Capitalism," is that the law is a male-dominated institution. Write an interpretation of *Trifles* in which you agree or disagree with this position.

3. Write a speech as if you were the prosecuting attorney asking for Minnie Wright's conviction for murder, *or* write one from the standpoint of her defense attorney, asking for her acquittal.

4. Classify the various kinds of evidence presented in the selections from the Apocrypha, Phillipps's *Famous Cases,* and the *New York Times.*

5. In an essay, explain how circumstantial evidence was used to convict the apprentice in Phillipps's "case of circumstantial evidence."

6. In an essay, provide a narrative and full analysis of one historical murder case from the "List of Cases" in the Appendix to these "Assignments" (see below). Include a cultural, geographical, or historical introduction to the case's era. If there was an official outcome to the case, your essay should agree or disagree with that outcome; if the case was unsolved, your essay should offer a possible solution. Almost all of the cases may be found under the heading "Murder" in the *New York Times Index* for the year given (the

beginning year of the reportage). Some cases span more than five years, so you should check the *Times Index* for at least ten years after the case *appears* to be over; new developments—appeals, new evidence—sometimes reopen a case. In some cases, there are magazine articles which you can locate by using *The Reader's Guide to Periodical Literature,* or other magazine indices, but you can complete your research of the case by using the *Times* alone.

7. Select one or two of the *Times* articles from your case (see "Assignment 6") and compare/contrast them with any of the five selections from the *Times* in "Documentary Materials" which are from decades *not* covered by your own case. What are the similarities and differences in the articles (how the facts were presented; what attitudes were displayed toward the accused and the victims, etc.)?

8. Retell your case (from "Assignment 6") as if it were a case from Phillipps's *Famous Cases of Circumstantial Evidence* or from Borges's *Universal History of Infamy.* In order to create such an imaginative retelling, you may have to invent or distort some of the original facts of your case.

Beyond This Chapter:

9. Choose materials from Chapter 6 on Jonestown and use methods derived from this chapter to explain in an essay how you would organize either the defense or the prosecution of Jim Jones for the "murder" of almost a thousand people at Jonestown.

10. For a longer research project and essay, compare two murders from eras widely separated in time; Colin Wilson's *A Casebook of Murder* (see "Sources") would be helpful in charting the different cultural aspects or sociology of crime. You and your classmates could pool results from "Assignment 6" to create a spectrum of cases over time.

11. Compare/contrast Glaspell's *two* versions of John Wright's murder: *Trifles,* from this chapter, and her earlier short story, "A Jury of Her Peers." (The short story is available in at least three different books —*The Best Short Stories of 1917;* Glaspell's own *Literature: Structure, Sound, and Sense* (1917); or in *Images of Women in Literature,* edited by Mary Anne Ferguson.)

12. Read Sophocles's play *Antigone* (many different editions are available), then, using *Trifles,* or a murder case in which an accused woman is the central figure, argue for or against the view that there is (or should be) a different standard of justice for men and women.

APPENDIX TO ASSIGNMENT 6: LIST OF CASES
(FROM W. KEITH KRAUS: *MURDER, MISCHIEF, AND MAYHEM*)

Note: An asterisk (*) designates an unsolved case.

1. The Sickles Tragedy, 1859
2. Mary Hill, 1868
3. John Smedick, 1868
4. *Benjamin Nathan, 1870
5. Edward H. Rulloff, 1870
6. Avery Putnam, 1871
7. James Fisk, 1872
8. William J. Starkey, 1872
9. *Kelsey Tar and Feather Outrage, 1872
10. Charles Goodrich, 1873
11. John McKenna, 1874
12. James Noe, 1875
13. Judge Chisolm, 1877
14. Staten Island Mystery, 1878
15. Mary Eliza Billings, 1878
16. The C. A. Cobb, Jr., Poison Case, 1878
17. Richard Harrison Smith, 1878
18. *Mary Stannard, 1878
19. Judge Elliot, 1879
20. Jane Hull, 1879
21. Jennie Cramer, 1881
22. Lamson-John Case, 1881
23. Captain A. C. Nutt and Nicholas Dukes, 1882
24. *Rose Clark Ambler, 1883
25. *The Rahway Mystery, 1887
26. Dr. P. H. Cronin, 1889
27. Helen Potts, 1891
28. Meyer's Insurance Case (Baum), 1893
29. Robert Ross, 1894
30. Blanche Lamont, 1895
31. Josephine Barnaby, 1895
32. Mrs. Henry H. Bliss, 1895
33. Benjamin Pitzel, 1895
34. William Guldensuppe, 1897
35. *Emeline Reynolds, 1898
36. Kate Adams, 1898
37. William Marsh Rice, 1900
38. Frank Young, 1904
39. William E. Annis, 1908
40. Lt. Giuseppe Petrosino, 1909

41. Ocey Snead, 1909

42. Avis Linnell, 1911

43. Louise Beatie, 1911

44. Herman Rosenthal (Becker Case), 1912

45. Mary Phagan, 1913

46. Mrs. William Bailey, 1914

47. Barnett Baff, 1914

48. Gaston Calmette, 1914

49. Dr. C. Franklin Mohr, 1915

50. *Charles Murray, 1915

51. Elizabeth Nichols, 1915

52. Arthur Warren Waite, 1916

53. F. R. Andrews, 1916

54. Mrs. Walter Wilkins, 1919

55. Daniel Kaber, 1919

56. Camillo Ciazzo, 1921

57. Luther Boddy, 1922

58. West End Bank Messenger Robbery, 1923

59. William Nelson McClintock, 1924

60. Dr. William Lilliandahl, 1927

61. Grace Budd, 1928

62. Alfred Lingle, 1930

63. Eugenia Cedarholm Mystery, 1930

64. *The 3X Murders (Mozynski), 1930

65. Zachery Smith Reynolds, 1932

66. E. A. Ridley, 1933

67. Samuel Drukman, 1935

68. Walter Liggett, 1935

69. *Peter Levine, 1938

70. Philadelphia Poisoning Ring, 1939

71. Mrs. Wayne Lonergan, 1943

72. *Sir Harry Oakes, 1943

73. William Earle Lynching, 1947

74. Janet Fay, 1949

75. Case of the Trenton Six, 1951

76. Pennsylvania Turnpike Case, 1953

77. Edward Bates, 1953

78. Brooklyn Teenage Killers, 1954

79. Judge Chillingworth, 1955

80. Joseph Aronowitz, 1955

81. Emmitt Till, 1955

82. Michael Farmer, 1957

83. Dr. John Bodkin Adams, 1957

84. Barbara Finch, 1959

SOURCES FOR FURTHER READING AND/OR RESEARCH

Asbury, Herbert. *The Gangs of New York.* New York: Alfred A. Knopf, 1928. An undocumented, but fascinating, view of the funky underworld of New York City from the nineteenth century through the 1920s.

De Lange, Nicholas. *Apocrypha: Jewish Literature of the Hellenistic Age.* New York: Viking, 1978. Good background on the Susanna story, as well as on Old Testament Apocryphal stories in general; includes another, slightly different, version of the Susanna story.

Hobsbawm, Eric. *Bandits.* Various editions. A political interpretation of murder and crime, especially those perpetrated by "outlaws" of many lands, including the United States.

Jones, Ann. *Women Who Kill.* New York: Holt, Rinehart, and Winston, 1980. Anecdotal writing, from a feminist perspective, about "prominent cases that obviously hit a social nerve."

Keylin, Arleen, and Arto DeMirjian, eds. *Crime: As Reported by the New York Times.* New York: Arno Press, 1976. With only one exception, these articles reprinted from the *Times* do not cover murders in the Appendix to this chapter's "Assignments." They do, however, cover many of the most notorious crimes of over a century of *Times* reporting, including assassinations and mass killings; excellent for comparisons with murders from the Appendix.

Kraus, W. Keith. *Murder, Mischief, and Mayhem.* Urbana: National Council of Teachers of English (NCTE), 1978. An excellent guide to original journalistic research into murders and other, usually neglected, historical incidents and characters.

Lewis, Janet. *The Wife of Martin Guerre; The Trial of Soren Qvist; The Ghost of Monsieur Scarron.* Currently available in Ohio University Press paperbacks. A series of three historical "novels of circumstantial evidence," based on cases from Phillipps's *Famous Cases of Circumstantial Evidence.*

McDADE, THOMAS. *The Annals of Murder: A Bibliography of Books and Pamphlets on American Murders from the Colonial Times to 1900.* Norman: University of Oklahoma Press, 1961. Does not include any of the murders from the Appendix, but does provide, in its annotations of numerous books and pamphlets, some sense of crime patterns before and during the nineteenth century.

NASH, JAY ROBERT. *Bloodletters and Badmen: A Narrative Encyclopedia of American Criminals from the Pilgrims to the Present.* New York: Evans, 1974. Conveniently arranged, alphabetical guide to hundreds of extremely bad people, with an extensive bibliography; individual entries are not footnoted and are somewhat casually written.

SAYERS, DOROTHY L., ED. *The Omnibus of Crime.* New York: Payson and Clarke, 1929. A British writer of detective novels arranged this extensive collection of fiction by both criminological and literary categories (e.g., "The Scientific and Medical Detective," "Tales of Magic," etc.).

TRILLIN, CALVIN. *Killings.* New York: Ticknor and Fields, 1984. "Attracted by stories of sudden death," Trillin writes about murders with an eye toward how unusual the commonplace can sometimes be; highly recommended reading.

WERTHAM, FREDERIC. *The Show of Violence.* Garden City: Doubleday, 1949. A psychiatrist's view of murder, not as a courtroom witness, but as an interpreter, often from a literary point of view; for example, in one chapter on a woman accused of murdering her children, we encounter "Medea in Modern Dress."

WILSON, COLIN. *A Casebook of Murder.* New York: Cowles, 1969. An almost R-rated attempt to provide a "philosophical" interpretation of the "changing patterns of murder in Western society," from the Elizabethan Age to modern times.

WOLFGANG, W. E., ED. *Studies in Homicide.* New York: Harper and Row, 1967. A collection of social-psychological essays, some out-of-date; includes Wolfgang's own interesting but controversial essay, "Subculture of Violence—A Socio-Psychological Theory."

EXPLORATIONS

1. Follow a local murder case (or other dramatic crime) in a local newspaper, and visit the courtroom during the trial. Compare your version of what happened as you observe the trial with the newspaper's version. In addition, determine if this case fits any of the patterns you have studied in this chapter.

2. Interview a police officer about murder, or other crimes, in your area. What kind of view of murder does the officer take: sociological; psychological; common-sense, individual-case, some other kind?

3. Interview a lawyer or a law professor about murder. Does the jurist you interview see any pattern in murders?

CHAPTER FIVE

Perspectives on Salem

The official prosecution of numerous women and men as witches and wizards in Salem, Massachusetts, in the 1690s has captured the imagination of people everywhere for almost three hundred years. Somewhat suddenly, village girls claimed to be attacked by witches who seemed to be all about them. It has been a drama which has somehow always remained news, in part because it deals with aspects of human behavior which defy easy definition, but also because the religious, political, and legal issues it raises are still part of our culture, and finally, simply because it is a haunting tale.

If you are unfamiliar with the Salem events, the first four selections in "Documentary Materials" may be the best place to begin: The passages from the Bible provided the Puritans—who felt the force of scripture literally—with the command to execute witches. The examination of Tituba, the West Indian slave in the household of the Salem Village minister, clearly indicates the presence of "heathen" folk who practiced magic arts; that her presence was tolerated for so long may demonstrate that, practically speaking, the devout Puritans did not "rid" themselves of the Devil, but simply fought him when they had the strength. The passages from two powerful Puritan ministers, Increase and Cotton Mather, show clearly how strong was the Puritans' belief in the real presence of supernatural forces all about them.

If you are already fairly familiar with the events, Whittier provides a nineteenth-century perspective in "Documentary Materials"—as does Hitchcock in Chapter 3. Both writers chart how the issues of Salem began to leave their historical traces in our culture. As a subject for two newly emerging fields of study—folklore and psychology—"seeing" or "imagining" the supernatural provided these two men with fascinating "raw" material: Folk beliefs persist even in the "more rational" nineteenth century, when there seemed to be scientific explanations for the phenomena. These beliefs also appear in literary art. In Hawthorne's case, perhaps for psychological reasons, his short story, "Alice Doane's Appeal," takes on the issues personally. He suggests that the power of Puritanism has left, in the New England world, blood traces not easily erased. (As a descendent of one of the Salem judges, Tituba's interrogator, he was in a position to know.)

Our century has seen the ground of Salem attract other disciplines and their blends: Historians (Ehrenreich and English) and social-psychologists (including Erikson) have tried to isolate the essence of the drama in more sociological, less emphatically religious terms. Medical interpretations have also helped to clarify some of the possibilities for interpreting the accusers' behavior, ranging from Matossian's essay on a possible chemical source of the outbreak of possessive fits by the afflicted girls, to Roueché's "Sandy," a modern tale, not about Salem, but about contagious hysteria among young people.

"Only" about twenty women and men (and two dogs) were executed in Salem in 1692 under very trying circumstances, insignificant numbers when compared to the many thousands burned in Europe during the seventeenth century. Yet those few executed in America have stirred up as much controversy as the thousands elsewhere. Why?

DISCURSIVE ESSAYS AND FICTIONS

SHORT STORY

NATHANIEL HAWTHORNE

The John Hathorne who interrogated Tituba at Salem (see "Documentary Materials") later became known as a hanging judge. His descendant, the

great New England regional writer Nathaniel Hawthorne, probably never
escaped the tremendous guilt he felt as a result of his ancestor's actions.
(He changed the spelling of his last name, but perhaps not dramatically
enough.) He also had an obsession with the Puritans' role in creating his
New England attitudes, especially concerning sin, guilt, and retribution,
all of which color his novels and short stories. "Alice Doane's Appeal"
—originally published in 1835 in a popular magazine (The Token)
—combines a fictional murder case with the Salem events, including one
of the crucial issues, the devil's use of spirits in human form called
"specters" (or, as it is often seen in British spelling, "spectres"), rooting
both in the actual soil of Salem's Gallows Hill where the witches were
executed. (See Hawthorne in "Sources" for the titles of his other stories
with Puritan themes.)

Alice Doane's Appeal

On a pleasant afternoon of June, it was my good fortune to be
the companion of two young ladies in a walk. The direction of our
course being left to me, I led them neither to Legge's Hill, nor to the
Cold Spring, nor to the rude shores and old batteries of the Neck, nor
yet to Paradise°; though if the latter place were rightly named, my
fair friends would have been at home there. We reached the outskirts
of the town, and turning aside from a street of tanners and curriers,
began to ascend a hill, which at a distance, by its dark slope and the
even line of its summit, resembled a green rampart along the road.
It was less steep than its aspect threatened. The eminence formed part
of an extensive tract of pasture land, and was traversed by cow paths
in various directions; but, strange to tell, though the whole slope and
summit were of a peculiarly deep green, scarce a blade of grass was
visible from the base upward. This deceitful verdure was occasioned
by a plentiful crop of "wood-wax," which wears the same dark and
glossy green throughout the summer, except at one short period,
when it puts forth a profusion of yellow blossoms. At that season,
to a distant spectator, the hill appears absolutely overlaid with gold,
or covered with a glory of sunshine, even beneath a clouded sky. But
the curious wanderer on the hill will perceive that all the grass, and
everything that should nourish man or beast, has been destroyed by
this vile and ineradicable weed: its tufted roots make the soil their

○ Legge's Hill, Cold Spring, etc.: all actual locations in Salem.

own, and permit nothing else to vegetate among them; so that a physical curse may be said to have blasted the spot, where guilt and frenzy consummated the most execrable scene that our history blushes to record. For this was the field where superstition won her darkest triumph; the high place where our fathers set up their shame, to the mournful gaze of generations far remote. The dust of martyrs was beneath our feet. We stood on Gallows Hill.

For my own part, I have often courted the historic influence of the spot. But it is singular how few come on pilgrimage to this famous hill; how many spend their lives almost at its base, and never once obey the summons of the shadowy past, as it beckons them to the summit. Till a year or two since, this portion of our history had been very imperfectly written, and, as we are not a people of legend or tradition, it was not every citizen of our ancient town that could tell, within half a century, so much as the date of the witchcraft delusion. Recently, indeed, an historian has treated the subject in a manner that will keep his name alive, in the only desirable connection with the errors of our ancestry, by converting the hill of their disgrace into an honorable monument of his own antiquarian lore, and of that better wisdom, which draws the moral while it tells the tale. But we are a people of the present, and have no heartfelt interest in the olden time. Every fifth of November,° in commemoration of they know not what, or rather without an idea beyond the momentary blaze, the young men scare the town with bonfires on this haunted height, but never dream of paying funeral honors to those who died so wrongfully, and, without a coffin or a prayer, were buried here.

Though with feminine susceptibility, my companions caught all the melancholy associations of the scene, yet these could but imperfectly overcome the gayety of girlish spirits. Their emotions came and went with quick vicissitude, and sometimes combined to form a peculiar and delicious excitement, the mirth brightening the gloom into a sunny shower of feeling, and a rainbow in the mind. My own more sombre mood was tinged by theirs. With now a merry word and next a sad one, we trod among the tangled weeds, and almost hoped that our feet would sink into the hollow of a witch's grave. Such vestiges were to be found within the memory of man, but

---

○ fifth of November: Guy Fawkes Day, originally a British holiday, celebrated with fireworks in honor of one of the conspirators who is alleged to have plotted to blow up King James and Parliament in 1605.

have vanished now, and with them, I believe, all traces of the precise spot of the executions. On the long and broad ridge of the eminence, there is no very decided elevation of any one point, nor other prominent marks, except the decayed stumps of two trees, standing near each other, and here and there the rocky substance of the hill, peeping just above the wood-wax.

There are few such prospects of town and village, woodland and cultivated field, steeples and country seats, as we beheld from this unhappy spot. No blight had fallen on old Essex; all was prosperity and riches, healthfully distributed. Before us lay our native town, extending from the foot of the hill to the harbor, level as a chess board, embraced by two arms of the sea, and filling the whole peninsula with a close assemblage of wooden roofs, overtopped by many a spire, and intermixed with frequent heaps of verdure, where trees threw up their shade from unseen trunks. Beyond was the bay and its islands, almost the only objects, in a country unmarked by strong natural features, on which time and human toil had produced no change. Retaining these portions of the scene, and also the peaceful glory and tender gloom of the declining sun, we threw, in imagination, a veil of deep forest over the land, and pictured a few scattered villages, and this old town itself a village, as when the prince of hell bore sway there. The idea thus gained of its former aspect, its quaint edifices standing far apart, with peaked roofs and projecting stories, and its single meeting-house pointing up a tall spire in the midst; the vision, in short, of the town in 1692, served to introduce a wondrous tale of those old times.

I had brought the manuscript in my pocket. It was one of a series written years ago, when my pen, now sluggish and perhaps feeble, because I have not much to hope or fear, was driven by stronger external motives, and a more passionate impulse within, than I am fated to feel again. Three or four of these tales had appeared in the "Token," after a long time and various adventures, but had encumbered me with no troublesome notoriety, even in my birthplace. One great heap had met a brighter destiny: they had fed the flames; thoughts meant to delight the world and endure for ages had perished in a moment, and stirred not a single heart but mine. The story now to be introduced, and another, chanced to be in kinder custody at the time, and thus, by no conspicuous merits of their own, escaped destruction.

The ladies, in consideration that I had never before intruded my performances on them, by any but the legitimate medium, through the press, consented to hear me read. I made them sit down on a moss-grown rock, close by the spot where we chose to believe that the death tree had stood. After a little hesitation on my part, caused by a dread of renewing my acquaintance with fantasies that had lost their charm in the ceaseless flux of mind, I began the tale, which opened darkly with the discovery of a murder.

———————— • ————————

A hundred years, and nearly half that time, have elapsed since the body of a murdered man was found, at about the distance of three miles, on the old road to Boston. He lay in a solitary spot, on the bank of a small lake, which the severe frost of December had covered with a sheet of ice. Beneath this, it seemed to have been the intention of the murderer to conceal his victim in a chill and watery grave, the ice being deeply hacked, perhaps with the weapon that had slain him, though its solidity was too stubborn for the patience of a man with blood upon his hand. The corpse therefore reclined on the earth, but was separated from the road by a thick growth of dwarf pines. There had been a slight fall of snow during the night, and as if nature were shocked at the deed, and strove to hide it with her frozen tears, a little drifted heap had partly buried the body, and lay deepest over the pale dead face. An early traveller, whose dog had led him to the spot, ventured to uncover the features, but was affrighted by their expression. A look of evil and scornful triumph had hardened on them, and made death so life-like and so terrible, that the beholder at once took flight, as swiftly as if the stiffened corpse would rise up and follow.

I read on, and identified the body as that of a young man, a stranger in the country, but resident during several preceding months in the town which lay at our feet. The story described, at some length, the excitement caused by the murder, the unavailing quest after the perpetrator, the funeral ceremonies, and other commonplace matters, in the course of which, I brought forward the personages who were to move among the succeeding events. They were but three. A young man and his sister; the former characterized by a diseased imagination and morbid feelings; the latter, beautiful and virtuous, and instilling something of her own excellence into the wild heart of her brother, but not enough to cure the deep taint of his nature. The third person was a wizard; a small, gray, withered man, with fiendish ingenuity in devising evil, and superhuman power to execute it, but senseless as an idiot and feebler than a child to all better purposes. The central scene of the story was an interview between this wretch and Leonard Doane, in the wizard's hut, situated beneath a range of rocks at some distance from the town. They sat beside a mouldering fire, while a tempest of wintry rain was beating on the roof. The young man spoke of the closeness of the tie which united him and Alice, the consecrated fervor of their affection from childhood upwards, their sense of lonely sufficiency to each other, because they only of their race had escaped death, in a night attack by the Indians. He related his discovery or suspicion of a secret sympathy between his sister and Walter Brome, and told how a distempered jealousy had maddened him. In the following passage, I threw a glimmering light on the mystery of the tale.

"Searching," continued Leonard, "into the breast of Walter Brome, I at length found a cause why Alice must inevitably love him. For he was my very counterpart! I compared his mind by each individual portion, and as a whole, with mine. There was a resemblance from which I shrunk with sickness, and loathing, and horror, as if my own features had come and stared upon me in a solitary place, or had met me in struggling through a crowd. Nay! the very same thoughts would often express themselves in the same words from our lips, proving a hateful sympathy in our secret souls. His education, indeed, in the cities of the old world, and mine in this rude wilderness, had wrought a superficial difference. The evil of his character, also, had been strengthened and rendered prominent by a reckless and ungoverned life, while mine had been softened and purified by the gentle and holy nature of Alice. But my soul had been conscious of the germ of all the fierce and deep passions, and of all the many varieties of wickedness, which accident had brought to their full maturity in him. Nor will I deny that, in the accursed one, I could see the withered blossom of every virtue, which, by a happier culture, had been made to bring forth fruit in me. Now, here was a man whom Alice might love with all the strength of sisterly affection, added to that impure passion which alone engrosses all the heart. The stranger would have more than the love which had been gathered to me from the many graves of our household—and I be desolate!"

——————————— • ———————————

Leonard Doane went on to describe the insane hatred that had kindled his heart into a volume of hellish flame. It appeared, indeed, that his jealousy had grounds, so far as that Walter Brome had actually sought the love of Alice, who also had betrayed an undefinable, but powerful interest in the unknown youth. The latter, in spite of his passion for Alice, seemed to return the loathful antipathy of her brother; the similarity of their dispositions made them like joint possessors of an individual nature, which could not become wholly the property of one, unless by the extinction of the other. At last, with the same devil in each bosom, they chanced to meet, they two on a lonely road. While Leonard spoke, the wizard had sat listening to what he already knew, yet with tokens of pleasurable interest, manifested by flashes of expression across his vacant features, by grisly smiles and by a word here and there, mysteriously filling up some void in the narrative. But when the young man told how Walter Brome had taunted him with indubitable proofs of the shame of Alice, and, before the triumphant sneer could vanish from his face, had died by her brother's hand, the wizard laughed aloud. Leonard started, but just then a gust of wind came down the chimney, forming itself into a close resemblance of the slow, unvaried laughter, by which he had been interrupted. "I was deceived," thought he; and thus pursued his fearful story.

———————— • ————————

"I trod out his accursed soul, and knew that he was dead; for my spirit bounded as if a chain had fallen from it and left me free. But the burst of exulting certainty soon fled, and was succeeded by a torpor over my brain and a dimness before my eyes, with the sensation of one who struggles through a dream. So I bent down over the body of Walter Brome, gazing into his face, and striving to make my soul glad with the thought, that he, in very truth, lay dead before me. I know not what space of time I had thus stood, nor how the vision came. But it seemed to me that the irrevocable years since childhood had rolled back, and a scene, that had long been confused and broken in my memory, arrayed itself with all its first distinctness. Methought I stood a weeping infant by my father's hearth; by the cold and blood-stained hearth where he lay dead. I heard the childish wail of Alice, and my own cry arose with hers, as we beheld the features of our parent, fierce with the strife and distorted with the pain, in which his spirit had passed away. As I gazed, a cold wind whistled by, and waved my father's hair. Immediately I stood again in the lonesome road, no more a sinless child, but a man of blood, whose tears were falling fast over the face of his dead enemy. But the delusion was not wholly gone; that face still wore a likeness of my father; and because my soul shrank from the fixed glare of the eyes, I bore the body to the lake, and would have buried it there. But before his icy sepulchre was hewn, I heard the voices of two travellers and fled."

———————————— • ————————————

Such was the dreadful confession of Leonard Doane. And now tortured by the idea of his sister's guilt, yet sometimes yielding to a conviction of her purity; stung with remorse for the death of Walter Brome, and shuddering with a deeper sense of some unutterable crime, perpetrated, as he imagined, in madness or a dream; moved also by dark impulses, as if a fiend were whispering him to meditate violence against the life of Alice; he had sought this interview with the wizard, who, on certain conditions, had no power to withhold his aid in unravelling the mystery. The tale drew near its close.

———————————— • ————————————

The moon was bright on high; the blue firmament appeared to glow with an inherent brightness; the greater stars were burning in their spheres; the northern lights threw their mysterious glare far over the horizon; the few small clouds aloft were burdened with radiance; but the sky, with all its variety of light, was scarcely so brilliant as the earth. The rain of the preceding night had frozen as it fell, and, by that simple magic, had wrought wonders. The trees were hung with diamonds and many-colored gems; the houses were overlaid with silver, and the streets paved with slippery brightness; a frigid glory was flung over all familiar things, from the cottage chimney to the steeple of the meeting-house, that gleamed upward to the sky. This living world, where we sit by our firesides, or go forth to meet beings like ourselves, seemed rather the creation of wizard power, with so much of resemblance to known objects that a man might shudder at the ghostly shape of his old beloved dwelling, and the shadow of a ghostly tree before his door. One looked to behold inhabitants suited to such a town, glittering in icy garments, with motionless features, cold, sparkling eyes, and just sensation enough in their frozen hearts to shiver at each other's presence.

———————————— • ————————————

By this fantastic piece of description, and more in the same style, I intended to throw a ghostly glimmer round the reader, so that his imagination might view the town through a medium that should take

off its every-day aspect, and make it a proper theatre for so wild a
scene as the final one. Amid this unearthly show, the wretched
brother and sister were represented as setting forth, at midnight,
through the gleaming streets, and directing their steps to a graveyard,
where all the dead had been laid, from the first corpse in that ancient
town, to the murdered man who was buried three days before. As
they went, they seemed to see the wizard gliding by their sides, or
walking dimly on the path before them. But here I paused, and gazed
into the faces of my two fair auditors, to judge whether, even on the
hill where so many had been brought to death by wilder tales than
this, I might venture to proceed. Their bright eyes were fixed on me;
their lips apart. I took courage, and led the fated pair to a new made
grave, where for a few moments, in the bright and silent midnight,
they stood alone. But suddenly there was a multitude of people
among the graves.

————————— • —————————

Each family tomb had given up its inhabitants, who, one by one,
through distant years, had been borne to its dark chamber, but now
came forth and stood in a pale group together. There was the gray
ancestor, the aged mother, and all their descendants, some withered
and full of years, like themselves, and others in their prime; there,
too, were the children who went prattling to the tomb, and there the
maiden who yielded her early beauty to death's embrace, before
passion had polluted it. Husbands and wives arose, who had lain
many years side by side, and young mothers who had forgotten to
kiss their first babes, though pillowed so long on their bosoms. Many
had been buried in the habiliments of life, and still wore their ancient
garb; some were old defenders of the infant colony, and gleamed
forth in their steel-caps and bright breastplates, as if starting up at
an Indian war-cry; other venerable shapes had been pastors of the
church, famous among the New England clergy, and now leaned with
hands clasped over their gravestones, ready to call the congregation
to prayer. There stood the early settlers, those old illustrious ones, the
heroes of tradition and fireside legends, the men of history whose
features had been so long beneath the sod that few alive could have
remembered them. There, too, were faces of former towns-people,
dimly recollected from childhood, and others, whom Leonard and
Alice had wept in later years, but who now were most terrible of all,
by their ghastly smile of recognition. All, in short, were there; the

dead of other generations, whose moss-grown names could scarce be read upon their tombstones, and their successors, whose graves were not yet green; all whom black funerals had followed slowly thither now reappeared where the mourners left them. Yet none but souls accursed were there, and fiends counterfeiting the likeness of departed saints.

The countenances of those venerable men, whose very features had been hallowed by lives of piety, were contorted now by intolerable pain or hellish passion, and now by an unearthly and derisive merriment. Had the pastors prayed, all saintlike as they seemed, it had been blasphemy. The chaste matrons, too, and the maidens with untasted lips, who had slept in their virgin graves apart from all other dust, now wore a look from which the two trembling mortals shrank, as if the unimaginable sin of twenty worlds were collected there. The faces of fond lovers, even of such as had pined into the tomb, because there their treasure was, were bent on one another with glances of hatred and smiles of bitter scorn, passions that are to devils what love is to the blest. At times, the features of those who had passed from a holy life to heaven would vary to and fro, between their assumed aspect and the fiendish lineaments whence they had been transformed. The whole miserable multitude, both sinful souls and false spectres of good men, groaned horribly and gnashed their teeth, as they looked upward to the calm loveliness of the midnight sky, and beheld those homes of bliss where they must never dwell. Such was the apparition, though too shadowy for language to portray; for here would be the moonbeams on the ice, glittering through a warrior's breastplate, and there the letters of a tombstone, on the form that stood before it; and whenever a breeze went by, it swept the old men's hoary heads, the women's fearful beauty, and all the unreal throng, into one indistinguishable cloud together.

——————————— • ———————————

I dare not give the remainder of the scene, except in a very brief epitome. This company of devils and condemned souls had come on a holiday, to revel in the discovery of a complicated crime; as foul a one as ever was imagined in their dreadful abode. In the course of the tale, the reader had been permitted to discover that all the incidents were results of the machinations of the wizard, who had cunningly devised that Walter Brome should tempt his unknown sister to guilt and shame, and himself perish by the hand of his twin-brother. I described the glee of the fiends at this hideous conception, and their eagerness to know if it were consummated. The story concluded with the Appeal of Alice to the spectre of Walter Brome; his reply, absolving her from every stain; and the trembling awe with which ghost and devil fled, as from the sinless presence of an angel.

The sun had gone down. While I held my page of wonders in the fading light, and read how Alice and her brother were left alone among the graves, my voice mingled with the sigh of a summer wind, which passed over the hill-top, with the broad and hollow sound as of the flight of unseen spirits. Not a word was spoken till I added that the wizard's grave was close beside us, and that the wood-wax had sprouted originally from his unhallowed bones. The ladies started; perhaps their cheeks might have grown pale had not the crimson west been blushing on them; but after a moment they began to laugh, while the breeze took a livelier motion, as if responsive to their mirth. I kept an awful solemnity of visage, being, indeed, a little piqued that a narrative which had good authority in our ancient superstitions, and would have brought even a church deacon to Gallows Hill, in old witch times, should now be considered too grotesque and extravagant for timid maids to tremble at. Though it was past supper time, I detained them a while longer on the hill, and made a trial whether truth were more powerful than fiction.

We looked again towards the town, no longer arrayed in that icy splendor of earth, tree, and edifice, beneath the glow of a wintry midnight, which shining afar through the gloom of a century had made it appear the very home of visions in visionary streets. An indistinctness had begun to creep over the mass of buildings and blend them with the intermingled tree-tops, except where the roof of a statelier mansion, and the steeples and brick towers of churches, caught the brightness of some cloud that yet floated in the sunshine. Twilight over the landscape was congenial to the obscurity of time. With such eloquence as my share of feeling and fancy could supply, I called back hoar antiquity, and bade my companions imagine an ancient multitude of people, congregated on the hillside, spreading far below, clustering on the steep old roofs, and climbing the adjacent heights, wherever a glimpse of this spot might be obtained. I strove to realize and faintly communicate the deep, unutterable loathing and horror, the indignation, the affrighted wonder, that wrinkled on every brow, and filled the universal heart. See! the whole crowd turns pale and shrinks within itself, as the virtuous emerge from yonder street. Keeping pace with that devoted company, I described them one by one; here tottered a woman in her dotage, knowing neither the crime imputed her, nor its punishment; there another, distracted by the universal madness, till feverish dreams were remembered as realities, and she almost believed her guilt. One, a proud man once, was so broken down by the intolerable hatred heaped upon him, that he seemed to hasten his steps, eager to hide himself in the grave hastily dug at the foot of the gallows. As they went slowly on, a mother looked behind, and beheld her peaceful dwelling; she cast her eyes elsewhere, and groaned inwardly yet with bitterest anguish, for there was her little son among the accusers. I watched the face of an ordained pastor, who walked onward to the same death; his lips moved in prayer; no narrow petition for himself alone, but embracing all his fellow-sufferers and the frenzied multitude; he looked to Heaven and trod lightly up the hill.

Behind their victims came the afflicted, a guilty and miserable band; villains who had thus avenged themselves on their enemies, and viler wretches, whose cowardice had destroyed their friends; lunatics, whose ravings had chimed in with the madness of the land; and children, who had played a game that the imps of darkness might have envied them, since it disgraced an age, and dipped a people's hands in blood. In the rear of the procession rode a figure on horseback, so darkly conspicuous, so sternly triumphant, that my hearers mistook him for the visible presence of the fiend himself; but it was only his good friend, Cotton Mather, proud of his well-won dignity, as the representative of all the hateful features of his time; the one blood-thirsty man, in whom were concentrated those vices of spirit and errors of opinion that sufficed to madden the whole surrounding multitude. And thus I marshalled them onward, the innocent who were to die, and the guilty who were to grow old in long remorse—tracing their every step, by rock, and shrub, and bro- ken track, till their shadowy visages had circled round the hill-top, where we stood. I plunged into my imagination for a blacker horror, and a deeper woe, and pictured the scaffold——

But here my companions seized an arm on each side; their nerves were trembling; and, sweeter victory still, I had reached the seldom trodden places of their hearts, and found the well-spring of their tears. And now the past had done all it could. We slowly descended, watching the lights as they twinkled gradually through the town, and listening to the distant mirth of boys at play, and to the voice of a young girl warbling somewhere in the dusk, a pleasant sound to wanderers from old witch times. Yet, ere we left the hill, we could not but regret that there is nothing on its barren summit, no relic of old, nor lettered stone of later days, to assist the imagination in appealing to the heart. We build the memorial column on the height which our fathers made sacred with their blood, poured out in a holy cause. And here, in dark, funereal stone, should rise another monument, sadly commemorative of the errors of an earlier race, and not to be cast down, while the human heart has one infirmity that may result in crime.

NARRATIVE ESSAY

BERTON ROUECHÉ

Berton Roueché has become known for his infectious essays in The New Yorker *on the detection of rare and unusual medical problems, about which he often writes as if the problems were mysterious "crimes." He uses the methods of fiction writers to convey the excitement of medical men and women who are confronted with sick, dying, or diseased individuals. For instance, the title piece in one of his essay collections,* Eleven Blue Men, *concerns a case of sodium* nitrite *poisoning which was the result of a wrongly filled salt (sodium* nitrate*) container in a cafeteria. Chapter 3 includes another of his "medical detection" essays, "The Emotion of Weirdness," which investigates an undangerous psychological mystery, that of* déjà vu.*

In the following selection, Sandy has caused a number of other children to become "afflicted." How she created this situation has implications for the study of the "afflicted" girls of Salem, although Roueché himself only glances in their direction once (in a reference to witch hunts). In this essay, the "medical detective" has a perhaps less poetic title—epidemiologist: one who studies epidemics, or widespread community diseases.

Roueché calls his essays "narratives of medical detection," and he accordingly uses fictional methods (scene-setting, characters, plot) to tell his story. The pieces remain essays, however, because he uses such nonfiction techniques as interviewing the participants and gathering information from authorities or from historical works to support the "plot." This "narrative," whether we see it as finally originating from a fiction or nonfiction impulse, relies on a high concentration of specific detail to convince us of the story's authenticity.

Sandy

Dr. Joel L. Nitzkin, chief of the Office of Consumer Protection, a section of the Dade County, Florida, Department of Public Health, sat crouched (he is six feet nine) at his desk in the Civic Center complex in downtown Miami, stirring a mug of coffee that his secretary had just brought in. It was around half past ten on a sunny Monday morning in May—May 13, 1974. His telephone rang. He put down his coffee and picked up the phone and heard the voice of a colleague, Martha Sonderegger, the department's assistant nursing director. Miss Sonderegger was calling to report that her Miami Beach unit had just received a call for help—for the services of a team of public-health nurses—from the Bay Harbor Elementary School. There had been a pipe break or a leak of some kind, Miss Sonderegger had been told, and the school was engulfed in a pall of poison gas. Many of the children were ill, and some had been taken to a neighborhood hospital by the rescue squad of the municipal fire department. Dr. Nitzkin listened, considered.

He said, "What do you think, Martha?"

"It sounds a little strange."

"I think so, too."

"But I'm sending a team of nurses."

"Yes," Dr. Nitzkin said. "Of course. And I think I'd better drive out to the school and take a look myself."

He thanked her and hung up—and then picked up the phone again. He made two quick calls. One was to an industrial hygienist named Carl DiSalvo, in the Division of Environmental Health. The other was to a staff physician named Myriam Enriquez, in the Disease Control Section. He asked Dr. Enriquez to meet him at once at his car; as for Mr. DiSalvo, he was already on his way to the school. Dr. Nitzkin untangled his legs and got up. He was out of his office in two easy, five-foot strides. His coffee cooled on his desk, untasted and forgotten.

———————————— • ————————————

Dr. Nitzkin is no longer associated with the Dade County Department of Public Health. He has moved up, both professionally and geographically, to Rochester, New York, where he now serves as director of the Monroe County Department of Health, and it was there, on a winter day, that I talked with him about the summons to the Bay Harbor Elementary School. His recollection was undimmed, indelible.

"I remember it was hot," he told me, standing at his office window and gazing down through the palm trees in his memory at the bare maples and last night's foot of new snow. "Warm, anyway —warm enough to make me think that the 'poison gas' at the school might have something to do with the air-conditioning system. And I remember my first sight of the school. The scene was complete pandemonium. It had the *look* of a disaster. We had to park half a block away, because the school parking lot was full of trucks and vans and cars of all kinds—all parked every which way. Ambulances. Fire equipment. Police cars. All with their flashers flashing. And the media—they were swarming. Newspaper reporters and photographers. Radio people with microphones. Television cameras from four local stations. And even—good God!—local dignitaries. Members of the Dade County School Board. Members of the Bay Harbor Town Council. And neighbors and passersby and parents all rushing around. I had never seen anything like it, and I had to wonder how come. But the explanation, it turned out, was simple enough. The school had called the fire department, and the fire department had called the rescue squad—and the media all monitor the fire department's radio frequency. There was one oasis of calm and order. That was the children. They had been marched out of the building in firedrill formation and were lined up quietly in the shade of some trees at the far end of the school grounds. There were a lot of them —several hundred, it looked like. Which was reassuring. I had got the impression that most of the school had been stricken by whatever the trouble was. Dr. Enriquez and I cut through the mob, looking for someone in charge. It turned out that the school principal was away somewhere at a meeting. We asked around and were finally directed to the head secretary. She was the person nominally in charge, but you couldn't say she was in control. Nobody was in control.

"She and Dr. Enriquez and I talked for a moment at the entrance to the building. The building was standard design for contemporary Florida schools. The entrance hall ran back to a cross corridor that led to the classrooms. The other school facilities were off the entrance hall. The offices, the clinic, and the library were on the right-hand side. On the left were the teachers' lounge, the cafetorium, and the kitchen. A cafetorium is a room that doubles as an auditorium and a cafeteria. The secretary gave us all the information she had. It was her understanding that there had been a gas leak of some kind. That was what she had heard. But she had seen the first victim with her own eyes. The first victim was an eleven-year-old girl in the fifth grade. I'll call her Sandy. Sandy was a member of a chorus of around a hundred and seventy-five fourth, fifth, and sixth graders who had assembled with the music teacher in the cafetorium at nine o'clock to rehearse for a schoolwide musical program. Halfway through the hour—this, I should say, was constructed later—she began to feel sick. She slipped out of the cafetorium. She was seen by some of the students but not by the teacher. She went across the hall to the clinic and went in and collapsed on a couch. The clinic staff was off duty at the moment, but the secretary happened to catch sight of her, and went in and found her lying there unconscious. She tried to revive her—with smelling salts!"

"My mother used to carry smelling salts," I said.

"Yes. It was rather sweet, I thought. Well, anyway, Sandy didn't respond, and that very naturally alarmed the secretary. And so she very naturally called for help. She called the fire department. Sandy was still unconscious when the fire-rescue squad arrived, and they didn't waste any time. They put her on a stretcher and took her off to the hospital—North Shore Hospital. Then another child got sick, and another, and another. That's when our nursing unit was called. Seven children were sick enough to also be rushed to the hospital after Sandy went. Around twenty-five others were sick enough to be sent home. The school called their parents, and they came and picked them up. Another forty or so were being treated here at the school. They were in the cafetorium." Dr. Nitzkin raised his eyebrows. "That's what the secretary said—in the *cafetorium!* Myriam Enriquez and I exchanged a look. Wasn't the cafetorium where Sandy became ill, I asked. Where the poison gas must have first appeared? The secretary looked baffled. She said she didn't know anything about that. She had first seen Sandy in the clinic. All she knew was that the sick children still at the school were being treated in the cafetorium.

"We left the secretary and went on into the school. I think we were both in the same uncomfortable state of mind. The situation still felt the way it had to Martha Sonderegger. It felt strange. There was also a strange smell in the place. We smelled it the minute we stepped into the hall. It wasn't unpleasant—just strong. We couldn't place it. Well, that was what Carl DiSalvo was here for. He would work it out. I hadn't seen him, but I knew he was somewhere in the building. We went on to the cafetorium. There was the sound of many voices. It sounded like a mammoth cocktail party. We went into a big room full of people, full of uniforms. Nurses. Police. Fire-rescue workers, in their white coveralls. And a lot of other people. The sick children were stretched out here and there. I could still smell the strange smell, but it was fainter—much fainter—here. Dr. Enriquez and I separated. She had her clinical tests to make. I was the epidemiologist. I walked around the room and looked, and talked to some of the children. The clinical picture was rather curious. There was an unusual variety of signs and symptoms. Headache. Dizziness. Chills. Abdominal pain. Shortness of breath. Weakness. I noticed two kids who were obviously hyperventilating, breathing very fast and very deep. That was an interesting symptom.

"I stood and thought for a moment. I began to get a glimmer of a glimmer. I went across the hall to an office and found a telephone and called the emergency room at North Shore Hospital and talked to the doctor on duty there. He knew about the children from the Bay Harbor school. He said they were in satisfactory condition. He said they seemed to be feeling better. He said he didn't have results on all of the lab tests yet, but the findings he *had* seen seemed to be essentially normal. My glimmer still glimmered. I started back to the cafetorium, and ran into DiSalvo. He had been looking for me. He had made a quick inspection of the physical environment of the building and he hadn't turned up any tangible factors—any gases or fumes or allergens—that could have caused any kind of illness. I mentioned the funny smell. He laughed. He had checked it out. It came from an adhesive used to secure a new carpet in the library. The adhesive was in no way toxic. Anyway, the carpet had been laid a good two weeks earlier. DiSalvo was satisfied with his preliminary findings, but he was going to settle down and do the usual full-scale comprehensive survey. I was satisfied, too. I was more than willing to drop the idea of a toxic gas. I had never really believed it. And I was also satisfied that we could rule out a bacterial or viral cause of the trouble. The incubation period—the interval between exposure and the onset of illness—was much too short. And the symptoms were also wrong.

"I left DiSalvo and went back to the cafetorium, and I remember looking at my watch. It was eleven-thirty. I had been at the school a scant twenty minutes. It felt like forever. But then, all of a sudden, things began to move. I entered the cafetorium this time by a side door at the kitchen end of the room, and there was a woman standing there—one of the kitchen staff. The dietitian, maybe. An authoritative woman, anyway. She called me over. And—Was it some look in my eye? I don't know. But she said, 'Aren't you a doctor?' I said I was. 'Well,' she said, 'then why don't you do something? Why don't you straighten out this mess? This is all perfectly ridiculous. You know as well as I do that there's nothing the matter with these kids. Get them up on their feet! Get them out of here! They're in the way! I have to start setting up for lunch.'

"I must have stood and gaped at her. I'd had a funny feeling —a deep-down, gut suspicion—from the very beginning of the case that there was something not quite right about it. I'd got a glimmer when I saw those two kids hyperventilating. Hyperventilation is a classic psychosomatic anxiety reaction. And now the truth finally hit me. A memory rose up in my mind. I knew what I was seeing here. Something very like this had happened just a year before in an elementary school in a little town in Alabama—Berry, Alabama. The dietician was right. But she was also wrong. She was right about there being nothing fundamentally the matter with the kids. But she was wrong in thinking that all those aches and pains and chills and nausea were illusory. They were real, all right. And this was a real epidemic. It was an epidemic of mass hysteria."

———————— • ————————

The word "hysteria" derives from the Greek *hystera,* meaning "uterus." This curious name reflects Hippocrates' notion of the point of origin of the disturbance. "For hysterical maidens," he wrote, "I prescribe marriage, for they are cured by pregnancy." His view prevailed in medicine until well into the nineteenth century, and is perhaps still prevalent in the lingering lay association of women and hysteria. The term "mass hysteria" is also a lay survival. The phenomenon is now preferably known to science as "collective obsessional behavior." Collective obsessions occur throughout the animal world (the cattle stampede, the flocking of starlings on the courthouse roof), and the human animal, despite—or maybe because of— its more finely tuned mentality, seems exquisitely susceptible to them. Manifestations among the human race take many forms. These range in social seriousness from the transient tyranny of the fad (skate-boards, Farrah Fawcett-Majors, jogging, Perrier with a twist) and the eager lockstep of fashion (blue jeans, hoopskirts, stomping boots, white kid gloves, the beard, the wig) to the delirium of the My Lai massacre and the frenzy of the race riot and the witch hunt. Epidemic obsessional behavior differs from its companion compulsions in one prominent respect. It is not, as Alan C. Kerckhoff and Kurt W. Back, both of Duke University, have noted in "The June Bug: A Study of Hysterical Contagion" (1968), "an active response to some element in the situation; it is a passive experience. The actors do not *do* something so much as something happens to them."

History is rich in eruptions of mass hysteria. An outbreak was reported toward the end of the first Christian century by Plutarch. In "Mulierum Virtutes," one of his several philosophical works, he refers to a mass "mental upset and frenzy" among the young women of Miletus (a then important port on the Aegean coast of what is now Turkey), in which "there fell suddenly upon all of them a desire for death, and a mad impulse toward hanging." The toll, if any, is not recorded. More recently, in 1936, a similar desire for death fell upon the citizens of Budapest. Its victims, eighteen in all, were mesmerized admirers of a popular song called "Gloomy Sunday." Lugubrious in words and music, it is a cry of despair from a lover whose loved one has died. The lyrics, in English translation, read in part:

> *Gloomy is Sunday, with shadows I spend it all.*
> *My heart and I have decided to end it all.*
> *Soon there'll be candles and pray'rs that are sad, I know.*
> *Let them not weep, let them know that I'm glad to go.*

Suicide is not a common component of morbid mass behavior. In fact, death of any kind is a rarity in such outbreaks. The maniacal speculation in tulip bulbs that swept ruinously through Holland in the seventeenth century was a phenomenon of more classic construction. So were the Children's Crusade of the early thirteenth century and the successive waves of the dancing mania which broke over most of Europe a century and a half later. The Children's Crusade had its beginning in the summer of 1212, when some twenty thousand German and some thirty thousand French children, exalted by a sudden and contagious conviction that Christian love would succeed where Christian arms had failed in the recovery of the Holy Land, left their homes and set out in mile-long swarms for the East. It ended

about a year later in Marseilles and several Italian ports, where differently inspired Christians rounded up most of the children and turned
them into cash. The girls were thrust into brothels, and the boys were
sold to agents of the Egyptian slave trade. The dancing mania is
usually taken to have been an overreaction to the abatement of the
protracted terrors of the Black Death in the mid-fourteenth century.
"As early as 1374," Ralph H. Major, in his "History of Medicine,"
notes, "large crowds of men and women, obsessed by a strange
mania, appeared on the streets of Aachen. Forming circles, hand in
hand, they danced around in wild delirium for hours and hours, quite
oblivious to the jeers and taunts of the onlookers. From Aachen the
malady spread to Liège, then to Utrecht, Cologne, and Metz. The
bands of dancers moved from town to town, finding everywhere new
recruits to swell their numbers." The nineteenth-century historian
J. F. K. Hecker, in his "Epidemics of the Middle Ages," adds, "Where
the disease was fully developed, the attacks were ushered in with
epileptiform seizures. The afflicted fell to the ground unconscious,
foaming from the mouth and struggling for breath, but after a time
of rest they got up and began dancing with still greater impetus and
renewed vigor. . . . Music appeared to be the sole means of combat-
ting this strange epidemic. . . . Soft, calm harmonies, graduated from
fast to slow, proved efficacious as a cure." The frenetic folk dance of
southern Italy called the tarantella is widely thought to be a relic of
that terpsichorean marathon.

Eruptions of epidemic hysteria in the modern world, though
numerous, have tended to be more modest in size. They have also,
like the 1973 outbreak in Berry, Alabama, which led Dr. Nitzkin to
suspect the nature of the episode at the Bay Harbor school, tended
to occur in schools or other closed communities, and to conceal their
functional origin behind a mask of organic illness.

——————— • ———————

Dr. Nitzkin turned away from the winter window. He sat on the edge
of his desk and crossed his legs. He reached down and scratched a
distant ankle. He raised his head and smiled. "The trouble at Berry
was a little unusual," he said. His smile widened. "It was a pruritus
—an itchy rash." His smile faded. "But it was otherwise very seriously typical. It was a small disaster. It went on and on. The outbreak
began on a Friday, there was a recurrence on Tuesday, and another
the following Friday. At that point, the school board closed the

school for the remainder of the term. A diagnosis of mass hysteria is largely a matter of exclusion. The investigators at Berry seem to have suspected hysteria pretty early, but they weren't able to convince the community that they had excluded all possibility of an organic cause. Hysteria is self-perpetuating. It doesn't just run its course. It must be promptly recognized and acted upon, or it will go on and on and get worse and worse. Well, I recognized it here. I was sure of that. I trusted DiSalvo's professionalism and plain good sense, and I was sure of my own clinical judgment. So it was up to me to act. But I was critically aware that I was taking a chance. The decision to close the school or allow it to stay open was no small thing. I looked around the room, and spotted a little group at the far end. I recognized the head secretary and two or three school-board people and somebody from the town council. That was the place to start. I went over, and they saw me coming. My height has its advantages. And I guess I looked decisive. I said I had an announcement to make, and they gave me their attention. I said that our Health Department investigation had eliminated the possibility of any toxic gas. I said there was also no evidence of any infectious disease. I called their attention to the hyperventilating kids. By that time, our little circle had grown. Some of the teachers drifted over, and some of the fire-rescue squad, and some of the police, and some parents, and some of the kids themselves. And, of course, the press. All of a sudden, I was talking into microphones, and flashbulbs were popping, and the television cameras were zooming in. I tell you, it was chilling. I had to believe I knew what I was doing. I took a deep breath, and said that it wasn't an outbreak of gas poisoning or any other kind of poisoning. It was an outbreak of hysteria—mass hysteria. I said I didn't know just how it had started, but I knew how to stop it. I said the only way to bring it under control was to get things back to normal. I asked that the cafetorium be cleared, so the kitchen staff could set it up for lunch. I asked that the children out on the school grounds be brought back into the building and sent to their classrooms. And the time to do it, I said, was *now*—right this minute.

"Then I held my breath. Nobody tried to challenge me or contradict me. Nobody said a word. But you should have seen their faces. The public-health nurses looked stunned. I saw Dr. Enriquez smiling and nodding. The parents of the sick children looked horrified and insulted—I was telling them their children were crazy. But most of the others—the teachers and the school-board people and the firemen and the head secretary—just stood there looking thoughtful. The truth was dawning. I think that maybe some of them had half suspected the truth all along. Well, I started in all over again. I gave them my reasons and my reasoning. I could see heads beginning to nod and faces starting to relax. And then, all of a sudden, the tension dissolved. The firemen and the police just sort of disappeared. People began to turn to each other and talk. The sick kids stopped looking so sick. The head secretary went out to the kitchen, and the teachers began to clear the room. It was all over.

"I mean, the *emergency* was over. There was still plenty of work to do. I still had to justify my decision—and not only to the school and the public. I had to explain it to the satisfaction of my office. I had made a bold move, and bold moves are not encouraged in the bureaucratic world. I had some very angry calls from parents. One mother demanded that I apologize to her child. I was finally able to convince her that being suggestible at the age of eleven was not a sign of insanity. But, thank God, I was lucky. The proof was forthcoming. I acquired one useful piece of information even before I left the cafetorium. A teacher came up to me at the end of my speech and said she was sure I was right. She said there could not have been any poison gas or fumes in the cafetorium, because when the first rehearsal class let out, and the first wave of illness broke, a second rehearsal class had marched into the cafetorium and spent the hour rehearsing, and none of the children in that class had been taken ill. So, gas or no gas, the cafetorium could not have been the site of the trouble. But it was in the cafetorium that the first victim—the girl I'm calling Sandy—took sick. How come?

"I hung around the school, trying to figure it out. It was amazing how quickly everything got back to normal. I talked to more teachers. I talked to some of the children. I talked with a neighborhood doctor who had been called when the trouble first began. They gave me a brainful of bits and pieces. I could see what had happened, but I couldn't see how it had happened. Sandy was what we call in epidemiology the index case. Everything that happened stemmed from her. But I couldn't find a clear connection. The timetable didn't seem to tell the right time. Sandy had slipped out of the cafetorium and collapsed in the clinic at about nine-thirty. But it wasn't until ten o'clock—until the nine-o'clock classes let out—that the wave of illness broke. Why did it take so long? And why did it happen when it did? I wandered around talking and listening, and trying to fit the pieces together. It's hard to remember now just how I did it. Did somebody tell me something? Or did I simply take a different look at something I already knew? Anyway, it suddenly all came together. The whole thing hung on coincidence—on two coincidences, actually. One of them had to do with Sandy and the fire-rescue people. They arrived at the school on the head secretary's summons a couple of minutes before ten. Sandy was still in her faint, or whatever it was. They lifted her onto a stretcher and carried her out and down the hall —at the very moment that the nine-o'clock classes, including the group rehearsing in the cafetorium, let out. The kids flowed out of the cafetorium. They saw Sandy passed out on a stretcher. They had seen her slip out of the rehearsal, and now they knew why. Something was wrong. And somebody reacted—I'm reconstructing now. Somebody complained of feeling sick. That triggered it. That's all it takes in these cases. Hysteria took over. And then the second coincidence happened. That was the neighborhood doctor. He arrived at the school, he saw the fire-rescue squad, he saw the children reacting —and he smelled the funny smell of the adhesive on the new library carpet. He thought it was the smell of something toxic. He said something to that effect to somebody. And the word spread. That pulled the trigger on the second barrel.

"When I went back to the office, I knew what had happened, and why, and how. The rest was documentation. I was confident that it would bear me out. And it did. DiSalvo's thorough investigation confirmed his preliminary study. The physical environment of the building was safe and clean. We also did a comprehensive clinical study. The heart of it was a student questionnaire. We found that a total of seventy-three children had reported at least some symptoms of illness—seventy-three out of a total enrollment of around four hundred and fifty. Most of them—sixty-three—were in either the fifth or the sixth grade. Most of the chief reactors were girls. Don't ask me why, but girls—young girls—seem to be more susceptible than boys. In the Berry outbreak, girls outnumbered boys by more than two to one. Anyway, we did a special study of the seven children who were hospitalized along with Sandy. All of them had been in the first rehearsal class, and they all knew Sandy. We looked into their psychological background, and came up with some interesting data. Five of the seven were girls. One of these had a clear history of hypochondria. Another was always sick or sickly. Another had a habit of hyperventilating in moments of stress. Another had come to school that day feeling vaguely ill. Another was one of Sandy's closest friends. One of the boys was a chronic discipline problem. The other boy was described by the school as highly excitable.

"The questionnaire provided some very interesting information. The comments of some of the children who reported feeling sick that morning were particularly revealing. These were mostly in response to the question 'When you got sick, did you know that other children were sick, too?' I'll read you some of the comments. One girl answered, 'Yes, because Sandy fainted.' Another wrote, 'Yes—a lot of kids. I started to feel sick between Music and Language Arts, and then they carried me outside.' Another girl answered, 'I just knew that a boy vomited.' Her only symptom was nausea. Another girl wrote, 'Yes—Sandy was sick.' And a boy—one of the few boys— wrote, 'Yes, and after Sandy got sick and there was a fire drill, and when everybody was walking out of the building, I felt like a small headache.' Well, you get the drift. We also talked to Sandy. She turned out to be pretty much as expected. I mean, she was the right type. She was attractive. She was a good student. She was precocious. And she was very popular. She was looked up to."

"She was a kind of leader?" I asked. "She set the pattern?"

"Yes," he said. "I think you could say that."

"But what about her?" I asked. "What made her get sick?"

Dr. Nitzkin looked at me. "Oh," he said. "Sandy was *really* sick. She had some sort of virus. All that standing and singing in place was too much for her. She just passed out."

ARGUMENTATIVE ESSAY

BARBARA EHRENREICH AND DEIRDRE ENGLISH

Ehrenreich and English argue that witches were persecuted in medieval Europe because they represented a threat to the orthodox, male-controlled approaches to religion and medicine. In this selection, the authors actually deny the direct relevance of their interpretation of witchcraft and medicine to the Salem events, mainly because those events took place "in an entirely different social context than the earlier European witch-craze." But the main points of their essay are worth considering in the context of Salem, if for no other reason than the fact that Puritan divines (regardless of the intensity of their personal beliefs) were a product of the European ideology of witch persecution.

The essay is a strong argument for the authors' central thesis that witches were "lay healers" whose persecution "marks one of the opening struggles in the history of man's suppression of women as healers." (Note that "man" here is gender-specific; it is not a generic, or all-inclusive, term for all people.) After a survey of witch hunting in Europe, the authors turn to a twofold classification of the main "crimes" witches were accused of: sexual contact with the devil, and healing. Three main agents are identified with their suppression, the Catholic Church, the State, and "university-trained" male doctors. For Ehrenreich and English, gender is a key agent in historical analysis; they take a militant stand almost immediately, in some cases quoting authorities only to undermine their positions. The result is a classic argumentative essay.

Witchcraft and Medicine in the Middle Ages

Witches lived and were burned long before the development of modern medical technology. The great majority of them were lay healers serving the peasant population, and their suppression marks one of the opening struggles in the history of man's suppression of women as healers.

The other side of the suppression of witches as healers was the creation of a new male medical profession, under the protection and patronage of the ruling classes. This new European medical profession played an important role in the witch-hunts, supporting the witches' persecutors with "medical" reasoning:

> . . . . Because the Medieval Church, with the support of kings, princes and secular authorities, controlled medical education and practice, the inquisition [witch-hunts] constitutes, among other things, an early instance of the "professional" repudiating the skills and interfering with the rights of the "nonprofessional" to minister to the poor. (Thomas Szasz, *The Manufacture of Madness*)

The witch-hunts left a lasting effect: An aspect of the female has ever since been associated with the witch, and an aura of contamination has remained—especially around the midwife and other women healers. This early and devastating exclusion of women from independent healing roles was a violent precedent and a warning: It was to become a theme of our history. The women's health movement of today has ancient roots in the medieval covens, and its opponents have as their ancestors those who ruthlessly forced the elimination of witches.

THE WITCH CRAZE

The age of witch-hunting spanned more than four centuries (from the 14th to the 17th century) in its sweep from Germany to England. It was born in feudalism and lasted—gaining in virulence —well into the "age of reason." The witch-craze took different forms at different times and places, but never lost its essential character: that of a ruling class campaign of terror directed against the female peasant population. Witches represented a political, religious and sexual threat to the Protestant and Catholic churches alike, as well as to the state.

The extent of the witch-craze is startling: In the late fifteenth and early sixteenth centuries there were thousands upon thousands of executions—usually live burnings at the stake—in Germany, Italy and other countries. In the mid-sixteenth century the terror spread to France, and finally to England. One writer has estimated the number of executions at an average of 600 a year for certain German cities —or two a day, "leaving out Sundays." Nine-hundred witches were destroyed in a single year in the Wertzberg area, and 1000 in and around Como. At Toulouse, four-hundred were put to death in a day. In the Bishopric of Trier, in 1585, two villages were left with only one female inhabitant each. Many writers have estimated the total number killed to have been in the millions. Women made up some 85 percent of those executed—old women, young women and children.*

Their scope alone suggests that the witch hunts represent a deep-seated social phenomenon which goes far beyond the history of medicine. In locale and timing, the most virulent witch hunts were associated with periods of great social upheaval

---

*We are omitting from this discussion any mention of the New England witch trials in the 1600's. These trials occurred on a relatively small scale, very late in the history of witch-hunts, and in an entirely different social context than the earlier European witch-craze.

shaking feudalism at its roots—mass peasant uprisings and conspiracies, the begin-
nings of capitalism, and the rise of Protestantism. There is fragmentary evidence—
which feminists ought to follow up—suggesting that in some areas witchcraft repre-
sented a female-led peasant rebellion. Here we can't attempt to explore the historical
context of the witch hunts in any depth. But we do have to get beyond some common
myths about the witch-craze—myths which rob the "witch" of any dignity and put
the blame on her and the peasants she served.

Unfortunately, the witch herself—poor and illiterate—did not leave us her
story. It was recorded, like all history, by the educated elite, so that today we know
the witch only through the eyes of her persecutors.

Two of the most common theories of the witch hunts are basically *medical* interpretations, attributing the witch craze to unexplain-
able outbreaks of mass hysteria. One version has it that the peasantry
went mad. According to this, the witch-craze was an epidemic of
mass hatred and panic cast in images of a blood-lusty peasant mob
bearing flaming torches. Another psychiatric interpretation holds
that the witches themselves were insane. One authoritative psychiatric historian, Gregory Zilboorg, wrote that:

> . . . millions of witches, sorcerers, possessed and obsessed were an
> enormous mass of severe neurotics [and] psychotics . . . for many years
> the world looked like a veritable insane asylum . . .

But, in fact, the witch-craze was neither a lynching party nor
a mass suicide by hysterical women. Rather, it followed well-
ordered, legalistic procedures. The witch-hunts were well-organized
campaigns, initiated, financed and executed by Church and State. To
Catholic and Protestant witch-hunters alike, the unquestioned authority on how to conduct a witch hunt was the *Malleus Maleficarum,*
or *Hammer of Witches,* written in 1484 by the Reverends Kramer and
Sprenger (the "beloved sons" of Pope Innocent VIII.) For three centuries this sadistic book lay on the bench of every judge, every witch-
hunter. In a long section on judicial proceedings, the instructions
make it clear how the "hysteria" was set off:

The job of initiating a witch trial was to be performed by either
the Vicar (priest) or Judge of the County, who was to post a notice
to

> direct, command, require and admonish that within the space of
> twelve days . . . that they should reveal it unto us if anyone know, see
> or have heard that any person is reported to be a heretic or a witch,

or if any is suspected especially of such practices as cause injury to men, cattle, or the fruits of the earth, to the loss of the State.

Anyone failing to report a witch faced both excommunication and a long list of temporal punishments.

If this threatening notice exposed at least one witch, her trial could be used to unearth several more. Kramer and Sprenger gave detailed instructions about the use of tortures to force confessions and further accusations. Commonly, the accused was stripped naked and shaved of all her body hair, then subjected to thumb-screws and the rack, spikes and bone-crushing "boots," starvation and beatings. The point is obvious: The witch-craze did not arise spontaneously in the peasantry. It was a calculated ruling class campaign of terrorization.

THE CRIMES OF THE WITCHES

Who were the witches, then, and what were their "crimes" that could arouse such vicious upper class suppression? Undoubtedly, over the centuries of witch hunting, the charge of "witchcraft" came to cover a multitude of sins ranging from political subversion and religious heresy to lewdness and blasphemy. But three central accusations emerge repeatedly in the history of witchcraft throughout northern Europe: First, witches are accused of every conceivable sexual crime against men. Quite simply, they are "accused" of female sexuality. Second, they are accused of being organized. Third, they are accused of having magical powers affecting health—of harming, but also of healing. They were often charged specifically with possessing medical and obstetrical skills.

First, consider the charge of sexual crimes. The medieval Catholic Church elevated sexism to a point of principle: The *Malleus* declares, "When a woman thinks alone, she thinks evil." The misogyny of the Church, if not proved by the witch-craze itself, is demonstrated by its teaching that in intercourse the male deposits in the female a homunculus, or "little person," complete with soul, which is simply housed in the womb for nine months, without acquiring any attributes of the mother. The homunculus is not really safe, however, until it reaches male hands again, when a priest baptises it, ensuring the salvation of its immortal soul. Another depressing fantasy of some medieval religious thinkers was that upon resurrection all human beings would be reborn as men!

The Church associated women with sex, and all pleasure in sex was condemned, because it could only come from the devil. Witches were supposed to have gotten pleasure from copulation with the devil (despite the icy-cold organ he was reputed to possess) and they in turn infected men. Lust in either man or wife, then, was blamed on the female. On the other hand, witches were accused of making men impotent and of causing their penises to disappear. As for female sexuality, witches were accused, in effect, of giving contraceptive aid and of performing abortions:

> Now there are, as it is said in the Papal Bull, seven methods by which they infect with witchcraft the venereal act and the conception of the womb: First, by inclining the minds of men to inordinate passion; second, by obstructing their generative force; third, by removing the members accommodated to that act; fourth, by changing men into beasts by their magic act; fifth, by destroying the generative force in women; sixth, by procuring abortion; seventh, by offering children to the devils, besides other animals and fruits of the earth with which they work much harm . . .
>
> *(Malleus Maleficarum)*

In the eyes of the Church, all the witches' power was ultimately derived from her sexuality. Her career began with sexual intercourse with the devil. Each witch was confirmed at a general meeting (the witches' Sabbath) at which the devil presided, often in the form of a goat, and had intercourse with the neophytes. In return for her powers, the witch promised to serve him faithfully. (In the imagination of the Church even evil could only be thought of as ultimately male-directed!) As the *Malleus* makes clear, the devil almost always acts through the female, just as he did in Eden:

> All witchcraft comes from carnal lust, which in women is insatiable . . . Wherefore for the sake of fulfilling their lusts they consort with devils . . . it is sufficiently clear that it is no matter for wonder that there are more women than men found infected with the heresy of witchcraft . . . And blessed be the Highest Who has so far preserved the male sex from so great a crime . . .

Not only were the witches women—they were women who seemed to be organized into an enormous secret society. A witch who was a proved member of the "Devil's party" was more dreadful than one who had acted alone, and the witch-hunting literature is obsessed with the question of what went on at the witches' "Sabbaths." (Eating of unbaptised babies? Bestialism and mass orgies? So went their lurid speculations . . .)

In fact, there is evidence that women accused of being witches did meet locally in small groups and that these groups came together in crowds of hundreds or thousands on festival days. Some writers speculate that the meetings were occasions for pagan religious worship. Undoubtedly the meetings were also occasions for trading herbal lore and passing on the news. We have little evidence about the political significance of the witches' organizations, but it's hard to imagine that they weren't connected to the peasant rebellions of the time. Any peasant organization, just by being an organization, would attract dissidents, increase communication between villages, and build a spirit of collectivity and autonomy among the peasants.

WITCHES AS HEALERS

We come now to the most fantastic accusation of all: The witch is accused not only of murdering and poisoning, sex crimes and conspiracy—but of *helping and healing.* As a leading English witch-hunter put it:

> For this must always be remembered, as a conclusion, that by witches we understand not only those which kill and torment, but all Diviners, Charmers, Jugglers, all Wizards, commonly called wise men and wise women . . . and in the same number we reckon all good Witches, which do no hurt but good, which do not spoil and destroy, but save and deliver . . . It were a thousand times better for the land if all Witches, but especially the blessing Witch, might suffer death.

Witch-healers were often the only general medical practitioners for a people who had no doctors and no hospitals and who were bitterly afflicted with poverty and disease. In particular, the association of the witch and the midwife was strong: "No one does more harm to the Catholic Church than midwives," wrote witch-hunters Kramer and Sprenger.

The Church itself had little to offer the suffering peasantry:

> On Sundays, after Mass, the sick came in scores, crying for help,—and words were all they got: "You have sinned, and God is afflicting you. Thank him; you will suffer so much the less torment in the life to

come. Endure, suffer, die. Has not the Church its prayers for the dead?"

(Jules Michelet, *Satanism and Witchcraft*)

When faced with the misery of the poor, the Church turned to the dogma that experience in this world is fleeting and unimportant. But there was a double standard at work, for the Church was not against medical care for the upper class. Kings and nobles had their court physicians who were men, sometimes even priests. The real issue was control: Male upper class healing under the auspices of the Church was acceptable; female healing as part of a peasant subculture was not.

The Church saw its attack on peasant healers as an attack on *magic,* not medicine. The devil was believed to have real power on earth, and the use of that power by peasant women—whether for good or evil—was frightening to the Church and State. The greater their satanic powers to help themselves, the less they were dependent on God and the Church and the more they were potentially able to use their powers against God's order. Magic charms were thought to be at least as effective as prayer in healing the sick, but prayer was Church-sanctioned and controlled while incantations and charms were not. Thus magic cures, even when successful, were an accursed interference with the will of God, achieved with the help of the devil, and the cure itself was evil. There was no problem in distinguishing God's cures from the devil's, for obviously the Lord would work through priests and doctors rather than through peasant women.

The wise woman, or witch, had a host of remedies which had been tested in years of use. Many of the herbal remedies developed by witches still have their place in modern pharmacology. They had pain-killers, digestive aids and anti-inflammatory agents. They used ergot° for the pain of labor at a time when the Church held that pain in labor was the Lord's just punishment for Eve's original sin. Ergot derivatives are the principal drugs used today to hasten labor and aid in the recovery from childbirth. Belladonna—still used today as an anti-spasmodic—was used by the witch-healers to inhibit uterine contractions when miscarriage threatened. Digitalis, still an impor-

_____

° ergot: drug which contracts blood vessels and relaxes muscles; it is derived from a fungus. See Mattossian's essay in "Essays from the Disciplines."

tant drug in treating heart ailments, is said to have been discovered by an English witch. Undoubtedly many of the witches' other remedies were purely magical, and owed their effectiveness—if they had any—to their reputation.

The witch-healer's methods were as great a threat (to the Catholic Church, if not the Protestant) as her results, for the witch was an empiricist: She relied on her senses rather than on faith or doctrine, she believed in trial and error, cause and effect. Her attitude was not religiously passive, but actively inquiring. She trusted her ability to find ways to deal with disease, pregnancy and childbirth—whether through medications or charms. In short, her magic was the science of her time.

The Church, by contrast, was deeply anti-empirical. It discredited the value of the material world, and had a profound distrust of the senses. There was no point in looking for natural laws that govern physical phenomena, for the world is created anew by God in every instant. Kramer and Sprenger, in the *Malleus,* quote St. Augustine on the deceptiveness of the senses:

> . . . Now the motive of the will is something perceived through the senses or the intellect, both of which are subject to the power of the devil. For St. Augustine says in Book 83: This evil, which is of the devil, creeps in by all the sensual approaches; he places himself in figures, he adapts himself to colors, he attaches himself to sounds, he lurks in angry and wrongful conversation, he abides in smells, he impregnates with flavours and fills with certain exhalations all the channels of the understanding.

The senses are the devil's playground, the arena into which he will try to lure men away from Faith and into the conceits of the intellect or the delusions of carnality.

In the persecution of the witch, the anti-empiricist and the misogynist, anti-sexual obsessions of the Church coincide: Empiricism and sexuality both represent a surrender to the senses, a betrayal of faith. The witch was a triple threat to the Church: She was a woman, and not ashamed of it. She appeared to be part of an organized underground of peasant women. And she was a healer whose practice was based in empirical study. In the face of the repressive fatalism of Christianity, she held out the hope of change in this world.

THE RISE OF THE EUROPEAN MEDICAL PROFESSION

While witches practiced among the people, the ruling classes were cultivating their own breed of secular healers: the university-trained physicians. In the century that preceded the beginning of the "witch-craze"—the thirteenth century—European medicine became firmly established as a secular science and a *profession*. The medical profession was actively engaged in the elimination of female healers —their exclusion from the universities, for example—long before the witch-hunts began.

For eight long centuries, from the fifth to the thirteenth, the other-worldly, anti-medical stance of the Church had stood in the way of the development of medicine as a respectable profession. Then, in the 13th century, there was a revival of learning, touched off by contact with the Arab world. Medical schools appeared in the universities, and more and more young men of means sought medical training. The church imposed strict controls on the new profession, and allowed it to develop only within the terms set by Catholic doctrine. University-trained physicians were not permitted to prac-tice without calling in a priest to aid and advise them, or to treat a patient who refused confession. By the fourteenth century their practice was in demand among the wealthy, as long as they continued to take pains to show that their attentions to the body did not jeopardize the soul. In fact, accounts of their medical training make it seem more likely that they jeopardized the *body*.

There was nothing in late medieval medical training that con-flicted with church doctrine, and little that we would recognize as "science." Medical students, like other scholarly young gentlemen, spent years studying Plato, Aristotle and Christian theology. Their medical theory was largely restricted to the works of Galen, the ancient Roman physician who stressed the theory of "complexions" or "temperaments" of men, "wherefore the choleric are wrathful, the sanguine are kindly, the melancholy are envious," and so on. While a student, a doctor rarely saw any patients at all, and no experimenta-tion of any kind was taught. Medicine was sharply differentiated from surgery, which was almost everywhere considered a degrading, menial craft, and the dissection of bodies was almost unheard of.

Confronted with a sick person, the university-trained physi-cian had little to go on but superstition. Bleeding was a common practice, especially in the case of wounds. Leeches were applied according to the time, the hour, the air, and other similar considerations. Medical theories were often grounded more in "logic" than in observation: "Some foods brought on good humours, and others, evil humours. For example, nasturtium, mustard, and garlic produced reddish bile; lentils, cabbage and the meat of old goats and beeves begot black bile." Incantations, and quasi-religious rituals were thought to be effective: The physician to Edward II, who held a bachelor's degree in theology and a doctorate in medicine from Oxford, prescribed for toothache writing on the jaws of the patient, "In the name of the Father, the Son, and the Holy Ghost, Amen," or touching a needle to a caterpillar and then to the tooth. A frequent treatment for leprosy was a broth made of the flesh of a black snake caught in a dry land among stones.

Such was the state of medical "science" at the time when witch-healers were persecuted for being practitioners of "magic". It was witches who developed an extensive understanding of bones and muscles, herbs and drugs, while physicians were still deriving their prognoses from astrology and alchemists were trying to turn lead into gold. So great was the witches' knowledge that in 1527, Paracelsus, considered the "father of modern medicine," burned his text on pharmaceuticals, confessing that he "had learned from the Sorceress all he knew."

THE SUPPRESSION OF WOMEN HEALERS

The establishment of medicine as a profession, requiring university training, made it easy to bar women legally from practice. With few exceptions, the universities were closed to women (even to upper class women who could afford them), and licensing laws were established to prohibit all but university-trained doctors from practice. It was impossible to enforce the licensing laws consistently since there was only a handful of university-trained doctors compared to the great mass of lay healers. But the laws *could* be used selectively. Their first target was not the peasant healer, but the better off, literate woman healer who competed for the same urban clientele as that of the university-trained doctors.

Take, for example, the case of Jacoba Felicie, brought to trial in 1322 by the Faculty of Medicine at the University of Paris, on charges of illegal practice. Jacoba was literate and had received some unspecified "special training" in medicine. That her patients were well off is evident from the fact that (as they testified in court) they had consulted well-known university-trained physicians before turning to her. The primary accusations brought against her were that

> ... she would cure her patient of internal illness and wounds or of external abscesses. She would visit the sick assiduously and continue to examine the urine in the manner of physicians, feel the pulse, and touch the body and limbs.

Six witnesses affirmed that Jacoba had cured them, even after numerous doctors had given up, and one patient declared that she was wiser in the art of surgery and medicine than any master physician or surgeon in Paris. But these testimonials were used against her, for the charge was not that she was incompetent, but that—as a woman—she dared to cure at all.

Along the same lines, English physicians sent a petition to Parliament bewailing the "worthless and presumptuous women who usurped the profession" and asking the imposition of fines and "long imprisonment" on any woman who attempted to "use the practyse of Fisyk." By the 14th century, the medical profession's campaign against urban, educated women healers was virtually complete throughout Europe. Male doctors had won a clear monopoly over the practice of medicine among the upper classes (except for obstetrics, which remained the province of female midwives even among the upper classes for another three centuries.) They were ready to take on a key role in the elimination of the great mass of female healers —the "witches."

The partnership between Church, State and medical profession reached full bloom in the witch trials. The doctor was held up the medical "expert," giving an aura of science to the whole proceeding. He was asked to make judgments about whether certain women were witches and whether certain afflictions had been caused by witchcraft. The *Malleus* says: "And if it is asked how it is possible to distinguish whether an illness is caused by witchcraft or by some natural physical defect, we answer that the first [way] is by means of the *judgement of doctors* . . ." [Emphasis added]. In the witch-hunts, the Church explicitly legitimized the doctors' professionalism, denouncing non-professional healing as equivalent to heresy: "If a woman dare to cure *without having studied* she is a witch and must die."

(Of course, there wasn't any way for a woman to study.) Finally, the witch craze provided a handy excuse for the doctor's failings in everyday practice: Anything he couldn't cure was obviously the result of sorcery.

The distinction between "female" superstition and "male" medicine was made final by the very roles of the doctor and the witch at the trial. The trial in one stroke established the male physician on a moral and intellectual plane vastly above the female healer he was called to judge. It placed him on the side of God and Law, a professional on par with lawyers and theologians, while it placed her on the side of darkness, evil and magic. He owed his new status not to medical or scientific achievements of his own, but to the Church and State he served so well.

THE AFTERMATH

Witch hunts did not eliminate the lower class woman healer, but they branded her forever as superstitious and possibly malevolent. So thoroughly was she discredited among the emerging middle classes that in the 17th and 18th centuries it was possible for male practitioners to make serious inroads into that last preserve of female healing—midwifery. Nonprofessional male practitioners—"barber-surgeons"—led the assault in England, claiming technical superiority on the basis of their use of the obstetrical forceps. (The forceps were legally classified as a surgical instrument, and women were legally barred from surgical practice.) In the hands of the barber surgeons, obstetrical practice among the middle class was quickly transformed from a neighborly service into a lucrative business, which real physicians entered in force in the 18th century. Female midwives in England organized and charged the male intruders with commercialism and dangerous misuse of the forceps. But it was too late—the women were easily put down as ignorant "old wives" clinging to the superstitions of the past.

BIBLIOGRAPHY

The Manufacture of Madness, by Thomas Szasz, M.D., Delta Books, 1971. Szasz asserts that institutional psychiatry is the modern version of the witch-hunts, with the patient in the role of the witch. We are indebted to him for first presenting witchcraft in the context of the struggle between professionals and lay healers. See especially the chapter on "The Witch as Healer."

Satanism and Witchcraft, by Jules Michelet. The Citadel Press, 1939. A mid-nineteenth-century work by a famous French historian. A vivid book on the Middle Ages, superstition and the Church, with a discussion of "satan as physician."

The Malleus Maleficarum, by Heinrich Kramer and James Sprenger, translated by Rev. Montague Summers. The Pushkin Press, London, 1928. Difficult medieval writing, but by far the best source for the day-to-day operations of the witch-hunts, and for insights into the mentality of the witch-hunter.

The History of Witchcraft and Demonology, by Rev. Montague Summers. University Books, New York, 1956. Written in the 1920's by a Catholic priest and defender—really!—of the witch-hunts. Attacks the witch as "heretic," "anarchist," and "bawd."

Witchcraft, by Pennethrone Hughes. Penguin Books, 1952. A general introduction and survey.

Women Healers in Medieval Life and Literature, by Muriel Joy Hughes. Books for Libraries Press, Freeport, New York, 1943. A conservatively written book, with good information on the state of academic medicine and on women lay doctors and midwives. Unfortunately, it dismisses the whole question of witchcraft.

The Witch-Cult in Western Europe, by Margaret Alice Murray. Oxford University Press, 1921. Dr. Murray was the first person to present the anthropological view, now widely accepted, that witchcraft represented, in part, the survival among the people of a pre-Christian religion.

A Mirror of Witchcraft, by Christina Hole. Chatto and Windus, London, 1957. A source-book of extracts from trial reports and other writings, mostly from English witch trials of the 16th and 17th centuries.

ESSAYS FROM THE DISCIPLINES

SOCIAL PSYCHOLOGY

KAI T. ERIKSON

This selection is taken from Erikson's book, Wayward Puritans: A Study in the Sociology of Deviance *(1966). The book as a whole*

*is a self-consciously "interdisciplinary effort" in which the author
combined historical examples of three sets of "deviants" in Puritan culture
—the followers of Anne Hutchinson, the Quakers, and the Salem witches
—with sociological concepts such as "deviancy."*

*In his book, Erikson argues that the Puritans defined those who
would threaten the religious status quo as deviant criminals; they thereby
gained the opportunity to hold on to their "stability" as a society
dominated by a single religious group. The Quakers, and then the
witches—the two groups with which we are most familiar today—
provided the Puritans with "recognizable" groups they could treat as
aliens and criminals.*

In other sections of Wayward Puritans, *Erikson analyzes
available crime data to show a remarkable consistency in the way the
courts treated deviants in the seventeenth century. In the following
selection, Erikson concentrates on some of the doctrines and attitudes
which set the tone for the Salem witch trials. He combines the
explanation of key Puritan doctrines (such as predestination) with a few
historical cases in order to demonstrate his main point here: that Puritan
justice is famous because of its "cold righteousness," not because of its
"fierceness."*

Puritanism and Deviancy

One of the most durable memories we have of old Massachusetts Bay is that the magistrates could be very cruel in their treatment
of offenders, burning ugly brands into their flesh, turning them out
into the wilderness, shaming them in the stocks and pillory, flogging
them with a heavy hand, severing their ears and mutilating their
noses, and sometimes even hanging them from the gallows. Students
of American history have long been attracted to this grisly subject,
not only the school children who learn something about Roger Williams and the witchcraft frenzy but whole generations of serious
scholars as well. Until late in the nineteenth century (and even well
into the twentieth) historians of Massachusetts wrote so much about
Puritan severity that one might have thought they were postponing
other relevant topics until they could come to terms with at least this
one compelling chapter of the past. Some of these historians were
looking for ways to exonerate the settlers of the Bay; others appeared
to feel an urgent sense of outrage over the atrocities they thought

they were reporting. Occasionally a writer like Nathaniel Hawthorne might draw an understanding portrait of the time without trying to take sides in those long dead disputes, but such men were easily outnumbered by the partisan observers around them—loyal apologists like John Palfrey or furious critics like James Truslow Adams.

Now historiography has come a long way since the nineteenth century and it would be absurd for us to be concerned because these writers did not observe modern conventions about neutrality in the study of the past. But even if we make lavish allowances for the fact that styles of scholarship have changed, we still have to admit that much of the material left to us gives us a poor angle of vision on colonial attitudes toward deviation. This material tells us a good deal about the Puritan appetite for persecution but almost nothing about the Puritan cosmology which lay behind it.

The fact seems to be that the punishment of crime in early Massachusetts was in many ways less severe than in other parts of the contemporary world, and this makes it difficult to understand why the colony should have earned such a lasting reputation for harshness. Perhaps the most terrifying thing about punishment in Massachusetts Bay, after all, was not its fierceness but its cold righteousness. Even the most merciless persecutions in other parts of the world were characterized by a degree of human sentimentality, if only because the participants were moved by feelings like rage, pity, revenge, or fear, but in Massachusetts Bay, justice was governed by a relentless kind of certainty. Little attention was paid to the motives of the offender, the grief of the victim, the anger of the community, or any other human emotion: the whole process had a flat, mechanical tone because it dealt with the laws of nature rather than with the decisions of men.

In order to understand this feature of Puritan justice, one should begin with the doctrine of predestination as it appeared in New England thinking. According to the Puritan reading of the Bible, as we have seen, there were only two important classes of people on earth—those who had been elected to everlasting life and those who had been consigned forever to hell. These decisions, of course, had been made before the people affected by them were born, and nothing they did in the course of their lives would have any influence on the outcome; yet the New England Puritans assumed that most men would sooner or later give evidence as to whether they were chosen or not. Persons who had felt grace would be so touched by the experience that they would develop a new sense of responsibility toward the community and slowly move into positions of leadership; persons who remained in doubt would stay in the middle ranks of the community and pursue their honest callings until they learned more of their fate; persons who had reason to fear the worst would drift sullenly into the lower echelons of society, highly susceptible to deviant forms of behavior. Thus the social structure of the Kingdom of God closely resembled that of the English nation, and it was obvious to the dullest saint that confirmed deviants belonged in the lowest of these ranks. If a man acts contemptuously toward authority and violates the norms of the community, God will not suddenly turn in wrath and reassign him to hell; but it is safe to assume that anyone who behaves in that fashion has not experienced and will not experience grace. He is not, as the term once implied, a "graceful" man.

Given these premises, Puritan attitudes toward punishment had a fairly simple logic. If a culprit standing before the bench is scheduled to spend eternity in hell, it does not matter very much how severely the judges treat him, for all the hardships and sufferings in the world will be no more than a faint hint of the torments awaiting him in the hereafter. In the ecclesiastical courts of medieval Europe, felons were sometimes sentenced to burn at the stake in the theory that this would represent an apt introduction to the fires of hell, and this is not wholly unlike the implicit notion which seems to have governed the courtrooms of New England. It was God, not the magistrates, who had sentenced the offender to everlasting suffering, and if the magistrates lashed a few stripes on his back or printed his skin with a hot iron, they were only doing what God, in His infinite wisdom, had already decreed. In a sense, then, the punishment of culprits was not only a handy method for protecting the public peace; it was an act of fealty to God.

The doctrine of predestination is often criticized as one of the cruelest of theologies since it condemns people to hell before they have had a chance to demonstrate whether they merit this fate or not. But it is important to understand that predestination was not just an article of dogma invented by people with hard imaginations: it was a description of life as the saints lived it, a natural explanation of happenings in the real world. God, they knew, was sovereign in all things, not only in broad natural cycles like the movement of the stars or the change of seasons, but in the most ordinary details of everyday life as well. Yet a number of things were difficult to explain in this world where nothing was left to human will or random chance: why, for example, are some men more gifted than others, some born to higher estates, some more fortunate in their daily enterprises? Clearly, God wills it that way:

> God Almighty, in his most holy and wise providence, hath so disposed of the condition of mankind, as in all times some must be rich and some poor, some high and eminent in power and dignities, others mean and in subjection.[1]

And so the notion of predestination took the two most evident "facts" of Puritan experience—the given knowledge that God governed the universe and the empirical observation that men differed from one another—and combined them with all the precision and economy of a scientific theory.

Now this was fatalism of a most exaggerated kind, but like so many tenets of Puritan theology it was seldom taken literally. It was necessary for the Puritans to feel that every movement of the universe was supervised directly by God, but it was also necessary for them to feel that people who infringe the rules of society were both morally and legally responsible for their own deviancies; and soon the Puritans developed the kind of legalistic solution for which their minds were so superbly trained. God, so the reasoning went, arranges every moment of human history in advance and regulates the affairs of men down to the smallest detail. Every act of man, then, whether it be a saintly deed or a frightful crime, has been fully preordained. Yet at the same time, God demands that each person *consent* to the future which has been chosen for him, so that he is always acting on the basis of his own volition in the very process of carrying out God's will. This is almost like saying that a man who finds himself falling from a tree will decide on the way down that this is what he really planned to do anyway, but it served the needs of New England theory well enough and was not a worse sophistry than many other strains of Puritan creed. From a legal point of view, then, the will of man stays wholly free and he accepts responsibility for whatever he does, not because he could have chosen to act otherwise but because he volunteered for this outcome in the first place. When one of the most gifted theorists in the colony tried to explain this tricky point,

---

[1]John Winthrop, "A Model of Christian Charity," *Winthrop Papers* (Boston: Massachusetts Historical Society, 1931), II, p. 282.

he could only assert a little lamely that God so organized the world
that men "should act freely, and yet that they should accomplish His
purposes by all their free actions."[2]

From a twentieth-century point of view, of course, there is a
very clear contradiction in this notion of criminal responsibility.

On the one hand, the deviant is doing little more than following a script which absolutely requires him to perform whatever delin-
quencies he is later punished for, and thus he cannot really be
"blamed" for his own misconduct—at least in the way we have since
learned to use the term. In this respect, punishment in Massachusetts
had an almost sacrificial quality: the culprit was asked to accept
punishment not because he could have "helped" it in any reasonable
sense but because the logic of the universe simply required it of him.

On the other hand, every offender who came before the bench
did so as a free man, entirely responsible for his own actions. He
could not plead that he had been forced into sin by God's decree or
that he came from a deprived background or that he was a victim of
circumstances or even that he did not know any better—for in the
very beginning he had made a contract with God to be an unregener-
ate sinner. There may be a certain dignity in this idea, after all,
because it gives every man credit for being the master of his own
destiny, but this may have been small consolation to those who had
to face the consequences of that ambiguity. As in our own day, the
Puritans found it convenient to assume that every human action had
a "cause" somewhere in the intricate machinery of nature, but this
did not make them feel for a moment that the person on whom this
cause had operated was any the less responsible for what he did.

There is no evidence that people in seventeenth-century New
England saw any contradiction in this notion, but it is a source of
continuing confusion to the later commentator. When one spends
many hours in the company of old records, it becomes increasingly
difficult to understand what the Puritans meant when they called
someone "guilty" or what they hoped to accomplish by punishing
him. A few examples might help illustrate the problem.

In 1638, a Dorothy Talbye was brought into court for murdering her child, a girl with the haunting and prophetic name "Difficult."
Mrs. Talbye's behavior both before and during her trial suggests that
she was by no means a competent person, even by the crude psychi-

---

[2]Quoted in Miller, *The New England Mind*, p. 193.

atric standards of that day. Winthrop thought that she was motivated by "melancholy and spiritual delusions" and attributed her crime to the fact that she was "so possessed with Satan, that he persuaded her (by his delusions, which she listened to as revelations from God) to break the neck of her own child, that she might free it from future misery." Despite this clinical impression she was hung in Boston and an excellent sermon preached on the occasion. Winthrop reports that she acted in a very undignified manner at her execution, refusing to repent, tearing off her hood as she stood on the scaffold, requesting to be beheaded rather than hanged ("giving this reason, that it was less painful and less shameful"), and struggling to free herself as she swung from the end of the rope. Whatever else might be said about this unfortunate woman, she most certainly did not die gracefully.[3]

In 1666, a woman named Jane Flanders was brought before the Essex County Court for "telling lies" and for "making debate among neighbors and casting great reproaches on several." The court found her "so distempered in her head" that she was prohibited from giving testimony at the trial; but this disability did not prevent her from being sentenced to "ten stripes on lecture day."[4]

And Cotton Mather, who knew a good deal about the subject, tells a story about one of the colony's first witches. Ann Cole had once been "a person of serious piety," he tells us, but one day she was "taken with very strange fits" and began to perform remarkable feats like speaking in Dutch, a language she presumably did not know. When her fits had abated, she admitted that she had made a covenant with the Devil and had sealed the bargain by permitting him to have "frequent carnal knowledge of her." It goes without saying that Mrs. Cole was promptly hanged, but it is Mather's description of the event which remains the most perplexing. "Upon this confession," he informs us, "the woman was executed, whereupon Ann Cole was happily delivered from the extraordinary troubles wherewith she had been exercised."[5] One is tempted to ask whether the judges had rid the community of a dangerous witch or had cured the lady of an annoying illness! And this is perhaps the main point: deviant behavior *was* a kind of illness, not an occasion for warmth or sympathy, to be sure, but an emergency condition which had to be

[3]Winthrop, Journal, I, pp. 282–283.
[4]Essex County Records, III, pp. 319–320.
[5]Mather, *Magnalia*, II, pp. 448–449.

treated with every resource at the community's disposal, whether or not the patient suffered any discomfort in the process.

This brings us to another curious feature of Puritan justice, the extraordinary efforts made by both magistrates and ministers to extract a formal expression of repentance from convicted felons. The main purpose of these expressions, of course, was to purge the person's soul and perhaps give him a chance to convince the rest of the community that he was not really a bad sort of fellow. Throughout the records we find any number of occasions in which the court softened its judgment upon receipt of a touching confession or an earnest promise of reform. But this is only half the story, for some of the most celebrated confessions in the history of the Bay, collected with meticulous care by people like Cotton Mather, were those uttered by doomed men on their last fateful walk to the gallows; and it is difficult to understand why so much importance was attached to them. Surely the culprit was not going to change his fate by being contrite at the last moment, nor was there any chance that the gesture would improve his prospects in the hereafter. It is important to remember, however, that repentance is a public ceremony of admission as well as a private act of contrition. To repent is to agree that the moral standards of the community are right and that the sentence of the court is just. To repent is to say (a phrase the Puritans loved to repeat) that one has "sinned against his own conscience" and entirely understands why the community has to punish or even kill him. (In this, again, as in so many other respects, the newer Puritanism of the Soviet Union seems to parallel the older Puritanism of New England.)

And here the circularities of Puritan theory meet together in a peculiar finale. The deviant plunges into a life of sin, impelled by forces beyond his control; yet in the final moment he is able to make a certain sense out of this inexorable process when he *consents* to the destiny which spells his destruction and when he stands on the scaffold and testifies that the laws about to destroy him are altogether reasonable and fair. In a sense, then, the victim is asked to endorse the action of the court and to share in the judgment against him, to move back into the community as a witness to his own execution. If the whole affair sounds a little like ritual sacrifice, we may all the more easily understand another element which may have been present in the Puritan attitude toward repentance—that the people of the community, vaguely aware of the contradictions of their own doctrine, were somehow anxious for the condemned man to forgive them.

MEDICAL HISTORY

MARY K. MATOSSIAN

Matossian's is not the first medical interpretation of Salem, medical "hysteria" having been suggested by others (see Hansen in the "Sources" for a full account). But her essay accepts an unusual pharmacological argument first made in 1976 by Linnda R. Caporael (see "Sources"), who attempted to prove that ergot, a rye fungus, was the actual agent of Salem "bewitchment." Caporael's essay was in turn rebutted (see Spanos and Gottlieb in "Sources"), and Matossian's essay is therefore both a review and a reassertion (with some new data) of an atypical position on Salem witchcraft, written for the nonspecialized scientific readers of American Scientist.

The heart of Matossian's argument is that the characteristics of the afflicted girls of Salem and the victims of ergotism, or ergot poisoning, are identical. Furthermore, ergotism is directly related to a set of specific weather conditions. In Salem in 1691–1692, these weather conditions existed. Since the afflicted girls showed symptoms of ergotism, they must have contracted the disease from infected rye.

Ergot and the Salem Witchcraft Affair

The witchcraft affair of 1692 had several peculiar aspects. In terms of the number of people accused and executed, it was the worst outbreak of witch persecution in American history. Accusations of witchcraft were made not only in Salem Village (now Danvers) but also in Andover, Beverly, Boxford, Gloucester, Ipswich, Newbury, Topsfield, and Wenham, all in Massachusetts, and in Fairfield County, Connecticut. The timing of the outbreak was strange, since it occurred 47 years after the last epidemic of witch persecution in England. No one has been able to prove why it occurred in 1692, and not some other year, or why it happened in Essex County, Massachusetts, and Fairfield County, Connecticut, and not in other counties.

In 1976 psychologist Linnda Caporael proposed an interesting solution to the problem of why various physical and mental symptoms appeared only in certain communities at certain times (1). She suggested that those who displayed symptoms of "bewitchment" in 1692 were actually suffering from a disease known as convulsive ergotism. The main causal factor in this disease is a substance called ergot, the sclerotia° of the fungus *Claviceps purpurea,* which usually grows on rye. Ergot is more likely to occur on rye grown on low, moist, shaded land, especially if the land is newly cultivated. The development of ergot is favored by a severely cold winter followed by a cool, moist growing season: the cold winter weakens the rye plant, and the spring moisture promotes the growth of the fungus.

People develop ergotism after eating rye contaminated by ergot. Children and teenagers are more vulnerable to ergotism than adults because they ingest more food per unit of body weight; consequently, they may ingest more poison per unit of body weight. Made up of four groups of alkaloids, ergot produces a variety of symptoms. Diagnosis may be difficult because many symptoms are not present in all cases.

According to current medical thinking, the symptoms of early and mild convulsive ergotism are a slight giddiness, a feeling of frontal pressure in the head, fatigue, depression, nausea with or without vomiting, and pains in the limbs and lumbar region that make walking difficult (2). In more severe cases the symptoms are formication (a feeling that ants are crawling under the skin), coldness of the extremities, muscle twitching, and tonic spasms° of the limbs, tongue, and facial muscles. Sometimes there is renal spasm and urine stoppage. In the most severe cases the patient has epileptiform° convulsions and, between fits, a ravenous appetite. He may lie as if dead for six to eight hours and afterward suffer from anesthesia of the skin, paralysis of the lower limbs, jerking arms, delirium, and loss of speech. He may die on the third day after the onset of symptoms.

○ sclerotia: the collection of threads in the fungus used for food storage during its dormant stage.
○ tonic spasms: continuous contractions of muscles.
○ epileptiform: resembling epileptic symptoms.

Animals suffering from convulsive ergotism may behave wildly, make loud, distressed noises, stop lactating, and die.

Caporael matched the symptoms and their epidemiology in 1692 with those in the above model. She was severely criticized by psychologists N. K. Spanos and Jack Gottlieb on the ground that the facts of the case fit the model very imperfectly *(3)*. I have concluded, after examining the Salem court transcript, the ecological situation, and recent literature on ergotism, that this objection is not as valid as originally perceived.

Previous attempts to explain the witchcraft affair of 1692 have been unsatisfactory. The work of historians Paul Boyer and Stephen Nissenbaum, for example, has been concerned with the social reactions to the symptoms of bewitchment, rather than the origin of the symptoms *(4)*. Other historians have attributed the outbreak to the tendency to make scapegoats of certain members of a community; although this is a widespread and chronic phenomenon, it is insufficient to explain the unique aspects of the case. New Englanders believed in witchcraft both before and after 1692, yet in no other year was there such severe persecution of witches.

The suggestion that the afflicted teenage girls in Salem Village were feigning their symptoms or, as Spanos and Gottlieb suggested, role-playing in the presence of social cues cannot explain the symptoms of the animal victims or of the other human victims who were apparently not stimulated by social cues. The suggestion made by an English professor, Chadwick Hansen, that the bewitched were suffering from hysteria is also unsatisfactory *(5)*. People in the afflicted communities may have been hysterical in the sense that they were excited and anxious, but such psychological stimuli alone have not been shown to be capable of producing an epidemic of convulsions, hallucinations, and sensory disturbances in any case in which a diagnosis of ergotism or other food poisoning was seriously considered and then ruled out *(6)*.

SYMPTOMS IN 1692

In Essex County, Massachusetts, 24 of 30 victims of "bewitchment" in 1692 suffered from convulsions and the sensations of being pinched, pricked, or bitten. According to English folk tradition, these were the most common specific symptoms of a condition called "bewitchment" *(7).* Hence, they were the symptoms most often mentioned in the court records, for the intent of the court proceedings was to prove "witchcraft," not to present a thorough medical case history.

Some of the other symptoms of "bewitchment" mentioned in the court record, like the most common symptoms, may also occur in cases of ergotism. These include temporary blindness, deafness, and speechlessness; burning sensations; seeing visions like a "ball of fire" or a "multitude in white glittering robes"; and the sensation of flying through the air "out of body." Three girls said they felt as if they were being torn to pieces and all their bones were being pulled out of joint. Some victims reported feeling "sick to the stomach" or "weak," having half of the right hand and part of the face swollen and painful, being "lame," or suffering from a temporary, painful urine stoppage. Three people and several cows died.

The Salem court record does not mention certain symptoms often associated with mild or early cases of ergotism, such as headache, nausea, diarrhea, dizziness, chills, sweating, livid or jaundiced skin, and the ravenous appetite likely to appear between fits. If these symptoms were present, they may not have been reported because they were not commonly associated with bewitchment. Nor does the court record establish whether or not the victims suffered relapses or how the cases ended.

Social cues in the courtroom may have stimulated some of the hallucinations, but such stimulation does not disprove a diagnosis of ergotism. Ergot is the source of lysergic acid diethylamide (LSD), which some mycologists believe can occur in a natural state *(8).* People under the influence of this compound tend to be highly suggestible. They may see formed images—for instance, of people, animals, or religious scenes—whether their eyes are open or closed *(9).* These hallucinations can take place in the presence or absence of social cues.

Symptoms similar to those mentioned in the Salem court record also appeared between May and September of 1692 in Fairfield County, Connecticut. A 17-year-old girl, Catherine Branch, suffered from epileptiform fits, pinching and pricking sensations, hallucinations, and spells of laughing and crying. On 28 October she died, after accusing two women of bewitching her. John Barlow, aged 24, reported that he could not speak or sit up and that daylight seemed to prevail even at night. He had pain in his feet and legs *(10).* These symptoms also suggest a diagnosis of ergotism.

EPIDEMIOLOGY

The victims of bewitchment in Essex County were mainly children and teenagers. Seven infants or young children are known to have developed symptoms or died. According to recent findings, nursing infants can develop ergotism from drinking their mother's milk (2).

Spanos and Gottlieb, citing the court record, asserted that the proportion of children among the victims in 1692 was less than that in a typical ergotism epidemic. However, in a recent epidemic of ergotism in Ethiopia, the ages of the victims were not much different from those in the Essex County epidemic of 1692: more than 80% of the Ethiopian victims were aged 5–34 (11).

There can be no doubt that rye was cultivated in Salem Village and in many other parts of Essex County in the late seventeenth century (12). The animal cases could have resulted from ingestion of wild grasses such as wild rye or cord grass, some of which in Essex County were also liable to ergot infection (13).

The first symptoms of bewitchment appeared in Salem Village in December 1691. Beginning about 18 April 1692, the pace of accusation increased. It slowed in June and then reached a peak between July and September. Exactly when the symptoms terminated is unknown. After 12 October 1692 there were no more trials for witchcraft, by order of the governor of Massachusetts. However, during the winter of 1692–93 in the area around Boston and Salem there were religious revivals, during which people saw visions (14).

If rye harvested in the summer of 1691 was responsible for the epidemic, why did no one exhibit any symptoms before December of that year? In the ergotism epidemics of continental Europe the first symptoms usually appeared in July or August, immediately after the rye harvest. But these episodes occurred in communities heavily dependent on rye as a staple crop and among people so poor that they had to begin eating the new rye crop immediately after the harvest. The situation was otherwise in New England. The diary of Zaccheus Collins, a resident of the Salem area during the epidemic, and probate inventories show that the rye crop often lay unthreshed in the barns until November or December if other food was abundant (15). Since ergot can remain chemically stable in storage for up to 18 months, stored rye might have been responsible for the symptoms of December 1691.

But if people normally delayed threshing rye until winter, why was there a peak of convulsive symptoms in the summer of 1692? Such a peak might be expected in time of food scarcity: was this the case in 1692?

Unfortunately the usual sources of information about food supply, government records, are missing for 1692, but data from tree rings indicate that in 1690, 1691, and 1692, the growing season in eastern New England was cooler than average. Diarists in Boston recorded that the winters of 1690–91 and 1691–92 were very cold *(16)*. Since rye is a crop that flourishes in cold weather when other crops fail, people may have been more dependent on rye and therefore may have begun consuming it earlier in the year. In coastal areas, such as Essex and Fairfield counties, cool conditions are usually also moist; ergot grows more rapidly in moist weather.

In several other years for which tree rings indicate especially cool weather, there were epidemics of convulsions. The most widespread epidemic in New England occurred in 1741. In 1795 a Salem epidemic, labeled "nervous fever," killed at least 33 persons *(17)*.

The growth of population in Salem Village provided an incentive for local farmers to utilize their swampy, sandy, marginal land. This land, if drained, was better suited to the cultivation of rye than other cereal crops. But this was the very type of land in which rye was most likely to be infected with ergot *(18)*. All 22 of the Salem households affected in 1692 were located on or at the edge of soils ideally suited to rye cultivation: moist, acid, sandy loams. Of the households, 16 were close to riverbanks or swamps and 15 were in areas shaded by adjacent hills. No part of Essex County is more than 129 m above sea level. As in Essex County, in southern Fairfield County, Connecticut, the predominant soil type was fine sandy loam, elevations were low, and the population was expanding *(19)*.

Beginning in the 1590s, the common people of England began to eat wheat instead of rye bread. The settlers in New England also preferred wheat bread but, troubled by wheat rust, in the 1660s they began to substitute the planting of rye for wheat. This dietary shift may explain why the witchcraft affair of 1692 occurred 47 years after the last epidemic of witch persecution in England *(20)*.

Although the limitations of surviving records make certainty impossible, the balance of the available evidence suggests that the witchcraft accusations of 1692 were prompted by an epidemic of ergotism. The witchcraft affair, therefore, may have been part of a largely unrecognized American health problem.

REFERENCES

1. L. R. Caporael. 1976. Ergotism: The Satan loosed in Salem? *Science* 192: 21–26.
2. B. Berde and H. O. Schild, eds. 1978. *Ergot Alkaloids and Related Compounds.* Springer.
3. N. P. Spanos and J. Gottlieb. 1976. Ergotism and the Salem Village witch trials. *Science* 194:1390–94.
4. P. Boyer and S. Nissenbaum. 1974. *Salem Village Possessed.* Harvard Univ. Press.
5. C. Hansen. 1969. *Witchcraft at Salem.* Braziller.
6. H. Mersky. 1979. *The Analysis of Hysteria.* London: Baillière Tindall.
   F. Sirois. 1974. *Epidemic Hysteria.* Copenhagen: Munksgaard.
   M. Gross. 1979. Pseudo-epilepsy: A study of adolescent hysteria. *Am. J. Psychiatry* 136:210–13.
7. P. Boyer and S. Nissenbaum, eds. 1977. *The Salem Witchcraft Papers.* New York: Da Capo Press.
   A. MacFarlane. 1970. *Witchcraft in Tudor and Stuart England.* London: Routledge & Kegan Paul.
   C. L. Ewen. 1933. *Witchcraft and Demonianism.* London: Frederick Muller.
   R. Scot. 1584. *The Discoverie of Witchcraft.* Reprinted 1973. Totowa, NJ: Rowman and Littlefield.
8. R. Emerson. 1973. Mycological relevance in the nineteen seventies. *Trans. Brit. Mycological Soc.* 60:363–87.
9. A. Hoffer and H. Osmond. 1967. *The Hallucinogens.* Academic Press.
   R. C. De Bold and R. C. Leaf, eds. 1967. *LSD, Man and Society.* Wesleyan Univ. Press.
   R. Blum. 1964. *Utopiates.* Atherton.
   M. Tarshis. 1972. *The LSD Controversy.* Thomas.
10. Wyllys Papers, Connecticut State Library, 23–29.
    J. M. Taylor. 1908. *The Witchcraft Delusion in Colonial Connecticut, 1647–1697.* Stratford, CT: J. E. Edward.
11. T. Demeke, Y. Kidane, and E. Wuhib. 1979. Ergotism, a report on an epidemic, 1977–78. *Ethiopian Med. J.* 17:107–14.
12. *Danvers Historical Collections.* 1926. Danvers, MA: Danvers Historical Society.
    Diary of Josiah Green. 1866, 1869, and 1900. *Essex Institute Historical Collections* 8:215–24, 10:73–104, and 36:323–30.
13. L. N. Eleutherius. 1974. Claviceps purpurea on Spartina in coastal marshes. *Mycologia* 66:978–86.
    S. K. Harris, 1975. *The Flora of Essex County, Massachusetts.* Salem, MA: Peabody Museum.
14. G. L. Burr, ed. 1914. *Narratives of the Witchcraft Cases, 1648–1706.* Scribners.
    C. Mather. N.d. *Diary.* Ungar.

15. Diary of Zaccheus Collins, Essex Institute, Salem.

A. L. Cummings. 1964. *Rural Household Inventories, 1675–1775.* Boston: Society for the Preservation of New England Antiquities.

16. Diary of Lawrence Hammond. 1891–92. *Mass. Hist. Soc. Proc.,* ser. 2, 7:160.

S. Sewall. 1972. *Diary.* Arno Press.

E. De Witt and M. Ames, eds. 1978. *Tree-Ring Chronology of Eastern North America.* Tucson: Univ. of Arizona Press.

H. C. Fritts and L. Conkey. Pers. comm. 1981.

17. Holyoke Papers and Salem Bills of Mortality, Essex Institute, Salem.

M. K. Matossian. 1982. Religious revivals and ergotism in America. *Clio Medica* 16:185–92.

18. O. Prescott, Jr. 1813. *A Dissertation on the Natural History and Medicinal Effects of the Secale Cornutam, or Ergot.* Boston: Cummings and Hilliard.

19. M. F. Morgan. 1930. *The Soils of Connecticut.* Bull. 320. Conn. Agriculture Station.

20. W. Harrison. 1587. *The Description of England.* Reprinted 1968. Cornell Univ. Press.

A. B. Appleby. 1979. Diet in sixteenth century England: Sources, problems and possibilities. In *Health, Medicine and Mortality in the Sixteenth Century,* ed. C. Webster, pp. 97–116. Cambridge Univ. Press.

DOCUMENTARY MATERIALS

THE BIBLE

OLD AND NEW TESTAMENTS

The following Biblical passages designate witchcraft as an evil which requires extremely strong remedies. While all of these passages have figured prominently in religious history, and as justification for witch hunts, one of the passages—that of the "familiar spirit," or satanic servant, of the witch at Endor who impersonated Samuel (1 Samuel 28) —is cited by Increase Mather in the excerpt included in this section from his Cases of Conscience *(1693). Its importance lies in the "fact" that it demonstrates the ability of satanic forces to imitate the image of an innocent person—that is, become his or her "specter"—without "consent."*

Passages on Witches

EXODUS 22:18

Thou shalt not suffer a witch to live.

DEUTERONOMY 18:10

There shalt not be found among you any that maketh his son or his daughter to pass through fire, or that useth divination, or an observer of times, or an enchanter, or a witch.

1 SAMUEL 15:23

For rebellion is as the sin of witchcraft, and stubbornness is as iniquity and idolatry. Because thou hast rejected the word of the Lord, he hath also rejected thee from being king.

1 SAMUEL 28:7–16

Then said Saul unto his servants, seek me a woman that hath a familiar spirit, that I may go to her, and enquire of her. And his servants said to him, behold, there is a woman that hath a familiar spirit at Endor.

And Saul disguised himself, and put on other raiment, and he went, and two other men with him, and they came to the woman at night: and he said, I pray thee, divine unto me by the familiar spirit, and bring me him up, whom I shall name unto thee.

And the woman said unto him, behold, thou knowest what Saul hath done, how he hath cut off those that have familiar spirits, and the wizards, out of the land: wherefore then layest thou a snare for my life, to cause me to die?

And Saul sware to her by the Lord, saying, as the Lord liveth, there shall no punishment happen to thee for this thing.

Then said the woman, whom shall I bring up unto thee? And he said, bring me up Samuel.

And when the woman saw Samuel, she cried with a loud voice:

and the woman spake to Saul, saying, why hast thou deceived me? for thou art Saul.

And the king said unto her, be not afraid: for what sawest thou? And the woman said unto Saul, I saw gods ascending out of the earth.

And he said unto her, what form is he of? And she said, an old man cometh up; and he is covered with a mantle. And Saul perceived that it was Samuel, and he stooped with his face to the ground, and bowed himself.

And Samuel said to Saul, why hast thou disquieted me, to bring me up? And Saul answered, I am sore distressed; for the Philistines make war against me, and God is departed from me, and answereth me no more, neither by prophets, nor by dreams: therefore I have called thee, that thou mayest make known unto me what I shall do.

Then said Samuel, wherefore then dost thou ask of me, seeing the Lord is departed from thee, and is become thine enemy?

GALATIANS 5:19–21

Now the works of the flesh are manifest, which are these: adultery, fornication, uncleanness, lasciviousness,

Idolatry, witchcraft, hatred, variance, emulations, wrath, strife, seditions, heresies,

Envyings, murders, drunkenness, revellings, and such like: of the which I tell you before, as I have told you in times past, that they which do such things shall not inherit the kingdom of God.

COURT RECORD

TITUBA AND JOHN HATHORNE

Tituba, also known as Tituba Indian (after her husband, John Indian), was a West Indian slave in the household of Samuel Parris, minister of Salem Village. She was clearly a palmist and conjuror, and had "entertained" the young girls in the Parris household with her magic. These girls, in February 1692, began having fits and appeared "bewitched." Tituba also baked—on advice from one of Parris's parishioners, conveyed to her by her husband—a "witchcake" (made with the urine of one of the afflicted girls) to cure one of the girls. Tituba, Sarah Good, and Sarah Osborne were the first women denounced as witches and questioned by the local magistrates, John Hathorne and Jonathan Corwin.

What follows is one of her several examinations. Her "pidgin English" has not been made to conform with Puritan English; in square brackets are the comments of the magistrates. Primarily because she confessed to witchcraft, she was not hanged. She remained in jail for over a year until she was ransomed by an unknown person who was willing to pay her jail costs in lieu of a slave's purchase-price from Parris, who had disowned her.

Although this is not an essay, it does embody patterns of persuasion or rhetoric on the parts of both Tituba and her examiners. (See the "Student Essay" for an interpretation of Tituba's pattern.)

The Examination of Tituba by John Hathorne
(March 1, 1691/1692)°

Q: Tituba, what evil spirit have you familiarity° with?

A: None.

Q: Why do you hurt these children?

A: I do not hurt them.

Q: Who is it then?

A: The devil for aught I know.

Q: Did you never see the devil?

A: The devil came to me and bid me serve him.

Q: Who have you seen?

A: Four women sometimes hurt the children.

○ March 1, 1691/1692: actually 1692, as the English and the Puritans did not accept January 1st as New Year's Day until 1752; for them, New Year's Day was the Feast of the Annunciation (March 25).
○ familiarity: contact with the devil (see "attendants," below).

Q: Who were they?

A: Goody° Osborne and Sarah Good and I do not know who the others were. Sarah Good and Osborne would have me hurt the children but I would not. She further said there was a tall man of Boston that she did see.

Q: When did you see them?

A: Last night at Boston.

Q: What did they say to you?

A: They said hurt the children.

Q: And did you hurt them?

A: No. There is four women and one man. They hurt the children and then lay upon me and they tell me if I will not hurt the children they will hurt me.

Q: But did you not hurt them?

A: Yes, but I will hurt them no more.

Q: Are you not sorry you did hurt them?

A: Yes.

Q: And why then do you hurt them?

A: They say hurt children or we will do worse to you.

Q: What have you seen?

A: A man come to me and say serve me.

Q: What service?

A: Hurt the children and last night there was an appearance° that said kill the children and I would no go on hurting the children they would do worse to me.

Q: What is this appearance you see?

° goody: a title (like "Mrs.") commonly used in Puritan society for those with low social status.

° appearance: one of a number of words, like "specter," "apparition," and "shape," which represents the figure or image of a person which could afflict or harass others; many assumed that the Devil orchestrated the movement of these appearances or specters.

A: Sometimes it is like a hog and sometimes like a great dog. [*This appearance she said she did see four times.*]

Q: What did it say to you?

A: The black dog said serve me but I said I am afraid. He said if I did not he would do worse to me.

Q: What did you say to it?

A: I will serve you no longer. Then he said he would hurt me and then he looks like a man and threatens to hurt me. [*She said that this man had a yellow bird that kept with him.*] He told me he had more pretty things that he would give me if I would serve him.

Q: What were these pretty things?

A: He did not show me them.

Q: What else have you seen?

A: Two rats, a red rat and a black rat.

Q: What did they say to you?

A: They said serve me.

Q: When did you see them?

A: Last night and they said serve me but I would not.

Q: What service?

A: Hurt the children.

Q: Did you not pinch Elizabeth Hubbard this morning?

A: The man brought her to me and made me pinch her.

Q: Why did you go to Thomas Putnam's last night and hurt his child?

A: They pull and haul me and make go.

Q: And what would have you do?

A: Kill her with a knife.

[*Lieutenant Fuller and others said at this time when the child saw these persons and was tormented by them that she did complain of a knife—that they would have her cut her head off with a knife.*]

Q: How did you go?

A: We ride upon sticks and are there presently.

Q: Did you go through the trees or over them?

A: We see no thing but are there presently.

Q: Why did you not tell your master?

A: I was afraid. They said they would cut off my head if I told.

Q: Would not you have hurt others if you could?

A: They said they would hurt others but they could not.

Q: What attendants° hath Sarah Good?

A: A yellow bird and she would have given me one.

Q: What meat did she give it?

A: It did suck her between her fingers.

Q: Did you not hurt Mr. Currin's child?

A: Goody Good and Goody Osborne told that they did hurt Mr. Currin's child and would have me hurt him too but I did not.

Q: What hath Sarah Osborne?

A: Yesterday she had a thing with a head like a woman with two legs and wings. Abigail Williams that lives with her uncle, Mr. Parris, said she did see this same creature and it turned into the shape of Goody Osborne.

Q: What else have you seen with Goody Osborne?

A: Another hairy thing. It goes upright like a man. It hath only two legs.

Q: Did you not see Sarah Good upon Elizabeth Hubbard last Saturday?

A: I did see her set a wolf upon her to afflict her. [*The persons with this maid did say that she did complain of a wolf. She further said that she saw a cat with Good at another time.*]

Q: What clothes doth the man go in?

A: He goes in black clothes, a tall man with white hair, I think.

° attendants: companions or "familiars," often animals, with whom a witch "trafficked" or cast spells.

Q: How doth the woman go?

A: In a white hood and a black hood with a top knot.

Q: Do you see who it is that torments these children now?

A: Yes, it is Goody Good. She hurts them in her own shape.

Q: And who is it that hurts them now?

A: I am blind now, I cannot see.

RELIGIOUS HISTORY

INCREASE MATHER

Increase Mather, a leading Puritan minister and theologian, confronted the central issue of "spectral evidence" in his book, Cases of Conscience Concerning Evil Spirits Personating Men *(1692). Could the Devil use a specter or apparition of a person, without that person's permission, to harass someone? But Increase Mather's drift toward discounting such evidence may have had as terrible an effect as did the belief in such evidence. When the judges couldn't get confessions, and when they began to lose faith in spectral evidence, they attracted more* visible and immediate *evidence of bewitchment. Some of the outlandish behavior at the hearings and trials—for example, the young girls were present and became visibly affected by the accused—therefore fulfilled their expectations.*

Mather follows a typical pattern of Puritan argument in this selection: He states a problem or "case," and then offers, first of all, scriptural support for his position on the argument; he next offers the examples of personal experience, about which he has read or which he knows of secondhand, as a second line of support. Each "case" ends with the implications of the previous arguments as they touch on Puritan society in general and on Salem witchcraft specifically.

[Cases of Spectral Evidence]

The first Case that I am desired to express my judgment in is this, whether it is not possible for the Devil to impose on the imagination of persons bewitched, and to cause them to believe that an innocent, yea that a pious person does torment them, when the Devil himself does it; or whether Satan may not appear in the shape of an innocent and pious, as well as a nocent° and wicked person, to afflict such as suffer by diabolical molestations?

The answer to the question must be affirmative; let the following arguments be duly weighed in the balance of the sanctuary.

. . . There are several Scriptures from which we may infer the possibility of what is affirmed.

We find that the Devil by the instigation of the witch at Endor° appeared in the likeness of the prophet Samuel. I am not ignorant that some have asserted that, which, if it were proved, would evert this argument, that is, that it was the true and not the delusive Samuel which the witch brought to converse with Saul. . . . If it were the Devil in his likeness, the argument seems very strong, that if the Devil may appear in the form of a saint in glory, much more is it possible for him to put on the likeness of the most pious and innocent saint on earth. There are [those] who acknowledge that a demon may appear in the shape of a Godly person, but not as doing evil. Whereas the Devil in Samuel's likeness told a pernicious lie, when he said, "Thou hath disquieted me." It was not in the power of Saul, nor of all the devils in hell, to disquiet a soul in heaven, where Samuel had been for two years before this apparition. Nor did the specter speak true, when he said, "Thou and thy sons shall be with me"; tho' Saul himself at his death went to be with the Devil, his son Jonathan did not so. Besides (which suits with the matter in hand) the Devil in Samuel's shape confirmed necromancy and cursed witchery. He that can in the likeness of saints encourage witches to familiarity with hell, may possibly in the likeness of a saint afflict a bewitched person. But this, we see from Scripture, Satan may be permitted to do.

———————— • ————————

. . . It is not usual for persons after their death to appear unto the living, but it does not therefore follow that the great God will not suffer this to be: for both in former and latter ages, examples thereof have not been wanting. No longer since than the last winter, there

○ nocent: harmful (opposite of "innocent").
○ witch of Endor: an important Biblical instance of a witch using an innocent person's specter (see "Passages on Witches from the Old and New Testaments" in this chapter).

was much discourse in London concerning a gentlewoman unto whom her dead son (and another whom she knew not) had appeared. Being then in London, I was willing to satisfy myself, by enquiring into the truth of what was reported, and on Feb. 23, 1691, my brother (who is now a pastor to a congregation in that city) and I discoursed the gentlewoman spoken of. She told us that a son of hers, who had been a very civil young man, but more airy in his temper than was pleasing to his serious mother, being dead, she was much concerned in her thoughts about his condition in the other world. But a fortnight after his death he appeared to her, saying, "Mother, you are solicitous about my spiritual welfare; trouble yourself no more, for I am happy," and so vanished. Should there be a continual intercourse between the visible and invisible world, it should breed confusion, but from thence to infer, that the great Ruler of the Universe will never permit anything of this nature to be, is an inconsequent conclusion. It is not usual for devils to be permitted to come and violently carry away persons through the air, several miles from their habitations; nevertheless, this was done in Swedeland about twenty years ago, by means of a cursed knot of witches there. And a learned physician now living, giveth an account of several children, who by diabolical frauds were stolen from their parents, and others left in their room; and of two [others], that in the nighttime a line was by invisible hands put about their necks, with which they had been strangled, but that some near them happily prevented it.

Let me further add here: it has very seldom been known, that Satan has personated innocent men doing an ill thing, but Providence has found out some way for their vindication: either they have been able to prove that they were in another place when the fact was done, or the like. So perhaps there never was an instance of any innocent person condemned in any court of judicature on earth, only through Satan's deluding and imposing on the imaginations of men, when nevertheless the witnesses, juries, and judges were all to be excused from blame.

———————— • ————————

I have myself known several of whom I ought to think that they are now in heaven, considering that they were of good conversation and reputed pious by those that had the greatest intimacy with them, of whom nevertheless some complained that their shapes appeared to them and threatened them. Nor is this answered by saying, we do not know but those persons might be witches: we are bound by the rule of charity to think otherwise. And they that censure any, merely because such a sad affliction as their being falsely represented by Satan has befallen them, do not do as they would be done by. I bless the Lord, it was never the portion alloted to me, nor to any relation of mine, to be thus abused; but no man knoweth what may happen to him, since "there be just men unto whom it happeneth according to the work of the wicked" (*Eccles.* 8, 14). But what needs more to be said, since there is one amongst ourselves whom no man that knows him, can think him to be a wizard, whom yet some bewitched persons complained of, that they are in his shape tormented. And the devils have of late accused some eminent person.

It is an awful thing which the Lord has done to convince some amongst us of their error: this then I declare and testify, that to take away the life of anyone, merely because a specter or devil, in a bewitched or possessed person does accuse them, will bring the guilt of innocent blood on the land, where such a thing shall be done. Mercy forbid that it should (and I trust that as it has not it never will be so) in New England. What does such an evidence amount unto more than this: either such a one did afflict such a one, or the Devil in his likeness, or his eyes were bewitched.

The things which have been mentioned make way for and bring us unto the second Case, which is to come under our consideration, that is, if one bewitched is struck down at the look or cast of the eye of another, and after that recovered again by a touch from the same person, is this not an infallible proof that the person suspected and complained of is in league with the Devil?

Answer: it must be owned that by such things as these witchcrafts and witches have been discovered more than once or twice, and that an ill fame, or other circumstances attending the suspected party, may be a ground for examination; but this alone does not afford sufficient ground for conviction, [just] as specters or devils appearing in the shapes of men that have been murdered, declaring that they were murdered by such persons and in such a place, may give just occasion to the magistrate for enquiry into the matter. One great witch-advocate confesseth that by this means murders have been brought to light; yet that alone, if the other circumstances did not concur, would not by the law of God take away the life of any man.

RELIGIOUS HISTORY

COTTON MATHER

In 1693, a year after his father's book had appeared, Cotton Mather
published The Wonders of the Invisible World *which, in part,*
had a similar effect: the casting into doubt of spectral evidence. In the
selection which follows (self-contained as in the original text) Cotton
Mather narrates a case of a friendly "apparition," or "appearance," as a
way of demonstrating that not just Satan, but God, has the means
necessary to set specters loose. (See Kibbey, in "Sources," for the
interesting Puritan tendency to equate divine and diabolical approaches to
problems.)

Since this is a self-contained narrative, the main interest is on
plot, but certainly Mather wishes to make clear that it is a firsthand
account (the "story written and signed" by Mr. Beacon himself), not
hearsay.

A Narrative of an Apparition
Which a Gentleman in Boston Had
of His Brother, Just Then Murdered
in London

It was on the second of May in the year 1687 that a most
ingenious, accomplished and well-disposed gentleman, Mr. Joseph
Beacon by name, about five a clock in the morning, as he lay, whether
sleeping or waking he could not say (but judged the latter of them),
had a view of his brother then at London, although he was now
himself at our Boston, distanced from him a thousand leagues. This
his brother appeared unto him, in the morning about five a clock at
Boston, having on him a Bengal° gown, which he usually wore with
a napkin tied about his head; his countenance was very pale, ghastly,

---

° Bengal: a heavy cloth, originating in India.

deadly, and he had a bloody wound on one side of his forehead. "Brother!" says the affrighted Joseph. "Brother!" answered the apparition. Said Joseph: "What's the matter, brother? How come you here!" The apparition replied: "Brother, I have been most barbarously and injuriously butchered, by a debauched, drunken fellow, to whom I never did any wrong in my life." Whereupon he gave a particular description of the murderer, adding: "Brother, this fellow changing his name, is attempting to come over to New England, in [the ships] *Foy,* or *Wild;* I would pray you on the first arrival of either of these, to get an order from the the Governor, to seize the person, whom I have now described; and then do you indict him for the murder of me your brother: I'll stand by you and prove the indictment." And so he vanished.

Mr. Beacon was extremely astonished at what he had seen and heard; and the people of the family not only observed an extraordinary alteration upon him, for the week following, but also have given me under their hands a full testimony that he then gave them an account of this apparition.

All this while Mr. Beacon had no advice of anything amiss attending his brother then in England; but about the latter end of June following, he understood by the common ways of communication, that the April before, his brother, going in haste by night to call a coach for a lady, met a fellow then in drink with his doxy in his hand: some way or other the fellow thought himself affronted with the hasty passage of this Beacon, and immediately ran into the fireside of a neighboring tavern, from whence he fetched out a fire-fork, wherewith he grievously wounded Beacon in his skull, even in that very part where the apparition showed his wound. Of this wound he languished until he died on the second of May about five a clock in the morning at London. The murderer, it seems, was endeavoring to escape, as the apparition affirmed, but the friends of the deceased Beacon seized him; and prosecuting him at law, he found the help of such friends as brought him off without the loss of his life; since which there has no more been heard of the business.

This history I received of Mr. Joseph Beacon himself, who a little before his own pious and hopeful death, which followed not long after, gave me the story written and signed with his own hand, and attested with the circumstances I have already mentioned.

JOURNALISM

JOHN GREENLEAF WHITTIER

Whittier was an amateur folklorist as well as a well-known poet in nineteenth-century America. He records here the persistence of legends associated with witchcraft. His desire to keep their charm, while explaining them away by science, is a noteworthy aspect of the book, The Supernaturalism of New England *(1847), from which this excerpt is taken. His reference in the first paragraph to the "days of the two Mathers" reflects his belief that they were the main supporters of superstitious attacks on witches and specters while, in fact, the matter was somewhat more complicated (as the two previous excerpts from the Mathers indicate). In any case, Whittier as a story teller is keenly interested in showing that the superstitions which haunted the Puritans still persisted in the nineteenth century.*

Whittier combines the roles of tale teller and learned commentator in these passages; after setting the scene appropriately, he offers anecdotes, but he also usually follows them up with the latest scientific data on the subject.

[Supernatural Phenomena]

One of their fables of a churchyard carcass raised and set a strutting.

Bishop Warburton *on Prodigies* °

Modern scepticism and philosophy have not yet eradicated the belief of supernatural visitation from the New England mind. Here and there—oftenest in our still, fixed, valley-sheltered, unvisited nooks and villages—the Rip Van Winkles of a progressive and restless population—may be still found devout believers worthy of the days of the two Mathers. There are those yet living in this very neighborhood who remember, and relate with an awe which half a century has not abated, the story of Ruth Blaye, the GHOST CHILD! Ruth

° prodigies: extraordinary and/or prophetic happenings.

was a young woman of lively temperament and some personal beauty. While engaged as the teacher of a school in the little town of Southampton, N.H. (whose hills roughen the horizon with their snowy outline within view of my window at this very moment), she was invited to spend an evening at the dwelling of one of her young associates. Suddenly, in the midst of unwonted gaiety, the young schoolmistress uttered a frightful shriek, and was seen gazing with a countenance of intense horror at the open window; and pointing with her rigid, outstretched arm at an object which drew at once the attention of her companions. Upon the sill of the window, those present saw, or thought they saw, a dead infant, which vanished before they could find words to express their surprise. The wretched Ruth was the first to break the silence. "It is *mine*—MINE—MY CHILD!" she shrieked; *"he has come for me!"* She gradually became more tranquil, but no effort availed to draw from her the terrible secret which was evidently connected with the apparition. She was soon after arrested and brought to trial for the crime of child-murder, found guilty, and executed at Portsmouth, N.H. I do not of course vouch for the truth of this story. "I tell the tale as 'twas told me."

Nearly opposite to my place of residence, on the south side of the Merrimack, stands a house which has long had a bad reputation. One of its recent inmates avers most positively that having on one occasion ventured to sleep in the haunted room, she was visited by a child-ghost which passed through the apartment with a most mournful and unbaby-like solemnity. Some of my unbelieving readers will doubtless smile at this, and deem it no matter of surprise that a maiden's slumbers should thus be haunted. As the old playwriter hath it:

> *She blushed and smiled to think upon her dream*
> *Of fondling a sweet infant (with a look*
> *Like one she will not name) upon her virgin knees.*

An esteemed friend—a lady of strong mind, not at all troubled with nervous sensibility, though not deficient in ideality—has told me that while living with an aged relative, who was at that time in the enjoyment of her usual health, she was terrified by the appearance of a dead body lying by the side of her relative, who was quietly sleeping in her bed. The old lady died soon after, and my friend avers that the corpse as it lay before her recalled in the most minute particulars her recollection of the apparition. She had seen the same before by the side of the living sleeper.

A respectable and worthy widow lady, in my neighborhood, professes to be clearly convinced that she saw the spectre of her daughter a little time before her death, while she was yet in perfect health. It crossed the room within a few feet of the mother, in broad day-light. She spoke, but no answer was returned; the countenance of the apparition was fixed and sorrowful. The daughter was at that time absent on a visit to a friend.

I could easily mention other cases some of which have occurred in my immediate vicinity, but the above may serve as a sample of all. I can only say that the character of these ghostseers, in most instances, precludes the idea of imposture or intentional exaggeration on their part. They were undoubtedly suffering under that peculiar disease of the organs of vision, or of the imaginative faculty, which is called "Spectral Illusion," of which so much has of late been written, and of which so little is really known. The case of Professor Hitchcock, detailed by himself in *The New Englander,* is one of the most striking on record. He had, day after day, visions of strange landscapes spread out before him—mountain and lake and forest—vast rocks, strata upon strata, piled to the clouds—the panorama of a world shattered and upheaved, disclosing the grim secrets of creation, the unshapely and monstrous rudiments of organic being. Equally remarkable is the case of Dr. Abel, of Lempster, N.H., as given by himself in *The Boston Medical Journal.* While totally blind he saw persons enter his apartment, and especially was he troubled with a grey horse which stood, saddled and bridled, champing his bit, by his bed-side. On one occasion he says:

> I seemed placed on the southern border of a plain, from which I could see a whole regiment of soldiers coming from the north. As they approached their number increased to thousands. Their dress was so splendid as to dazzle my sight. Their movements were generally quick, often forced and halting and forming into two columns, facing each other and extending in line as far as the eye could reach. They would then break up and march in different directions, often driving each other in large companies. I felt peculiarly gratified in seeing large groups of little boys running and jumping before and after the troops —many of them dressed in a light blue frock with a scarlet sash. These movements continued through the day till near sunset, when the field was cleared until after ten o'clock, when I saw them returning, but

they took a westward movement, and soon disappeared. Among the great variety of moving objects which I have seen, their motion has been from right to left, with very few exceptions, as that of marches and countermarches of the soldiers. It was common to see two objects moving in the same direction, while one would move much faster than the other, and pass by.

To the persons who are the subjects of this illusion the phantoms are real enough—all the more so that they are creations of their own—pictures from within projected outward by the force of Imagination —that tyrant of the mind, enslaving the senses which were intended for its guard against error, and making even their apparently natural action the medium of falsehood. Most readers will remember the account which, about a year ago, circulated through all the newspapers of a spectre seen in Warner, N.H., by two men while watching by the bedside of a dying neighbor. A red, unnatural light filled the room; a stranger suddenly stood beside them, and fixed his eyes upon the dying man who writhed and shrunk beneath the ghastly scrutiny. On the disappearance of the spectre, the sick man made an effort to speak, and in broken words confessed that many years before he had aided in the murder of the man whose spectral image had just left them. This statement, if I recollect rightly, was made under oath. It is but proper, however, to mention, that it has been intimated that the *spirit* seen on this occasion was none other than one of Deacon Gile's sprites of the distillery—one of those bottle imps which play as fantastic tricks with those who uncork them, as *Le Diable Boiteux*° of the old French novelist did with the student of Salamanca.

———————— • ————————

I am reminded of a story somewhat in point. An old strolling woman who, all along the valley of the Piscataqua, was known as a fortune-teller, and was even suspected of witchcraft, called once at my grandfather's house while he was absent. The young girls naturally enough employed her in delineating their future fortunes, but it unluckily chanced that just in the midst of the soothsaying my grandfather's heavy boot-fall was heard on the staircase. All was now consternation, for the stout-hearted, clear-headed old gentleman entertained a very emphatic contempt for all the petty superstitions of his neigh-

° Le Diable Boiteux: *The Crippled Devil* (1707), a novel by Alan Rene Le Sage.

borhood and times; and so far as ridicule and sarcasm went, he was as unsparing and merciless toward the pretenders to magic, as Saul was to the "wizards and women with familiar spirits" in his day. The teacup with its occult deposits, so profoundly significant to initiated eyes, was hastily put aside, and the old sorceress, who had some reason for regarding my grandfather as her evil genius, threw herself upon a bed, where she lay for two hours in a kind of trance, defying all efforts to awaken her. At length she started up, and shook back her grey locks from her eyes, declaring that *"she had had a sweet breezing spell!"* Her young questioners took note of the fact that during her seeming sleep, the sky was overcast and wild gusts of wind swept down the river, upsetting wherries, and playing all manner of mad pranks with the marketboats of their brothers coming home from Portsmouth. Is there not something in this to remind one of Lapland wind-making and cloud-compelling Norna?°

STUDENT ESSAY

Assignment 3: Analyze Tituba's testimony as presented in this chapter, using *what* she said, the *way* she said it, or both.

RITA ARMSTRONG

Tituba—A Credit to Her Craft

As a slave and known conjurer, Tituba was an extremely susceptible target for the accusations of witchcraft in Salem Village; yet she shrewdly exploited these very same aspects of her vulnerability in artful manipulation of her predicament. Indeed, though it may seem that the three women initially accused were, more or less, equally assailable in that none of them were respected in the community, Tituba may have had an upper hand by being a slave in the town minister's household and by her previous experience as a conjurer—a trickster, a manipulator.

○ Norna: Norse goddess who determines both human and divine destinies.

Surely, as Minister Parris' household slave, Tituba was privy not only to firsthand observation of the physical and verbal fits of Betty Parris and Abigail Williams, but probably, also to highly informative conversations between Parris and neighboring ministers who had been called in for their advice. Thus, when Tituba was summoned for questioning by the magistrates, in the presence of the afflicted girls, she already had a familiarity with their "tormented seizures" and was not so readily thrown into a panic by their demonstrations, as were Sarah Good and Sarah Osborne. Furthermore, this would explain Tituba's otherwise inexplicable knowledge of Ann Putnam's descriptions of torment, as was evidenced in her testimony:

Q. And what would have you do?

A. Kill her with a knife.

Lieutenant Fuller and others said at this time when the child saw these persons and was tormented by them that she did complain of a knife, that they would have her cut her head off with a knife.[1] In following testimony, Tituba further exploited her inside information and cleverly allied herself with the afflicted girls by confirming their allegations and their descriptions of Sarah Osborne's familiar. For Tituba, unlike Good and Osborne, had the insight to corroborate the statements of her accusers, who were, by then, the focus of village-wide praying, fasting, and solicitude; and thus allied herself, not only with the girls, but with everyone in their attempts to uncover the Devil's work. Records of Tituba's examination seemingly manifest an active cooperation on her part—testifying (in Boyer's and Nissenbaum's words) "volubly and in great detail, even volunteering a description of the devil."[2] While Good and Osborne replied to the magistrates' questions with terse and even impertinent denials of the accusations, Tituba responded with verbosity and contrition, conceding the charges against her.

However, though Tituba's confession was profuse, it was not verbose in the strictest sense of the word; indeed, her elaborate responses were much more than repetitive wordiness—each statement had a definite function. She shrewdly exonerated herself from direct blame by begging coercion when asked why she had hurt the children: "They say hurt children or we [the Devil and witches] will do worse to you."[3] In addition, she further established her spiritual regeneration by describing several occasions on which she refused to torment the children though under duress. Throughout her testimony, she artfully diverted suspicion from herself with detailed descriptions of those who enjoined her cooperation. And when asked to identify these persons, Tituba carefully named only Sarah Good and Sarah Osborne, though she had previously testified that four women had afflicted the girls. Quite cleverly, she claimed ignorance in identifying two of the witches, and perceptively accused the two women most open to suspicion—insuring the validity of her statements.

For establishing her own innocence was not her only concern —her husband, John Indian, was also under suspicion. When the magistrates had questioned Sarah Osborne, she implicated John Indian "by claiming that she had been attacked by a thing like an Indian, all black."[4] As with her other concerns, Tituba deftly handled this problem during her testimony. She affirmed that the four witches were accompanied by a tall man garbed in black, but added that the man was from Boston—thereby eliminating her spouse as a suspect.

To say the least, Tituba's testimony was most skillful: while feigning cooperation, she avoided further vengeance from the afflicted girls, she validated her own statements by confirming those of the girls, she diverted suspicion from herself and John Indian to highly credible suspects, and she established her spirit's restoration. Indeed, one is not left with the impression that Tituba's life laid in the hands of the magistrates. With cunning, subtlety, and insight, she was as much in control of the situation as a defendant could possibly be; she was truly a credit to her craft—to trickery and manipulation.

NOTES

1. Examination of Tituba Indian from William E. Woodward, *Records of Salem Witchcraft* (1864) in David Levin, *What Happened in Salem?* (New York: Harcourt, Brace and World, 1960), p. 7.
2. Paul Boyer and Stephen Nissenbaum, *Salem Possessed* (Cambridge, Mass.: Harvard University Press, 1974), p. 3.
3. Woodward, p. 6.
4. Allen Weinstein and R. Jackson Wilson, *Freedom and Crisis* (New York: Random House, 1974), p. 82.

BIBLIOGRAPHY

Blassingame, John W. *The Slave Community: Plantation Life in the Antebellum South.* New York: Oxford University Press, 1972.
Boyer, Paul, and Stephen Nissenbaum. *Salem Possessed: The Social Origins of Witchcraft.* Cambridge, Mass.: Harvard University Press, 1974.
Hansen, Chadwick. *Witchcraft at Salem.* New York: George Braziller, 1969.
Levin, David. *What Happened in Salem?* New York: Harcourt, Brace and World, 1960.
Nevins, Winfield S. *Witchcraft in Salem Village in 1692.* New York: Burt Franklin, 1976.
Weinstein, Allen, and R. Jackson Wilson. *Freedom and Crisis: An American History.* New York: Random House, 1974.

QUESTIONS FOR DISCUSSION

Within This Chapter:

1. According to Ehrenreich and English, what is the relationship between witchcraft and medicine?

2. Why did the "mass hysteria" in Sandy's school take place?

3. Does reading Hawthorne's story make you a believer in witches, or a skeptic?

4. Are any of Hawthorne's principal characters (the Doanes, Brome, the wizard) deviants by Erikson's definition?

5. Which parts of Tituba's testimony match Matossian's symptoms or characteristics of ergot poisoning?

6. What current folklore about witches resembles the material in any of the stories told about them in this chapter?

Using Other Chapters:

7. How does Hawthorne create an "American scene" (refer to Chapter 1) in "Alice Doane's Appeal"?

8. Are the specters and apparitions narrated by the Mathers testable by Gibson's criteria? (See question 9 in Chapter 4.)

9. How would Danto (see Chapter 4) classify the murderer, Walter Doane, in "Alice Doane's Appeal"?

10. Are the residents of Jonestown (see Chapter 6) caught up by a form of "mass hysteria"?

ASSIGNMENTS

WITHIN THIS CHAPTER:

1. Both Matossian's and Roueché's essays (as well as the books by Hansen and Starkey cited in "Sources") suggest medical interpretations of the Salem events. In an essay, distinguish between a medical and a historical interpretation of the events.

2. Assume the accused in Salem really were witches; then select one of the following disciplines and argue for its being the most important approach to arrive at a comprehensive interpretation of Salem: sociology, psychology, history, law, literature, or folklore.

3. Analyze Tituba's testimony as presented in this chapter, using *what* she said, the *way* she said it, or both.

4. Hawthorne's "Alice Doane's Appeal" attempts to portray a real murder in the context of both a Gothic scene (his scary delivery of the tale to two impressionable young women) and that of the actual execution spot of the Salem witches. By blending all three of these elements (actual murder; Gothic tale; Salem events) Hawthorne demonstrates a consistent view of human nature and behavior. In an essay, present your interpretation of this view.

5. A number of essays in this chapter suggest that because a clear majority (two-thirds) of both accusers and accused were women, the Salem events should be treated as a feminist issue. Using these essays (and any of the other "Sources"), evaluate the feminist approach to Salem.

6. Select a real participant in the trials and, referring to current standards and attitudes regarding evidence, describe the nature, and predict the outcome, of your participant's trial on the basis of current practice.

BEYOND THIS CHAPTER:

7. Using "Alice Doane's Appeal," and any of the other Hawthorne short stories listed in "Sources," analyze Hawthorne's attitudes toward the Puritans and the Salem events. Look especially at the

extent to which he is a faithful commentator on the details or the psychological truth of the era.

8. Select a real participant in the Salem trials—either an accused witch or wizard—and analyze her or his case in the same way you approached the murder case in "Assignment 6" of Chapter 4: "Investigating Murder." Then write a narrative and analysis of the case, either agreeing or disagreeing with the official outcome.

9. Select a fictional character in Arthur Miller's play, *The Crucible,* or in Esther Forbes's short novel, *A Mirror for Witches,* and evaluate the accuracy of their fictional portrayal based on your understanding of the real person (from your reading in this chapter or in the documentary materials available in Levin's or Boyer and Nissenbaum's books—see "Sources").

10. A key issue at Salem was "spectral evidence"—the likelihood that the Devil could use a person's "specter" or image (with or without that person's "permission") to harass others. Evaluate the different interpretations of "spectral evidence," in part using the selections from Whittier in this chapter, and Hitchcock in Chapter 3.

11. After studying the materials in this chapter and those in Chapter 6, "Approaching Jonestown," can you make any generalizations about "mass" movements which involve religious dimensions? In an essay, list and defend the generalizations you have discovered.

12. Compare Increase and Cotton Mather's uses of psychological or optical phenomena with the examples found in Hitchcock's letter and Gibson's essay, both in Chapter 3.

SOURCES FOR FURTHER READING AND/OR RESEARCH

BOYER, PAUL, AND STEPHEN NISSENBAUM, EDS.   *Salem-Village Witchcraft: A Documentary Record of Local Conflict in Colonial New England.* Belmont, Calif.: Wadsworth, 1972. An excellent sourcebook, more extensive than Levin's (see below); provides many archival materials previously unpublished.

————. *Salem Possessed: The Social Origins of Witchcraft.* Cambridge: Harvard University Press, 1974. A highly recommended cross-disciplinary (sociology, economics, geography) reinterpretation of Salem, emphasizing the competition between Salem and Salem Village (now called Danvers). See "Explorations" No. 1, below.

————. *Salem Witchcraft Papers: Verbatim Transcripts of the Legal Documents of the Salem Witchcraft Outbreak of 1692.* 3 vols. New York: Da Capo Press, 1977. The definitive collection of legal transcripts of testimony and other papers.

CAPORAEL, LINNDA R. "Ergotism: The Satan Loosed in Salem?" *Science* 192 (April 2, 1976), pp. 21–26. The first essay to suggest that ergotism was the primary cause of the afflicted girls' behavior; it offers a medical or physiological hypothesis. (See also Spanos and Gottlieb, below.)

DEMOS, JOHN PUTNAM. *Entertaining Satan: Witchcraft and the Culture of New England.* New York: Oxford University Press, 1984. Cross-disciplinary "community study" of the pre-Salem, seventeenth-century folk who *survived* witchcraft accusations; attempts a mixture of biographical, psychological, sociological, and historical portraits.

FORBES, ESTHER. *A Mirror for Witches.* Boston: Houghton Mifflin, 1928; various later reprints. A convincing historical novel of a young woman's belief that she is a witch; set in the vicinity of Salem in the 1680s.

HANSEN, CHADWICK. *Witchcraft at Salem.* New York: Braziller, 1969; reprint, New York: Mentor, 1970. A carefully documented argument that medical hysteria in the context of widespread belief *in,* and limited practice *of,* actual witchcraft was responsible for the Salem outbreak.

HAWTHORNE, NATHANIEL. "The Gentle Boy"; "Main Street"; "The Maypole of Merrymount"; "The Minister's Black Veil"; "Young Goodman Brown." Available in numerous editions of Hawthorne's works, these short stories portray in great detail Hawthorne's vision of the Puritans as a people obsessed with sin and witchcraft.

KIBBEY, ANN. "Mutations of the Supernatural: Witchcraft, Remarkable Providences, and the Power of Puritan Men." *American Quarterly* 34 (Summer 1982), pp. 125–148. Carefully documents two important and related issues: (1) that the result of witches doing Satan's work strangely resembled God's own wrathful punishments; and (2) if witches had such powers, their skills were threatening to the exclusively male ministry.

LEVIN, DAVID. "Salem Witchcraft in Recent Fiction and Drama." *New England Quarterly* 28 (1955), pp. 537–546. A helpful review of a number of literary works on Salem, including Miller's *The Crucible* and Forbes's *A Mirror for Witches;* argues for the quality of Forbes's novel.

————. *What Happened in Salem?* New York: Harcourt, Brace and World, 1960. An excellent casebook/collection of testimonies and contemporary accounts, as well as texts of Forbes's *A Mirror for Witches* and Hawthorne's "Young Goodman Brown."

MAPPER, MARC. *Witches and Historians.* Huntington, W. Va.: Krieger, 1980. Collection of essays, including "medical and psychological explanations"; reprints the Caporeal, and the Spanos–Gottlieb, essays cited in these "Sources."

MILLER, ARTHUR. *The Crucible* (1953). Many editions available. Usually interpreted as a cautionary parable, warning against American McCarthyism of the 1950s, while telling of Puritan repression in the 1690s.

SPANOS, NICHOLAS P., AND JACK GOTTLIEB. "Ergotism and the Salem Village Witch Trials." *Science* 194 (Dec. 24, 1976), pp. 1390–1394. A very detailed rebuttal of Caporael's essay (cited above), arguing that the "general features of the crisis did not resemble an ergotism epidemic."

STARKEY, MARION. *The Devil in Massachusetts.* New York: Knopf, 1950. A "narrative history" from a Freudian or psychoanalytical viewpoint; well-documented and very readable.

UPHAM, CHARLES W. *Salem Witchcraft.* Originally published in two volumes in 1867; various reprints available. Outdated, but still a helpful sourcebook.

WILLIAMS, CHARLES. *Witchcraft.* Originally published in 1941; various reprints available. A British Catholic novelist's analysis/exploration of the witchcraft phenomena, mainly in Europe, but with a chapter on Salem.

WILLIAMS, SELMA R. *Riding the Nightmare: Women and Witchcraft.* New York: Athenaeum, 1978. Feminist interpretation, with fascinating illustrations from both the popular and fine arts.

EXPLORATIONS

1. A visit to Salem would be the ideal exploration. Much of the "stuff" about Salem witchcraft has been commercialized, but numerous sites and museums remain which are worth visiting. The Essex Institute, for example, or the Peabody Museum, both on Essex Street, will help set the historical and geographical context for your visit, while the Witch House and other historic buildings on Chestnut Street will help to establish the atmosphere of the era. You should set your course for *Salem,* but you should know that, in the seventeenth century, Salem Village (now called Danvers) was actually a community separate from Salem, which is the older of the two communities. Keep in mind this simple distinction: Witchcraft, if it happened, occurred mostly in Salem Village; prosecution, if it happened, was carried out in Salem. Boyer and Nissenbaum argue in *Salem Possessed*—see "Sources"—that comprehending the geographical and economic differences between Salem Village and Salem is essential for understanding the Salem witchcraft events.

2. The novel and film *The Exorcist* made quite a stir in popular culture in the 1970s because it showed an on-going relationship between the Catholic Church and satanism. Interview a priest, minister, or rabbi to get a sense of how these religious leaders and their congregations regard witches and witchcraft.

3. Do a survey in a large class, or in a central place like a cafeteria, of people's attitudes toward witchcraft or satanism. Create your own set of questions, but include items like these: Do you believe witches exist today? If so, what should we do, if anything, about them? (If you did "Exploration No. 2," compare your results.)

CHAPTER SIX

Approaching Jonestown

When the 914 members of Rev. Jim Jones's People's Temple took part in a mass "suicide" in Guyana, on November 18, 1978, many of us must have had the same reaction as the reporter James Reston, Jr.—that this was surely "an event unique in human history." The "suicides"—some have called them "murders"—were in themselves horrible reminders of a cult gone over the edge, but the catastrophe also included the murder of U.S. Representative Leo Ryan from California, who had gone to investigate reports of wrongdoings at Jonestown, and who ended up being the first congressman ever to be assassinated.

As a number of selections in this chapter make reasonably clear, Jim Jones's church in its early phase was a curious mixture of fundamentalist black religious spirit and socialist political organizing. Jones started as a minister, but he became a little Stalin. To many of his followers, who would have been insulted by the label "cult," he was simply Dad, an omnipotent Father with Old Testament powers and New Testament charity.

It is easy to be shocked by the ideas and images of this chapter; it is much harder to begin to understand their origins. If this is your first contact with the world of Jim Jones, the third selection in the "Documentary Materials"—Lindsey's "How Rev. Jim Jones Gained His Power Over Followers," one of the first newspaper overviews of

Jones's career, which appeared immediately after the disaster—is a good place to start. Then turn to Rensberger's and Greenberg's essays in the first section, and Hall's in the second: All three of these will provide an overview of the history and progress of the People's Temple.

Eventually, whether you have read about this movement before or are just coming to it now, you will have to confront the "Transcript of a Tape of the Last Moments at Jonestown" in "Documentary Materials," a terrible but necessary document for your understanding of Jonestown. We are used to firsthand video news of wars and other disasters, but rarely, if ever, is there a record such as this. Here we have a religious leader taking his flock quite literally to the Promised Land. In order to place the transcript in the context of the history of the People's Temple, you should read Deborah Layton Blakey's "Affidavit" which predicted the mass suicide.

The selection by Shiva Naipaul, in "Discursive Essays," is a more personal reaction to Jonestown and its place in Guyanese culture. Naipaul, of Indian parentage but born in Jamaica, interpreted the events as part of a cycle of frustrated black rule in the Third World.

A fair amount of evidence indicates that Jim Jones modeled his church—with one obvious exception—on the Father Divine Peace Mission Movement. The exception is important: Father Divine was a black leader of a mainly black church, and although Jones claimed some American Indian blood, his was a mainly black church led by a white minister. In the 1930s and 1940s the black anthropologist Arthur Huff Fauset studied Father Divine and other cult leaders. His observations and conclusions are in "Essays from the Disciplines," and they offer still another approach to the world of Jim Jones.

Cults are not simply what "other" people join. You may have observed that, even to this day, people of many ages (although predominantly the young) are attracted to cults. The 1980s have seen the rise and fall of some quite dramatic cults: the MOVE group in Philadelphia, for example, or the Rajneesh commune in Oregon. Whether the People's Temple was the logical extension of cult life, or an obvious exception to it, is for you to decide.

DISCURSIVE ESSAYS

EDITORIAL

BOYCE RENSBERGER

Boyce Rensberger's essay on Jonestown appeared on the Op-Ed (opinion-editorial) page of the New York Times *ten days after the deaths occurred. His task was to place the People's Temple events in historical context, in effect arguing that theirs was not a unique event but one example in a long tradition of messianic cults. Drawing examples from history, psychology, and anthropology, Rensberger attempts to lead the reader toward a potentially controversial thesis: that "the rise of the California-based cult, its retreat to Guyana and its cataclysmic end have ample precedent."*

Rensberger offers a single thesis, or central argument, originally set forth by his title, that "Jonestown has many precedents," but he organizes his support or proof in two distinct ways. In the first half of the essay, he offers a long catalog of specific cults from history; the "precedents" for, or predecessors of, the People's Temple. In the second half, he outlines a psychological, sociological, and religious profile of "what is common to nearly all the movements." The reader who already knows something about the People's Temple from other newspaper or TV reports will, in effect, be completing Rensberger's argument by noticing that most of the publicized characteristics of Jones's movement match this "profile."

We don't usually define newspaper writing as "cross-disciplinary," but Rensberger's essay serves as a good example of journalism by a writer who has done his homework in several fields.

Jonestown Has Many Precedents

Had they died for a cause in which everyone could believe, they would have been called martyrs. But the members of the People's Temple shared a belief system that, though surely coherent and laudable to them, seems to others tragically misguided and even psychotic.

Yet from what psychologists know of the human mind and from what anthropologists know of how peoples have behaved when their belief systems were threatened, it is clear that the rise of the California-based cult, its retreat to Guyana and its cataclysmic end have ample precedent.

Indeed, the birth and death of the People's Temple fits a pattern repeated many times in many cultures. An examination of these phenomena sheds light on the nature of the universal human need not only for an explanation of the unknown but of the personal need for acceptance by society.

The evidence is that whenever a group has been made to feel that its belief system is no longer generally shared or, at a minimum, respected, something radical happens.

A common pattern is for a small group to find that its traditional values are no longer respected in a changing larger culture. A new cult is typically messianic, emerges, often with a charismatic leader who promises his followers that the millennium is coming and that they will be prepared for while the evil larger society will be cast into darkness.

Among the best known examples are the cargo cults of New Guinea and Melanesia. Christian missionaries arrived in the last century and persuaded the islanders that their religion and way of life were inferior to the ways of Europe and America. Rocked by such teachings from people with obvious material wealth and power, new cults emerged, blending Christian and native concepts and preaching that a return to fundamental values would usher in a utopian age in which Melanesians would dominate Europeans. The concept of the meek inheriting the earth—the strong made weak and the weak strong—has been a feature of messianic cults everywhere.

As the Western impact on the Pacific Islands continued, with military forces replacing missionaries in World War II, utopia-promising cults continued to emerge and fade.

To Western eyes, the most poignant instances involved the belief that God was labeling crates of cargo for delivery from the skies to the Melanesians but that Westerners were intercepting the shipments. To prepare for the millennium when the cargo would reach its rightful owners, Melanesian groups built elaborate airstrips and warehouses.

Many American Indians suffered a similar destruction of native culture with the westward migration of white settlers. In 1870 the

Ghost Dance religion emerged in Nevada and swept through several tribes of Indians. A Paiute medicine man had had a vision that a new era was coming in which the ungodly would be punished and the native Americans restored to a promised land. To prepare themselves they were to learn the rituals of the Ghost Dance.

Even in Western cultures messianic cults have been common. "It's easy for us to look on the People's Temple as aberrant, but they reflect a phenomenon that runs through many cultures, including our own," said Dr. Theodore Schwartz, an anthropologist. "America has had a long history of similar religious cults."

Among the better known of these are the Shakers, the Mennonites, the Amish, the Jehovah's Witnesses, Father Divine's Peace Mission and Aimee Semple McPherson's Church of the Foursquare Gospel.

The Millerites, whose predicted dates of apocalypse came and went, finally modified their beliefs to survive as today's Seventh Day Adventists. The Mormons, once viewed as bizarre, migrated to the Utah wilderness and became respectable. All the world's great religions, of course, began as tiny sects repudiating the beliefs of the majority.

As many sociologists have observed, the idea of going off into the wilderness to start a new way of life is a thoroughly American tradition. Over its two centuries this country has seen the founding and, usually, the foundering of scores of utopian communities and religious sects.

The United States was, after all, founded by minority religious groups seeking freedom from persecution. The pioneers who pushed the frontier westward were often driven by a need to find a place where their belief systems could be lived out without harassment from others.

California was, for most, the geographical end of the search for a Promised Land, and, perhaps for that reason, the beginning of the psychological search. Dr. Charles Glock, a sociologist who has studied California cults, agrees that the country has always spawned new cults but believes that the social turbulence of the 1960's increased the rate.

He suspects that the rise of new cults probably peaked about 1974. Prominent today are such groups as the Rev. Sun Myung Moon's Unification Church, Scientology, the Hare Krishna movement and Synanon.

What is common to nearly all the movements is that they began as small bands of people who suffered what anthropologists call "relative deprivation"—not necessarily in the material sense. The hypothesis deals with people who feel they are being deprived of influence in the mainstream even though they adhere to the proper values and "live right." Such people feel a need to band together for the social approval society denies them.

"It's a feeling," said Dr. Mervyn Meggitt, an anthropologist who has studied the phenomenon, "that people are redefining the world in a way that excludes us even though we are doing the proper thing. We are abiding by the word of God but others have taken control of society."

Scorned belief systems, it appears, do not automatically wither. The believers seek reassurance and, if there is a leader prepared to unite them, a new cult emerges. It provides the social approval that individuals need and concentrates the momentum of individual dedication to a cause into a small religious counterculture. The almost universal expectation is that someday God will put it all aright.

The success of a cult often depends on the presence of an effective, often charismatic, leader who knows how to deliver the approbation so needed by his followers.

Such leaders often accumulate and display great personal wealth, something outsiders believe ought to arouse resentment among followers. Examples include Father Divine, Rev. Ike, and Garner Ted Armstrong. In fact, it appears that followers often take pride in their leader's wealth, seeing in it evidence that God is indeed rewarding the godly.

In a way, so-called brainwashing procedures condense the historical process that spawns cults into a program of altering the belief systems of individuals. Victims are subjected to personal degradation and isolation from approval until they begin to question the rightness of their beliefs.

At this point a new set of beliefs, approved by the brainwashers, is introduced. As the victim demonstrates acceptance of the beliefs, both material rewards and social approbation are delivered. So powerful is the need for these, psychologists suggest, that belief systems that satisfy the needs are embraced more strongly.

In the formation of cults, one other psychological mechanism is at play—the effect of power on the leader. As the leader becomes the embodiment of the group's hopes for a millennium, his ability to separate himself from his office can be severely tested.

Often enough the very qualities that push him to leadership impel him further. He identifies so closely with the prophets of his belief system—Jesus, Lenin, Mohammed, whomever—that his decisions as leader are regarded as infallible or divinely inspired and, therefore, quite capable of overriding the older tenets of belief.

The process is familiar to psychiatrists who have seen countless persons whose behavior develops almost imperceptibly over a period of years from unremarkable patterns into full-blown delusional psychosis. "In our mental hospitals," Dr. Schwartz said, "you'll find many people who are a cult of one. They don't all find followers."

Followers of such a leader, as were the settlers at Jonestown—most of them very much excluded from the mainstream of American life—may find the only source of social approbation for their belief system lies in obeying in dictates of their leader.

Willingly going to one's death for a cause that transcends death is, of course, a proud and noble tradition in the history of religion.

REPORT

JOEL GREENBERG

Greenberg offers here a report on a single symposium on Jonestown held at the 1979 annual meeting of the American Psychological Association, at which a number of psychologists offered their interpretations of Jones's drive for power and how he used it. In their view, Jones was eventually destroyed by the creation of an over-dependent flock. In a sense, his drive for absolute power over them led almost inevitably to his need for them to "die" for him, at first symbolically (during "white nights") and then, actually.

 The symposium participants argued that Jones first used a series of successful psychological maneuvers to build an organization of dependent followers; their dependence was deepened by what one researcher has called the "basic techniques of political control," such as the expropriation of private property and the break-up of family units. The analysts began with a primarily psychological look at Jones and his flock, but soon turned to more social-psychological or even social-political viewpoints.

 Since this is a report from Science News, *a general-information*

science magazine, Greenberg summarizes a number of papers presented at
the conference. He concentrates on rendering the main points and some of
the research of the three speakers (Lasaga, Singer, and Ulman).
Greenberg does not, therefore, offer his own interpretation of the events.
By combining quotations from the speakers and samples from their
research, he does, however, give a continuous narration of the history of
Jones's movement, from recruitment to collective "suicide."

Jim Jones: The Deadly Hypnotist

For Dad's Eyes Only: If you were to die tonight of a natural death
and your wishes were to follow the leader who you appoint, I
would give my life as I would for you at any moment for the
cause . . . I would proceed on my own to subdue as many enemies
I could get hold of . . . also killing myself.

—CLIFF G.

As the world was to learn in the fall of 1978, the sentiments
expressed by People's Temple member Cliff G. in his letter to "Dad"
—leader Jim Jones—were not those of just one isolated, radical devo-
tee of Jones's cult in Guyana. Indeed, it is now clear that many of the
more than 900 mass suicide victims at Jonestown participated willingly with a common bond of fanatical devotion that was incomprehensible to outsiders. One temple member recently was quoted as
saying: "Had I been in Jonestown on Nov. 18, 1978, I would have
been the first in line to take the poison, if I had been so honored."

In the year since that grisly slaughter in the forest-shrouded
commune, behavioral scientists have been conducting their own
"psychological autopsies" on the forces that would ultimately drive
members of an entire community to knowingly drink grape punch
laced with lethal amounts of cyanide. If the results of such studies
have not yet produced definitive explanations, they have begun to
shed light on Jones's awesome power and control over his "flock."
And in the end, it was this very twisted and primitive idea of power
that dictated the downfall of Jonestown and its "father."

The cloistered, no-escape world of the Guyana compound was
but the final phase of a calculated series of steps designed by Jones
to achieve what University of Miami psychologist José I. Lasaga
describes as "mass hypnosis at a social level . . . a unique process of

group regression° that led to a full acceptance of the leader's delusional system."

That process, analyzed in a symposium earlier this year at the annual meeting of the American Psychological Association, began with careful selection of Jones's followers. "They were people who were highly dissatisfied with the American way of life," says Lasaga, "either because of personal and family frustrations, or because of social frustrations—like racial discrimination—or because of political idealism—people longing for a more just form of social organization."

But it is one thing to identify unhappy and dissatisfied persons, and another to convince them that the solutions to their worries lie in one man: Jim Jones. According to some psychologists, Jones often began this task by creating an air of deception that might have been envied even by the CIA (which, coincidentally, Jones frequently singled out to his followers as a potent enemy of the People's Temple). "The recruitment was very sophisticated . . . Jones was a modern master of deception," says Margaret Thaler Singer, a clinical psychologist at the University of California in San Francisco.

From interviews with Jonestown survivors and temple defectors, Singer detailed various recruitment scenarios: A potential recruit who seemed "impressionable" was investigated first by Jones's emissaries, who would rummage through the person's garbage can and report on discarded letters, food preferences and other clues. In some instances, two temple members would visit the home of a prospective recruit. While one member initiated conversation, the other would ask to use the bathroom, where he or she would copy names of doctors and types of medications off pill bottles. Temple members also would phone a recruit's relatives and, under the pretense of conducting a survey, gather vital information such as date and place of birth and years of residence in California, where the church was located.

Armed with such information (it was frequently taped to the inside of his lectern), Jones would demonstrate his "magical powers" at the next lecture attended by the recruit. In a typical lecture, Jones might preach that he "sensed the presence" of a woman about 45 years of age who had diabetes and was under the care of a Dr.

○ regression: a psychoanalytical term referring to a person's psychological movement "backwards" to a less mature state.

Johnson. The listening woman, of course, would be "deeply impressed," according to Singer.

Convinced of their leader's "divine" powers, new members usually would faithfully submit to what Lasaga describes as the "basic techniques of political control" employed by Jones:

- Control of his followers' property and income. As mandated by the temple, all personal property and social security checks were to be turned over to Jones—rendering the followers fully dependent on him as a provider . . . "like a child in relation to his father," Lasaga says. Indeed, many referred to Jones as "Dad."

- Weakening of family ties. "Jones tried to weaken the relationship between husband and wife, and he was personally involved in a large number of extramarital affairs," Lasaga notes. But Jones's quest to "become the most important love object in the whole community" went beyond that. His sexual partners—both women and men—were often forced to stand before the community and testify to Jones's sexual prowess. In one instance, Jones forced Larry Layton (who was later to be charged with the murder of Congressman Leo Ryan and four others) to submit to a homosexual act in the presence of a women with whom Layton was romantically involved; Jones also broke up another of Layton's romances by simply taking the woman away from him. "Larry's sister, Deborah, remembers how she watched her brother's mental condition deteriorate as he became more and more caught up in the almost hypnotic-like spell cast over him by the charismatic Jim Jones," reports Richard Barrett Ulman, assistant professor of psychiatry at the New York Medical College.

- Institution of a sociopolitical caste system. A strict power pyramid consisted of Jones at the top, from where he oversaw a planning commission, and enforcement guards, or "angels." "The common people were absolutely powerless," Lasaga says.

- The no-escape society. Most members came to believe that leaving Jonestown was out of the question. The reasons were both geographic (isolation in a dense jungle) and political—escape was equated with treason and subject to severe punishment. According to Ulman, Jones warned black temple members that if they ventured into the outside world, they would be herded into concentration camps. "He convinced white members that they were under CIA investigation and would be tracked down, tortured, imprisoned and killed if they did not go along with his dictates," reports Ulman.

- Control over verbal expression. "Overt criticism was harshly punished, and a zealous spy network reported all expressions of dissent to Jones," Lasaga says. "In this type of society most people behave like little children who do not dare express their feelings because of their fear of a terribly punitive father, and this means there is no room for external dissent."

- Cognitive and emotional control of the mind. This aspect of Jones's character permeated the entire community of Jonestown. Ultimately it set the stage for one of the most astonishing instances of mass suicide in history. "There was a process of continuous indoctrination carried out by Jones," notes Lasaga. "On the other hand . . . no outside sources of information were available to the community except those which had received his explicit approval. Let us emphasize the tremendous psychological power of these techniques."

Such indoctrinations took place for hours each day both through powerful loudspeakers and lengthy, exhausting speeches by Jones. Members were frequently interrogated in front of the others about their political ideas—which invariably led to expressions of identification with their leader. "This caused in many cases a problem of cognitive dissonance [a state of tension caused by conflict between one's attitudes and behaviors]," Lasaga says, "and it is highly probable that sooner or later those who internally disagreed tried to persuade themselves that what they were forced to say was not completely false."

Lasaga and others have compared Jones's methods with those of a hypnotist. Several researchers have conceptualized hypnosis "as an interpersonal process in which the hypnotist requires the subject to close all his channels of communication with the external world except one: the voice of the hypnotist," according to Lasaga. "Since there are no other channels available to check the truth of the hypnotist's statements, his or her voice becomes a substitute for reality. . . . It is mass hypnosis at a social level."

The group meetings at Jonestown, he says, were "a frightful

emotional experience" that went far beyond the mass contagion of most evangelistic services. Jones's nonstop diatribes were always woven around "the Truth." But his speeches were frequently punctuated with the public humiliation of individuals; sometimes, according to investigators, he would have certain members remove their clothes in front of the group and participate in bizarre boxing matches—often pitting an elderly person against a strong, young man. Paddle-beatings were used on breakers of the strict rules.

But the most haunting of rituals, reflecting Jones's preoccupation with death, were the suicide rehearsals. During so-called "white nights," about 50 rifle-toting members would go from cabin to cabin to round up members as sirens blared. As described by Deborah Layton (according to Ulman): "A mass meeting would ensue. Frequently . . . we would be told that the jungle was swarming with mercenaries and that death could be expected at any minute . . . we were informed that our situation had become hopeless and that the only course of action open to us was a mass suicide for the glory of socialism. We were told that we would be tortured by mercenaries if we were taken alive. Everyone, including the children, was told to line up. As we passed through the lines, we were given a small glass of red liquid to drink. We were told that the liquid contained poison and that we would die within 45 minutes. We all did as we were told."

As well as the group's vulnerability, what Jones played upon —and what finally turned such rehearsals into the real thing—was the "self-hatred" of not only his followers but of himself. As one member wrote, "Dear Dad and Savior—I have many times been so disgusted with myself . . . I hate being old I hate it . . . I know you are the truth and the way . . . I hope I die before I ever betray you." Such letters, says Ulman, "suggest that whatever agony was in these people's lives before they joined the People's Temple was not merely mirrored in Jonestown but rather shaped by Jones so as to give their pain and anguish the seeming virtue of self-sacrifice and ennoblement."

As for their leader himself, Jones's own self-hatred was evident in his constant need for omnipotence, to be loved by everyone and to be everyone's "best" lover. "Everyone had to say he [Jones] was the only true heterosexual man in the world . . . to compensate for his feelings of inferiority," Lasaga says. "He was bisexual, but he 'hated' homosexuals—as he demonstrated by punishing them.

Therefore, he hated himself . . . there was tremendous cognitive dissonance."

To help cope with his own internal struggles—and those of his followers—Jones turned to drugs. "He was a very heavy user of amphetamines," says Singer. And to temple members, Jones dispensed vast amounts of Quaaludes, Demerol, Valium, morphine and Thorazine to control behavior, according to the researchers. These all appeared to contribute to the community's steady withdrawal from reality and to the final tragedy.

In such an atmosphere, says Ulman, "a pathological, collective regression may take place whereby the leader and followers become partners in a form of group decompensation.° In a sense they are victims of each other. . . . [Jones] stripped the group of the ability to fight for their lives, [and] their acquiescence and adulation probably contributed to his weakening hold on reality."

What most group members sought, Ulman says, was "to magically merge with their idealized omnipotent leader in hopes of overcoming their lack of a positive self-image and correspondingly healthy self-esteem. Unfortunately, the price they paid was total masochistic surrender to Jim Jones."

To Lasaga, "Jonestown was a minitotalitarian state ruled by the primitive mind of a paranoiac." Jones had to be "reassured every day that people would die for him." The mass suicide, he adds, was the ultimate "orgasm of power."

DESCRIPTIVE ESSAY

SHIVA NAIPAUL

Naipaul's experience in Guyana after *the Jonestown events was recorded in a full-length book with the appropriate title,* Journey to Nowhere: A New World Tragedy *(1980), from which this selection has been taken. Naipaul is especially informative on the relationship between*

○ decompensation: in "compensation" an individual attempts to do something to "make up" for a certain lack; in "decompensation" an individual is a victim of his own drive to control others totally, with the resultant loss of self-control or self-maintenance.

Guyanese politics and Jones's California "radicalism." He attempts to answer the question: "Why Guyana?"

By piling up details and incidents of the unsavory activities of both Jones and his host country, Naipaul attempts a satiric portrait of both parties. This particular section from his book is mainly based on research in Guyanese newspapers, although the information is also used to give a chronological account of Jones's entry into Guyanese society. Although it is clear that Naipaul has relied on others, many of his judgments are presumably his own, like his reference to "the most notorious of Burnham's criminal courtiers."

[Guyana Welcomes Jones]

It was on Christmas Day 1974 that the following advertisement appeared in Guyana's *Daily Chronicle:* "The Blind See! The Deaf Hear! The Crippled Walk!"

The Greatest Healing Ministry Through Christ on Earth Today had arrived in town.

This modern-day Apostolic ministry, readers of the *Chronicle* were told, was in the process of establishing an agricultural mission in Guyana. It was their intention to assist the Government in its feeding, clothing and housing of the Guyanese people. One Eugene Chaikin, described as a wealthy California attorney, asserted that Pastor Jones was the most loving, Christ-like human being he had ever met. After this testimonial, there was a curious little digression: the People's Temple, the advertisement said, was well known for its support of local governments. But the text soon reverted to the matter at hand. Pastor Jones, it continued, possessed all nine gifts of the Holy Spirit. He had been able to cure thousands of "every kind of affliction!!!" It gave as an example a young woman whose X-rays had revealed holes in the bone as large as twenty-five-cent pieces. Pastor Jones had assured her that she would be all right, and, after his laying on of hands, the pain—which no sedative had been able to ease—had vanished. This was typical of the miraculous Power of Christ which channeled itself through Pastor Jones. The public was invited to attend a healing service where they would see with their own eyes the restorations performed by the wonderful powers with which Pastor Jones had been invested. This performance would take place at the Sacred Heart Church on December 29. The Catholics were praised for the ecumenical spirit they had shown in allowing one of their churches to be the venue of this supernatural display.

Dutifully, the *Chronicle* supplied an account of the service on December 30. It had been a great success. "Long before the service started, Guyanese from all walks of life, many of them old and infirm, deaf, blind, paralysed . . . filled the pews and aisles of the church. Scores of others . . . crowded the doors and the churchyard to witness the ceremony." Miracle after miracle was performed that afternoon in Georgetown. Pastor Jones chose at random people he said were sick. One woman was told that she was suffering from a pain in the head and had a cancerous growth. The woman agreed that he had diagnosed correctly and was told to go to the bathroom. She reappeared a few minutes later, loudly proclaiming that she had cast off the growth and that the pain in her head was gone. A man suffering from knee pains jumped for joy after Pastor Jones had prayed for him; a woman's stomachache disappeared; another announced that her high blood pressure had been cured. The Catholics, who, days before, had been congratulated for their ecumenical spirit, were suddenly upset. Nothing, however, could now be done about that.

A Jesuit priest, Father Morrison, recalled the day in late 1974 when a group of "very presentable" young Americans had come to see him. They told him of the pioneering work they were engaged on up in the northwest; they had come to Guyana, they said, because they wanted to help the developing countries of the world. It all sounded so very good, so wonderfully Christian. Here were all these young people showing their love not only by word but by deed. Practical Christianity—that was what he thought the People's Temple stood for. The presentable, courteous Americans had a favor to ask of him. Would it be possible for them to use the Sacred Heart Church for one of their services? From its pulpit they would announce the good news of their ministry. He discussed their request with the parish council. The chairman liked the idea. So did Father Morrison. Guyana was in bad shape physically and spiritually. It needed all the help it could get. He felt that given a chance, those young men and women could light some candles in the Guyanese darkness. Permission was granted for the service.

Father Morrison was not prepared for the advertisement that followed. Not once had they hinted to him that it was to be a "healing" service, a platform for the self-display of their Pastor.

"I was horrified. It was so terrible, so disgusting, what they had gone and done."

He argued for its cancellation—without success. The Charismatics° would not hear of it. They were extremely curious and wanted to see what the healing would be like. Others argued that cancellation would be contrary to the ecumenical spirit. The show went on as scheduled.

The Temple representatives wept when Father Morrison accused them of having deceived him.

"Wept?"

"Weeping was one of their favorite tactics. They would use tears as propaganda. They were most adept at projecting hurt feelings."

They had no idea how the misunderstanding could have come about. They thought they had made themselves clear. They had never intended to deceive him. Oh, dear! Oh, dear! So they wept before him and wrung their hands.

But the damage had been done.

(The Temple's use of tears as a weapon was mentioned to me by someone else. On this occasion, it involved an attempted real-estate transaction in Georgetown. The owner did not want to sell at the price that was offered, but the Temple's representatives were persistent. They would telephone and call upon her at all hours of the day and night. On one of these visits, a Temple female started to cry. "If only you knew what would happen to me if I don't get you to agree! Do you love me? Do you care about me? Does the fate of another human being not matter to you? If you really loved me and cared for me as a human being you would sell your house." The owner was flabbergasted. She argued with them. How could she buy another house with the money they would give her? They replied that she need not buy another house. She could go to Jonestown. There she would not need money; there all her needs would be met

---

° the Charismatics: a group within a church who believe in the more immediate, direct demonstration of their faith, without necessarily relying on designated ministers or passive forms of worship.

and she would experience perfect fulfillment and happiness. She was spared, however, when the Temple became interested in another property and swiftly discarded her.)

Thus did Jim Jones and the People's Temple come to socialist Guyana—with tears, deception and voodoo.

———————— • ————————

It is hardly a cause for astonishment, given the history, beliefs and practices of the People's Temple as we now know them to have been, that Jim Jones should have been drawn to Guyana; and it is equally unastonishing that the Guyana of Forbes Burnham,° given its history, beliefs and practices, should have accepted him. Guyana, over recent years, has shown a predilection for welcoming, assisting and sheltering strange people, a weakness springing from a peculiar sort of gangsterism that can contain within itself both corrupt cynicism of the highest order and ideological motivation. "You're a stupid black man," Burnham is reported to have said to the architect who refused to inflate his estimates. That outburst reveals the complex nature of Burnhamite gangsterism. It is about being Black and Third World as well as about being rich; it is a point of view. Within that point of view, criminality, nationalism, corruption, altruism of a kind, can all coexist. What holds them together is the personality of the Big Black Chief who operates, so to speak, by institutionalizing his manias, lusts and fantasies. This makes him and his country— which is no more than a projection of his caprice—vulnerable to appropriate calls from the wild.

For instance, in 1971 a dope dealer from Bermuda came to Guyana to drum up support for a so-called Black Peoples Congress. The Government obliged with a handout. However, the Black Peoples Congress is yet to take place. Then there was the man who claimed to be an Angolan freedom fighter. He was honored with Guyanese citizenship. It turned out that he was an American black in flight from the police. Like the Bermudan, he was also involved in the dope trade.

○ Forbes Burnham: dictatorial president of Guyana, who came to power in 1964 with American support. He died in 1985, after leading his country from being a relatively prosperous West Indian British colony to one of the poorest independent Caribbean countries.

These were not isolated pieces of bad luck. The Bermudan and the pseudo-Angolan belong to a common pattern of vaguely ideological misadventure. After he had committed murder on his Trinidad commune, it was to Guyana that Michael X° had fled. There he was met at the airport by a Minister of the Government and given the red-carpet treatment. (Admittedly, at that stage, the murders had not yet come to light; but the less than salubrious past of the man now calling himself Michael X was well known.) The state-owned *Chronicle* published a photograph of the Minister and his guest gazing deep into each other's eyes. Beneath the photograph was the caption "When Two Revolutionaries Meet."

Less controversial, perhaps, but equally revealing of the mood of Guyanese hospitality, was the visit of the American Black Power activist and theorist Stokely Carmichael. He had originally been invited to Guyana by a dissident group of academics and students. But they quickly dissociated themselves from him when they heard the sort of things he was saying. "All the talk was of bloodshed and fighting," a member of the group said to me. "He said Black Power meant African power. He said we had to learn how to kill. It was the wrong message for a place like Guyana. We had had enough of racial killing by then." Carmichael was not left either embarrassed or marooned by their hasty desertion: he was quickly picked up by the People's National Congress and, like Michael X, given the red-carpet treatment by the Guyanese Government.

Toward the end of 1978, *The New York Times,* reporting from Georgetown, stated that there were at least four Americans wanted back at home for an assortment of crimes—rape, murder, armed robbery, blackmail—who were living in Guyana under Government protection. One of these had been made a senior training official in the National Service. "This is a position of considerable responsibility," a "Soviet-bloc source" was quoted as saying. "The Government wouldn't give him the job if it didn't have faith in him."

○ Michael X: a Trinidadian—his name was homage to the black American civil-rights activist Malcolm X—who worked for "Black Power" in London in the 1960s. His career, which verged on petty crime, turned really nasty, and he was executed for murder in the 1970s.

But the most notorious of Burnham's criminal courtiers is a black preacher from Tennessee calling himself Rabbi Washington. Back home, where he is known as David Hill, he is wanted by the police on charges of blackmail and violence. But in Guyana, where he surfaced in 1972, he is a figure of consequence. He has created around himself a religious sect—the House of Israel— which espouses a messianic doctrine of black redemption. His Guyanese followers adorn themselves in the colors of the ruling party, which also happen to be the national colors. They arrive by the busload to take part in Government-sponsored rallies and parades; they help to break up Opposition meetings. In a sugar strike called by a union unfriendly to the Government, they played the part of scab labor. The Rabbi lives in considerable style. His benefactors have, in addition, provided his organization with two farms. The House of Israel calls itself "Burnham's Church." It has even included him in its theology: the Comrade Leader is Moses; the Rabbi is Aaron.

There was nothing extraordinary, therefore, in the warm welcome extended by the Guyanese Government to Jim Jones and his People's Temple. Agricultural communes staffed by the disciples of various (largely black) American sects and cults were springing up all over the Guyanese interior. (The agricultural vogue, though, does not benefit the Indian population of Guyana—the country's traditional farmers. Most of them have their requests for land refused. Occasionally, what they do have is actually taken away from them. The most recent case concerned a livestock cooperative whose lands were seized at gunpoint and turned over to supporters of the People's National Congress. I have a photograph arising out of that incident. It shows a smiling Parliamentary Secretary, wearing a dashiki, standing in a field and looking on as a couple of the new owners ride about on a tractor. Beside him are posted armed guards, presumably on the lookout for any of the dispossessed who might be thinking of making some trouble.) When Jim Jones described Guyana to his flock as "paradise," he knew what he was talking about. He was an ideal applicant: he had money, he had hundreds of devoted disciples, he had good contacts in California, he knew what politics was about. Guyana had the land, the protective privacy and the ideological cloak of feeding, housing and clothing the people. It was a marriage made in heaven.

ESSAYS FROM THE DISCIPLINES

ANTHROPOLOGY

ARTHUR HUFF FAUSET

> *Former members of the People's Temple have stated that Jim Jones was fascinated by the success of Father Divine's religious, political, and economic organizing among black Americans in the decades preceding World War II. Indeed, Jones actually visited the remnants of this movement after Father Divine had died, and even attempted to win over Father Divine's wife and parishioners to the People's Temple.*
>
> *Fauset's urban-anthropological study emphasizes the "functionalism" of Father Divine's organization. According to Fauset, black urban cults are able to transform "social needs by means of secular enterprises." The resemblances between Father Divine's organization and Jones's church are obvious and quite striking. In addition to his analysis of Father Divine, Fauset included in his longer study,* Black Gods of the Metropolis *(1944), numerous "field observations" he had undertaken to gauge the temper of members of various black cults. The passage in the Appendix to this selection represents such a visit by Fauset to a small business run by mission members.*
>
> *The main section of Fauset's report attempts an honest but critical appraisal of American society in the early 1940s. He carefully notes, for example, the fact that American blacks dreaded long-distance travel because of difficulties in obtaining food and lodging. Although the Appendix presents its "interviewer" somewhat neutrally, it is likely to have been Fauset himself. This "field observation" report has a wealth of telling detail which establishes Fauset as a careful interviewer. Note, for example, the interviewees' indignation when they get the drift of the question about Father Divine's "wayward children."*

Father Divine Peace Mission Movement

It is when we come to the Father Divine Peace Mission Movement that the function of the cult to transform social needs by means of secular enterprises is most clearly demonstrated. Here these transformations achieve a plane of efficiency and a scope which in some instances lift them clear of the realm of amateurism, and establish them with those other secular expressions in America which have culminated in the concept of "big business."

Perhaps the only substantial difference, morphologically, between the functional forms which have developed in this movement and those forms which have been produced in the ordinary processes of big business in our country, is that in the Father Divine Peace Mission Movement these forms are functional by-products rather than end-products.

Many critics who see in the Father Divine Peace Mission Movement nothing but a "racket" probably miss this important functional implication. Such people, observing that many patrons of the Peace restaurants and of the three-cent (without tips) shoe shine parlors are not members of the cult, opine that these secular expressions should in no way be related to the religious expression.

It is true that many people who benefit by the functions of the movement have no vital interest in the movement itself, but this probably has no more significance than the fact that most people using an electric light bulb for reading purposes have no knowledge of or interest in the processes by which the lamp was created. The essential fact is that out of an attempt, through the Father Divine Peace Mission Movement, to resolve a need of a segment of humanity, numerous significant functional transformations have ensued.

A perusal of the advertisements in a recent copy of the *New Day* confirms the point. More than fifty of these advertisements are of business establishments which are directly or indirectly connected with the Peace Mission Movement. It is to be assumed that there are many more such establishments controlled by individuals and groups which have not advertised in the *New Day*.

Among the enterprises advertised in this particular issue are the following: automobile accessories and repairs; garages; cabinet makers; coal, ice, oil distributors; barbers; free employment agency; express and hauling; food distribution; jewelry; women's wear; laundries; notions; radios and repair; restaurants; shoe repair; tailors and cleaners.

The most spectacular economic function of the Father Divine Peace Mission Movement develops out of its real estate holdings. The "extensions," of which there are scores, are really hotels. This is of the utmost significance in the life of Negroes, for, quite apart from the item of expense in which these hotels are distinguished by the amazingly low cost of services rendered (usually two dollars a week room rent, and fifteen cents a meal with no tips allowed), the significant fact lies in this: here we have a functional transformation with regard to a very vital need of American Negroes growing out of the general practice of American hostelries to refuse to receive them.

To a degree probably unknown or unsuspected by people outside the racial group, the psychology of an entire race, numbering nearly fifteen million people, has been conditioned by this need. White Americans look forward to travel as one of life's richest boons; but the American Negro contemplates travel in the United States with a degree of misgiving amounting to dread. A Negro, when setting out on a trip, either must have every stopover very carefully arranged in advance, or he must see to it that he does not arrive at an unknown place too late in the evening to shop around for accommodations; otherwise he is likely to be compelled to spend the night out of doors and without anything to eat.

It would seem that this need should have been met many years ago, but little has developed to ameliorate this condition. Now, however, the Father Divine Peace Mission Movement, a religious undertaking, is in the process of meeting such a need through the functional transformation described above. It is hardly to be wondered at that the name "Promised Land" has been bestowed upon the choicest of these extensions located in the beautiful Hudson River Valley and the Catskill Mountains.*

---

*When the Father Divine Peace Mission Movement purchased the extension at Krum Elbow, across the river from the Hyde Park residence of President Roosevelt, a cartoonist on the Chicago *Daily News* thought to enliven his sheet with a drawing with the title "At Krum Elbow."

He pictured a little black urchin standing with hat in hand on President Roosevelt's doorstep at Hyde Park. Two empty milk bottles still remained at the doorstep of the President's house, one of them containing the usual message to the milkman. The President of the United States was pictured coatless, standing behind a screen door and looking even more perplexed than might have been the case had he been confronted suddenly by a troop of Nazi parachuters. The Negro boy is calling up to him, "Father Divine wants t' know kin he borry yo' lawn-mo?" Below the cartoon is another caption which reads, "DON'T FORGET YOUR GOOD NEIGHBOR POLICY, FRANKLIN!"

In this connection it is of interest to note also that the man who recently was elected president of the North and South American Hotel Keepers' Association, a cultural organization for the promotion of hemispherical good-will, is himself the

How the Father Divine Peace Mission Movement functions in an analogous manner on the political-economic plane is demonstrated in the following report by Floyd Calvin in the June 22, 1935, issue of the Pittsburgh *Courier,* a Negro weekly:

FATHER DIVINE THREATENS BOYCOTT AGAINST MILK COMPANIES—MAKES PROBE OF POLITICS TOWARDS RACE

It now looks like something more than the usual perfunctory gestures in Harlem's economic battles will come of the threatened boycott by Father Divine against milk companies if they don't employ colored drivers and mechanics. The "placating" letters sent to "Father" by Sheffield and Borden were promptly turned down when Divine replied that the companies had evaded the point—that they did not employ colored drivers and mechanics, which he specifically requested that they do. . . .

"Under further investigation, both within your stores and connections and especially with the public drivers on the streets of the city of New York and elsewhere, I do not find drivers non-discriminated according to your information given in your letter. If your concern is to be looked upon as equitable, we are looking forward for an immediate change in your staff of drivers on the public streets, especially in Harlem, by immediately placing 50% of a different color than what you now have."

These functional implications are again demonstrated in the Righteous Government program, which is the name of a specific

---

manager of a well-known hotel in Harrisburg, Pennsylvania, against whom a suit was brought, under the Pennsylvania Equal Rights Act, for refusing to permit five Negroes in an interracial group to be served in the dining room of his hotel.

It should be remembered that properties owned by the Father Divine Peace Mission Movement in the Promised Land are only a small fraction of the real estate holdings of the movement, and do not include the immensely valuable parcels of real property in a score or more locations in New York City. *See* Richard S. Bird, in the *New York Times Magazine,* July 2, 1939. Since this study was made, the Father Divine Peace Mission Movement has purchased a pretentious hotel building located on the shore at Brigantine Beach, scarcely five minutes drive from Atlantic City. How religious and class lines break down in the face of an economic compulsion is clearly reflected in the clientele of this hotel, which includes Negroes from every social and occupational avenue of life. Note already has been made of increasing Philadelphia holdings.

effort within the movement to guide the entire politico-economic and educational motivation of the movement. The Righteous Government program was launched in January 1936, at a special convention of the followers of Father Divine called the International Righteous Government Convention. A Righteous Government platform was drawn up, which in addition to being a rare piece of legalistic exposition (containing as it does whole speeches by the leader) embraces nearly all the principles operative in the cult, and thereby points to its truly functional character:

1.   The Righteous Government is to be interracial, international, interreligious, interdenominational, and non-partisan.
2.   It is to be bound by the following principles:
    a.   The entire human race is essentially one.
    b.   Peace in the human race is to be established by eradicating prejudice, segregation and division among people, and promoting the welfare of every living creature.
    c.   Equal opportunity for every individual without regard to race, creed, and color.

There are fourteen general planks. Of these, eight refer to injustices involving race, creed, and color. There are twelve purely economic planks and three educational provisions, also a special amendment calling for legislation "imposing the penalty for first degree murder on all members of lynch mobs killing or fatally injuring any person, together with a fine of Ten or Twenty Thousand Dollars to be paid by the county wherein the lynching occurs, to the estate of the injured or deceased person."

Thus the Father Divine Peace Mission Movement, which essentially is a religious organization, in effect becomes the mechanism by which various social urges, particularly those of its leaders and more socially dynamic members, may find outlets of expression. By making it possible for agencies to be established to fulfill these needs, it tends to transform these urges into the imperatives of American culture. It would appear that the Father Divine Peace Mission Movement outstrips the other cults in the extent to which it demonstrates these functional characteristics. This undoubtedly is due to a greater social awareness as well as a superior organizational capacity on the part of the leadership of the Father Divine Peace Mission Movement. Still it is clear that lurking within the framework of each of the cults are the seeds and roots of the same general tendency.

APPENDIX

Four women in a Father Divine Peace Mission dress shop: Three of these were about fifty years of age, and the fourth a younger woman, about thirty-five. All but one had come from outside New York City, one from the South, another from Kansas, and the third from Cincinnati. The interviewer entered the shop about 10:30 one summer evening, when all four were working over sewing machines or with scissors. When the interviewer asked them if they would mind enlightening him a bit about the Father Divine movement, one of the older women said she doubted that anything she could say would help him because each person had to get his understanding of the Father in his own way. The best way would be for him to read the *New Day* and attend the meetings, another said. The third one remarked, "Not any one of us got the divine revelation in the same way, and if a million people enter into the spirit, they will enter in a million different ways." They discussed among themselves the worthwhileness of talking with the interviewer. They said if he had come merely out of curiosity, it was doubtful if anything they might say would help him. Besides, they had their own understanding, but only Father and the *New Day* could speak with authority. Nothing they would say could be accounted the gospel truth.

One of the older women was more inclined to talk than any of the others. The interviewer addressed himself to her, and told her he was puzzled by a few things in the Peace Mission Movement. For example, he was unable to note any praying, and since he had come up in a church where prayer was an important part of the service, was he correct in believing that Father Divinites did not pray? She said that the interviewer was wrong. She quoted from the Bible, "Prayer is the expression of the heart's desire." She said every word that a person might utter could be a prayer. Our very breathing is a prayer. Especially everything about us that causes us to be grateful is a prayer. The fact is that the followers of Father Divine do not pray in the way others do because prayer assumes that God is far off somewhere and you have to petition him. But God is here with us (Father Divine). It no longer is necessary to send a petition to him.

He is in our midst, sees us and knows us. And that is why, instead of praying in the usual way, they say over and over, "Thank you, Father!" The youngest woman then spoke up. She said yes, that prayer is on their lips constantly, and it makes them very happy. When she goes to bed she can feel that prayer beating within her. When she turns in her bed, her very muscles and tissues say, "Thank you, Father," and it makes her very happy.

The interviewer asked them about baptism. They told him that baptism in the old sense has been done away with. Water baptism was a form. Now we are baptized in the spirit. They told him it is like cotton; when you plant the seed, you say you are planting cotton; when it begins to shoot up, you say you must tend the cotton; when you find it in full bloom, you say you must pick the cotton; then you say you must seed it. Yet all the while you are not talking about the cotton at all. Only the final product is the cotton, and only that is useful. All the rest is useless and worse than useless, because if it gets mixed in with the final product it will spoil it. So it is with baptism with water. All these things lead up to the spiritual life, but they are not the spiritual life. Once this life is attained, all these other things are useless and could even be harmful. Father Divine has come to do away with all harmful things.

The interviewer asked if it were true that most of Father Divine's followers once had been very wayward children. This question stirred considerable resentment. The women as much as told him that his question was insulting. If anyone would look, they said, he would see for himself. The interviewer had been present at various meetings. Did it appear to him that most of the followers belonged to the scum of the earth? Did they seem to be bums and criminals? One of the older women said she had grown up in a fine home, with splendid surroundings and background. In certain respects there were things in her home which were not provided for in Father's life. But she had forsaken these in order to live a life of evangelical faith.

All these women protested that they had not come to Father Divine because of a sense of dereliction, but because they felt his call. The youngest woman said she had begun to find the call more than four years ago in Cincinnati. She kept asking herself, "Can Father Divine be God?" She went to her room and prayed constantly to God to let her know whether or not Father Divine was God. None of her immediate family was a follower. One morning, about three o'clock, a voice spoke out to her. It said, "I am God, and you will find me in the body of Father Divine. Have no fear; you will be saved." It was a most thrilling moment for her, she said. She could hardly wait for morning to come. When finally it had arrived, she went downstairs and told other members of her family. They laughed at her and derided her. She went over to the local Peace Mission. There she found sympathy and comfort. Within four months the call to be near the presence of God was so strong that she left Cincinnati and came to New York City, where she has been ever since. She is so glad she let the bit be placed in her mouth!

One of the older women said she had had a very good home with fine surroundings as a girl, but that she had been very petulant, obstinate, willful, and ungrateful for everything she received from her loving parents. She constantly found fault, picked quarrels, and the like. Then she came under the influence of Father Divine's teachings. Her entire nature has changed. She lives a life of complete happiness. She never finds fault. She never argues or gets into quarrels. Life is a happy song. She loves her work; thinks nothing of beginning very early in the morning and finishing at five o'clock the next morning. In fact, she said, and her friends said the same for themselves, sometimes she was not altogether glad to go to sleep; life was so beautiful and wonderful. They spoke of the Rosebuds' singing. These songs are inspirations of Father. He will put a song on your lips and when you utter it, everyone will join in. Some of the Rosebuds are children of the followers, and others have come right off the streets. They live pure, evangelical lives, and are devoted to Father. There are more than one hundred of these alone. Also there are Crusaders among the boys. These refute the claim that all the followers of Father Divine are old people. They told me that followers of Father Divine do not use the term "Heaven" when referring to one of his hostels. This is a derisive term used by outsiders. Actually there is a heaven for every individual, and that heaven is within. Only that. Color is completely out with Father Divine's followers. Father Divine himself has no color. He is the expression of everybody and everything.

SOCIOLOGY

JOHN R. HALL

In this long, carefully documented study of Jonestown, sociologist John R. Hall first discusses what he feels are the inadequate *explanations of*

*Jonestown—such as historical precedents, Jones's irrationality, cult
behavior, and brainwashing. He then turns to a sociological analysis
based on the idea that the People's Temple was an "apocalyptic sect";
that is, a religious group which expects a radical—(if not supernatural)—
change to be effected in the world through direct divine intervention (such
as Christ's Advent, or the "coming" of the Lord to scourge the unjust).
The implications of such an analysis, Hall argues, reveal the reasons
why this particular sect chose mass suicide, when the majority of others
have not.*

    *The form of this essay is polemical. Hall first disposes of certain
current interpretations as he moves toward his own interpretation. In
reaching this goal, Hall also surveys the basic historical research
concerning the "facts" of Jonestown in the context of interpretations of
religious and sociological concepts, such as Adventism and communal
discipline.*

The Apocalypse at Jonestown

    The events of November 1978 at Jonestown, Guyana have been
well documented, indeed probably better documented than most
incidents in the realm of the bizarre. Beyond the wealth of "facts"
that have been drawn from interviews with survivors of all stripes,
there remain piles of as yet unsifted documents and tapes. If they can
ever be examined, these will perhaps add something in the way of
detail, but it is unlikely they will change very much the broad lines
of our understanding of Jonestown. The major dimensions of the
events and the outlines of various intrigues are already before us. But
so far we have been caught in a flood of instant analysis. Some of this
has been insightful, but much of the accompanying moral outrage
has clouded our ability to comprehend the events themselves. We
need a more considered look at what sort of social phenomenon
Jonestown was, and why, and how the Reverend Jim Jones and his
staff led the 900 people at Jonestown to die in mass murder and
suicide. On the face of it, the action is unparalleled and incredible.

    The news media have sought to account for Jonestown largely
by looking for parallels in history. Yet we have not been terribly
enlightened by the examples they have found, usually because they
have searched for cases that bear the outer trappings of the event but
have fundamentally different causes. Thus, at Masada, in 73 A.D. the

Jews who committed suicide under siege by Roman soldiers knew their fate was death, and they chose to die by their own hands rather than at those of the Romans. In World War II Japanese kamikaze pilots acted with the knowledge that direct, tangible, strategic results would stem from their altruistic suicides, if they were properly executed. And in Hitler's concentration camps, though there was occasional cooperation by Jews in their own executions, the Nazi executioners had no intentions of dying themselves.

Besides pointing to parallels that don't quite fit, the news media have portrayed Jim Jones as irrational—a madman who had perverse tendencies from early in his youth. They have labelled the Peoples Temple a "cult," perhaps in the hope that a label will suffice when an explanation is unavailable. And they have quite correctly plumbed the key issue of how Jones and his staff were able to bring the mass murder/suicide to completion, drawing largely on the explanations of psychiatrists who have suggested the concept of "brainwashing" as the answer.

But Jones was crazy like a fox! Though he may have been "possessed" or "crazed," both the organizational effectiveness of the Peoples Temple for more than fifteen years and the actual carrying out of the mass murder/suicide show that Jones and his immediate staff knew what they were doing.

Moreover, the Peoples Temple only became a cult when the media discovered the tragedy at Jonestown. As an Indiana woman whose teenager died there commented: "I can't understand why they call the Peoples Temple a cult. To the people, it was their church. . . ."[1]

It is questionable whether the term cult has any sociological utility, for as Harold Fallding has observed, it is a pejorative term most often used by members of one religion to describe a heretical or competing religion, of which they disapprove (1974, p. 27).[2] Of course, even if the use of the term "cult" in the press has been sloppy and inappropriate, some comparisons—for example, to the Unification church, the Krishna Society, and the Children of God—have been quite apt. But these comparisons have triggered a sort of guilt by association. In this view, Jonestown is not such an aberrant case among numerous exotic and bizarre religious cults. The only thing stopping some people from "cleaning up" the cult situation is the constitutional guarantee of freedom of religion.[3]

Finally, the brainwashing concept is an important but nevertheless incomplete basis for understanding the mass murder/suicide.

There can be no way to determine how many people at Jonestown freely chose to drink the cyanide-laced Flav-r-ade distributed after word was received of the murders of U.S. Representative Leo Ryan and four other visitors at the airstrip. Clearly, over 200 children and an undetermined number of adults were murdered. Thought control and blind obedience to authority—brainwashing—surely account for some additional number of suicides. But the obvious cannot be ignored—that a substantial number of people, brainwashed or not, committed suicide. Since brainwashing occurs in other social organizations besides the Peoples Temple, it can only be a necessary but not a sufficient cause of the mass murder/suicide. The coercive persuasion involved in a totalistic construction of reality may explain in part *how* large numbers of people came to accept the course proposed by their leader, but it leaves unanswered the question of *why* the true believers among the inhabitants of Jonestown came to consider "revolutionary suicide" a plausible course of action.

In all the instant analysis of Jones' perversity, the threats posed by cults, and the victimization of people by brainwashing, there has been little attempt to account for Jonestown sociologically or as a religious phenomenon. The various facets of Jonestown remain as incongruous pieces of seemingly separate puzzles, and we need a close examination of the case itself in order to try to comprehend it.

In the following discussion, based on ideal-type analysis and *verstehende* sociology° (Weber, 1977, pp. 4–22), I will suggest that the Peoples Temple Agricultural Project at Jonestown was an apocalyptic sect. Most apocalyptic sects gravitate toward one of three ideal typical possibilities—preapocalyptic Adventism,° preapocalyptic war, or postapocalyptic other-worldly grace. Insofar as the Adventist group

---

○ ideal-type analysis and "verstehende" sociology: in Max Weber's approach, true "understanding" (translation of the German, *verstehende*) "consists in placing the act in an intelligible and more inclusive context of meaning" *(Economy and Society)*, including the *motive* for an act. In reaching this "understanding," it is helpful to propose the "ideal-type," or pure form, of the social group being studied. Thus, Hall suggests that the People's Temple, because of its beliefs and behavior, was an "ideal-type" of an "other-worldly sect."

○ Adventism: the belief in the Advent or (second) Coming of Christ, who will end human history by rewarding the just and punishing sinners; some Adventist groups have actually predicted a specific day for the Apocalypse—the catastrophic end of the earth.

takes on a communal form, it comes to approximate the postapocalyptic tableau of other-worldly grace. Jonestown, I argue, was caught
on the saddle of the apocalypse: it had its origins in the vaguely
apocalyptic revivalist evangelism of the Peoples Temple in the
United States, but the Guyanese communal settlement itself was an
attempt to transcend the apocalypse by establishing a "heaven-on-
earth." For various reasons this attempt was frustrated. The Jonestown group was drawn back into a preapocalyptic war with the
forces of the established order, and thus "revolutionary suicide"
came to be seen as a way of surmounting the frustration, of moving
beyond the apocalypse to heaven, albeit not on earth.

In order to explore this idea, let us first consider the origins of
Jonestown and the ways in which it subsequently came to approximate the ideal typical other-worldly sect. Then we can consider
certain tensions within the Jonestown group with respect to its other-
worldly existence in order to understand why similar groups did not
(and are not likely to) encounter the same fate.

JONESTOWN AS AN OTHER-WORLDLY SECT

An other-worldly sect, as I have described it in *The Ways Out*
(1978), is a utopian communal group that subscribes to a comprehensive set of beliefs based on an apocalyptic interpretation of current history. The world of society-at-large is seen as totally evil, in
its last days, at the end of history as we know it. It is to be replaced
by a community of the elect—those who live according to the revelation of God's will. The convert who embraces such a sect must,
therefore, abandon any previous understanding of life's meaning and
embrace the new world view, which itself is capable of subsuming
and explaining the individual's previous life, the actions of the sect's
opponents, and the demands that are placed on the convert by the
leadership of the sect. The other-worldly sect typically establishes its
existence on the "other" side of the apocalypse by withdrawing from
"this" world into a timeless heaven-on-earth. In this millennial kingdom,° those closest to God come to rule. Though democratic consen-

---

° millennial kingdom: specifically the thousand-year reign of Christ on earth, as
predicted in *Revelations* 20:1–7; but often, more generally, any post-historical period in
which the good have come to power.

suality° or the collegiality of elders may come into play, more typically a preeminent prophet or messiah, who is legitimated by charisma or tradition, calls the shots in a theocratic organization of God's chosen people.

The Peoples Temple had its roots in amorphous revivalistic evangelical religion, but in the transition to the Jonestown Agricultural Mission it came to resemble an other-worldly sect. The Temple grew out of the interracial congregation Jim Jones had founded in Indiana in 1953. By 1964 the Peoples Temple Full Gospel Church was federated with the Disciples of Christ (Kilduff and Javers, 1978, p. 20). Later, in 1966, Jones moved with 100 of his most devout followers to Redwood Valley, California. From there they expanded in the 1970s to San Francisco and Los Angeles, which were more promising locales for liberal, interracial evangelism. In these years before the move to Guyana, Jones largely engaged himself in the manifold craft of revivalism. He learned from others he observed—Father Divine in Philadelphia and David Martinus de Miranda in Brazil—and Jones himself became a purveyor of faked miracles and faith healings (*Newsweek,* December 4, 1978, pp. 55–56). By the time of the California years, the Peoples Temple was prospering financially from its somewhat shady tent meeting-style activities and from a variety of other money-making schemes. It was also gaining political clout through the deployment of its members for the benefit of various politicians and causes.

These early developments make one wonder why Jones did not establish a successful but relatively benign sect like the Jehovah's Witnesses, or, alternatively, why he did not move from a religious base directly into the realm of politics, as did the Reverend Adam Clayton Powell when he left his Harlem congregation to go to the U.S. House of Representatives. The answer seems twofold.

In the first place, Jim Jones appears to have had limitations both as an evangelist and as a politician. He simply did not succeed in fooling key California religious observers with his faked miracles. And for all his political support in California politics, Jones was not always able to draw on his good political "credit" when he needed it. A certain mark of political effectiveness is the ability to sustain power in the face of scandal. By this standard, Jones was not totally

---

° consensuality: a voluntary association of individuals who reach a decision through collective consultation, but not necessarily by voting, or by "majority rule."

successful in either Indiana or California. There always seemed to be investigators and reporters on the trails of his various questionable financial and evangelical dealings (Kilduff and Javers, 1978, pp. 23–25, 35–38).

Quite aside from the limits of Jones' effectiveness, the very nature of his prophecy directed his religious movement along a different path from either worldly politics or sectarian Adventism. Keyed to the New Testament Book of Revelations, Adventist groups receive prophecy about the apocalyptic downfall of the present evil world order and the second coming of Christ to preside over a millennial period of divine grace on earth. For all such groups, the Advent itself makes irrelevant social action to reform the institutions of this world. Adventist groups differ from one another in their exact eschatology of the last days, but the groups that have survived, e.g., the Seventh Day Adventists and Jehovah's Witnesses, have juggled their doctrines that fix an exact date for Christ's appearance. They have thus moved away from any intense chiliastic° expectation of an imminent appearance to engage in more mundane conversionist activities that are intended to pave the way for the Millennium (Clark, 1949, pp. 34–50; Lewy, 1974, p. 265).

Reverend Jones himself seems to have shared the pessimism of the Adventist sects about reforming social institutions in this world —for him, the capitalist world of the United States. It is true that he supported various progressive causes, but he did not put much stake in their success. Jones' prophecy was far more radical than those of contemporary Adventist groups: he focused on imminent apocalyptic disaster rather than on Christ's millennial salvation, and his eschatology therefore had to resolve a choice between preapocalyptic struggle with "the beast" or collective flight to establish a postapocalyptic kingdom of the elect. Up until the end, the Peoples Temple was directed toward the latter possibility.

Even in the Indiana years Jones had embraced an apocalyptic view. The move from Indiana to California was justified in part by his claim that Redwood Valley would survive nuclear holocaust (Krause, Stern, and Harwood, 1978, p. 29). In the California years the apocalyptic vision shifted to CIA persecution and Nazi-like extermi-

---

° chiliasm: a synonym for "millennialism," or the belief in the coming of Christ's kingdom on earth; but "chiliasm" has the ring of greater urgency, i.e., Christ is coming *quite* soon.

nation of blacks. In California also, the Peoples Temple gradually became communalistic in certain respects. It established a community of goods, pooled resources of elderly followers to provide communal housing for them, and drew on state funds to act as foster parents by establishing group homes for displaced youths.

In its apocalyptic and communal aspects, the Peoples Temple more and more came to exist as an ark of survival. Jonestown—the Agricultural Project in Guyana—was built, beginning in 1974, by an advance crew that by early 1977 still amounted to less than 60 people, most of them under 30. The mass exodus of the Peoples Temple to Jonestown really began in 1977 when the Peoples Temple was coming under increasing scrutiny in California.

In the move to Guyana, the group began to concertedly exhibit many dynamics of an other-worldly sect, although it differed in ways that were central to its fate. Until the end, Jonestown was similar in striking ways to contemporary sects like the Children of God and the Krishna Society (ISKCON, Inc.). Indeed, the Temple bears a more than casual, and somewhat uncomfortable, resemblance to the various Protestant sects that emigrated to the wilderness of North America beginning in the seventeenth century. The Puritans, Moravians, Rappites, Shakers, Lutherans, and many others like them sought to escape religious persecution in Europe by setting up theocracies where they could live out their own visions of the earthly millennial community. So it was with Jonestown. In this light, neither disciplinary practices, the daily round of life, nor the community of goods at Jonestown seem so unusual.

The disciplinary practices of the Peoples Temple—as bizarre and grotesque as they may sound—are not uncommon aspects of other-worldly sects. These practices have been played up in the press in an attempt to demonstrate the perverse nature of the group, in order to "explain" the terrible climax to their life. But, as Erving Goffman has shown in *Asylums* (1961), sexual intimidation and general psychological terror occur in all kinds of total institutions, including mental hospitals, prisons, armies, and even nunneries. Indeed, Congressman Leo Ryan, just prior to his fateful visit to Jonestown, accepted the need for social control: ". . . . you can't put 1,200 people in the middle of a jungle without some damn tight discipline" (quoted in Krause, Stern, and Harwood, 1978, p. 21). Practices at Jonestown may well seem restrained in comparison to practices of, say, seventeenth-century American Puritans who, among other things, were willing to execute "witches" on the testimony of respected churchgoers or even children. Meg Greenfield observed in *Newsweek*, in reflecting on Jonestown, that "the jungle is only a few yards away" (December 4, 1978, p. 132). It seems important to recall that some revered origins of the United States lie in a remarkably similar "jungle."

Communal groups of all types, not just other-worldly sects, face problems of social control and commitment. Rosabeth Kanter (1972) has convincingly shown that successful communal groups in the nineteenth-century United States often drew on mechanisms of mutual criticism, mortification, modification of conventional dyadic sexual mores,° and other devices in order to decrease the individual's ties to the outside or to personal relationships within the group and thus to increase the individual's commitment to the collectivity as a whole.

Such commitment mechanisms are employed most often in religious communal groups, especially those with charismatic leaders (Hall, 1978, pp. 225–26). Other-worldly communal groups, where a special attempt is being made to forge a wholly new interpretation of reality, where the demand for commitment is especially pronounced, in a word, where it is sectarian—these groups have tremendously high stakes in maintaining commitment. Such groups are likely to seek out the procedures that are the most effective in guaranteeing commitment. After all, defection from "the way" inevitably casts doubt on its sanctity, no matter how it is rationalized among the faithful. Thus, it is against such groups that the charges of brainwashing, chicanery, and mistreatment of members are leveled most often. Whatever their basis in fact, these are the likely charges of families and friends who see their loved ones abandon them in favor of committing material resources and persona to the religious hope of a new life. Much like other-worldly sects, families suffer a loss of legitimacy in the defection of one of their own.

The abyss that comes to exist between other-worldly sects and the world of society-at-large left behind simply cannot be bridged. There is no encompassing rational connection between the two realities, and therefore the interchange between the other-worldly sect and people beyond its boundaries becomes a struggle either between

---

° dyadic sexual mores: when the standard for a community is heterosexual love between two adults.

"infidels" and the "faithful" from the point of view of the sect, or between rationality and fanaticism from the point of view of outsiders. Every sectarian action has its benevolent interpretation and legitimation within the sect, and a converse interpretation is given from the outside. Thus, from inside the sect, various practices of "confession," "mutual criticism," or "catharsis sessions" seem necessary to prevent deviant world views from taking hold within the group.

In the Peoples Temple, such practices included occasional enforced isolation and drug regimens for "rehabilitation" that were like contemporary psychiatric treatment. From the outside, all this tends to be regarded as brainwashing, but insiders will turn the accusation outward, claiming that it is those in the society-at-large who are brainwashed. Though there really can be no resolution to this conflict of interpretations, the widespread incidence of similar patterns of "coercive persuasion" outside Jonestown suggests that its practice there was not so unusual, at least within the context of other-worldly sects, or total institutions in general for that matter.

What is unusual is the direction that coerceive persuasion or brainwashing took. Jones worked to instill devotion in unusual ways —ways that fostered the acceptibility of "revolutionary suicide" among his followers. During "white nights" of emergency mobilization, he conducted rituals of proclaimed mass suicide, giving "poison" to all members, and saying they would die within the hour. According to one defector—Deborah Blakey—Jones "explained that the poison was not real and we had just been through a loyalty test. He warned us that the time was not far off when it would be necessary for us to die by our own hands" (cited in Krause, Stern, and Harwood, 1978, p. 193). This event initially left Blakey "indifferent" to whether she "lived or died." A true believer in the Peoples Temple was more emphatic. Disappointed by the string of false collective suicides, he said in a note to Jones that he hoped for "the real thing" so that they could all pass beyond the suffering of this world.[4]

Some people yielded to Jim Jones only because their will to resist was beaten down; others—including many "seniors," the elderly members of the Peoples Temple—felt they owed everything to Jim Jones, and they provided him with a strong core of unequivocal support. Jones apparently allowed open dissension at "town meetings" because, with the support of the seniors, he knew he could prevail. Thus, no matter what they wanted personally, people learned to leave their fates in the hands of Jim Jones and to accept what he demanded. The specific uses of coercive persuasion at Jonestown help to explain how (but not why) the mass murder/suicide was implemented. But it is the special use, not the general nature, of brainwashing that distinguishes Jonestown from most other-worldly sects.

Aside from brainwashing, a second major kind of accusation about Jonestown, put forward most forcefully by Deborah Blakey, concerns the work discipline and diet there. Blakey swore in an affidavit that the work load was excessive and that the food served to the average residents of Jonestown was inadequate. She abhorred the contradiction between the conditions she reported and the privileged diet of Reverend Jones and his inner circle. Moreover, because she had dealt with the group's finances, she knew that money could have been directed to providing a more adequate diet for everyone.

Blakey's horal sensibilities notwithstanding, the disparity between the diet of the elite and that of the average Jonestowner should come as no surprise: it parallels Erving Goffman's (1961, p. 48ff.) description of widespread hierarchies of privilege in total institutions. Her concern about the average diet is more to the point. But here, other accounts differ from Blakey's report. Maria Katsaris, a consort of Reverend Jones, wrote her father a letter extolling the virtues of the Agricultural Project's "cutlass" beans that were used as a meat substitute (Kilduff and Javers, 1978, p. 109). And Paula Adams, who survived the Jonestown holocaust because she resided at the Peoples Temple house in Georgetown, expressed ambivalence about the Jonestown community in an interview after the tragedy. But she also remarked: "My daughter ate very well. She got eggs and milk everyday. How many black children in the ghetto eat that well?"[5]

The accounts of surviving members of Jones' personal staff and inner circle, like Katsaris and Adams, are suspect, of course, in exactly the opposite way to those of people like the "Concerned Relatives." But the inside accounts are corroborated by at least one outsider, *Washington Post* reporter Charles Krause. On his arrival at Jonestown in the company of U.S. Representative Leo Ryan, Krause noted that "contrary to what the Concerned Relatives had told us, nobody seemed to be starving. Indeed, everyone seemed quite healthy" (Krause, Stern, and Harwood, 1978, p. 41).

It is difficult to assess these conflicting views. Beginning early in the summer of 1977, Jones set in motion the mass exodus of some 800 Peoples Temple members from California. Though Jonestown could adequately house only about 500 people at that time, the population climbed quickly well beyond that mark. At the same time the population mushroomed beyond the agricultural potential of the settlement. The exodus also caused Jonestown to become top heavy with less productive seniors and children. Anything close to agricultural self-sufficiency thus became a more elusive and long-range goal.

As time wore on during the group's last year of existence, Jones himself became more and more fixated on the prospect of a mass emigration from Guyana, and in this light, any sort of long-range agricultural-development strategy seemed increasingly irrational. According to *The New York Times,* the former Jonestown farm manager, Jim Bogue, suggested that the agricultural program would have succeeded in the long run if it had been adhered to.[6] But with the emerging plans for emigration, it was not followed and thus became merely a charade for the benefit of the Guyanese Government.

This analysis would seem to have implications for the *internal* conflicts about goals at Jonestown. Jim Jones' only natural son, Stephan Jones, and several other young men in the Peoples Temple came to believe in Jonestown as a socialist agrarian community, not as an other-worldly sect headed up by Jim Jones. Reflecting about his father after the mass murder/suicide, Stephan Jones commented: "I don't mind discrediting him, but I'm still a socialist, and Jim Jones will be used to discredit socialism. People will use him to discredit what we built. Jonestown was not Jim Jones, although he believed it was."[7]

The seniors, who provided social security checks, gardened, and produced handicraft articles for sale in Georgetown in lieu of heavy physical labor, and the fate of agricultural productivity both reinforce the assessment that Jim Jones' vision of the Peoples Temple approximates the other-worldly sect as an ideal type. In such sects, as a rule, proponents seek to survive *not* on the basis of productive labor, as in more "worldly utopian" communal groups, but on the basis of patronage, petty financial schemes, and the building of a "community of goods" through prosyletization (Hall, 1978, p. 207). This was the case with Jonestown. The community of goods that Jones built up is valued at more than $12 million. As a basis for satisfying collective wants, any agricultural production at Jonestown would have paled in comparison to this amassed wealth.

But even if the agricultural project itself became a charade, it is no easy task to create a plausible charade in the midst of relatively infertile soil reclaimed from dense jungle. This would have required the long hours of work that Peoples Temple defectors described. Such a charade could serve as yet another effective means of social control. In the first place, it gave a purposeful role to those who envisioned Jonestown as an experimental socialist agrarian community. Beyond this, it monopolized the waking hours of most of the populace in exhausting work, and it gave them a minimal—though probably adequate—diet on which to subsist. It is easy to imagine that many city people, or those with bourgeois sensibilities in general, would not find this their cup of tea in any case. But the demanding daily regimen, however abhorrent to the uninitiated, is widespread in other-worldly sects.

Various programs of fasting and work asceticism have long been regarded as signs of piety and routes to religious enlightenment or ecstasy. In the contemporary American Krishna groups, an alternation of nonsugar and high-sugar phases of the diet seems to create an almost addictive attachment to the food that is community dispersed (Hall, 1978, p. 76; cf. Goffman, 1961, pp. 49–50). And we need look no later in history than to Saint Benedict's order to find a situation in which the personal time of participants was eliminated for all practical purposes, with procedures of mortification for offenders laid out by Saint Benedict in his *Rule* (1975; cf. Zerubavel, 1977). The concerns of Blakey and others about diet, work, and discipline may have some basis, but probably they have been exaggerated. In any case, they do not distinguish Jonestown from other-worldly sects in general.

One final public concern with the Peoples Temple deserves mention because it parallels so closely previous sectarian practices. The Reverend Jim Jones is accused of swindling people out of their livelihoods and life circumstances by tricking them into signing over their money and possessions to the Peoples Temple or to its inner circle of members. Of course Jones considered this a "community of goods," and he correctly pointed to a long tradition of such want satisfaction among other-worldly sects. In an interview just prior to the tragedy, Jones cited Jesus' call to hold all things in common.[8] There are good grounds to think that Reverend Jones carried this philosophy into the realm of a con game. Still it should be noted that in the suicidal end, Jones did not benefit from the wealth in the way a large number of other self-declared prophets and messiahs have.[9]

Like its disciplinary practices and its round of daily life, the community of goods in the Peoples Temple at Jonestown emphasizes its similarities to other-worldly sects—both the contemporary ones labelled cults by their detractors and historical examples that are often revered in retrospect by contemporary religious culture. The elaboration of these affinities is in no way intended to suggest that we can or should vindicate the duplicity, the bizarre sexual and psychological intimidation, and the hardships of daily life at Jonestown. But it must be recognized that the settlement was much less unusual that some of us might like to think. The practices that detractors find abhorrent in the life of the Peoples Temple at Jonestown prior to the final "white night" of murder and suicide are the core nature of other-worldly sects. Therefore, it should come as no surprise that practices like those at Jonestown are widespread, both in historical and contemporary other-worldly sects. Granted that the character of such sects—the theocratic basis of authority, the devices of mortification and social control, and the demanding regimen of everyday life—predisposes people in such groups to respond to the whims of their leaders, no matter what fanatic and zealous directions they may take. But given the widespread occurrence of other-worldly sects, the other-worldly features of Jonestown are insufficient in themselves to explain the bizarre fate of its participants. If we are to understand the unique turn of events at Jonestown, we must look to certain distinctive features of the Peoples Temple— traits that make it unusual among other-worldly sects—and we must try to comprehend the subjective meanings of these features for some of Jonestown's participants.

PERSECUTION AT JONESTOWN

If the Peoples Temple was distinctive among other-worldly sects, it is for two reasons. First, the group was more thoroughly integrated racially than any other such group today. Second, the Peoples Temple was distinctively protocommunist in ideology. Both of these conditions, together with certain personal fears of Jim Jones (mixed perhaps with organic disorders and assorted drugs), converged in his active mind to give a special twist to the apocalyptic quest of his flock. Let us consider these matters in turn.

In the Peoples Temple, Jim Jones had consistently sought to transcend racism in peace rather than in struggle. The origins of this approach, like most of Jones' early life, are by now shrouded in myth. But it is clear that Jones was committed to racial harmony in his Indiana ministry. In the 1950s his formation of an interracial congregation met with much resistance in Indianapolis, and this persecution was one impetus for the exodus to California (Kilduff and Javers, 1978, pp. 16–17, 19–20, 25).[10] There is room for debate on how far Jones' operation actually went toward achieving racial equality, or to what degree it simply perpetuated racism, albeit in a racially harmonious microcosm (Kilduff and Javers, 1978, pp. 86–7; Krause, Stern, and Harwood, 1978, p. 41). But the Peoples Temple fostered greater racial equality and harmony than that of the larger society, and in this respect it has few parallels in present-day communal groups.[11] It also achieved more racial harmony than is evidenced in mainstream religious congregations. The significance of this cannot be assayed easily, but one view of it has been captured in a letter from a 20-year-old Jonestown girl. She wrote to her mother in Evansville, Indiana that she could "walk down the street now without the fear of having little old white ladies call me nigger."[12]

Coupled with the commitment to racial integration and again in contrast to most other-worldly sects, the Peoples Temple moved strongly toward ideological communism. Most other-worldly sects practice religiously inspired communism—the "clerical" or "Christian" socialism that Marx and Engels railed against (1959, p. 31). But few if any to date have flirted with communism in the theories of Marx, Lenin, and Stalin. By contrast, it has become clear that, whatever the contradictions other socialists point to between Jones' messianism and socialism (Moberg, 1978), the Reverend Jim Jones and his staff considered themselves socialists. In his column, "Perspectives from Guyana," Jones (1978, p. 208) maintained that "neither my colleagues nor I are any longer caught up in the opiate of religion. . . ." (reprinted in Krause, Stern, and Harwood, 1978, p. 208). Though the practices of the group prior to the mass murder/suicide were not based on any doctrinaire Marxism, at least some of the recruits to the group were young radical intellectuals, and one of the group's members, Richard Tropp, gave evening classes on radical political theory.[13] In short, radical socialist currents were unmistakably present in the group.

It is perhaps more questionable whether the Peoples Temple was religious in any conventional sense of the term. Of course, all utopian communal groups are religious in that they draw true believers together who seek to live out a heretical or heterodox interpretation of the meaningfulness of social existence. In this sense, the Peoples Temple was a religious group, just as Frederick Engels (1964a; 1964b) once observed that socialist sects of the nineteenth century were similar in character to primitive Christian and Reformation sects. Jim Jones clearly was more self-conscious religious than were the leaders of the socialist sects. Though he preached atheism and did not believe in a God that answers prayer, he did embrace reincarnation. A surviving resident of Jonestown remembers him saying that "our religion is this—your highest service to God is service to your fellow man." On the other hand, it seems that the outward manifestations of conventional religious activity—revivals, sermons, faith healings—were, at least in Jim Jones' view, calculated devices to draw people into an organization that was something quite different. It is a telling point in this regard that Jones ceased the practice of faith healings and cut off other religious activities once he moved to Jonestown. Jones' wife, Marceline, once noted that Jim Jones considered himself a Marxist who "used religion to try to get some people out of the opiate of religion."[14] In a remarkable off-the-cuff interview with Richard and Harriet Tropp—the two Jonestown residents who were writing a book about the Peoples Temple—Jones reflected on the early years of his ministry, claiming: "What a hell of a battle that [integration] was—I thought 'I'll never make a revolution, I can't even get those fuckers to integrate, much less get them to any communist philosophy.' "[15]

In the same interview, Jones intimated that he had been a member of the U.S. Communist party in the early 1950s. Of course, with Jones' Nixonesque concern for his place in history, it is possible that his hindsight, even in talking with sympathetic biographers, did not convey his original motives. In the interview with the Tropps, Jones also hinted that the entire development of the Peoples Temple, down to the Jonestown Agricultural Project, derived from his communist beliefs. This interview and Marceline Jones' comment give strong evidence of Jim Jones' early communist orientation. Whenever this orientation began, the move to Jonestown was predicated on it.

The socialist government of Guyana was generally committed to supporting socialists seeking refuge from capitalist societies, and they apparently thought that Jones' flexible brand of Marxism fit well within the country's political matrix. By 1973 when negotiations with Guyana about an agricultural project were initiated, Jones and his aides were professing identification with the world historical communist movement.

The convergence of racial integration and crude communism gave a distinctly political character to what in many other respects was an other-worldly religious sect. The injection of radical politics gave a heightened sense of persecution to the Jonestown Agricultural Project. Jim Jones himself seems both to have fed this heightened sense of persecution to his followers and to have been devoured by it himself. He manipulated fears among his followers by controlling information and spreading false rumors about news events in the United States (Moberg, 1978, p. 14). With actual knowledge of certain adversaries and fed by his own premonitions, Jones spread these premonitions among his followers, thereby heightening their dedication. In the process, Jones disenchanted a few members who became Judas Iscariots and who in time brought the forces of legitimated external authority to "persecute" Jones and his true believers in their jungle theocracy.

The persecution complex is a stock-in-trade of other-worldly sects. It is naturally engendered by a radical separation from the world of society-at-large. An apocalyptic mission develops in such a way that persecution from the world left behind is taken as a sign of the sanctity of the group's chosen path of salvation. Though racial and political persecution are not usually among the themes of other-worldly persecution, they do not totally break with the other-worldly way of interpreting experience. But the heightened sense of persecution at Jonestown did reduce the disconnection from society-at-large that is the signature of other-worldly sects.

Most blacks in the United States have already experienced persecution; and if Jim Jones gave his black followers some relief from a ghetto existence (which many seem to have felt he did), he also made a point of reminding those in his group that persecution still awaited them back in the ghettos and rural areas of the United States. In the California years, for example, the Peoples Temple would stage mock lynchings of blacks by the Ku Klux Klan as a form of political theater (Krause, Stern, and Harwood, 1978, p. 56). And, according to Deborah Blakey, Jones "convinced black Temple members that if they did not follow him to Guyana, they would be put into concentration camps and killed" (quoted in Krause, Stern, and Harwood, 1978, p. 188).

Similarly, white socialist intellectuals could easily become paranoid about their activities. As any participant in the New Left movement of the 1960s and early 1970s knows, paranoia was a sort of badge of honor to some people. Jones exacerbated this by telling whites that the CIA listed them as enemies of the state.

Jones probably impressed persecution upon his followers to increase their allegiance to him. But Jones himself was caught up in a web of persecution and betrayal. The falling-out between Jones and Grace and Tim Stoen seems of primary importance here. In conjunction with the imminent appearance of negative news articles, the fight over custody of John Victor Stoen (Grace's son whom both Jones and Tim Stoen claimed to have fathered) triggered Jones' 1977 decision to remove himself from the San Francisco Temple to Guyana (Krause, Stern, and Harwood, 1978, p. 57).[16]

We may never know what happened between the Stoens and Jones. According to Terri Buford, a former Jonestown insider, Tim Stoen left the Peoples Temple shortly after it became known that in the 1960s he had gone on a Rotary-sponsored speaking tour denouncing communism.[17] Both sides have accused the other of being the progenitors of violence in the Peoples Temple.[18] To reporters who accompanied Representative Ryan, Jones charged that the Stoen couple had been government agents and provocateurs who had advocated bombing, burning, and terrorism.[19] This possibility could have been regarded as quite plausible by Jones and his staff because they possessed documents about similar alleged FBI moves against the Weather Underground and the Church of Scientology.[20] The struggle between Jones and the Stoens thus could easily have personified to Jones the quintessence of a conspiracy against him and his work. It certainly intensified negative media attention on the Temple.

For all his attempts to curry favor with the press, Jones failed in the crucial instance: the San Francisco investigative reporters gave much coverage to the horror stories about the Peoples Temple and Jones' custody battle. Jones may well have been correct in his suspicion that he was not being treated fairly in the press. After the mass murder/suicide, the managing editor of the *San Francisco Examiner* proudly asserted in a January 15, 1979 letter to the *Wall Street Journal* that his paper had not been "morally neutral" in its coverage of the Peoples Temple.[21]

The published horror stories were based on the allegations by defectors—the Stoens and Deborah Blakey being foremost among them. We do not know how true, widespread, exaggerated, or isolated the incidents reported were. Certainly they were generalized in the press to the point of creating an image of Jones as a total ogre. The defectors also initiated legal proceedings against the Temple, and the news articles began to stir the interest of government authorities in the operation. These developments were not lost on Jim Jones. In fact, the custody battle with the Stoens seems to have precipitated Jones' mass suicide threat to the Guyanese government. Not coincidentally, according to Jim Jones' only natural son, Stephan, the first "white night" drills for mass suicide were held at this point. Stephan Jones connects these events with the appearance of several negative news articles.[22]

With these sorts of events in mind, it is not hard to see how it happened that Jim Jones felt betrayed by the Stoens and the other defectors, and persecuted by those who appeared to side with them —the press and the government foremost among them. In September 1978 Jones went so far as to retain the well-known conspiracy theorist and lawyer, Mark Lane, to investigate the possibility of a plot against the Peoples Temple. In the days immediately following, Mark Lane—perhaps self-servingly—reported in a memorandum to Jones that "even a cursory examination" of the available evidence "reveals that there has been a coordinated campaign to destroy the Peoples Temple and to impugn the reputation of its leader." Those involved were said to include the U.S. Customs Bureau, the Federal Communications Commission, the Central Intelligence Agency, the Federal Bureau of Investigation, and the Internal Revenue Service.[23] Lane's assertions probably had little basis in fact. Although several of these agencies had looked into certain Temple activities independently, none of them had taken any direct action against the Temple, even though they may have had some cause for so doing. The actual state of affairs notwithstanding, with Lane's assertions Jones had substantiation of his sense of persecution from a widely touted conspiracy theorist.

The sense of persecution that gradually developed in the Peoples Temple from its beginning and increased markedly at Jonestown must have come to a head with the visit of U.S. Representative Leo Ryan. The U.S. State Department has revealed that Jones had agreed to a visit by Ryan, but that he withdrew permission when it became known that a contingent of Concerned Relatives as well as certain members of the press would accompany Ryan to Guyana.[24] Among the Concerned Relatives who came with Ryan was the Stoen couple; in fact, Tim Stoen was known as a leader of the Concerned Relatives group.[25] Reporters with Ryan included two from the *San Francisco Chronicle,* a paper that had already pursued investigative reporting on the Peoples Temple, as well as Gordon Lindsay, an independent newsman who had written a negative story on the Peoples Temple for publication in the *National Enquirer* (this article was never published) (Krause, Stern, and Harwood, 1978, p. 40). This entourage could hardly have been regarded as objective or unbiased by Jones and his closer supporters. Instead, it identified Ryan with the forces of persecution, personified by the Stoens and the investigative press, and it set the stage for the mass murder/suicide that had already been threatened in conjunction with the custody fight.

The ways in which the Peoples Temple came to differ from more typical other-worldly sects are more a matter of degree than of kind, but the differences profoundly altered the character of the scene at Jonestown. Though the avowed radicalism, the interracial living, and the defector-media-government "conspiracy" are structurally distinct from one another, Jim Jones incorporated them into a tableau of conspiracy that was intended to increase his followers' attachment to him but ironically brought his legitimacy as a messiah into question, undermined the other-worldly possibilities of the Peoples Temple Agricultural Project, and placed the group on the stage of history in a distinctive relationship to the apocalypse.

JONESTOWN AND THE APOCALYPSE

Other-worldly sects by their very nature are permeated with apocalyptic ideas. The sense of a decaying social order is personally experienced by the religious seeker in a life held to be untenable, meaningless, or both. This interpretation of life is collectively affirmed and transcended in other-worldly sects that purport to offer heaven-on-earth beyond the apocalypse. Such sects promise the grace of a theocracy in which followers can sometimes really escape the "living hell" of society-at-large. Many of the Reverend Jones' followers seem to have joined the Peoples Temple with this in mind. But the predominance of blacks, the radical ideology of the Temple, the persistent struggle against the defectors, and the "conspiracy" that formed around them in the minds of the faithful gave the true believers' sense of persecution a more immediate and pressing aura, rather than an other-worldly one.

Jones used these elements to heighten his followers' sense of persecution from the outside, but this device itself may have drawn into question the ability of the supposed charismatic leader to provide an other-worldly sanctuary. By the middle of October 1978, a month before Representative Ryan's trip in November, Jones' position of preeminent leadership was beginning to be questioned not only by disappointed religious followers, but also by previously devoted seniors, who were growing tired of the endless meetings and the increasingly untenable character of everyday life, and by key proponents of collective life, who felt Jones was responsible for their growing inability to deal successfully with Jonestown's material operations.

Once these dissatisfied individuals circumvented Jones' intelligence network of informers and began to establish solidarity with one another, the conspiracy can be said truly to have taken hold within Jonestown itself. If the times were apocalyptic, Reverend Jones was like the revolutionary millenarians described by Norman Cohn (1970) and Gunther Lewy (1974). Rather than successfully proclaiming the postapocalyptic sanctuary, Jones was reduced to declaiming the web of "evil" powers in which he was ensnared and to searching with chiliastic expectation for the imminent cataclysm that would announce the beginning of the kingdom of righteousness.

Usually other-worldly sects have a sense of the eternal about them—having escaped this world, they adopt the temporal trappings of heaven, which amounts to a timeless bliss of immortality (Hall, 1978, pp. 72–79). But Jim Jones had not really established a postapocalyptic heavenly plateau. Even if he had promised this to his followers, it was only just being built in the form of the Agricultural Project. And it was not even clear that Jonestown itself was the promised land. Jones did not entirely trust the Guyanese government, and he was considering seeking final asylum in Cuba or the Soviet Union. Whereas other-worldly sects typically assert that heaven is at hand, Jones could only hold it out as a future goal—one that became more and more elusive as the forces of persecution tracked him to Guyana. Thus, Jones and his followers were still within the throes of the Apocalypse as they conceived it—the forces of good fighting against the evil and conspiratorial world that could not tolerate a living example of a racially integrated American socialist utopia.

In the struggle against evil, Jones and his true believers took on the character of what I have termed a "warring sect," fighting a decisive Manichean° struggle with the forces of evil (Hall, 1978, pp. 206–207). Such a struggle seems almost inevitable when political rather than religious themes of apocalypse are stressed. And it is clear that Jones and his staff acted at times within this militant frame of reference. For example, they maintained armed guards around the settlement, held "white night" emergency drills, and even staged mock CIA attacks on Jonestown. By so doing, they undermined the plausibility of an other-worldly existence. The struggle of a warring sect takes place in historical time, where one action builds on another and decisive outcomes of previous events shape future possibilities. The contradiction between this earthly struggle and the heaven-on-earth Jones would have liked to proclaim (e.g., in "Perspectives from Guyana") gave Jonestown many of its strange juxtapositions—of heaven and hell, of suffering and bliss, of love and coercion. Perhaps even Jones himself, for all his megalomaniacal ability to transcend the contradictions that others saw in him, and that caused him to be labeled an "opportunist," could not endure the struggle for his own immortality. If he were indeed a messianic incarnation of God, as he sometimes claimed, presumably Jones could have either won the struggle of the warring sect against its evil persecutors or delivered his people to the bliss of another world.

In effect, Jones had brought his flock to the point of straddling the two sides of the apocalypse. Had he established his colony beyond the unsympathetic purview of defectors, Concerned Relatives, investigative reporters, and government agencies, the other-worldly tableau perhaps could have been sustained with less repressive methods of social control. As it was, Jones and the colony experienced the three interconnected limitations of group totalism that Robert Jay Lifton (1968, p. 129) described with respect to the Chinese Communist Revolution—diminishing conversions, inner antagonism of disillusioned participants to the suffocation of individuality, and increasing penetration of the "idea-tight milieu control"° by outside

○ Manichean: the struggle between two opposing and equal forces (good and evil) in the universe.
○ "idea-tight milieu control": Robert Jay Lifton's phrase (from his books *Thought Reform* and *Revolutionary Immortality*) for an environment in which only a limited number of "correct" and "incorrect" ideas circulate.

forces.[26] As Lifton noted, revolutionaries are engaged in a quest for immortality. Other-worldly sectarians short-circuit this quest in a way by the fiat of *asserting* their immortality—positing the timeless heavenly plateau that exists *beyond* history as the basis of their every-day life. But under the persistent eyes of external critics and because Jones himself exploited such "persecution" to increase his social control, he could not sustain the illusion of other-worldly immortality.

On the other hand, the Peoples Temple could not achieve the sort of political victory that would have been the goal of a warring sect. Since revolutionary war involves a struggle with an established political order in unfolding historical time, revolutionaries can only attain immortality in the widescape victory of the revolution over the "forces of reaction." Ironically, as Lifton pointed out, even the initial political and military victory of the revolutionary forces does not end the search for immortality. Even in victory, revolution can be sustained only through diffusion of its principles and goals. But, as Max Weber (1977, p. 1121) observed, in the long run it seems impossible to maintain the charismatic enthusiasm of revolution; more pragmatic concerns come to the fore, and as the ultimate ends of revolution are faced off against everyday life and its demands, the question for immortality fades, and the immortality of the revolutionary moment is replaced by the myth of a grand revolutionary past.

The Peoples Temple could not begin to achieve revolutionary immortality in historical time because it could not even pretend to achieve any victory against its enemies. If it had come to a pitched battle, the Jonestown defenders—like the Symbionese Liberation Army against the Los Angeles Police Department S.W.A.T. Team—would have been wiped out.

But the Peoples Temple could create a kind of immortality that is not really a possibility for political revolutionaries. They could abandon apocalyptic hell by the act of mass suicide. This would shut out the opponents of the Temple. They could not be the undoing of what was already undone, and there could be no recriminations against the dead. It could also achieve the other-worldly salvation Jones had promised his more religious followers. Mass suicide bridged the divergent public threads of meaningful existence at Jonestown—those of political revolution and religious salvation. It was an awesome vehicle for a powerful statement of collective solidarity by the true believers among the people of Jonestown—that they would rather die together than have their lives together subjected to gradual decimation and dishonor at the hands of authorities regarded as illegitimate.

Most warring sects reach a grisly end. Occasionally they achieve martyrdom, but if they lack a constituency, their extermination is used by the state as proof of its monopoly on the legitimate use of force. Revolutionary suicide is a victory by comparison. The event can be drawn upon for moral didactics, but this cannot erase the stigma that Jonestown implicitly places on the world that its members left behind. Nor can the state punish the dead who are guilty, among other things, of murdering a United States Congressman, three newsmen, a Concerned Relative, and those many Jonestown residents who did not willingly commit suicide.[27]

Though they paid the total price of death for their ultimate commitment and though they achieved little except perhaps sustenance of their own collective sense of honor, those who won this hollow victory still cannot have it taken away from them. In the absence of retribution, the state search for the guilty who have remained alive and the widespread outcry against cults take on the character of scapegoating.[28] Those most responsible are beyond the reach of the law. Unable to escape the hell of their own lives by creating an other-worldly existence on earth, they instead sought their immortality in death, and left it to others to ponder the apocalypse that they have unveiled.[29]

NOTES

1. *Louisville Courier-Journal,* 23 December 1978, p. B1.
2. Fallding does not want to "plunge into relativism," so he tries to retrieve the term "cultism" for sociological use by defining it as ascribing sacred status to anything in the profane, actualized world. But this just displaces the problem of "false religion" onto the definition of "profane," which itself can only be defined within a religious perspective!
3. Even the constitutional guarantee is under fire. Prior to the Jonestown events, the U.S. Justice Department (texts in Krause, Stern, and Harwood, 1978, pp. 171–85) had carefully examined the legal issues involved in investigating religious sects, and determined against such action. But since Jonestown, there have been suggestions, for example by William Randolph Hearst, in the *San Francisco Examiner* (10 December 1978, p. 28), and a law professor, Richard Delgado, in the *New York Times* (27 December 1978, p. A23), that totalitarianism in the name of

religion should not qualify for constitutional protection. Also, the *Washington Post* (16 December 1978, p. 3) reports that mainline churches have been reexamining their stands on freedom of religion in light of the Jonestown events.

4. *San Francisco Examiner,* 6 December 1978, p. 10.
5. *San Francisco Examiner,* 10 December 1978, p. 9.
6. *New York Times,* 24 December 1978, pp. 1, 20.
7. *San Francisco Examiner,* 10 December 1978, p. 9.
8. *San Francisco Examiner,* 3 December 1978, p. 16.
9. The list of these religious swindlers, if it is kept by God's angels someplace, must be a long one indeed! Some would want to suggest that even in the end, Jim Jones plotted to make off with the loot. One theory holds that he planned to escape with his personal nurse at the conclusion of the cyanide poisonings. But this theory seems far-fetched to the *New York Times* (25 December 1978, p. 15) reporter who attended the Guyanese coroner's inquest where it was proposed. It did not account either for the bequeathing of Temple assets to the Communist party of the Soviet Union or for the suicidal "lost hope" that Jones expressed in the taped portion of the mass murder/suicide episode.
10. *Time,* December 4, 1978, p. 22.
11. Only one contemporary, explicitly interracial communal group immediately comes to mind—Koinonia Farm in Georgia, a Christian group founded in the 1940s.
12. *Louisville Courier-Journal,* 23 December 1978, p. B1.
13. *San Francisco Examiner,* 8 December 1978, p. 1.
14. *New York Times,* 26 November 1978, p. 20.
15. *San Francisco Examiner,* 8 December 1978, p. 16.
16. Kilduff and Javers (1978, pp. 77–78) cite the imminent appearance of negative news articles as a cause of Jones' departure.
17. *New York Times,* 1 January 1979, p. 35.
18. *San Francisco Examiner,* 6 December 1978, p. 1; *Louisville Courier-Journal,* 22 December 1978, p. 5.
19. *San Francisco Examiner,* 3 December 1978, p. 14.
20. *New York Times,* 6 December 1979, p. 16; *Columbia (Mo.) Tribune,* 6 January 1979, p. 6.
21. "Letter to the Editor," *Wall Street Journal,* 5 January 1979, p. 21.
22. *San Francisco Examiner,* 17 December 1978, p. 5.
23. *New York Times,* 4 February 1979, pp. 1, 42.
24. *San Francisco Examiner,* 16 December 1978, p. 1.
25. *New York Times,* 1 January 1979, p. 35.
26. The Peoples Temple perhaps had already begun to undergo the third of Lifton's limitations—the "law of diminishing conversions"—before the move from San Francisco to Guyana.

27. On the trip into Jonestown with Ryan, Peoples Temple lawyer Mark Lane told reporter Charles Krause (1978, p. 37) that perhaps ten percent of Jonestown residents would leave if given a chance but "90 percent . . . will fight to the death to remain." The U.S. State Department originally suppressed the tape recording of the mass murder/suicide, but I have listened to a pirated copy of it, and the event clearly involved a freewheeling discussion of alternatives, with vocal support as well as pointed resistance voiced for the proposed "taking of the potion." (*New York Times,* 10 December 1978, p. A28; 25 December 1978, p. A16).

28. *Washington Post,* 16 December 1978, p. 3; *New York Times,* 27 December 1978, p. A23.

29. In addition to the references cited in this article, it is based on personal interviews by the author conducted in Georgetown, Guyana, and in California during the summer of 1979.

REFERENCES

BENEDICTUS, SAINT. *The Rule of Saint Benedict.* NY: Doubleday, 1975. (Originally written c. 525?).

CLARK, ELMER T. *The Small Sects in America.* 1st rev. ed. NY: Abingdon-Cokesbury Press, 1949.

COHN, NORMAN. *Pursuit of the Millennium.* 2nd ed. NY: Oxford University Press, 1970. (Originally published 1957).

ENGELS, FREDERICK. "The Peasant War in Germany." In *Karl Marx and Frederick Engels on Religion.* Edited by Reinhold Niebuhr. NY: Shocken, 1964a. (Originally published 1850).

ENGELS, FREDERICK. "The Book of Revelation." In *Karl Marx and Frederick Engels on Religion.* Edited by Reinhold Niebuhr. NY: Shocken, 1964b. (Originally published 1883).

FALLDING, HAROLD. *The Sociology of Religion.* Toronto: McGraw-Hill Ryerson, 1974.

GOFFMAN, ERVING. *Asylums: Essays on the Social Situations of Mental Patients and Other Inmates.* Garden City: Doubleday Anchor, 1961.

GREENFIELD, MEG. "Heart of Darkness." *Newsweek,* December 4, 1978, p. 132.

HALL, JOHN R. *The Ways Out: Utopian Communal Groups in an Age of Babylon.* Boston: Routledge and Kegan Paul, 1978.

JONES, JIM. "Perspectives from Guyana." *People's Forum,* January 1978. (Reprinted in Krause, Stern, and Harwood [1978, pp. 205–210]).

KANTER, ROSABETH MOSS. *Commitment and Community.* Cambridge: Harvard University Press, 1972.

KILDUFF, MARSHALL, AND JAVERS, RON. *The Suicide Cult: The Inside Story of the People's Temple Sect and the Massacre in Guyana.* NY: Bantam, 1978.

KRAUSE, CHARLES, STERN, LAWRENCE M., AND HARWOOD, RICHARD. *Guyana Massacre: The Eyewitness Account.* NY: Berkeley Books, 1978.

LEWY, GUNTHER. *Religion and Revolution.* NY: Oxford University Press, 1974.

LIFTON, ROBERT J. *Revolutionary Immortality: Mao Tse-tung and the Chinese Cultural Revolution.* NY: Vintage, 1968.

MARX, KARL, AND ENGELS, FREDERICK. "Manifesto of the Communist Party." In *Marx and Engels: Basic Writings on Politics and Philosophy.* Edited by Lewis S. Feuer. Garden City: Doubleday Anchor, 1959. (Originally published 1848).

MOBERG, DAVID. "Prison Camp of the Mind." *In These Times,* December 13, 1978, pp. 11–14.

WEBER, MAX. *Economy and Society.* Edited by G. Roth and Claus Wittich. Berkeley and Los Angeles: University of California Press, 1977. (Originally published 1922).

ZERUBAVEL, EVIATAR. "The Benedictine Ethic and the Spirit of Scheduling." Paper read at the meetings of the International Society for the Comparative Study of Civilizations, Milwaukee, April, 1978.

DOCUMENTARY MATERIALS

COURT RECORD

DEBORAH LAYTON BLAKEY

Unlike many other predictions of catastrophe often publicized in our society, Deborah Blakey's has the terrible distinction of having come true. She joined the People's Temple in the early 1970s, and reached the important post of Financial Secretary. Her mother and older brother, Larry, were also members. Her growing disillusionment with Jones is carefully laid out in her affidavit, which was published in the June 16, 1978, San Francisco Chronicle, *almost exactly five months before the tragedies at Jonestown. Congressman Leo Ryan, one of the few officials who followed up on her charges, did so in part because they were echoed by other returning members of the Guyanese commune, as well as by relatives of those still there.*

An affidavit is a legal document, a statement made under oath before an official. Its value depends in part upon the reputation for truthfulness of the person who makes the statement, but also on the statement's correspondence to reality. Both of these matters are left to the reader to judge. The document itself combines a narrative of Blakey's Temple life with her observations of Jones and other events. Her thesis or main point is clearly spelled out in Item 1 of her affidavit.

Affidavit of Deborah Layton Blakey
Re the Threat and Possibility of Mass Suicide by Members of the People's Temple

1. The purpose of this affidavit is to call to the attention of the United States government the existence of a situation which threatens the lives of United States citizens living in Jonestown, Guyana.

2. From August, 1971 until May 13, 1978, I was a member of the People's Temple. For a substantial period of time prior to my departure for Guyana in December, 1977, I held the position of Financial Secretary of the People's Temple.

3. I was 18 years old when I joined the People's Temple. I had grown up in affluent circumstances in the permissive atmosphere of Berkeley, California. By joining the People's Temple, I hoped to help others and in the process to bring structure and self-discipline to my own life.

4. During the years I was a member of the People's Temple, I watched the organization depart with increasing frequency from the professed dedication to social change and participatory democracy. The Rev. Jim Jones gradually assumed a tyrannical hold over the lives of Temple members.

5. Any disagreement with his dictates came to be regarded as "treason." The Rev. Jones labelled any person who left the organization a "traitor" and "fair game." He steadfastly and convincingly maintained that the punishment for defection was death. The fact that severe corporal punishment was frequently administered to Temple members gave the threats a threatening air of reality.

6. The Rev. Jones saw himself as the center of a conspiracy. The identity of the conspirators changed from day to day along with his erratic world vision. He induced the fear in others that, through their contact with him, they had become targets of the conspiracy. He

convinced black Temple members that if they did not follow him to Guyana, they would be put into concentration camps and killed. White members were instilled with the belief that their names appeared on a secret list of enemies of the state that was kept by the C.I.A. and that they would be tracked down, tortured, imprisoned, and subsequently killed if they did not flee to Guyana.

7. Frequently, at Temple meetings, Rev. Jones would talk nonstop for hours. At various times, he claimed that he was the reincarnation of either Lenin, Jesus Christ, or one of a variety of other religious or political figures. He claimed that he had divine powers and could heal the sick. He stated that he had extrasensory perception and could tell what everyone was thinking. He said that he had powerful connections the world over, including the Mafia, Idi Amin, and the Soviet government.

8. When I first joined the Temple, Rev. Jones seemed to make clear distinctions between fantasy and reality. I believed that most of the time when he said irrational things, he was aware that they were irrational, but that they served as a tool of his leadership. His theory was that the end justified the means. At other times, he appeared to be deluded by a paranoid vision of the world. He would not sleep for days at a time and talk compulsively about the conspiracies against him. However, as time went on, he appeared to become genuinely irrational.

9. Rev. Jones insisted that Temple members work long hours and completely give up all semblance of a personal life. Proof of loyalty to Jones was confirmed by actions showing that a member had given up everything, even basic necessities. The most loyal were in the worst physical condition. Dark circles under one's eyes or extreme loss of weight were considered signs of loyalty.

10. The primary emotions I came to experience were exhaustion and fear. I know that Rev. Jones was in some sense "sick," but that did not make me any less afraid of him.

11. Rev. Jones fled the United States in June, 1977, amidst growing public criticism of the practices of the Temple. He informed members of the Temple that he would be imprisoned for life if he did not leave immediately.

12. Between June, 1977 and December, 1977, when I was ordered to depart for Guyana, I had access to coded radio broadcasts from Rev. Jones in Guyana to the People's Temple headquarters in San Francisco.

13. In September, 1977, an event which Rev. Jones viewed as a major crisis occurred. Through listening to coded radio broadcasts and conversations with other members of the Temple staff, I learned that an attorney for former Temple member Grace Stoen had arrived in Guyana, seeking the return of her son, John Victor Stoen.

14. Rev. Jones has expressed particular bitterness toward Grace Stoen. She had been Chief Counselor, a position of great responsibility within the Temple. Her personal qualities of generosity and compassion made her very popular with the membership. Her departure posed a threat to Rev. Jones' absolute control. Rev. Jones delivered a number of public tirades against her. He said that her kindness was faked and that she was a C.I.A. agent. He swore that he would never return her son to her.

15. I am informed that Rev. Jones believed that he would be able to stop Timothy Stoen, husband of Grace Stoen and father of John Victor Stoen, from speaking against the Temple as long as the child was being held in Guyana. Timothy Stoen, a former Assistant District Attorney in Mendocino and San Francisco counties, had been one of Rev. Jones' most trusted advisors. It was rumored that Stoen was critical of the use of physical force and other forms of intimidation against Temple members. I am further informed that Rev. Jones believed that a public statement by Timothy Stoen would increase the tarnish on his public image.

16. When the Temple lost track of Timothy Stoen, I was assigned to track him down and offer him a large sum of money in return for his silence. Initially, I was to offer him $5,000. I was authorized to pay him up to $10,000. I was not able to locate him and did not see him again until on or about October 6, 1977. On that date, the Temple received information that he would be joining Grace in a San Francisco Superior Court action to determine the custody of John. I was one of a group of Temple members assigned to meet him outside the court and attempt to intimidate him to prevent him from going inside.

17. The September, 1977, crisis concerning John Stoen reached major proportions. The radio messages from Guyana were frenzied and hysterical. One morning, Terry J. Buford, public relations advisor to Rev. Jones, and myself were instructed to place a telephone call to a high-ranking Guyanese official who was visiting the United States and deliver the following threat: unless the government of Guyana took immediate steps to stall the Guyanese court action regarding

John Stoen's custody, the entire population of Jonestown would extinguish itself in a mass suicide by 3:00 P.M. that day. I was later informed that Temple members in Guyana placed similar calls to other Guyanese officials.

18. We later received radio communication to the effect that the court case had been stalled and that the suicide threat was called off.

19. I arrived in Guyana in December, 1977. I spent a week in Georgetown and then, pursuant to orders, traveled to Jonestown.

20. Conditions at Jonestown were even worse than I had feared they would be. The settlement was swarming with armed guards. No one was permitted to leave unless on a special assignment and these assignments were given only to the most trusted. We were allowed to associate with Guyanese people only while on a "mission."

21. The vast majority of the Temple members were required to work in the fields from 7 A.M. to 6 P.M. six days per week and on Sunday from 7 A.M. to 2 P.M. We were allowed one hour for lunch. Most of this hour was spent walking back to lunch and standing in line for our food. Taking any other breaks during the workday was severely frowned upon.

22. The food was woefully inadequate. There was rice for breakfast, rice water soup for lunch, and rice and beans for dinner. On Sunday, we each received an egg and a cookie. Two or three times a week we had vegetables. Some very weak and elderly members received one egg per day. However, the food did improve markedly on the few occasions which there were outside visitors.

23. In contrast, Rev. Jones, claiming problems with his blood sugar, dined separately and ate meat regularly. He had his own refrigerator which was stocked with food. The two women with whom he resided, Maria Katsaris and Carolyn Layton, and the two small boys who lived with him, Kimo Prokes and John Stoen, dined with the membership. However, they were in much better physical shape than everyone else since they were also allowed to eat the food in Rev. Jones' refrigerator.

24. In February, 1978, conditions had become so bad that half of Jonestown was ill with severe diarrhea and high fevers. I was seriously ill for two weeks. Like most of the other sick people, I was not given any nourishing foods to help recover. I was given water and a tea drink until I was well enough to return to the basic rice and beans diet.

25. As the former financial secretary, I was aware that the

Temple received over $65,000 in Social Security checks per month. It made me angry to see that only a fraction of the income of the senior citizens in the care of the Temple was being used for their benefit. Some of the money was being used to build a settlement that would earn Rev. Jones the place in history with which he was so obsessed. The balance was being held in "reserve." Although I felt terrible about what was happening, I was afraid to say anything because I knew that anyone with a differing opinion gained the wrath of Jones and other members.

26. Rev. Jones' thoughts were made known to the population of Jonestown by means of broadcasts over the loudspeaker system. He broadcast an average of six hours per day. When the Reverend was particularly agitated, he would broadcast for hours on end. He would talk on and on while we worked in the fields or tried to sleep. In addition to the daily broadcasts, there were marathon meetings six nights per week.

27. The tenor of the broadcasts revealed that Rev. Jones' paranoia had reached an all-time high. He was irate at the light in which he had been portrayed by the media. He felt that as a consequence of having been ridiculed and maligned, he would be denied a place in history. His obsession with his place in history was maniacal. When pondering the loss of what he considered his rightful place in history, he would grow despondent and say that all was lost.

28. Visitors were infrequently permitted access to Jonestown. The entire community was required to put on a performance when a visitor arrived. Before the visitor arrived, Rev. Jones would instruct us on the image we were to project. The workday would be shortened. The food would be better. Sometimes there would be music and dancing. Aside from these performances, there was little joy or hope in any of our lives. An air of despondency prevailed.

29. There was constant talk of death. In the early days of the People's Temple, general rhetoric about dying for principles was sometimes heard. In Jonestown, the concept of mass suicide for socialism arose. Because our lives were so wretched anyway and because we were so afraid to contradict Rev. Jones, the concept was not challenged.

30. An event which transpired shortly after I reached Jonestown convinced me that Rev. Jones had sufficient control over the minds of the residents that it would be possible for him to effect a mass suicide.

31. At least once a week, Rev. Jones would declare a "white night," or state of emergency. The entire population of Jonestown would be awakened by blaring sirens. Designated persons, approximately fifty in number, would arm themselves with rifles, move from cabin to cabin, and make certain that all members were responding. A mass meeting would ensue. Frequently during these crises, we would be told that the jungle was swarming with mercenaries and that death could be expected at any minute.

32. During one "white night," we were informed that our situation had become hopeless and that the only course of action open to us was a mass suicide for the glory of socialism. We were told that we would be tortured by mercenaries if we were taken alive. Everyone, including the children, was told to line up. As we passed through the lines we were given a small glass of red liquid to drink. We were told that the liquid contained poison and that we would die within 45 minutes. We all did as we were told. When the time came when we should have dropped dead, Rev. Jones explained that the poison was not real and that we had just been through a loyalty test. He warned us that the time was not far off when it would become necessary for us to die by our own hands.

33. Life at Jonestown was so miserable and the physical pain of exhaustion was so great that this event was not traumatic for me. I had become indifferent as to whether I lived or died.

34. During another "white night," I watched Carolyn Layton, my former sister-in-law, give sleeping pills to two young children in her care, John Victor Stoen and Kimo Prokes, her own son. Carolyn said to me that Rev. Jones had told her everyone was going to have to die that night. She said that she would probably have to shoot John and Kimo and that it would be easier for them if she did it while they were asleep.

35. In April, 1978, I was reassigned to Georgetown. I became determined to escape or die trying. I surreptitiously contacted my sister, who wired me a plane ticket. After I received the ticket, I sought the assistance of the United States Embassy in arranging to leave Guyana. Rev. Jones had instructed us that he had a spy working in the United States Embassy and that he would know if anyone went to the embassy for help. For this reason, I was very fearful.

36. I am most grateful to the United States government and Richard McCoy and Daniel Weber, in particular, for the assistance they gave me. However, the efforts made to investigate conditions in

Jonestown are inadequate for the following reasons. The infrequent visits are always announced and arranged. Acting in fear for their lives, Temple members respond as they are told. The members appear to speak freely to American representatives, but in fact they are drilled thoroughly prior to each visit on what questions to expect and how to respond. Members are afraid of retaliation if they speak their true feelings in public.

37. On behalf of the population of Jonestown, I urge that the United States Government take adequate steps to safeguard their rights. I believe that their lives are in danger.

I declare under penalty of perjury that the foregoing is true and correct, except as to those matters stated on information and belief and as to those I believe them to be true.

Executed this 15th day of June, 1978, at San Francisco, California.

DEBORAH LAYTON BLAKEY

HISTORICAL DOCUMENT

JIM JONES

Jim Jones obsessively recorded many of his speeches at Jonestown. He even left the tape recorder on during the last moments of his doomed community. The experience of listening to the tape of this final hour is not recommended to anyone. It is a chilling experience, possibly unique in both human and historic terms. Nevertheless, the tape gives an unusually direct view of Jones and his community. Reading the transcript which follows is an easier experience, because the cries of the Jonestown children are not heard.

The transcript covers the period of time when Congressman Ryan and his party of relatives, media people, and People's Temple members, having left Jonestown, reached the airstrip where their planes were waiting to take them back to the Guyanese capital, Georgetown. A number of Jones's men, with the help of Larry Layton (Deborah Layton Blakey's brother, who was pretending to defect) attacked the party and killed Ryan and others. In his remarks to the crowd, Jones uses this

*attack as an event which requires them to commit suicide, otherwise more
congressmen like Ryan, or more Guyanese forces (unlike those who ran
into the "bush" during the attack at the airstrip) will come and destroy
their community.*

*The transcript is an accurate version (within the limits explained
below) of a copy of the tape which was presumably smuggled out of
Guyana and eventually sold in the open market in the United States. Its
authenticity has not been questioned by those who have studied Jonestown
extensively, and it is only one of the hundreds of tapes gathered up by
Guyanese and American authorities in the aftermath of the disaster.*

*What is printed here is my version of the tape, the result of
having listened to it and having studied two shorter versions of it
published by the* New York Times, *and by Mark Lane in his book
on Jonestown,* The Strongest Poison *(see "Sources"). The tape
appears to be "edited," that is, there are a number of interruptions,
caused either by joining two related tracks together, or even by Jones
starting and stopping the recorder. In any case, there is a sense of a
continuous development of events. When there is no chance of deciphering
a word or phrase I have said so; most of the time I have presented what
appeared to me and others to be the correct passage. I have not, however,
included every instance of audience response (cheers or applause, for
example), nor have I indicated every instance of background cries or the
moments when it appears as if the tape is being "stopped" or "edited."*

*With a general knowledge of Jonestown, the reader will understand
most of the action in the tape. The names which appear in the transcript
belong to those who had, for the most part, dramatic parts to play in the
final Jonestown hours. Tim Stoen and Deanna Mertle (later Jeanne
Mills) were both leaders in the movement to expose Jones as a "dictator."
Among those "defectors" from Jonestown who left with Ryan, Patty
Parks was killed, but Jim Cobb survived. Two major speakers include Jim
McElvane, who was a member of Jones's security staff, and Christine
Miller, who had a reputation for complaining. Both died. Ryan's "aide"
mentioned in the transcript as having died was Jackie Speier, who—
although wounded by gunfire—survived. The "Oliver woman" is Beverly
Oliver, a member of The Concerned Relatives who was trying desperately
to see her sons at Jonestown. She was also wounded at the airstrip.*

*One major figure in the transcript needs special mention: Jones
speaks a number of times of protecting "Ujar" and of his refusal to
"deliver them Ujar." In the Rose and Reiterman–Jacobs books on Jones
(see "Sources") the authors have accurately identified "Ujar" as the
nickname of Don Sly, the man who attempted to stab Congressman Ryan
when the congressional party was still at Jonestown. At this point in the
excitement, Jones is explaining about all the trouble they are going to*

*have because he will refuse to give Don Sly up to the authorities. (Later,
in part because of Jones's slurred speech, a number of his listeners mistake
the name "Dwyer" for "Ujar." Dwyer, an American consular officer,
was not in fact at Jonestown at that moment. He was at the airstrip,
wounded.)*

*This is a transcript of a spontaneous interchange, mostly between
Jones and a few of his followers, characterized by Jones's particular style
of oratory. Note, for example, the repetition of key phrases throughout
Jones's speeches ("not only are we in a compound situation; not only are
there those . . ."), pseudo-Biblical sayings ("the violent shall take it by
force"), and the statements which generate applause or other audience
response, as in a revival sermon ("I've lived with—for all; I'll die for
all.")*

Transcript of a Tape of the Last Moments at Jonestown

JONES: [*Music.*]—how very much I've tried my best to give you
a good life. [*Voices.*] In spite of all that I've tried, a handful of our
people, with their lies, have made our life impossible. No way to
detach ourself from what's happened today. Not only are we in a
compound situation, not only are there those who have left and
committed the betrayal of the century, some have stolen children
from others and they are in pursuit right now to kill them, because
they stole their children. And we are sitting or waiting on a powder
keg. I don't think this is what we want to do with our babies. I don't
think that's what we had in mind to do with our babies. It was said
by the greatest of prophets from time immemorial: no man really
takes my life from me, I lay my life down. So to sit here and wait
for the catastrophe that's going to happen on that airplane—it's going
to be a catastrophe. It almost happened here. Almost happened—the
Congressman was nearly killed here. You can't steal people's children. You can't take off with people's children without expecting a
violent reaction. And that's not so unfamiliar to us, either, even if we,
even if we were Judeo-Christian, if we weren't communists. The
world opinion suffers violence and the violent shall take it by force.

If we can't live in peace, then let's die in peace. [*Applause.*] We've been so betrayed. We have been so terribly betrayed. [*Music and singing.*] But we've tried. And as Jack Malcolm [?] said—I don't know where he's at right this moment—hi, Jack—he said if this only worked one day, it was worthwhile. [*Applause.*] Thank you. What's going to happen here in a matter of a few minutes is that one of those people on that plane is going to shoot the pilot; I know that. I didn't plan it, but I know it's going to happen. They're gonna shoot that pilot and down comes that plane into the jungle. And we had better not have any of our children left when it's over. Because they'll parachute in here on us. I'm going to be just as plain as I know how to tell you. I've never lied to you—never have lied to you. I know that's what's gonna happen. That's what he intends to do and he will do it. He'll do it. What's with being so bewildered with many, many pressures on my brain, seeing all these people behave so treasonous, there was just too much for me to put together, but I now know what he was telling me. And it'll happen. If the plane gets in the air even. So my opinion is that you be kind to children, and be kind to seniors, and take the potion like they used to take in ancient Greece, and step over quietly; because we are not committing suicide—it's a revolutionary act. We can't go back; they won't leave us alone. They're now going back to tell more lies, which means more congressmen. And there's no way, no way we can survive. Anybody. Anyone that has any dissenting opinion, please speak. Yes. [*Question not audible.*] You can have an opportunity, but if the children are left, we're going to have them butchered. We can make a strike, but we'll be striking against people that we don't want to strike against. We'd like to get the people who caused this stuff; and some, if some people here are prepared and know how to do that, to go in town and get Timothy Stoen, but there's no plane. There's no plane. You can't catch a plane in time. He's responsible for it. He [*Stoen*] brought these people to us. He and Deanna Mertle.° The people in San Francisco° will not, not be idle over this. They'll not take our death in vain, you know. Yes.

° Deanna Mertle: ex-Jones-follower, leader of the Concerned Relatives Movement; changed her name to Jeannie Mills after leaving Temple (see "Sources").

° San Francisco: the home base of the People's Temple, with which Jonestown is in radio contact; Jones hints a number of times that his people back in San Francisco can avenge their suicide.

CHRISTINE MILLER: Is it too late for Russia?

JONES: At this point, it's too late for Russia. They killed. They started to kill. That's why it makes it too late for Russia. Otherwise, I'd say, yes, sir, you bet your life. But it's too late. I can't control these people. They're out there. They've gone with guns. And it's too late. Once we kill anybody—at least, that's the way I've always put my lot with you. If one of my people do something, that's me. And they say I don't have to take the blame for this, but I don't live that way. They said, deliver up Ujar, who tried to get the man back here. Ujar, whose mother's been lying on him, and lying on him, and trying to break up this family. And they're all agreed to kill us by any means necessary. Do you think I'm going to deliver them Ujar? Not on your life. [*Voices:* "No!"] No.

MAN: I know a way to find Stoen if it'll help us.

JONES: No. You're not going. You're not going. You're not going. I can't live that way. I cannot live that way. I've lived with, for all, and I'll die for all. [*Applause.*] I've been living on hope for a long time, Christine, and I appreciate—you've always been a good agitator. I like agitation because you have to see two sides of one issue, two sides of a question. But what those people are gonna get done and what they get through will make our lives worse than hell —will make us, will make the rest of us not accept it. When they get through lying, they posed so many lies between there and that truck that we are—we are done in as far as any other alternative.

MILLER: Well, I say let's make an air—airlift to Russia. That's what I say. I don't think nothing is impossible, if you believe it.

JONES: How are we going to do that? How are you going to airlift to Russia?

MILLER: Well, I thought they said if we got in an emergency, they gave you a code to let them know.

JONES: No, they didn't. They gave us a code that they'd let us know on that issue, not us create an issue for them. They said that we, if they saw the country coming down they'd give us a code. They'd give us a code. We can check on that and see if it's on the code. Check with Russia to see if they'll take us in a minute but otherwise we die. I don't know what else to say to these people. But to me death—death is not a fearful thing. It's living that's cursed.

[*Applause.*] I have never, never, never, never seen anything like this before in my whole life. I've never seen people take the law and do —in their own hands and provoke us and try to purposely agitate mothers of children. There is no need to finish us; it's not worth living like this. Not worth living like this.

MILLER: I think that there were too few who left for 1,200 people to give them their lives for those people that left.

JONES: Do you know how many left?

MILLER: Oh, twenty-odd. That's a small—

JONES: Twenty-odd.

MILLER: —compared to what's here.

JONES: Twenty-odd. But what's gonna happen when they don't leave? I hope that they could leave. But what's gonna happen when they don't leave?

MILLER: You mean the people here?

JONES: Yeah, what's going to happen to us when they don't leave, when they get on the plane and the plane goes down?

MILLER: I don't think they'll go down.

JONES: You don't think they'll go down? I wish I could tell you you're right, but I'm right. There's one man there [*Larry Layton*] who blames, and rightfully so, Debbie [*Layton*] Blakey for the murder— for the murder of his mother, and he'll—he'll stop that pilot by any means necessary. He'll do it. That plane'll come out of the air. There's no way you fly a plane without a pilot.

MILLER: I wasn't speaking about that plane. I was speaking about a plane for us to go to Russia.

JONES: How—to Russia? You think Russia's gonna want—no— [*stammers*]. You think Russia's gonna want us with all this stigma? We had some value, but now we don't have any value.

MILLER: Well I don't see it like that. I mean, I feel like that as long as there's life there's hope. That's my faith.

JONES: Well, some—everybody dies. Some place that hope runs out, because everybody dies. I haven't seen anybody yet didn't die. And I like to choose my own kind of death for a change. I'm tired of being tormented to hell, that's what I'm tired of. Tired of it.

[*Applause.*] To have other people's lives in my hands, and I certainly don't want your life in my hands. I'm going to tell you, Christine, without me, life has no meaning. [*Applause.*] I'm the best thing you'll ever have. I want—want—I have to pay; I'm standing with Ujar. I'm standing with those people. They're part of me. I could detach myself —my attorney says—detach myself. No, no, no, no, no. I never detach myself from any of your troubles. I've always taken your troubles right on my shoulders. And I'm not going to change that now. It's too late. I've been running too long. Not going to change now. [*Applause.*] Maybe the next time you'll get to go to Russia. The next time round. This is—what I'm talking about now is the dispensation of judgment. This is a revolutionary, a revolutionary suicide council. I'm not talking about self—self-destruction. I'm talking about what we have no other road. I will put your call; we will put it to the Russians. And I can tell you the answer now, because I'm a prophet. Call the Russians and tell them to see if they'll take us.

MILLER: I said I'm not ready to die.

JONES: I don't think you are.

MILLER: But I know what you mean.

JONES: I don't think you are.

MILLER: But I look at all the babies and I think they deserve to live.

JONES: I agree with you. But don't they deserve much more— they deserve peace.

MILLER: We all came here for peace.

JONES: And we've—have we had it?

MILLER: No.

JONES: I tried to give it to you. I've laid down my life, practically. I've practically died every day to give you peace. And you still not have any peace. You look better than I've seen in a long while but it's still not the kind of peace I want to give you. A person's a fool who continues to say that you're winning when you're losing. Win one, lose two. What? [*Noise in background.*] I didn't hear you, ma'm, you'll have to speak up. Ma'm, you'll have to speak up.

WOMAN: [*Inaudible.*]

JONES: That's a sweet thought. Who said that? [*Voices.*] Come on up and speak again, honey [*inaudible*]. It's taking off. No plane is taking off. Suicide. They have done it. Stoen has done it. Somebody ought to—somebody—can they talk—can they not talk to San Francisco to see that Stoen does not get by with this infamy. Infamy. He has done the thing he wanted to do—have us destroyed.

MILLER: When you—when you—when we destroy ourselves we're defeated. We let them, the enemy, defeat us.

JONES: Did you see *I Live to Fight No More Forever* °?

MILLER: Yes, I saw that.

JONES: Did you not have some sense of pride and dignity in that man who would not subject himself to the will and whim of people who tell that they're gonna come in whenever they please and push into our house; come when they please; take who they want to; talk to who they want to. Does this help living? That's not living, to me. [*Voices:* "No!"] That's not freedom. That's not the kind of freedom I sought.

MILLER: But I think where they made their mistake was when they stopped to rest. If they had gone on, they would have made it. But they stopped to rest.

MAN: Will you hold this? Just hold that. We made that day; we made a beautiful day. And let's make it a beautiful day. [*Applause.*]

JONES: We win when we go down. Tim Stoen has nobody else to hate. Has nobody else to hate. Then he'll destroy himself. I'm speaking here not as the administrator—I'm speaking as a prophet today. I wouldn't step in this seat and talk so serious if I didn't know what I was talking about. And if there's any way to call back the immense amount of damage that's going to be done, but I cannot separate myself from the pain in my people. You can't either, Christine, if you stop to think about it. You can't separate yourself. We walked too long together.

○ I Live to Fight No More Forever: the title of a film, using the inaccurately quoted slogan of Chief Joseph of the Nez Perce Indians. Chief Joseph, after a number of successful battles against U. S. troops in 1877, eventually surrendered because his tribe was freezing and starving. He said: "From where the sun now stands I will fight no more forever."

MILLER: I know that. But I still think, as an individual, I have a right to—

JONES: You do, and I'm listening.

MILLER: —to say what I think, what I feel. And I think we all have a right to our own destiny as individuals.

JONES: Right.

MILLER: And I think I have a right to choose mine and everybody else has a right to choose theirs.

JONES: Yes. I'm not criticizing my people. What's that? [*Inaudible*]—said that today. That's what twenty people said today with their lies.

MILLER: Well, I think I still have a right to my own opinion.

JONES: I'm not taking it from you. I'm not taking it from you.

MCELVANE: Christine, you're only standing here because he was here in the first place. So I don't know what you're talking about, having an individual life. Your life has been extended to the day that you're standing there because of him.

JONES: I guess she has as much right to speak as anybody else to. What did you say, Ruby? [*Voice.*] Well, you'll regret that this very day if you don't die. You'll regret it if you do though you don't die. You'll regret it.

MILLER: Damnest thing. So many people.

JONES: I saved them. I saved them, but I made my example. I made my expression. I made my manifestation and the world was ready, not ready for me. Paul said I was a man born out of due season. I've been born out of due season, just like all we are, and the best testimony we can make is to leave this goddamn world. [*Applause.*]

WOMAN: You must prepare to die.

MILLER: I'm not talking to her. Will you let—would you let her or let me talk?

JONES: Keep talking.

MILLER: Would you make her sit down and let me talk while I'm on the floor or let her talk? [*Other woman talking inaudibly.*]

JONES: But how can you tell the leader what to do if you live? [*Many voices, inaudible.*] I've listened to you. You asked me about Russia. I'm right now making a call to Russia. What more do you suggest? I'm listening to you. You've yet to give me one slight bit of encouragement. I just now instructed him to go there and do that. [*Voices.*] Everybody hold it. We didn't come—hold it. Hold it. Hold it. Hold it. That song—[*voices*]. Lay down your burdens. I'm gonna lay down my burden. Down by the riverside. Shall we lay them down here by the side of Guyana? What is the difference? No man didn't take our lives. Right now. They haven't taken them. But when they start parachuting out of the air, they'll shoot some of our innocent babies. I'm not—I didn't accept this, Christine. They've got to shoot me to get through to some of these people. I'm not letting them take Ujar. Can you let them take Ujar? [*Voices:* "No!"]

MILLER: —see John die?

JONES: What's that?

MILLER: You mean you want to see John—

JONES: I want to see—[*lots of voices*]. Please, please, please, please, please, please, please.

MILLER: Are you certain that you think—you think more of him than other children here?

JONES: John, John.

MILLER: But you're saying—

JONES: John, John. But do you think I'd put John's life above others? If I put John's life above others I wouldn't be standing with Ujar. I'd send John out, out, to go out on the driveway tonight.

MILLER: You're talking of John—they're young.

JONES: I know. But he's no different to me than any of these children here. He's just one of my children. I don't prefer one above another. I don't prefer him above Ujar. I can't do that. I can't separate myself from your actions or his actions. If you done something wrong, I'd stand with you. If they wanted to come and get you, they'd have to take me.

MAN: We're all ready to go. If you tell us we have to give our lives now, we're ready. I'm pretty sure all the rest of the sisters and brothers are with me.

JONES: Some months I've tried to keep this thing from happening. But I see now it's the will—it's the will of Sovereign Being that this happened to us. That we lay down our lives in protest against what's been done. That we lay down our lives to protest at what's being done. The criminality of people. The cruelty of people. Who walked out of here today? Do you know who walked out? Mostly white people. [*Voices.*] Mostly white people walked. I'm so grateful for the ones that didn't—those who knew who they are. There's no point—there's no point to this. We are born before our time. They won't accept us. And I don't think we should sit here and take any more time for our children to be endangered, because if they come after our children, we give them our children, then our children will suffer forever.

MILLER: [*Inaudible.*]

JONES: I have no quarrel with you coming up. I like you. I personally like you very much.

MILLER: People get hostile when you try to—

JONES: Oh well, some people do. But then—there's only—some people do. Put it that way. I'm not hostile. You had to be honest and you say—if you want to run, you'd run with them because anybody could have run today. They were the ones—do. I know you're not a runner. And I—your life is precious to me. It's as precious as John's. And I don't—what I do I do with weight and justice and judgment. I have weighed it against all evidence.

MILLER: And that's all I've got to say.

JONES: What comes now, folks, what comes now?

MCELVANE: Everybody hold it.

JONES: Say peace. Say peace. Say peace. Say peace. What's come? Don't let—take Dwyer on down to the East House. Take Dwyer.

WOMAN: Everybody be quiet please.

JONES: —got some respect for our lives.

MCELVANE: That means sit down, sit down, sit down.

JONES: They know. [*Sigh.*] I tried so very, very hard. They're trying over here to see what's going to happen. Who is it?

[*Voices.*] Get Dwyer out of here before something happens to him. Dwyer. I'm not talking about Ujar. I said Dwyer. Ain't nobody gonna take Ujar. I'm not letting' 'em take Ujar. Tell 'em, folks, it's easy. It's easy. Yes, my love.

WOMAN: At one time, I felt just like Christine here, but after today I don't feel anything because the biggest majority of the people that left here for a fight and I know it really hurt my heart because—

JONES: Broke your heart, didn't it?

WOMAN: It broke my heart completely. All of this year the white people had been with us and they're not a part of us. So we might as well end it now; because I don't see—

JONES: The Congressman has been murdered. [*Music.*] Well, it's all over, all over. What a legacy, what a legacy. What's the Red Brigade° doing? They're the only ones who made any sense anyway. They invaded our privacy. They came into our home. They followed us 6,000 miles away. The Red Brigade showed them justice. The Congressman's dead. Please get us some medication. Simple. It's simple, there's no convulsions with it. It's just simple. Just, please, get it. Before it's too late. The G.D.F.° will be here. I tell you, get movin', get movin', get movin'. [*Voices.*] Don't be afraid to die. You'll see people land out here. They'll torture some of our children. They'll torture our people. They'll torture our seniors. We cannot have this. Are you going to separate yourself from whoever shot the Congressman? I don't know who shot him. [*Voices:* "No!"] They speak their piece, and those that had a right to go, and they had a right to—how many are dead? Aw, God, Almighty God. Huh. Patty Park is dead? [*Voices.*]

WOMAN: Some of the others who endure long enough in a safe place to write about the goodness that's been brought—

JONES: I don't know how in the world they're ever going to write about us. It's just too late. The Congressman's dead. The Congressman's aide's dead. Many of our traitors are dead. They're all laying out there dead. [*Voices.*] I didn't. But my people did. My people

○ Red Brigade: Jonestown's security force.
○ G.D.F.: Guyanese Defense Forces, the national army.

did. They're my people. [*Voices.*] And they've been provoked too much. They've been provoked too much. What's happened here has been an act of provocation. [*Voices.*]

WOMAN: [*Inaudible.*] I'm satisfied, O.K.? I said if there's any way we could do to get them to give Ted something so he won't have to let them go through, O.K.? And I'm satisfied.

JONES: That's right. Good. Yes, yes, yes.

WOMAN: And I appreciate you for everything. You're the only —you're the only—you're the only, and I appreciate you. [*Applause.*]

JONES: Please can we hasten? Can we hasten with that medication? You don't know what you've done. I tried. [*Applause, voices, music.*] They [*G.D.F.*] saw it happen and ran in the bush and dropped the machine guns. Never in my life. But they'll be more. But we've got to move. Are you gonna get that medication here? You've got to move. Marcelline, about forty minutes.

WOMAN: Do—have to know when the people are standing there in the aisles, go stand in the radio room yard, everybody get behind a table and back this way. O.K.? There's nothing to worry about. Everybody keep calm; and try and keep your children calm. And all those children that help, let the little children in and reassure them. They're not crying from pain; it's just a little bitter tasting, they're not crying out of any pain. Annie Miguel, can I please see you back—

MCELVANE: —what I used to do before I came here. So let me tell you about it. It might make a lot of you feel a little more comfortable. Sit down and be quiet, please. One of the things that I used to do— I used to be a therapist. And the kind of therapy that I did had to do with reincarnation in past life situations. And every time anybody had an experience of going into a past life, I was fortunate enough through Father [*Jones*] to be able to let them experience it all the way through their death, so to speak. And everybody was so happy when they made that step to the other side.

JONES: When you step to—there's nothing you can do but step that way. It's the only way to step. The choice is not ours now. It's out of our hands.

MCELVANE: If you have a body that's been crippled, suddenly you have the kind of body that you want to have. It feels good, but never felt so good, I tell you. You've never felt so good as how that feels.

JONES: And I do hope that those attorneys will stay where they belong and don't come up here. What is it? What is it? It what? It's hard. It's hard. It's hard. Only at first is it hard. It's hard only at first. Living you're looking at death. It only looks—living is much, much more difficult. Raise it up every morning and not knowing what's going to be the night's bringing. It's much more difficult. It's much more difficult.

WOMAN: I just want to say something for everyone that I see that is standing around, or crying. This is nothing to cry about. This is something we could all rejoice about. We could be happy about this. They always told us that we could cry when you're coming into this world. So we're leaving it, and we're leaving it peaceful, I think we should be—should be happy about this. [*Voices:* "That's right!"] I was just thinking about Jim Jones. He just has suffered and suffered and suffered. We have the honor guard and we don't even have a chance to [*inaudible*]. I want to say one more thing. One more thing I want to say. That's not all of us—that's not all that's left. That's just a few that has got [*inaudible*]. I'm looking at so many people crying. I wish you would not cry. I bless thy father and the children. I've been here about—[*applause*]—I've been here one year and nine months. And I never felt better in my life, not in San Francisco, but until I came to Jonestown. I had a—life. I had a beautiful life. I don't see nothing that I should be crying about. We should be happy. At least I am. That's all I came to say. [*Applause, music.*]

WOMAN: —good to be alive today. I just like to thank Dad, 'cause he was the only one that stood up for me when I needed him. And thank you, Dad.

WOMAN: I'm glad that you're my brothers and sisters. I'm glad to be here. [*Voices.*] O.K.

JONES: Please, for God's sake, let's get on with it. We've lived —we've lived as no other people lived and loved. We've had as much of this world as you're gonna get. Let's just be done with it. Let's be done with the agony of it. [*Applause.*] It's far, far harder to have to walk through every day, die slowly, and from the time you're a child till the time you get gray, you're dying—[*inaudible*] dishonest, and I'm sure that they'll—they'll pay for it. They'll pay for it. This is a revolutionary suicide. This is not a self-destructive suicide. So they'll pay for this. They brought this upon us. And they'll pay for that. I leave that destiny to them. [*Voices*]—wants to go with their child has a right to go with their child. I think it's humane. I want to go—I want to see you go, though. They can take me and do what they want—whatever they want to do. I want to see you go. I don't want to see you go through this hell no more. No more. No more. No more. We're trying. If everybody—relax. The best thing you do to relax and you won't have a problem. You'll have no problem with the thing, if you just relax.

MAN: —a great deal because it's Jim Jones. And the way the children are laying there now. I'd rather see them lay like that than to see them have to die like the Jews did, which was pitiful anyhow. And I just like to thank Dad for giving us life, and also death. And I appreciate the fact, the way, our children are going. Because, like Dad said, when they come in, what they're going to do to our children—they're going to massacre our children. And also the ones that they take, capture, they're gonna just let them grow up and be dummies, like they want them to be and not grow up to be a person like the one and only Jim Jones. So I'd like to thank Dad for the opportunity for letting Jonestown be not what it could be, but what Jonestown is. Thank you, Dad. [*Applause.*]

JONES: It is not to be feared. It is not to be feared. It is a friend. It's a friend. Sitting there show your love for one another. Let's get gone. Let's get gone. We had nothing we could do. We can't separate ourselves from our own people for twenty years lying in some old rotten nursing home—taking us through all these anguish years. They took us and put us in chains and that's nothing. This business, that business, there's no comparison to that, to this. They've robbed us of our land, they've taken us and driven us and we tried to find ourselves. We tried to find a new beginning, but it's too late. You can't separate yourself from your brother and your sister. No way I'm going to do it. I refuse. I don't know who fired the shot. I don't know who killed the Congressman. But as far as I'm concerned I killed him. You understand what I'm saying. I killed him. He had no business coming. I told him not to come.

WOMAN: Right. Right. [*Music, children crying.*]

JONES: I, with respect, die with the beginning of dignity. Lay down your life with dignity. Don't lay down with tears and agony. There's nothing to death. It's like Mac said, it's just stepping over to another plane. Don't be this way. Stop this hysterics. This is not the way for people who are socialists or communists to die. No way for us to die. We must die with some dignity. We must die with some dignity. We have no choice. Now we have some choice. Do you think they're gonna allow this to be done? And allow us to get by with this? You must be insane—children, it's just something to put you to rest. Oh. God. [*Child crying:* "I want my momma."] Mother, mother, mother, mother, mother, please. Mother, please. Please. Please. Don't do this. Don't do this. Lay down your life with your child. But don't do this. Free at last. [*Applause.*] Keep—keep your emotions down. Keep your emotions down. Children, it will not hurt. If you'll be— if you'll be quiet. If you'll be quiet. [*Children crying.*] It's never been done before, you say. It's been done by every tribe in history. Every tribe facing annihilation. All the Indians of the Amazon are doing it right now. They refuse to bring any babies into the world. They kill every child that comes into the world, because they don't want to live in this kind of a world. So be patient. Be patient. Death is—I tell you, I don't care how many screams you hear—I don't care how many anguished cries—death is a million times preferable to spend more days in this life. If you knew what was ahead of you—if you knew what was ahead of you, you'd be glad to be stepping over tonight. Death, death, death is common to people. And the Eskimos, they take death in their stride. Let's be digni—let's be dignified. If you quit telling them they're dying—if you adults would stop some of this nonsense—adults, adults, adults, I call on you to stop this nonsense. I call on you to quit exciting your children, when all they're doing is going to a quiet rest. I call on you to stop this now, if you have any respect at all. Are we black, proud, and socialists—or what are we? Now stop this nonsense. Don't carry this on anymore. You're exciting your children. No, no sorrow that it's all over. I'm glad it's over. Hurry. Hurry, my children. Hurry. [*Inaudible*]—hands of the enemy. Hurry, my children, hurry. There are seniors out here that I'm concerned about. Hurry. I don't want any of my seniors to this mess. Quickly, quickly, quickly, quickly, quickly. Let's just—good knowing you. No more pain. No more pain, I said now. No more pain. Jim Cobb is laying on the airfield dead at this moment. [*Applause.*] Remember, the Oliver woman said she—she'd come over and kill me if her son wouldn't stop her. These—these are the people—the peddlers of hate. All we're doing is laying down our lives. We're not letting them take our lives. We're laying down our lives. Peace in their lives. They just want peace.

MAN: I'd like to say that my—my so-called parents are filled with so much hate and [*Jones:* "Stop this, stop this, stop this crying and hollering"] treachery. I think you people out here should think about what your relatives were and be glad that the children are being laid to rest. And I'd like to say that I thank Dad for making me strong to stand with it all and make me ready for it. Thank you.

JONES: All they do is take a drink. They take it to go to sleep. That's what death is, sleep. I'm tired of it all.

WOMAN: Everything we could have ever done—most loving thing all of us could have done and it's been a pleasure walking with all of you in this revolutionary struggle. No other way I would rather go than to give my life for socialism, communism, and I thank Dad very, very much.

ANOTHER WOMAN: Dad's love and nursing, goodness and kindness and bring us to this land of freedom. His love—his mother was the advance—the advance guard to socialism. And his love and his presence will go on forever unto the fields of—

JONES: Where is the vat, the vat, the vat, where is the vat with the green "C"° in it?

WOMAN: —go on forever unto the sign. And thank you, Dad.

JONES: —the vat with the green "C" in it. Please, bring it here so the adults can begin. You don't—don't fail to follow my advice. You'll be sorry. You'll be sorry. You'll be sorry. We do it—than that they do it. Have trust. You have to step across. We used to think this world was—this world was not our home, and it sure isn't—we were saying, it sure wasn't. Don't want to tell them. All he's doing—if they will tell them—assure these—can't some people assure these children

---

° green "C": while this refers to the cyanide poison, Jones may have been using a euphemism ("sea").

of the relaxation of stepping over to the next plane? They set an example for others. We said—1,000 people who said—we don't like the way the world is. Take our life from us. We laid it down, we got tired. We didn't commit suicide, we committed an act of revolutionary suicide protesting the conditions of an inhumane world. [*Organ music.*]

JOURNALISM

ROBERT LINDSEY

> *This news "bio" appeared eight days after the Jonestown disaster. It basically summarizes accurately and neutrally the key events in Jones's career. The section titled "Chronology of Desperate Warnings" is especially helpful in setting the stage for Ryan's visit. (Some commentators have argued that as the publicity increased, so did the likelihood of Jones's "cracking" and moving towards the mass "suicide.")*
>
> *Although this is for the most part an objective account, Lindsey does emphasize (fairly, given the available information) that Jones, according to "experts," was "almost certainly insane at the end of his life."*

How Rev. Jim Jones Gained His Power over Followers

LOS ANGELES, Nov. 25—He promised utopia and delivered death. And when warnings came of how it might end—and they came for more than a year—almost no one listened.

The Rev. Jim Jones, who died with hundreds of his followers in Guyana last weekend, sprang out of dreary poverty in an industrial backwater of Indiana. At 16, he came under the influence of a woman at least four years older than he was who aroused his social conscience, and at 19, he began teaching a brand of Christian goodness as pure as that preached by Jesus himself in the Sermon on the Mount.

As he grew older, Mr. Jones fought racism, championed black

causes, built nursing homes for the elderly, clothed the needy, rehabilitated drug addicts and prostitutes, became an early opponent of the Vietnam War, and campaigned for government aid to feed and house the poor.

But, according to interviews with friends, relatives, religious leaders and others who knew Jim Jones in the 47 years of a curious life, he was not always what he appeared to be.

He was a handsome, shy youth of 19 when he first mounted a pulpit. He became a faith healer who built a theocratic dictatorship that used religion to camouflage a bitter class hatred and a fascination with Marxism that his wife said took root when he was a teen-ager.

ADMIRED FUNDAMENTALIST PREACHER

Mr. Jones became a bisexual, according to several of his aides. He was arrested here for lewd conduct at a theater frequented by homosexuals. He demanded that scores of women in his church submit to him. From his pulpit, he ranted for hours on the evils of sexual temptation, but used his own charm, dark good looks and overt suggestions of sexuality to help maintain his spell over female followers.

He was a brilliant organizer and a spell-binding preacher who patterned his style after that of Father Divine, the vastly popular and successful black fundamentalist preacher of the 1930's through 1960's, many of whose followers considered him the personification of God.

He was a skilled manipulator of the political process whose style of mixing religion with social activism was so plausible that he was courted by political leaders and appointed to important government positions in Indianapolis and San Francisco.

And experts say he was, near the end of his life, almost certainly insane.

LIKED CHURCH'S AUTONOMY

In the late 1950's, he gravitated to the Christian Church (Disciples of Christ), a middle-of-the-road Protestant denomination. In 1960, that church listed the People's Temple in Indianapolis as a branch. In its subsequent moves to California and then to Guyana, The People's Temple maintained the affiliation.

The church gives each congregation substantial autonomy, is considered liberal on social issues and permits each congregation to select its own pastor and nominate him for ordination—all features that attracted Mr. Jones. He was ordained in the church in February 1964, three years after obtaining a degree in secondary education from Butler. He had then served as pastor of the People's Temple for more than a decade.

He remained in Indianapolis until 1965, and for the most part, was in the mainstream of clerical and civic life, although his emphasis on helping the poor, especially blacks, made him conspicuous.

Several other changes occurred in Mr. Jones during these years: He began to claim that he could perform miracles, he demonstrated a remarkable skill for organizing projects, he realized the political value of a large religious congregation and he began to enjoy power.

A turning point had come in the early 1950's. After attending a service in Philadelphia conducted by Father Divine, he told friends how impressed he had been and said that he was determined to change his own style. Ross E. Case, one of his aides, recalled this week:

"He was always talking about sex, or Father Divine, or Daddy Grace, and was envious of how they were adored by their people and the absolute loyalty they got. Jim wanted all that affection and loyalty for himself."

During his dozen years in Indianapolis, he had started to urge his parishioners to call him "Father," and to address his wife as "Mother."

Aides later said that he began to fake healings during this period, using cooperative church members to claim that he had miraculously cured them, or using the intestines of animals as evidence to show that he had exorcised cancer from congregants. At the same time, there were some followers who alleged that he had actually cured them of arthritis or other ailments.

His wife worked closely with him as his church grew. They began to help poor blacks as well as whites, opening soup kitchens, helping poor people get jobs and establishing facilities for the elderly. In 1961, the couple had a son and named him Stephan Gandhi Jones.

SAFE HAVEN IN CALIFORNIA

In 1965, Mr. Jones announced to his congregation that the world would be engulfed by a devastating thermonuclear war on July 15, 1967, and that it was therefore necessary to move to a safe haven in northern California. He led about 70 families to Redwood Valley near Ukiah, a rural town set in the redwoods of Mendocino County, one of the places scouted by Mr. Case.

About half of these colonizers were black, and their arrival shocked some townspeople, but members of the group kept to themselves and were eventually considered good neighbors who worked hard and did not bother other people.

California has long had a reputation as a fertile ground for persuasive authority figures/religious leaders who offered easy answers to complex problems and offered to make decisions for their followers.

Dr. Louis J. West, chairman of the Department of Psychiatry at the University of California at Los Angeles, explained: "They expect California to be a utopia. But some get disillusioned when they get here, and they get mixed up with cults, because they promise them the ties they are seeking. To lots of these people the cults look like utopia."

His intelligence, soft-spoken friendliness and seemingly earnest search for a better world impressed people in the conservative California town. In 1966, he was appointed chairman of the county grand jury. Robert Winslow, the judge who made the appointment, recalled:

"He was a very bright, humanistic person. He didn't seem to be a socialist. They were nice, concerned people. Their most significant characteristic was that they wanted to come to the aid of anyone in trouble. Jones wasn't a fanatic when I knew him, although people were emotionally dependent upon him. The people in his community built their entire lives around Jones and his church."

Although he was accepted socially and in the political establishment, few people attended his church. Then in October 1968, Timothy Stoen, a politically liberal Stanford University Law School graduate and a deputy district attorney, began to attend his services, largely, he said later, because of the emphasis on helping the poor.

The next year, he sold almost everything he owned to become

a church member and an aide to Mr. Jones. He was, he said, influenced by the assassination of Dr. Martin Luther King, Jr.

Thomas E. Martin, the Mendocino County probation officer, said that Mr. Stoen's enrollment was a turning point. "He was highly respected in the community," Mr. Martin said, "and this gave the church instant credence."

UTOPIA IN SOUTH AMERICA

Mr. Jones had moved ahead with plans to relocate his congregation in Guyana, which he said would be a socialist utopia where all races could mix in peace and work for the common good. After he arrived in Guyana, he increasingly preached about dark forces that were out to shut down his experiment in communal living.

When the minister left San Francisco, he left behind an "administrative department," to which he spoke nightly via short-wave radio, and in code, to deal with "traitors." Defectors were bombarded with threats of beatings and killings, and at least one member, Christopher Lewis, was murdered in San Francisco in December, 1977, although the police never established that the crime was connected with Mr. Jones. Still, Mr. Lewis's death was constantly cited by the administrative department—a kind of enforcement squad—to dissident members as a warning to keep quiet. Mr. Stoen said that Mr. Jones took any critical comment about the commune as a personal attack and said that anyone who left the church deserved to die.

Warnings to officials that something was seriously wrong in Guyana began in the summer of 1977. Mrs. Mobley said that she made 100 copies of the 1977 *New York Times* interview in which Mrs. Jones admitted her husband's longtime contempt for religion and his affection for Marxism and sent them to every politician whose name she could find, beginning with President Carter.

"I warned them that something like this was going to happen," she said in an interview, as she broke into tears. "But nobody would listen."

CHRONOLOGY OF DESPERATE WARNINGS

More precise warnings and signals from Jones himself on what was about to happen began to come last spring:

April 10—Relatives of the church members living in Guyana issued a statement accusing Mr. Jones of "human rights violations" and quoted him as having told a member: "I can say without hesitation that we are devoted to a decision that it is better even to die than to be constantly harassed from one continent to the next."

April 18—Mr. Jones replied, confirming the possibility of mass suicide, writing in part: "Dr. Martin Luther King reaffirmed the validity of ultimate commitment when he told his Freedom Riders: 'We must develop the courage of dying for a cause.' We likewise affirm that before we will submit quietly to the interminable plotting and persecution of this politically motivated conspiracy, we will resist actively, putting our lives on the line if it comes to that. . . . We chose as our motto, Not like those who march submissively into gas ovens, but like the valiant heroes who resisted in the Warsaw ghetto."

June 15—Deborah Layton Blakey, after leaving the commune in May, said in an affidavit and in newspaper interviews that Mr. Jones was "obsessed with his place in history" and had paranoia of "maniacal" proportions. She told of rehearsals for mass suicide. She said that Mr. Jones had said that the purpose of the suicides was to "create an international incident" and that commune members were so broken by the fear of the minister and by exhaustion that they could not escape and might follow his orders to kill themselves.

June 22—A former member, James Cobb, charged in a lawsuit filed against Mr. Jones in San Francisco that Mr. Jones was planning "mass murder that would result in the death of minor children not old enough to make voluntary and informed decisions about serious matters of any nature, much less insane proposals of collective suicide."

STATE DEPARTMENT FOUND NO BASIS

Meanwhile, many former members of the group sought help from the State Department, which responded that it had investigated the charges and found no basis for action, and a few newspapers began looking into the allegations.

Relatives of church members in Guyana at last prevailed on a San Francisco Bay area Congressman, Leo J. Ryan, to investigate the charges, and it was his visit that precipitated the mass suicide.

In his final days, there were reports that Mr. Jones, more than ever, harangued against the forces that were out to get him, against heterosexual relations between church members, and, according to a church member who visited the commune in September, he repeatedly accused the male defectors from the church of being homosexuals.

His wife, Marcie, was near his side when Jones died. Witnesses said that his last words were: "Mother . . . Mother . . ."

Mrs. Baldwin, Marceline Jones's mother, visited the commune in Guyana for three weeks and left only a few days before the Ryan party arrived.

In a curious interview that she gave to an Indiana newspaper after the mass suicide and killings, she said she still believed that her daughter and son-in-law had done good works and respected the commune in Guyana. Her daughter's last words to her were, "I have lived, not just existed."

The bodies of Jim and Marceline Jones were on their way home today, to be buried in Richmond, Ind.

STUDENT ESSAY

Assignment 1. At least six disciplines have claimed to offer the most helpful explanation of Jones or Jonestown: sociology, psychology, social-psychology, anthropology, history, and religion. Select one of these as the class or course in which you would choose to study Jones or Jonestown to the greatest advantage. Use a key concept or methodology associated with your choice to analyze Jones.

SHERRY JOHNSON

Jim Jones: Man or Monster?

Who was the Reverend Jimmy Jones? Was he a rebellious fanatical religious leader or a severely emotionally disturbed man? During the last few months of his life, Jones seemed to be a mixture of psychological disorders. One disorder I have isolated involves antisocial or sociopathic behavior. To be even more specific, I believe Reverend Jones was a "manipulative personality," which is one form of the many antisocial behaviors.

The antisocial person has trouble controlling his need for superiority. He has a need to overcome inner feelings of self-hate, isolation, and emptiness (Leaff 92). Jones relied on his followers to boost
his self-esteem. He sought admiration, plus absolute loyalty from his
followers. In order to make his followers dependent on him, he
required them to turn all their money and property over to him. He
acted as their provider and even encouraged them to call him "Father" and "Dad" (Greenberg 379).

To continue this study of manipulative behavior in Jones, let
us look at "The Antisocial Personality" by Louis Leaff, M.D. Leaff
refers to a book called *The Manipulator* by Ben Bursten in order to
describe the characteristics of the "manipulative personality" (Leaff
96). The manipulator forms an object relationship or, as Bursten puts
it, a "complementary relationship" with another person so that they
can fulfill each other's needs (Leaff 96). For instance, Jones's need for
love and power led him to the weak, the jobless, the elderly, and
those dissatisfied with American life. He offered them a better society
in return for their love and loyalty. Jones weakened family ties by
becoming sexually involved with many of the members (Greenberg
379). He had affairs with both men and women, and was "the most
important love object of the community" (Greenberg 379).

Generally the manipulator has no concern for the other person
except as a need-satisfying object (Leaff 98). Leaff refers to Bursten's
view that the manipulator must feel like he is "putting something
over" on the other person; the manipulator has feelings of contempt
and devaluation for the other person but increases his self-esteem
and gives himself a sense of power (Leaff 98). During his speeches,
Jones would publicly humiliate individuals or have them participate
in bizarre acts in front of the congregation, such as having them
undress or giving them paddle-beatings (Greenberg 379).

If we probe a little deeper, we see that the "manipulative personality" is also a type of narcissistic personality. Leaff sees the
narcissist's inner feelings as objects of "dark shadowy persecutors, a
world of danger and paranoid fear" (Leaff 98). The narcissist needs
to identify with an "all-good, all-powerful person," so he can be
protected from danger and persecution (Leaff 98). Jones related to
God for this protection, but the sicker he became the more he believed that he was the "Savior." Out of fear of persecution and
destruction of his church, he moved his people to Guyana. In another
view, the narcissistic or manipulative person has a need to control,

and he uses power to suppress the aggression he sees in others (Leaff 99). Jones controlled his followers with fear of punishment, by brainwashing, by frequent political interrogations, by withdrawal of information about the world, and by dispensing to them drugs to control their minds (Greenberg 379–380). For example, he told the black members that if they left the People's Temple, they would be put in concentration camps, and he told the white members that they were being investigated by the CIA (Greenberg 379).

In the end, the members lost all hold on reality and their submission reinforced Jones' own paranoid fears about the world. We could assume that he actually believed that the only way to save his people was through a mass suicide. Furthermore, the mass suicide was a way to ensure that his name would go down in history. That was the final manipulation for him.

LIST OF WORKS CITED

GREENBERG, JOEL. "Jim Jones: The Deadly Hypnotist." *Science News,* Dec. 1, 1979: 378–379, 382.

LEAFF, LOUIS, M.D. "The Antisocial Personality: Psychodynamic Implications." In William H. Reed, ed. *The Psychopath: A Comprehensive Study of Antisocial Disorders and Behaviors.* New York: Brunner, 1978, 79–117.

QUESTIONS FOR DISCUSSION

WITHIN THIS CHAPTER:

1. What characteristics did Jonestown share with other "messianic" cults?

2. The title of Greenberg's essay on Jones directs the reader's attention to Jones as a kind of "hypnotist." Is this an accurate summation of the article?

3. What features of the life and culture of Guyana made that country a likely home for Jones and his followers?

4. How did Jones's movement resemble Father Divine's?

5. What are the differences between a "messianic" sect, as Rensberger argues, and an "apocalyptic" sect, as Hall argues?

6. How well does the "Affidavit" predict the attitudes and events suggested by the "Transcript"?

7. Examine any of Jones's arguments for collective suicide in the "Transcript." How does he try to convince his followers to act in this horrible way?

USING OTHER CHAPTERS:

8. Will historians, archaeologists, or writers (like McPhee in Chapter 1) ever search for the ruins of Jonestown? Explain your answer.

9. Can you make an argument for understanding Jonestown as a medical problem in ways similar to Matossian's argument for ergot poisoning at Salem in Chapter 5?

10. Would Jones's religious views fit Erikson's definition of "deviancy" (see Chapter 5)?

ASSIGNMENTS

WITHIN THIS CHAPTER:

1. At least six disciplines have claimed to offer the most helpful explanation of Jones or Jonestown: sociology, psychology, social-psychology, anthropology, history, and religion. Select one of these as the course or class in which you would choose to study Jones or Jonestown to the greatest advantage. Use a key concept or methodology associated with your choice to analyze Jones.

2. Write an analysis of the ways in which Jones tried to convince his flock to commit suicide using Blakey's "Affidavit," Greenberg's report, and the "Transcript."

3. Based on your reading of the materials in this chapter, write a short story or sketch of life at Jonestown.

4. In an essay, demonstrate with specific examples how accurate Blakey's "Affidavit" was in "predicting" what finally happened in Jonestown.

5. Officially, the People's Temple was a branch of the Disciples of Christ, a large Protestant church. Is there a difference between a "cult" and a "church"? Using the materials in this chapter and any other information available (perhaps from the history of religion or about the charismatic movements in various churches today), define the term "cult" in relation to "church" or "religion."

6. Assume that a much longer delay had ensued between the events of Congressman Ryan's death and the final meeting of the Jonestown residents. Write a speech to be delivered either by Christine Miller (see "Transcript") or by yourself (taking the role of one of the residents) in which you argue against the collective suicide. Do not take the easy way out: You should assume at least some level of personal belief in Jones and Jonestown.

7. How closely did Jim Jones model his movement on Father Divine? Write an essay comparing the two movements.

BEYOND THIS CHAPTER:

8. According to James Reston, Jr. (see "Sources"), the 1970 novel *The Parallax View* by Loren Singer and the 1974 film based on it directed by Alan J. Pakula were almost required reading and viewing in the increasingly paranoid world of Jim Jones in 1978. Read the novel, or view the film, and then explain its relevance to an understanding of Jonestown.

9. Using the methods or ideas—especially those concerning "place"—in Chapter 1, "The American Scene," describe and explain how the principal locations of Jones's movement (Indiana, California, and Guyana) interacted with the ideas and events of his career.

10. Le Guin's story, "Mazes," in Chapter 2, suggests that the perception of events may limit our understanding of events so severely that we can become unbalanced mentally. Explain how this psychological situation applies to the lives of the Jonestown residents.

11. Numerous essays in Chapter 2 offer new perspectives on ways of thinking. Select one or two of these alternative perspectives to explore the psychology of either Jones or one of his followers.

12. Write the summation speech of either the prosecutor or the defense attorney to the imaginary court which is trying the case of Jim Jones, who has been charged with the deaths of the Jonestown community. (You may wish to refer to the various trial procedures in either Chapter 4 on murder, or Chapter 5 on Salem.)

SOURCES FOR FURTHER READING AND/OR RESEARCH

THE ASSASSINATION OF REPRESENTATIVE LEO J. RYAN AND THE JONESTOWN GUYANA TRAGEDY. Washington, D.C.: Government Printing Office, 1979. This very helpful official government report, available on microfilm at Government Depository libraries, reprints many newspaper articles and testimony from hearings.

FEINSOD, ETHAN. *Awake in a Nightmare: Jonestown—The Only Eyewitness Account.* New York: Norton, 1981. Uses the eyewitness recollections of Odell Rhodes, a Jonestown resident who escaped the end; rings true with the details only a survivor would know.

KILDUFF, MARSHALL, AND RON JAVERS. *The Suicide Cult: The Inside Story of the People's Temple Sect and the Massacre in Guyana.* New York: Bantam, 1978. A book similar to Krause's since Javers was also in the Ryan party. Kilduff had already been interested in Jones's case for two years prior to the final disaster.

KRAUSE, CHARLES A., AND THE STAFF OF THE *WASHINGTON POST.* *Guyana Massacre: The Eyewitness Account.* New York: Berkley, 1978. A detailed account of the end of Jonestown which is especially good on the details of the attack on Ryan, since the primary author was a member of his party.

LANE, MARK. *The Strongest Poison.* New York: Hawthorne, 1980. Lane, and Charles Garry, although they competed with one another, were lawyers for Jones. They cooperated long enough to make their escape from the slaughter on November 18th; Lane ultimately came to feel that the residents were "murdered" by Jones and his guards, and he presents in this book many details and much documentary material not available elsewhere. His title comes from the English poet and visionary William Blake: "The strongest poison ever known/Came from Caesar's laurel crown."

LEVI, KEN, ED. *Violence and Religious Commitment: Implications of Jim Jones's People's Temple Movement.* University Park: Penn State University Press, 1982. Essays on Jonestown from a number of different disciplines including Stanley Hauerwas's helpful "Self-Sacrifice as Demonic: A Theological Response to Jonestown."

LEWIS, GORDON K. *"Gather with the Saints at the River," the Jonestown Guyana Holocaust of 1978: A Descriptive and Interpretative Essay on Its Ultimate Meaning from a Caribbean Viewpoint.* Rio Piedras: University of Puerto Rico, Institute of Caribbean Studies, 1979. Although its title promises more than it could possibly deliver, this pamphlet has the advantage of setting the events and lessons of Jonestown in the context of Caribbean society and politics.

McKELWAY, ST. CLAIR, AND A. J. LIEBLING. "Who Is This King of Glory?" In St. Clair McKelway, *True Tales from the Annals of Crime and Rascality.* New York: Random House, 1950. An excellent portrait of Father Divine and his movement.

MILLS, JEANNIE. *Six Years with God: Life inside Reverend Jim Jones' People's Temple.* New York: A & W, 1979. Under their real name of Mertle, the author and family experienced the early years of the People's Temple in California. Includes information on Jones's Father Divine visit and photos of Temple activities such as healings and staged KKK lynchings.

NUGENT, JOHN PETER. *White Night: The Untold Story of What Happened Before—and Beyond—Jonestown.* New York: Rawson, Wade, 1979. Helpful information on the political and cultural background of Jones, including material on his relation to Father Divine and the Third World.

PARKER, PAT. "Jonestown," from *Jonestown and Other Madness.* Ithaca, N.Y.: Firebrand Books, 1985. A powerful poem which "argues" that "Black people do not commit suicide"; Parker's poem concentrates on racism: "Jim Jones was not the cause/he was the result/of 400 years/of not caring." Highly recommended.

PFAFF, WILLIAM. "Reflections: The People's Temple." *The New Yorker,* December 18, 1978, pp. 57, 60, 63. Covers ground similar to Rensberger's essay, but Pfaff is somewhat more speculative and philosophical about the implications of Jonestown for American society.

REITERMAN, TIM, AND JOHN JACOBS. *Raven: The Untold Story of the Rev. Jim Jones and His People.* New York: Dutton, 1982. Extremely thorough book, with very dense and convincing detail. Based on numerous interviews with survivors and relatives of those who perished, as well as extensive use of Jonestown tapes; includes a large number of photos of the participants.

RESTON, JAMES, JR. *Our Father Who Art in Hell: The Life and Death of Jim Jones.* New York: Times Books, 1981. Very fine book, certainly not as detailed as Reiterman's, but more interpretative. Uses many of the Jonestown tapes as well as tapes of FCC-monitored communications of Jonestown with San Francisco from 1977 to 1978.

ROSE, STEVE. *Jesus and Jim Jones: Behind Jonestown.* New York: Pilgrim Press, 1979. A religious (Protestant) analysis, with numerous appendices, including a 1977 "Temple Agricultural Report" and various communications from the "parent" church, The Disciples of Christ.

WASHINGTON, JOSEPH R. *Black Sects and Cults.* Garden City, N.Y.: Doubleday, 1972. Argues that the "similarities between black religion and the evangelistic religion of whites are more and greater" than the similarities (which *do* exist) between African and black-American religious practices.

WITTEN, MANLEY. "Guyana: The Autopsy of Disbelief." *Lab World* 30 (March 1979), pp. 14–19. A convincing indictment of the U.S. government's medical and military staff who assumed charge of the Jonestown bodies; a legal, medical, and professional (coroner's) point of view.

YEE, MIN S., AND THOMAS N. LAYTON. *In My Father's House: The Story of the Layton*

Family and the Reverend Jim Jones. New York: Holt, Rinehart and Winston, 1981. More details about the Layton family than you'll care to know, but nonetheless a fairly honest inside look at one of Jones's important families.

EXPLORATIONS

1. If there is a religious commune or similar group in your area, monitor the local press and media coverage of the group. Does the commune or group have an identifiable public image? Do there seem to be any preconceptions about the group held by the media?

2. Interview a religious leader in your community about issues like "cults" or independent religious groups.

3. In some religious organizations there are members who take a "charismatic" or more active view of worship. How do such members interact with the organization as a whole?

APPENDIX

Reference Styles

Encountering a batch of essays with different reference styles is like entering a thorny thicket with numerous competing branches. Not only do a number of disciplines have their own styles, but the Modern Language Association (which provides leadership in this area to most English instructors) has, in effect, sanctioned at least three different styles over the years. Regularizing all of the selections in this text, by making all of the reference styles uniform, would prove not only difficult, but detrimental: You need to learn how the different disciplines handle this crucial problem of identifying sources. I have, therefore, decided to leave all of the reference styles intact, but in this Appendix I have identified the particular style of references used in each selection.

It is my experience that virtually all instructors have their own preferences on the matters of notes and bibliography; often they use one of a number of research guides, if not the *Modern Language Association (MLA) Handbook* itself. Therefore, I have limited the list below to six of the most inclusive groupings. The trend across the disciplines is toward the elimination of separate "notes" at the bottom of the page, or even at the end of a piece, but a great variety of styles still persists.

I believe that in the long run this textbook will be easier for you to use than most readers because it shows how these different styles operate across the disciplines in practice. In virtually all styles, the list of works cited, or bibliography, at the end *also* varies. This text will probably not, however, be a substitute for a standard research guide or for the instructor's own advice.

SIX MAJOR REFERENCE STYLES

Most referenced papers are written in styles 3, 4, and 5; 6 is an informal style which, by definition, has no set pattern. And, although you may encounter 1 and 2 in your own reading, they are no longer used for writing papers.

1. Classical MLA: both footnotes or endnotes and bibliography offered; the note would include only the city of publication and date (if a book); Latin abbreviations, *ibid.* (i.e., on the same page) and *op. cit.* (i.e., in the same book, but with different page number), were required for second or third notes to the same title:

> 1. Gertrude Stein, *Narration* (Chicago, 1935), p. 18.
> 2. *Ibid.*
> 3. *Op. cit.*, p. 20.

2. Old MLA (pre-1984): both notes and bibliography offered, but the note would include full publication data; subsequent notes for same title would use a "short form" of the original title:

> 1. Gertrude Stein, *Narration* (Chicago: University of Chicago Press, 1935), p. 18.
> 2. Stein, p. 24.

3. New MLA: documentation is provided in parentheses immediately in the text, using the author's last name or a short form of the title from a "List of Works Cited" at the end:

> Gertrude Stein argued against chronological order for her stories (Stein 18).

4. American Psychological Association or APA/name and year: the author's name, year of title, and page reference are inserted directly into the text, usually in parentheses; an alphabetical list of references is found at the end:

By 1964 the People's Temple Full Gospel Church was federated with the Disciples of Christ (Kilduff and Javers, 1978, p. 20).

5. Scientific/number: a number in parentheses following quoted or cited material in the text refers to a numbered list of references at the end of the article; depending upon the discipline, that list may be chronological, alphabetical, or follow the order in which the references appear in the text:

In 1795 a Salem epidemic, labeled "nervous fever," killed at least 33 persons (17).

6. Informal/in-text: numerous writers refer to sources within their texts *without* one of the formal or organized styles as outlined above; these essays may be technically "unfootnoted," but they nevertheless guide readers to sources if they wish to follow up on them:

Tolstoy, in his memoir *Childhood, Boyhood, and Youth,* relates an even more elaborate encounter with *déjà vu.*

THE ESSAYS: REFERENCE STYLES

CHAPTER 1 THE AMERICAN SCENE

Le Sueur, "Old Andy Comes to the North Star Country":
No particular style; the entire essay relies on author's version of folk and other oral sources.

McPhee, "The Search for Marvin Gardens":
None; presumably McPhee has used some historical sources for sections of this essay, but he does not cite them.

Trillin, "Newport, Ky.—Across the River":
Really none at all. Much of the essay is based on personal contacts and interviews, and these are not cited in any formal way. (They could have been, but the essay appeared in *The New Yorker,* which does not use footnoted essays.) In other essays, Trillin often uses

local newspapers for information and though he may have done so in this essay, he does not say so.

Stewart, U.S. 40 (excerpts):
The three individual pieces use no formal reference style, but the volume as a whole has a bibliography which lists numerous sources from which Stewart may have gathered his historical material.

Lehn, "Atmospheric Refraction and Lake Monsters":
Scientific/number style, with a numbered list at the end of the article; Lehn varies the usual system by including a number of content notes as well.

Loftis, "What? Three Man-High Birds":
None.

Wilford, "Is It Lake Champlain's Monster?":
Informal journalistic references (identifying interviewees) and citations (Lehn's article in *Science* can be tracked down, even though a full citation was not given).

CHAPTER 2 MECHANISMS OF MIND

Pye, [Designing a Draining Rack]:
This excerpt, like the book from which it was taken, concentrates on a practitioner's experience and knowledge and uses no obvious *verbal* sources. There are, however, numerous photographs of objects from books and of actual objects which serve as *visual* sources for Pye's analyses.

Turing, "Computing Machinery and Intelligence":
There are no references in this section of the essay.

Gregory, "Seeing as Thinking: An Active Theory of Perception":
No formal style; Gregory cites a number of figures (B. F. Skinner, the behavioral psychologist; the Gibsons, experimental psychologists), but he does not direct the reader to specific sources.

Bolter, "Turing's Game":

Parenthetical short-form citations (author, title, and page number) lead the reader to the Annotated Bibliography at the end of Bolter's book. I have reproduced the relevant section of that bibliography after the selection. (Such a bibliography takes the place of "content" notes, since the author is commenting on his sources here instead of in separate notes.)

Crovitz, "The Form of Logical Solutions":

Scientific/number style. The numbered references at the end of the essay appear in the order of citation.

Gardner, "Sidney Sackson's Patterns":

No formal style. In some cases, a specific parenthetical citation is made; in other instances only a reference to the name of an important authority (Popper or Carnap) is found. You would have to consult a library card catalog to pursue these names or to have access to general works of popular science (like those by Gardner himself, listed in "Sources").

Box, "A Plus *and* A Minus for Basic English Translation":

Informal references to titles of pieces translated.

CHAPTER 3 VISIONS

Melnechuk, "The Dream Machine":

As a popular article in *Psychology Today*, this essay has no formal reference style. Accompanying the article were a number of boxed quotations (from the *Nature* article, and from Freud's essays on dreams) and diagrams (for example, of EEG waves during waking and different stages of sleep) which could indirectly lead you toward some other sources. The only exceptions to this pattern are references to another essay which appeared in a 1978 issue of *Psychology Today*, and to Crick and Mitchison's essay in *Nature*.

Roueché, "An Emotion of Weirdness":

Roueché uses an informal, in-text reference style, naming author, title, and date for the items from which he quotes. You would have to do some work (find the exact month and page numbers, for example) if you wanted to look up his sources.

Freud, "The Interpretation of Dreams":
None; encyclopedia articles do not usually contain references.

Jung, "On the Nature of Dreams":
Jung uses a modified version of Classical MLA style, often with very abbreviated references to his sources. Because he is describing an aspect of his own more general system of psychology (dream-interpretation), he uses the notes to direct the reader to his other books and essays on related subjects. Thus, note 2 refers to "pars. 343ff" ("paragraphs 343 and those following") of "The Practical Use of Dream-Analysis," a related essay printed in the same volume of *The Collected Works of C. G. Jung* as the essay you have just read (see "Sources").

Gibson, "On the Relation between Hallucination and Perception":
Scientific style; numbers lead you to the list of references at the end (in order of their appearance in the article).

Stewart, "Dream Theory in Malaya":
None; based almost exclusively on his own experiences, Stewart offers no citations. His only specific reference—to H. D. Noone— would be helpful only if you happen to discover Noone's brother's book, *In Search of the Dream People* (see "Sources").

CHAPTER 4 INVESTIGATING MURDER

Danto, "A Psychiatric View of Those Who Kill":
APA/name and year, with alphabetical list of references at the end.

Rifkin, "Patriarchy, Law, and Capitalism":
Modified form of the Classical MLA style. Uses footnotes which include author, title, date, and page numbers; subsequent notes have *"Id.,"* for *"ibid."* (meaning that the source is the same as the previous footnote) and *"supra"* (meaning that the source is the same as one

above in a designated note). Thus, note 12, *"Id.* at 257," means that the source for note 12 is the same as that for note 11, but that note 12 refers to page 257 (while note 11 refers to page 228).

Parr, "The Murder of Kelsey: A Crime That Escaped Punishment":
Old MLA style is used; subsequent notes are short versions of the *first* time a title was used. The separate bibliography is alphabetical by title in this case, since all the sources are newspaper articles with no identified authors. Although using the "column" numbers makes research in newspapers slightly easier, many instructors would consider it to be optional to include them in citations.

CHAPTER 5 PERSPECTIVES ON SALEM

Roueché, "Sandy":
Roueché uses an informal, in-text method, since he gives us the author, title, and date of an essay such as "The June Bug," but not the title of the source-journal, its specific date, or page numbers. We would have to consult a periodical index, or the relevant scientific index or abstract, to find the details omitted. Roueché obviously relies on extensive personal interviews. Although these could be cited formally at the end of the essay, he chooses not to.

Ehrenreich and English, "Witchcraft and Medicine in the Middle Ages":
In a number of instances, the authors use an in-text, mainly parenthetical method of noting sources; author and title mentioned in parentheses are then found in a bibliography at the end of the pamphlet from which this excerpt is taken, but specific pages are not cited. (The style, therefore, is a very abbreviated version of New MLA.) There are, however, a number of instances in which an authority is cited ("Zilboorg" or "many writers") without any further clear reference to sources: In this case, you must judge the validity of the argument on its own merits, since the source is unclear.

Erikson, "Puritanism and Deviancy":
Slightly modified Old MLA style throughout. Archival records are cited in short or subsequent form as in note 4, "Essex County Rec-

ords, III, pp. 319–320," which is the short form of a full, earlier reference: *Records and Files of the Quarterly Courts of Essex County, Massachusetts, 1636–1682,* edited by George Francis Dow (Salem, Mass.: The Essex Institute).

Matossian, "Ergot and the Salem Witchcraft Affair":

Scientific style: A number in parentheses following data or a statement which needs footnoting leads the reader to a numbered list of "References" at the end of the essay. Matossian does not cite a particular page of the source; she simply lists the source. This, of course, would place the obligation on the reader to find a particular page by going to the original source.

I. Mather, [Cases of Spectral Evidence]:

Mather uses informal or in-text references, usually to the Bible; he also discusses incidents about which he has read (without offering the sources).

Whittier, [Supernatural Phenomena]:

Whittier uses an informal, in-text, and somewhat casual approach. The reader would have to do much of the work in tracking down an article and date, for example, when Whittier cites only author and journal (e.g., Hitchcock in *The New Englander,* or Abel in *The Boston Medical Journal*). In one instance, that of Hitchcock, I found the full reference in *Poole's Index to Periodical Literature,* the nineteenth-century equivalent to today's *Reader's Guide to Periodical Literature.*

Armstrong, "Tituba—A Credit to Her Craft":

Old MLA style is used. Note 3, for example, uses the short form, the author's name, to refer to the reference cited in note 1.

CHAPTER 6 APPROACHING JONESTOWN

Rensberger, "Jonestown Has Many Precedents":

Rensberger uses a very informal (perhaps typically journalistic) method of citing authorities, giving only their names and academic field. If readers wish to pursue a specific authority's work in depth, they must consult general indices such as the *Reader's Guide to Periodical*

Literature or the *Social Science Index,* or more specific indices like *Psychological Abstracts* or *Sociological Abstracts.*

Greenberg, "Jim Jones: The Deadly Hypnotist":

Despite the fact that this is a report in a science-news journal, it does not use any scientific reference style. Like Rensberger's essay, Greenberg's piece cites authorities (in psychology and psychiatry), but interested readers who wish to pursue the subject would have to consult the general essay indices or a specialized index like *Psychological Abstracts* for essays which have been published by the cited authorities.

Naipaul, [Guyana Welcomes Jones]:

Naipaul's informal, in-text references to newspapers, such as the Guyanese *Daily Chronicle* or the *New York Times,* provide sometimes sufficient ("Christmas Day, 1974"), sometimes unhelpful ("toward the end of 1978") guidance to the sources.

Fauset, "Father Divine Peace Mission Movement":

Fauset combines both content footnotes and references to some of his sources, but for the most part he simply refers to "recent" newspapers he has studied or meetings he has attended. In this regard, then, he is using an informal but unhelpful system.

Hall, "The Apocalypse at Jonestown":

Hall's essay uses a somewhat unusual combination of (1) APA references (name, date, and occasionally page) for mainly sociological or conceptual issues, and (2) a modified Old MLA style for most factual acknowledgments. It is therefore a double reference system which separates theoretical and factual notes, the former through in-text parenthetical references, the latter through traditional footnote numbering.

Lindsey, "How Rev. Jim Jones Gained His Power over Followers":

Lindsey uses journalistic forms of citation—"according to several of his aides" or "experts say"—which do not permit easy verification or subsequent development as research sources. For the most part, a news essay like this may lead to other sources and articles if the reader looks up additional articles in the same or other newspapers. Some of the authorities or contacts have been interviewed by Lindsey. The quality of the reporter's work and the newspaper in which the article appears help to determine the validity of the interviews.

Johnson, "Jim Jones: Man or Monster?":

New MLA style (citations include author's name and page number; "List of Works Cited" at the end).

Contents

According to Discipline

Contents
According to Rhetorical Style

About the Author

TOM ZANIELLO has taught composition, literature, and film classes at Northern Kentucky University for fifteen years. He has a keen interest in teaching cross-disciplinary topics, and has published on folk and pop culture, on traditional literary figures, and on the relationships among the arts. His undergraduate major at Tufts University was English, but he earned the equivalent of a minor in biology and has taught science in a junior high school. His doctorate in English is from Stanford University. With his family, in the United States and in England, he is almost always in pursuit of one more ancient monument, one more perfect ethnic or regional dish, and one more unusual essay topic.